KARL BARTH'S THEOLOGICAL EXEGESIS

Karl Barth's Theological Exegesis

The Hermeneutical Principles of the Römerbrief *Period*

Richard E. Burnett

WILLIAM B. EERDMANS PUBLISHING COMPANY
GRAND RAPIDS, MICHIGAN

Originally published 2001
by J. C. B. Mohr (Paul Siebeck), Tübingen, Germany
© 2001 J. C. B. Mohr (Paul Siebeck)
All rights reserved

US hardcover edition published 2004
This paperback edition published 2019
by Wm. B. Eerdmans Publishing Co.
4035 Park East Court SE, Grand Rapids, Michigan 49546
www.eerdmans.com

ISBN 978-0-8028-7820-5

Library of Congress Cataloging-in-Publication Data

Burnett, Richard E., 1963–
Karl Barth's theological exegesis: the hermeneutical principles of the Römerbrief period / Richard E. Burnett.
   p.   cm.
Revision of the author's thesis (doctoral) — Princeton Theological Seminary, 2001.
Includes bibliographical references (p.) and indexes.
ISBN 0-8028-7820-5 (pbk.   )
1. Barth, Karl, 1886-1968. 2. Bible — Criticism, interpretation, etc. — History — 20th century. 3. Barth, Karl, 1886-1968. Römerbrief. 4. Bible. N.T. Romans — Commentaries — History and criticism. I. Title.
BS500.B37B87 2004
220.6'092 — dc22   2004040487

for
Martha

Contents

Foreword ix
Preface xiii

Chapter 1 Introduction 1

Chapter 2 A Hermeneutical Manifesto:
                Barth's Hermeneutical Discovery in Context 13

   A. The Priority of Exegesis over Hermeneutics 14
   B. Karl Barth's Commitment to Theological Exegesis 23
   C. The Post-War Appraisal of Barth's Hermeneutic 31
   D. Karl Barth's Problem with "The Hermeneutical Problem" 35
   E. The Being of God is the Hermeneutical Problem: Background to Barth's Discovery . 41
   F. From Special Hermeneutics to General Hermeneutics 50
   G. The School of the Holy Spirit 56

Chapter 3 *Sachlicher, Inhaltlicher, Wesentlicher* 65

   A. Karl Barth's "Turn to the Bible" 65
   B. Wilhelm Herrmann: A *Sachlicher* Approach 70
   C. What Exactly is *die Sache* of the Bible 74
   D. The Whole in Light of its Parts and the Parts in Light of the Whole 78
   E. The Challenge of Interpreting "What is There" Dialectically 84
   F. Truth and Memory 86

Chapter 4 Entering into the Meaning of the Bible 95

   A. A Scientific Approach to Exegesis 96
   B. A Living Context 100
   C. Active Participation 111
      1. No Reading Out Without Reading In 112
      2. Like Through Like 114
      3. Until I Almost Forget That I Am Not the Author 117

Chapter 5 With More Attention and Love 125

A. *With* or *About* the Author 125
B. The Historical-Pyschological Approach of Paul Wernle 128
C. Beyond Religious Personality and Experience 134
D. A Short History of the Empathetic Tradition of Interpretation 142
   1. Johann Gottfried von Herder 143
   2. Friedrich Daniel Ernst Schleiermacher 149
   3. Wilhelm Dilthey 158
   4. Ernst Troeltsch and Georg Wobbermin 166
   5. The Young Karl Barth (Pre-1915) 169
      a. "Modern Theology and Work in the Kingdom of God" 171
      b. "The Christian Faith and History" 176
E. A Hermeneutics of Love and Trust 184
   1. No Art of Empathy can Offer the Slightest Substitute 185
   2. A Relationship of Faithfulness 192
   3. An Emergency Clause 197
   4. *Caritas*: an Excursus 207
      a. Love is a Gift, a Miracle 208
      b. Love is Always for Another 210
      c. To Love is to Receive and be a Witness 213

Chapter 6 The Meaning of the Bible Itself 221

A. The Language and the Content are One 221
B. The Service of Historical Criticism 230
C. The Art of Paraphrasing 240
D. Calvin as Exemplar 250

Chapter 7 Conclusion 255

Appendix 1 The Historical Background of the Preface to the First Edition of Barth's *Römerbrief* 265

Appendix 2 The Preface Drafts to the First Edition of Barth's *Römerbrief*. 277

Bibliography 293
Indexes 307

Foreword

The hermeneutics of Karl Barth have never been well understood in the English-speaking world. Two major interpretive approaches dominated the scene up through the mid-1990s. The first, reflecting a preoccupation with the debates over demythologization in the 1950s, began with the assumption that Barth's hermeneutics can best be understood through a comparison with Rudolf Bultmann. The glaring weakness of this approach was that Barth's hermeneutics were not allowed to become a subject of interest in their own right. The focus was too narrow, too restrictive, to allow that to happen. Barth's early exegetical work was of some interest – but only insofar as it could be shown to have influenced Bultmann in the same period. And his later reflections were dismissed by means of labels like "revelational hermeneutics." This was the approach favored by theological 'liberals.' It was typically wedded to a depiction of Barth's theological development which posited a shift away from dialectical theology towards a dogmatic theology grounded in a method of analogy around 1931 – which strengthened the tendency towards dismissal of Barth's later hermeneutical reflections as the product of a 'neo-orthodox' or kerymatic theologian.

When a reaction finally set in to this one-sided approach, it made itself guilty of a new one-sidedness. The so-called 'Yale School', reacting against the almost exclusive concentration of 'liberals' on Barth's theoretical statements on hermeneutics, looked almost completely away from such statements in order to focus attention upon Barth's actual exegesis of Scriptural passages. In defense of this procedure, it was frequently pointed out that Barth himself had said that the proper order was first exegesis and then hermeneutics (as an a posteriori reflection on a prior engagement with texts). But such a defense fails to convince. Once Barth has done the work of reflecting on the hermeneutics implicit in his exegetical procedures, ought we not to take such theoretical statements seriously? We might wish to repeat the experiment, passing through his exegesis to his 'theory' to see if the 'theory' is justified by his practice. But surely, that would still require close attention to the 'theory' as well? More often that not, however, the Yale theologians contented themselves with teasing their own theories out of Barth's exegetical practice. Not surprisingly, given their preoccupation with exegesis, they regularly concluded that Barth really had no hermeneutical 'principles' at all in any customary sense of the word. His hermeneutics were strictly ad hoc in character; the description of strategies devised for use in relation to particular textual challenges without further prescriptive value. The claim was made that Barth understood biblical texts to have the character of a 'realistic narrative' – something between a factual report and a symbolic expression of the interior condition of an author – which rendered interpretation of them largely immune to any systematic (well-ordered) hermeneutical approach. Interest in the referent of biblical language waned. Attention was focussed instead on questions concerning the power of language to disclose meaning and to form persons, and the use of language as tools for socializing new members into religious communities. In raising these questions, the Yale School helped prepare the way for more recent 'postmodern' readings of Barth's hermeneutics. There is a certain irony in this; the members of the Yale School were much more conservative than their 'postmodern' successors. Indeed, I do not think I do this movement an injustice when I describe it as the last (and, in many ways, the greatest) achievement of American 'neo-orthodoxy.' The one thing it shared with its 'liberal' counterpart was the picture of Barth's development in terms of a 'second conversion' – though in this case, the alleged departure from dialectical theology was valued positively.

What has changed since these efforts were made is that most Barth scholars today recognize that the thought of a 'second turn' or 'break' in Barth's development cannot stand up to close scrutiny. Barth was and remained a dialectical theologian. The significance of this advance for an understanding of Barth's hermeneutics is not far to seek. One cannot expect to arrive at an adequate understanding of Barth's hermeneutics if one begins with the assumption that Barth's early reflections on hermeneutics were joined to the later only on the formal level of similar interests and motives. There is a material continuity which evidences itself throughout, from the first Romans commentary right on through the Church Dogmatics.

The present work marks the dawn of a new era. Against depictions of Barth's early theology as merely exegetical and lacking in the kind of serious hermeneutical reflection that characterized Bultmann's work in the same period, Richard Burnett mines the unpublished drafts of the preface to the first edition of Romans to show: 1) that it is not the case that Barth's hermeneutics were formed only as a grudging response to unexpected criticism and that, therefore, he never took any real interest in the subject; 2) that the first is true because Barth's hermeneutical commitments did not come late but were very close to fully formed as early as 1918; 3) that Barth did indeed have hermeneutical 'principles' which were understood by him to be relevant for interpreting not just the Bible but any piece of literature whatsoever; and 4) that Barth remained attached to these 'principles' well after 1931 (demonstrating the continuity in his thinking on the subject). Most importantly, Burnett has initiated a much needed effort to bring Barth into conversation with Schleiermacher, depicting Barth's efforts in the field of hermeneutics as an attempt to overcome the Schleiermacherian tradition from within. More work will need to be done in this area, but Burnett has pointed the way forward.

The highest compliment I can pay to Richard Burnett is that he has achieved in this work a living incarnation of the kind of hermeneutics Karl Barth advocated. Watching him wrestle, page after page, with the meaning of the preface drafts is like watching someone try to wring every last drop of water out of a wet towel; it is almost exhausting to watch and I am sure it was exhausting to do. This is the kind of thing that only happens where love is the driving motivation. To his credit, Burnett never loses sight of the need for 'creativity' and 'elasticity' in the interpretive process. The results are compelling and constitute a serious challenge to those who would grant to Barth but a small role in the history of hermeneutics in the nineteenth and twentieth centuries.

Bruce Lindley McCormack
Weyerhaeuser Professor of Systematic Theology
Princeton Theological Seminary (USA)

Preface

The present volume is only a slightly revised version of my 2001 doctoral dissertation, written for Princeton Theological Seminary. It represents my attempt to come to terms with questions I have been wrestling with for more than a decade and a half.

I began reading Karl Barth seriously at the beginning of my junior year in college. At the same time I was introduced to historical-criticism and became enthusiastic about the fruit it could bear. When I came to seminary, I signed up for as many New Testament courses as I could fit into my schedule. I enjoyed and remained enthusiastic about studying the Bible "critically." Yet somehow I was still not satisfied. Gradually, I realized there had to be more to biblical exegesis than reckoning with the various historical circumstances and sources behind the text. Fortunately, at the end of my first year, I came upon a copy of Hans Frei's *The Eclipse of Biblical Narrative: A Study in Eighteenth and Nineteenth Century Hermeneutics*. It took me years to understand what is really at issue in this book. After seminary, I packed it in my suitcase and meditated on it while studying at the University of Tübingen. Later, as a pastor, I continued to reflect on Frei and Barth, and specifically the latter's call to an approach to the task of exegesis which he claimed was 'more critical.' It was also as a pastor that I came face to face with the same sort of problem Barth alludes to somewhat bitterly in the preface to the second edition of his *Römerbrief*:

> I know what it means to have to go into the pulpit year in and year out, obliged to understand and explain, and wanting to do so, yet being unable to do it because we were given almost nothing at the university except the famous "respect for history," which despite the beautiful expression means simply the renunciation of every earnest, respectful understanding and explanation.

After a few years in the pastorate, I entered the S.T.M. program at Yale University Divinity School in order to sort out some of these issues and do further research on Frei. There I was introduced to the so-called 'Yale School' of theologians (notably Professors David Kelsey, George Lindbeck, and Brevard Childs), to Gadamer's *Wahrheit und Methode* by Professor Cyril O'Regan, to deconstructionists, and to all sorts of post-modernists who talked a lot about hermeneutics (even though most of them claimed they were not interested in hermeneutics).

In 1993, I entered the Ph.D. program at Princeton Theological Seminary and came under the tutelage of Dr. Bruce McCormack, my *Doktorvater*, who challenged me to think more dogmatically about the topic of hermeneutics than I had ever thought about it before. He also pointed me in the direction of the preface drafts to the first edition of Barth's *Römerbrief*. Professor McCormack's reputation as a Barth scholar and as one of the leading theologians of our day is well-known both in the United States and abroad. What is perhaps not so well-known is his devotion to his students. His advice throughout the process of writing my dissertation and his guidance throughout the entire doctoral program was invaluable. His willingness to take time to read, to critique, and to discuss many things with me, was a labor of love and exemplified the kind of *Nachdenken* and *Mitdenken*, the kind of *Aufmerksamkeit* and *Liebe*, that is so important in Karl Barth's hermeneutics. For Professor McCormack's help I will be forever grateful. I am also thankful for Professor Diogenes Allen, above all for his kindness and Christian character which were a great source of encouragement to me throughout my years at Princeton but also for introducing me to Austin Farrer, "the one genius of the English church" (as C.S. Lewis referred to him), whose own approach to exegesis also shed important light on this project.

I am greatly indebted to Dr. Hans-Anton Drewes, editor of the Karl Barth *Gesamtausgabe* and director of the Karl Barth-Achiv in Basel, Switzerland, who read my manuscript in its entirety and offered me indispensable advice. His knowledge of Barth and his keen editorial eyes saved me from many mistakes. I also thank my friend, D. Paul La Montagne, for his help in preparing this work for publication. His expertise in theology, computers, and editing proved to be very important for the final production of this volume. I, nevertheless, am responsible for all mistakes, as well as any undo repetition of Barth's statements from his *Römerbrief* prefaces (which, given the richness of some of them, often seemed unavoidable).

I must also thank my mother, Ruth, and my father, the late Reverend Robert E. Burnett, for their lives of humble Christian service and their effort to bring me up in the nurture and admonition of the Lord. My indebtedness to them goes beyond words. I thank the congregations of The Second English Presbyterian Church of Amwell, New Jersey, and The First Presbyterian Church of Waynesville, North Carolina for their patience with me as I tried to be their pastor while writing my dissertation. I am also grateful to the Montreat Presbyterian Church and to Mrs. Kate Simpson for their support, and a very special word of thanks goes to the Reverend Dr. Calvin Thielman who has been a mentor and father in the faith to me for many years. I am also grateful to Professor Martin Hengel, my sponsor while I studied at the University of Tübingen, who graciously recommended my dissertation for publication. I also thank Mr. Georg Siebeck and Mr. Bill Eerdmans, and am honored to have this work published by J.C.B. Mohr (Paul Siebeck) and William B. Eerdmans.

Finally, I wish to thank my wife, Martha, the mother of our four children, Robert Knox, Hanna Ruth, Carl Austin, and Collin Brock. She has taught me more about love than I deserve to know, and I dedicate this book to her.

If Protestant theology is to recover once more from its emaciation, and it is by no means certain that it will, our Old and New Testament scholars will, without prejudice to what they do as historians (as an avocation!), be theological exegetes, and as such really also work in obedience to "the truth."

Karl Barth, "Von der Paradoxie des 'positiven Paradoxes' Antworten und Fragen an Paul Tillich" (1923)

Chapter 1
Introduction

Karl Barth's break with liberalism in the summer of 1915 is the most important event that has occurred in theology in over two hundred years. It should come as no surprise, therefore, that the precise nature of Barth's break with liberalism continues to be analyzed. Many books have dealt with this topic, but the most important to appear in recent years has been Bruce McCormack's *Karl Barth's Critically Realistic Dialectical Theology: Its Genesis and Development 1909-1936*.[1] This study has overturned Hans Urs von Balthasar's thesis, which prevailed for nearly half a century, that Barth's break actually consisted of two breaks, "two conversions," "two decisive turning-points," the first occurring sometime during the First World War, which was a turn from liberal theology to dialectical theology, culminating in the second edition of his *Römerbrief* (1922), and the second occurring in the late 1920s, which was a turn "from dialectic to analogy," culminating in his little book on Anselm which he wrote in 1931 entitled *Fides Quaerens Intellectum*. McCormack has shown that although there were various shifts in Barth's development, there was actually only one break, that which occurred in the summer of 1915, and that analogy never simply replaced dialectic but co-existed with it in Barth's thought from at least 1920 on, and that Barth's theology was always inherently dialectical from the first edition of his *Römerbrief* (1919) through the *Church Dogmatics,* in the sense that it presupposed a *Realdialektik* of the veiling and unveiling of God in revelation. The upshot of all this is that we now have a new paradigm, a new periodization of Barth's development, which has not only further dismantled the largely Anglo-American myth of a neo-orthodox Barth, but has also shown, because of "a single material insight" which began to emerge in Barth's thought in the summer of 1915, "that Barth was from first to last a theologian (and not a philosopher turned theologian as von Balthasar and those who followed in his wake seemed to imply)."[2]

A new day has clearly dawned in Barth studies. But as pioneering as McCormack's work has been and as much insight as he has given us into the social, political, cultural, philosophical, and theological antecedents leading up

---

[1] Bruce L. McCormack, *Karl Barth's Critically Realistic Dialectical Theology: Its Genesis and Development 1909-1936* (Oxford: Clarendon Press, 1995).

[2] McCormack, *Karl Barth's Critically Realistic Dialectical Theology*, p. 20.

to Barth's break with liberalism, many important questions remain. What was Barth's relationship to Kant prior to his break with liberalism and throughout his *Römerbrief* period? What was his relationship to the reformers, to Luther, to Calvin? And above all, what was Barth's relationship to Schleiermacher? The significance of this latter question can hardly be overestimated. Barth recognized the significance of Schleiermacher's legacy perhaps more than anyone else of his generation. Prior to his break with liberalism he had been a deeply devoted disciple of Schleiemacher. At the end of his career he questioned whether Schleiermacher was not only *the* church father of the nineteenth century but of the twentieth century as well.[3] Even after his break, in his introductory lecture to his course on Schleiermacher in Göttingen on Nov.11, 1923, he said:

> Schleiermacher merits detailed historical consideration and study even if only because he was the one in whom the great struggle of Christianity with the strivings and achievements of the German spirit in 1750-1830, in whose light or shadow we still stand today, took place in a way which would still be memorable even if he were dead and his theological work had been transcended. ... But Schleiermacher is not dead for us and his theological work has not been transcended. If anyone still speaks today in Protestant theology as though he were still among us, it is Schleiermacher. We *study* Paul and the reformers, but we *see* with the eyes of Schleiermacher and think along the same lines as he did. This is true even when we criticize or reject the most important of his theologoumena or even all of them. Wittingly or willingly or not, Schleiermacher's method and presuppositions are the typical ferment in almost all theological work.[4]

There has been a great deal of discussion in the last several decades about Karl Barth's relationship to Schleiermacher. Many have claimed that Barth's treatment of Schleiermacher was not always fair. Indeed some have argued that especially in the period immediately following his break, his "critique was seriously mistaken at every juncture."[5] Barth himself said of those early years:

> It is certain that what I thought, said, and wrote from that year [1916] on, I simply did without him, and that his spectacles were not sitting on my nose as I was expounding the Epistle to the Romans. He was no longer a 'church father' for me. It is further certain, however, that this 'without him' implied a rather sharp 'against him.' On occasion,

---

[3] Karl Barth, "Nachwort" in F.D.E. Schleiermacher, *Schleiermacher-Auswahl*, ed. Heinz Bolli (Munich: Siebenstern-Taschenbuch-Verlag, 1968), p. 290; ET "Concluding Unscientific Postscript on Schleiermacher," trans. George Hunsinger in *The Theology of Schleiermacher* (Grand Rapids: William B. Eerdmans, 1982), p. 261. Hereafter cited as "Nachwort."

[4] Karl Barth, *Die Theologie Schleiermachers 1923/24*, ed. Dietrich Ritschl (Zürich: Theologischer Verlag Zürich, 1978), p. 1; ET *The Theology of Schleiermacher*, trans. Geoffrey Bromiley (Grand Rapids: William B. Eerdmans, 1982), xiii. Hereafter cited as *Die Theologie Schleiermachers*.

[5] Terrence Tice, "Interviews with Karl Barth and Reflections on his Interpretation of Schleiermacher," *Barth and Schleiermacher: Beyond the Impasse?*, ed. J. Duke & R. Streetman (Philadelphia: Fortress Press, 1988), p. 55.

I intentionally made that explicit. Yet I really did not do it — since 'old love never fades' — without a deep inner regret that it could not be otherwise.[6]

Suffice it to say, no account of Barth's break with liberalism can be considered complete apart from a thorough examination of his relationship to Schleiermacher. The following study seeks, in part, to contribute to a further understanding of this very deep and complex relationship. Though it makes no pretense of being complete in any sense, it does focus on a theme that deeply concerned them both.

More has been written about Schleiermacher's hermeneutics in the last hundred years than about any other topic related to him. Yet very little has been written about Barth's relationship to Schleiemacher's hermeneutics. This is surprising not only because of the enormous influence of Schleiermacher's hermeneutics throughout the twentieth century, but also because Barth himself recognized it from early on. In his 1923/24 Göttingen lectures on Schleiermacher, Barth chose Schleiermacher's hermeneutics from the four theological works selected to represent his greatest achievement as a scholar, for the following reason: "I am choosing for this purpose his hermeneutics, partly because of the principal importance of the material, for if a theologian of this significance wants to explain to us from what standpoint he reads and understands other writings, and especially the Bible, will not this apparently specialized question be in a very special way the place where everything is decided?"[7] Barth, of course, could have chosen from a number of other works, but the primary reason he seems to have chosen Schleiermacher's hermeneutics as among his "most *mature* and *decisive*" is because "here we shall have the chance to get to know Schleiermacher at his best and most brilliant, in his natural strength, on his home ground, for, to use his own expression, he was a virtuoso in the field whose method hermeneutics describes."[8] Barth's analysis of Schleiermacher's hermeneutics in his Göttingen lectures is as nuanced and erudite as one can find in the early 1920s. Yet it also reflects the level of understanding, the depth of engagement, of one who knows exactly where he stands in relationship to it. The following study seeks to demonstrate that Barth *did* know where he stood in relationship to Schleiermacher's hermeneutics and knew from a much earlier period than most have realized.

In 1965, in the second edition of his epoch-making work, *Wahrheit und Methode*, Hans-Georg Gadamer referred to the first edition of Karl Barth's

---

[6] Barth, "Nachwort," p. 296.
[7] Barth, *Die Theologie Schleiermachers*, p. 318; ET p. 178.
[8] Barth *Die Theologie Schleiermachers*, pp. 9, 318; ET pp. xviii, 178.

Römerbrief as "a virtual hermeneutical manifesto."[9] This is an intriguing claim because the word hermeneutics does not even appear in any of the editions of Barth's *Römerbrief* and because the theme of hermeneutics, apart from a few remarks in the prefaces, is nowhere specifically addressed. Unfortunately, Gadamer never elaborated on this claim, nor has anyone else provided a substantive explanation of it. It is the purpose of this study, however, to demonstrate that Gadamer was basically correct in referring to the first edition of Barth's *Römerbrief* as "a virtual hermeneutical manifesto," and the reason is because it challenged the hegemony of a reigning hermeneutical tradition, that of Friedrich Schleiermacher. To state it precisely, this study seeks to advance the thesis that an important part of Karl Barth's attempt to break with liberalism was his attempt to overcome the hermeneutical tradition of Friedrich Schleiermacher – a tradition which was emerging before him and extended well beyond him yet took definitive shape in him – and that Barth's attempt to overcome this hermeneutical tradition is reflected throughout his *Römerbrief* period and particularly in his attempt to engage in what he referred to as "theological exegesis." Before I suggest why this study is important, however, it is necessary to address one particular issue which no consideration of this topic can avoid.

McCormack has argued that Karl Barth's break with liberalism and subsequent theological revolution came about as the result of "a single material insight" and not primarily as the result of a shift in theological method. This is an important claim because "having identified a shift in theological method as the most significant," many interpreters, according to McCormack, have "had a tendency to give to methodological questions a prominence that they simply did not have in Barth's development when that development is viewed genetically – that is, from a standpoint within the development itself."[10] The following study seeks not to challenge this claim regarding the priority of content over method but, on the contrary, to underscore and deepen it, even if in an effort to contribute to a fuller account of Barth's break with liberalism, it also seeks to take one step beyond it.

Barth could indeed say from the beginning of his theological revolution, as he did throughout his career, that "*methodus est arbitraria*." Nowhere is this better illustrated than in his talk about method and hermeneutics in the first half-volume of his *Church Dogmatics*, where we repeatedly come across statements such as "When God's Word is heard and proclaimed, something takes place that for all our hermeneutical skill cannot be brought about by her-

---

[9] Hans-Georg Gadamer, *Wahrheit und Methode*, 2nd ed. (Tübingen: J.C.B. Mohr [Paul Siebeck], 1965), p. 481 (Hereafter cited as "Wahrheit und Methode"); ET *Truth and Method*, trans. Joel Weinsheimer and Donald G. Marshall (New York: Crossroad, 1992), p. 581.

[10] McCormack, *Karl Barth's Critically Realistic Dialectical Theology*, p. viii.

meneutical skill," or "The only proper thing to do here is to renounce altogether the search for a method of hearing God's Word, for an unequivocally correct description of its entry into man, into the realm of his experiences, attitudes and thoughts."[11] From such statements it might appear that Barth was simply indifferent to hermeneutics or the question of method. This is certainly how many interpreted him after World War II and throughout the 1960s. More recently, however, a younger generation of scholars has suggested that Barth's emphasis on the priority of content over method, specifically his emphasis on the priority of actual exegesis over hermeneutical theory, makes him more an exemplar or precursor of 'post-modern' or 'post-critical' thought. One such scholar, Mary Kathleen Cunningham, has for such reasons said that Barth's hermeneutic is basically "*ad hoc*," that he offers only "*ad hoc* hermeneutical principles." Explaining the reason for her own procedure, she says:

> Moving from an examination of Barth's hermeneutical comments to a study of his exegesis does not honor the pattern of Barth's thinking, neither the unsystematic nature of his thought, nor his commitment to proceed from the particular to the general. Constructing a systematic hermeneutics out of what are essentially ad hoc remarks and then drawing conclusions about Barth's exegesis on the grounds of these generalizations can lead one to distort his scriptural interpretation.[12]

There is much to affirm here for it is certainly true that Karl Barth insisted on moving from the particular to the general and that there are dangers in drawing conclusions about his understanding of the exegetical task on the basis of generalizations rather than on the basis of his actual exegesis. (Barth was fond of saying "*Latet periculum in generalibus!*" "Danger lurks in generalities!" and this certainly applies to any discussion of his exegesis.) It is also true that Barth's thought is unsystematic in the sense that it is not governed by any system, and that he did not construct a systematic hermeneutics.[13] But it is quite another matter, it seems to me, to characterize Barth's hermeneutic as basically "*ad hoc*" or to claim that he offers only "*ad hoc* hermeneutical principles." Barth's hermeneutic, on the contrary, as this study seeks to demonstrate on the basis of an examination of the *Römerbrief* period, can hardly be described as *ad hoc*. Indeed quite apart from where they came from or how he got them (which is the main reason they cannot be referred to as *ad hoc*), there are hermeneutical principles manifest in Barth's writings throughout this period, par-

---

[11] KD I/1:153, 192; CD I/1:148, 184.

[12] Mary Kathleen Cunningham, *What Is Theological Exegesis? Interpretation and Use of Scripture in Barth's Doctrine of Election* (Valley Forge, PA: Trinity Press International, 1995), p. 14.

[13] I would argue that Barth's theology, on the other hand, is systematic in the sense that it reflects the fact that not everything can be said about God at once and that when talking about God some things ought to be said before others.

ticularly in the prefaces to the various editions of his *Römerbrief*, and Barth defended these principles throughout his career.

Again, however, this is not to suggest that Barth had a systematic or what since Schleiermacher has been called a general hermeneutic. Nor is it to suggest that what sparked Barth's revolution was his discovery of a new method. To repeat, Karl Barth's theological revolution emerged in the summer of 1915 out of a single material insight which did not occur as a result of applying *a priori* hermeneutical principles. Yet what this study seeks to highlight is the fact that the immediate consequence of this single material insight was a new understanding of the exegetical task which is reflected in the first edition of his *Römerbrief*. The hermeneutical principles emerging out of Barth's new understanding of the exegetical task, in other words, cannot be understood apart from this single material insight, but they are sufficiently formal to warrant attention. It is important to emphasize that these principles are not hard and fast rules. They do not serve to predict the outcome of any piece of actual exegesis or even preclude the possibility of arriving at very different interpretations of the same text.[14] But they do indicate how Barth approached the task of exegesis, and it is in closely examining these principles that we see as clearly as anywhere that Barth was indeed, as McCormack has said, "from first to last a theologian."

There are at least three reasons why this study is important. The first is because an in-depth study of the hermeneutical principles of Barth's *Römerbrief* period has yet to appear. A number of articles, dissertations, and book-length studies on Barth's exegesis have appeared in the German and English-speaking worlds in the last few decades.[15] In this country, among the most notable are two recently published Yale dissertations, Paul McGlasson's *Jesus and Judas: Biblical Exegesis in Barth*, and Mary Cunningham's book which I alluded to earlier, *What Is Theological Exegesis? Interpretation and Use of Scripture in Barth's Doctrine of Election*. Both of these studies have the virtue of maintaining Barth's priority of actual exegesis over hermeneutical reflection, but neither, frankly, tell us very much about Barth's theological exegesis.[16] In the

---

[14] What George Hunsinger says about certain patterns of thought in Barth's theology applies also to his hermeneutical principles. It would be false to suppose "that, because one understands how a lens works, one also understands the nature of an object on which the lens is focused. Just as a lens is merely a device for seeing and not the object perceived, so the patterns are merely instruments of perception and not Barth's argument itself. The difference between a lens and these patterns, however, is that the patterns are embedded in the object of perception rather than external to it." George Hunsinger, *How To Read Karl Barth: The Shape of His Theology* (Oxford: University Press, 1991), pp. vii-viii.

[15] Most of these are listed in the bibliography.

[16] Paul McGlasson, *Jesus and Judas: Biblical Exegesis in Barth* (Atlanta: Scholars Press, 1991). I have reviewed Cunningham's book in *Pro Ecclesia* 4:4, pp. 499-501. Another Yale

German-speaking world, however, much more serious attention has been given to Barth's hermeneutic. Walter Lindemann's book, *Karl Barth und die Kritische Schriftauslegung,* and Nicolaas Bakker's *In der Krisis der Offenbarung: Karl Barths Hermeneutik, dargestellt an seiner Römerbrief-Auslegung* are two among several important works which carefully examine Barth's hermeneutic and specifically his hermeneutical principles.[17] Thus far, however, no study has focused primarily on the hermeneutical principles of Barth's *Römerbrief* prefaces nor how such principles might be understood in light of the hermeneutical tradition of Schleiermacher.[18]

The second reason why this study is important is because, in addition to all the secondary literature, a considerable amount of primary literature shedding light on Barth's understanding of the exegetical task has surfaced in recent years. Barth's personal correspondence with Eduard Thurneysen, of course, has shed a great deal of light on Barth's thinking in his early years, particularly with respect to exegesis. But more recent volumes of the *Gesamtausgabe* have shed even more light. Until 1978, for example, with the publication of Barth's 1923/24 Göttingen lectures on Schleiermacher, few knew that Barth had dealt specifically with Schleiermacher's hermeneutics. Furthermore, with the publication of two volumes of his writings from 1905-1914 in the last decade and a volume of his confirmation instruction from 1909-1921 in 1987, we now have more insight than ever into Barth's thinking before his break with liberalism, not least of all with respect to his understanding of the Bible and the exegetical task.[19] Likewise the publication of Barth's first cycle of lectures on

---

dissertation yielding a similar result is Kathryn Greene-McCreight's *Ad Litteram: Understandings of The Plain Sense of Scripture in the Exegesis of Augustine, Calvin and Barth of Genesis 1-3* (Ann Arbor, MI: UMI, 1994).

[17] Walter Lindemann, *Karl Barth und die kritische Schriftauslegung* (Hamburg-Bergstedt: Herbert Reich-EvangelischerVerlag, 1973). Nicolaas T. Bakker, *In der Krisis der Offenbarung: Karl Barths Hermeneutik, dargestellt an seiner Römerbrief-Auslegung* (Neukirchen-Vluyn: Neukirchener Verlag, 1974).

[18] Two studies, however, are worthy of mention. Helmut Kirschstein's *Der souveräne Gott und die heilige Schrift: Einführung in die biblische Hermeneutik Karl Barths* (Aachen: Shaker Verlag, 1998) is the most comprehensive study of Barth's hermeneutic to date. It considers Barth's hermeneutic in relation to the hermeneutical tradition of Schleiermacher but it does not do so in significant detail or specifically with respect to the *Römerbrief* period. Frederick Herzog's unpublished Th.D. dissertation, "The Possibility of Theological Understanding: An Inquiry in the Presuppositions of Hermeneutics in Theology," which began under Barth whom Herzog credits with having "pointed out the direction in which I was to follow," deals broadly with Barth's hermeneutic in relationship to Schleiermacher's (again, however, not with respect to the *Römerbrief* period), but, judging by its conclusions, did not have the benefit of materials which would have given him deeper insight into it. It was completed at Princeton Theological Seminary in 1953 under Paul Lehmann.

[19] See p. 171n.183 and p. 45n.137 below.

dogmatics, the *Göttingen Dogmatics*, coming as they do on the heels of the *Römerbrief* period, yield considerable insight into these matters, even though a conscious effort has been made not to read later insights back into this earlier period.[20] But by far the most important sources of information to appear in recent years are the preface drafts to the first edition of Barth's *Römerbrief*, which were made available thanks to Herbert Anzinger's careful transcription of Barth's handwritten manuscripts and were first published in 1985 in the *Gesamtausgabe* edition of *Der Römerbrief (Erste Fassung) 1919* edited by Hermann Schmidt.[21]

Barth wrote six different drafts for his preface to the first edition of his *Römerbrief* before he settled on the one which is in the published edition. These are available here for the first time in English in the Appendix to this volume and they are significant for several reasons. Beyond giving us the rare opportunity to see a work of Barth's in progress, placing us, as Hermann Schmidt says, "in the fortunate position to be able to look at the author in his workshop,"[22] these preface drafts yield many new insights into Barth's understanding of the exegetical task at one of the most decisive turning points in his career. Michael Beintker has said:

> Barth had of course already separated himself by the time of the first edition of his *Römerbrief* from the liberalizing tendency of his earlier years. He now approaches the Bible in that manner which shall remain determinative and valid for the entirety of his work. In contrast to historical-critical biblical exegesis, whose right he did not deny, he wanted to press forward to the theological understanding of the biblical texts – a task which he saw had been brought to extinction by limiting exegesis to historical analysis. Barth's exegesis was led by a hermeneutic which is able to see our world within the world of Paul's *Romans*. ... In the drafts of the preface Barth reflected on his hermeneutic even more extensively than in the programmatic preface of the published edition. ... the fact is, the first *Römerbrief* edition with its program of a thoroughly theological understanding of the text is to be seen as a fundamental building block in the history of biblical hermeneutics in this century, or even as an exceptional, pioneering accomplishment in this field.[23]

Moreover, contrary to those who might have thought that his hermeneutical remarks in his famous preface to the second edition were "essentially *ad hoc*"

---

[20] Though I have sought to avoid a backwards historical argument, I *do* make references to the *Göttingen* and *Church Dogmatics* and other later materials for two reasons: first, because Barth himself sometimes makes reference in his later writings to his own thought processes in the *Römerbrief* period, and second, because Barth continued to use concepts and vocabulary out of his *Römerbrief* period, it is important to follow the trajectory of some of these thoughts at various points (which I do occasionally, though largely in the footnotes).

[21] Karl Barth, *Der Römerbrief (Erste Fassung) 1919*, ed. Hermann Schmidt (Zürich: Theologischer Verlag Zürich, 1985), pp. 581-602.

[22] Barth, *Der Römerbrief (Erste Fassung) 1919*, editor's preface, xv.

[23] Michael Beintker, "Der Römerbrief von 1919," *Verkündigung und Forschung* 30:2, 1985, p. 23.

responses to the charges of his critics,[24] the preface drafts to the first *Römerbrief* edition are also significant because they demonstrate not only that Barth had clear, self-conscious hermeneutical convictions from the very beginning, but that he clearly anticipated his contemporaries' objections to them. In any case, they shed considerable light on much that Barth says in his prefaces to the second and third editions of his *Römerbrief* and, contrary to those who have sought to drive a wedge between the first and second editions, show significant points of continuity.

Finally, a third reason why this study is important is because no theologian since John Calvin has been more committed to biblical exegesis than Karl Barth. There are over fifteen thousand biblical references throughout the *Church Dogmatics* and more than two thousand examples of detailed exegesis of specific biblical passages. In addition to his other books, commentaries, articles, sermons, and publications, there are still many unpublished materials that demonstrate the seriousness of Barth's commitment to biblical exegesis. Barth's contribution is clearly unprecedented in modern theology. No other modern theologian has even come close to producing the volume of exegesis he produced. Yet the significance of Barth's achievement as a biblical exegete continues to be assessed. Unlike his early contemporaries who tried to dismiss him as a proof-texting "concordance exegete," scholars have tended in recent years – even those largely sympathetic to Barth – to characterize his contribution as basically aberrant, anomalous, something which owes more to his "tremendous creativity" and "genius" than to anything else.[25] Even my teacher, Brevard Childs, a student and longtime admirer of Barth's theology, has recently stated:

> Karl Barth's name emerges above all others in the 20th century as providing the most ambitious attempt to construct church dogmatics on the foundation of biblical exegesis. One only has to compare Barth's sustained use of detailed exegesis throughout his dogmatics with Brunner, Althaus, Niebuhr, Tillich, and Ebeling, to name only a few, to see what a remarkably different world he had entered from that of his contemporaries. Yet for various reasons Barth's exegesis, for all its brilliant insights and massive stimulus, remained a "virtuoso performance" (the term is Paul McGlasson's) which could not be duplicated and which left little lasting impact either on the biblical academy or on the church. Here the contrast with the enduring biblical contribution of the Reformers is painfully evident.[26]

---

[24] A collection of all the published reviews of the first edition of Barth's *Römerbrief* can be found in the Center for Barth Studies in Luce Library at Princeton Theological Seminary.

[25] Cunningham, *What Is Theological Exegesis?*, p. 14.

[26] Brevard Childs, "Toward Recovering Theological Exegesis" in *Pro Ecclesia* 6 (1997), p. 19. In 1969, Childs said: "When one reads Jülicher's brilliant and learned treatment of Romans, the book emerges from a few shattered walls and ruins. And yet when you read Barth on Romans, whether you agree with his interpretation or not, you know you have confronted someone who understands Paul. It reminds one, again, of Augustine or Chrysostom." ("Karl

This is a serious charge which I believe calls into question not only the significance of Karl Barth's contribution as a biblical exegete but the significance of his entire theology. If Barth's exegesis was essentially a "virtuoso performance," something having more to do with his own creativity and genius than with what Scripture actually says, then his theology – on the basis of its own presuppositions and standards – will not stand. Barth insisted throughout his career that his move had been first to the Bible then to dogma, but if this first move began with exegesis which was essentially ill-founded or merely the product of his own idiosyncratic insights, then his entire theology – again, by its own presuppositions and standards – can hardly be judged as anything else but a "false start." Anyone who has read Barth for very long knows that his entire theological enterprise stands or falls on the basis of exegesis. "Does it stand in Scripture?" This is the presupposition and test of all dogma. This is what really mattered most to Barth; and not just in his early years but in his later years as well.[27] Thus, given the significance of the role of exegesis, at least in Barth's own mind, before pronouncing any final verdict over his exegesis on the basis of whether it has made any "lasting impact" on the church or academy (which is perhaps still too early to tell) or whether it is capable of being "duplicated" or was merely the product of a "virtuoso" (neither of which, for reasons I hope to make clear, he would have seen as good), perhaps it is

---

Barth as Interpreter of Scripture" in *Karl Barth and the Future of Theology*, ed. David L. Dickerman (New Haven: Yale Divinity School Association, 1969), p. 35). Among others who refer to Barth as an exegetical "virtuoso" is Mark I. Wallace, "Karl Barth's Hermeneutic: A Way Beyond the Impasse," *Journal of Religion* 68 (July 1988), p. 408. See also Paul Avis, "Karl Barth: The Reluctant Virtuoso," *Theology* 86 (May 1983), pp. 164-171.

[27] Robert C. Johnson recounts being in one of Barth's seminars in the late 1950s when "a spirited and somewhat convoluted debate" over Barth's method arose, "a debate that moved from one complex issue to two others, and from each of these to two others, and so on. ... The dispute continued in white heat for more than an hour, in the course of which – peering over his glasses on the end of his nose – Barth smoked his pipe, sipped his wine, and refrained from speaking even one word. Then when the debate was at the point of moving into the second hour, it suddenly occurred to one of the students that there was a potential consultant present, a resource person who might conceivably be able to shed some light on the problem or adjudicate the dispute. This student turned and ricocheted the original question that had begun the debate to Barth. Not to be dramatic, but simply to report: there literally was a full minute of heavy silence, in which everyone simply stared at the table. And then Barth said, looking across the morass of complex issues that had been spread on the table (and to all appearances he was entirely serious), 'If I understand what I'm trying to do in the *Church Dogmatics*, it is to listen to what Scripture is saying and tell you what I hear.'" To which Johnson adds: "There was another full minute of silence; and when it was broken, it was not broken verbally but by the noise of chairs in which there was squirming and shifting. And when someone finally did say something (and a great deal more was said), it was said in quite another vein." See "The Legacy of Karl Barth" in *Karl Barth and the Future of Theology*, ed. David L. Dickerman (New Haven: Yale Divinity School Association, 1969), pp. 3-4.

worthwhile to take a closer look at what Barth was really trying to do, what he was up against and trying to overcome, and see if there are specific exegetical principles he employed which might still be worthy of our attention.

In my effort to do so, I will attempt in Chapter 2 to describe the context out of which Barth's so-called "hermeneutical manifesto" was born. Chapter 3 will examine his most important hermeneutical principle, namely, his attempt to read the Bible according to its subject matter, content, and theme. Chapter 4 will analyze what might best be called Barth's "hermeneutics of participation." Chapter 5 will further elaborate his understanding of participation but specifically with respect to the author. Here I will seek to describe the hermeneutical tradition of Schleiermacher, which I refer to as "the empathetic tradition of interpretation," and Barth's relationship to it both before and after his break with liberalism. Finally, Chapter 6 will explore the significance of Barth's effort to interpret the Bible "according to the meaning of the Bible itself."

Chapter 2

A Hermeneutical Manifesto:
Barth's Hermeneutical Discovery in Context

On May 2, 1962, Karl Barth stood before the students and faculty of Princeton Theological Seminary and was asked this question: "Sir, would you comment briefly on, or would you tell us the names of some of the schools in Europe that are actively engaged in hermeneutics, and what we may expect, if anything important, in the future from this discipline?" Softly, slowly, with a heavy Swiss accent, the seventy-six-year-old theologian responded in English:

> The situation has become more and more obscured. The theme of hermeneutics has come up, more and more people speak of hermeneutics – every young man in a different way – and I regret that in discussing 'hermeneutics' the texts themselves come short, you see? They are discussing the question of language, of translation, of application, and so on. I have always preferred to do the thing, to try to explain, to understand texts. And now they are fighting especially in the different schools of the 'Bultmannites,' because there are different Bultmann-schools now, and they are fighting on this methodological basis. I can't like this thing. I'm not involved in it, I look, I see, I read it, but I would prefer they would write commentaries or deliver sermons or write, let us say, a good theology of the New Testament, a better one – yes. Instead of that they are thinking round and round, how do we understand instead of trying to understand and then make a jump in the water to see if they are able to swim![1]

Though stated in his twilight years, these comments are consistent with the position Barth had taken toward the theme of hermeneutics throughout his career. Karl Barth was always more interested in interpreting the Bible than discussing methods of *how* to interpret the Bible. His reasons for maintaining this priority go to the very heart of his theology, and to understand this priority is to understand something very important about the theological revolution he launched in the early part of the twentieth century. Unfortunately, to the extent this priority has been recognized at all, Barth's reasons for maintaining it have never been widely understood. Indeed, perhaps more so today than ever, they have been widely misunderstood.

Underscoring the priority of exegesis over hermeneutics in Barth's thought may seem like an odd way to introduce a study of his hermeneutics, but it is necessary because any attempt to discuss Barth's hermeneutics apart from an

---

[1] Karl Barth, "Gespräch in Princeton I," Question #14, *Gespräche, 1959-1962*, ed. Eberhard Busch (Zürich: Theologischer Verlag Zürich, 1995), p. 507.

understanding of this priority is to misunderstand his hermeneutics fundamentally. To understand the role of this priority in Barth's hermeneutics, it is necessary to understand his specific reasons for maintaining it, and perhaps the best way to understand these reasons is to consider this priority briefly in light of his overall career beginning with his *Römerbrief* period through the 1960s. This is what I will attempt to do in sections A, B, and C of this chapter. In section D, I will try to analyze why Barth maintained this priority from a systematic theological perspective. In section E, I will try to sketch the rise of hermeneutics in the nineteenth and early part of the twentieth century, with its opposing priority of hermeneutics over exegesis which provides important background to Barth's revolution. Finally, in section F, I will outline how Barth proposed to *overcome* the priority of hermeneutics over exegesis in his *Church Dogmatics*, and in section G, I will show that this was actually his aim from the very beginning and how it is reflected in his approach to the task of exegesis in his *Römerbrief* period.

A. The Priority of Exegesis Over Hermeneutics

As a matter of historical interest in the genesis and development of his theology, it is significant that Karl Barth did not come to a conviction regarding the priority of exegesis over hermeneutics gradually or in the course of his later theological development. It was a conviction he held from the very beginning of his theological revolution, and his struggle to draft a fitting preface to the first edition of his commentary on Paul's *Epistle to the Romans* is an expression of that conviction. Throughout the spring and summer of 1918, less than three years after his celebrated break with liberalism, Barth debated with himself and his friend, Eduard Thurneysen, whether or not to include a few preliminary remarks regarding his own understanding of the exegetical task. He realized that the approach he had taken in his attempt to interpret *Romans* would be considered highly controversial by many of his contemporaries and that it would be important to try to preempt some of their criticisms by providing a rationale for why he went about the task of interpretation as he did. But after laboring for several months over several different preface drafts which did provide some rationale for his approach, and after weighing the opinions of his two most trusted advisers, Nelly, his wife, and Thurneysen (both of whom discouraged him from adding a longer preface), Barth decided not to elaborate or provide any substantive explanation of his views regarding the exegetical task in his preface or anywhere else in his commentary. He would simply let the substance of his commentary speak for itself. This decision, seen in retrospect, has to be judged an unfortunate one.[2]

The consequence was that most readers of the first edition of Barth's *Römerbrief* did not know what to make of it. They did not recognize the hermeneutical challenge it represented. Even those favorably disposed to its basic message simply did not know what to make of Barth's method of exposition. Reviewers criticized its exegetical method more than anything else about it. Many questioned whether it should even be called a commentary.[3] They simply did not understand where Barth was coming from or how he could say the things he said in the name of an 'exegesis' of Paul's *Epistle to the Romans*. Adolf Jülicher, probably the most esteemed New Testament scholar of his day, called Barth a "gnostic," a "pneumatic," an "Alexandrian."[4] With Karl Ludwig Schmidt, he compared Barth to Marcion.[5] Wilhelm Loew and Hans Windisch joined Jülicher in calling Barth a "gnostic."[6] Robert Epprecht

---

[2] An account of Barth's attempt to draft a preface to the first edition of the *Römerbrief* is provided in Appendix 1, "The Historical Background of the Preface to the First Edition of Karl Barth's *Römerbrief*."

[3] Philipp Bachmann, "Der Römerbrief verdeutscht und vergegenwärtigt," *Neue Kirchliche Zeitschrift* 32 (1921), pp. 517-547; Jules Breitenstein, *La Semaine religieuse de Genève: journal evangelique protestant*, 1919, 10.5 (1919), p. 19; Ernst Miescher, *Christlicher Volksfreund: Blätter zur Förderung christlichen Glaubens und Lebens* 45:6 (8.2.1919), p. 71; Karl Müller, "Karl Barths' Römerbrief," *Reformierte Kirchenzeitung* 71 (1921), pp. 103-105; Rudolf Steinmetz, *Theologisches Literaturblatt* 41 (1920), pp. 323-325.

[4] Adolf Jülicher, "Ein moderner Paulusausleger" *Die christliche Welt* 34 (1920), pp. 453-457. Also contained in Jürgen Moltmann, ed., *Anfänge der dialektischen Theologie* I (Munich: Christian Kaiser, Verlag, 1962), pp.87-98. Hereafter cited as *Anfänge*; ET "A Modern Interpreter of Paul," *The Beginnings of Dialectical Theology*, trans. Keith R. Crim, ed. James M. Robinson, (Richmond, VA: John Knox Press, 1968), pp. 72-81.

[5] Karl L. Schmidt, "Marcion und wir. Die Gegenwartsbedeutung von Harnacks Marcion," in *Kartell-Zeitung. Organ des Eisenacher Kartells akademisch-theologischer Vereine* 31 (1920/21), pp. 83-85. This is the source of Barth's comment in his preface to the second edition of his *Römerbrief* (hereafter cited as Rom II), "When I was in the midst of the work, Harnack's book on *Marcion* appeared. Anyone who is acquainted with it and who only leafs through my book will know at once why I must mention it. Certain striking parallels also startled me when I looked at the first reviews of that work. I would like, however, to ask the reader to look carefully both here and there and not to praise or condemn me too quickly as a Marcionite. In the decisive points we simply do not agree. Even before the appearance of Harnack's book, Jülicher placed me with Marcion, Harnack himself with Thomas Münzer, and Walther Koehler, if I am not mistaken, with Kaspar Schwenckfeld. I might take this occasion to raise the question of whether this favorite pastime of the theological historians of passing out old and even ancient heretical labels should have taken place before they came to more agreement among themselves? Perhaps it will be to my credit, as the one labeled this time, if I am amazed at how varied the nominations of the three scholars are." See Rom II, pp. xvi-xvii.

[6] Wilhelm Loew, "Noch einmal Barths Römerbrief," *Die Christliche Welt* 34 (1920), pp. 585-587. Hans Windisch, *Theologische Literaturzeitung* 45 (1920), pp. 200-201.

echoed Jülicher's charge that he was a "Neo-Paulinist."[7] Paul Wernle and Friedrich Hadorn referred to him as a "biblicist."[8]

Reviewers of the first edition of the *Römerbrief* (hereafter cited as Rom I) saw it as the product of a variety of influences. Carl Mennicke claimed it was the product of sheer "dogmatism."[9] Ernst Gerber said it was the product of "antinomistical" (Kantian) thought.[10] Rudolf Steinmetz said it was the product of "impressionistic" tendencies.[11] Philipp Bachmann said it was the product of "enthusiasm" and "pneumatic-prophetic exegesis."[12] The young Rudolf Bultmann said it was the product of "enthusiastic revivalism."[13] The young Emil Brunner said it was "naive," though not in the common sense but in the "Schillerian sense."[14] Some complained it was too unscientific, others that it was too scientific, too abstract, too philosophical.[15] Some, like Adriaan van Veldhuizen, said it was "edifying" and would "be of special help to pastors preparing Bible studies."[16] Others said it was not edifying at all.[17]

Paul Wernle, professor of New Testament and Church History at Basel, renowned liberal churchman, and most distinguished Swiss reviewer of Rom I, referred to Barth as a "biblicist" because he simply could not understand how Barth could interpret the apostle Paul so uncritically, so sympathetically, with so much "*Kongenialität*."[18] Wernle admitted that with respect to his own views, "I know I do not have the whole Paul on my side, nor do I even want that. I want to hold on to that which speaks to my heart and conscience, to that

---

[7] Jülicher, *Anfänge*, p. 90; ET p. 75. In his review, "Der Römerbrief von Karl Barth," *Religiöses Volksblatt: Organ für kirchlichen Fortschritt* 51 (1920), pp. 182-184, Robert Epprecht claimed Barth did not care at all about the "historical Jesus" and cared more about Paul than about the simple Gospel of Jesus, more about Paul's teachings than the Sermon on the Mount.

[8] Friedrich Wilhelm Hadorn, *Berner Tagblatt* 32:33 (24.1.1920), p. 2; Paul Wernle, "Der Römberbrief in neuer Beleuchtung," *Kirchenblatt für die reformierte Schweiz* 34 (1919), pp. 163-164, 167-169.

[9] Carl Mennicke, "Auseinandersetzung mit Karl Barth," *Blätter für religiösen Sozialismus* 2 (1920), pp. 5-8.

[10] Ernst Gerber, "Ein neues Buch über den Römerbrief," *Brosamen: Evangelisches Volksblatt* 32:17 (27.4.1919), p. 3.

[11] Steinmetz, *Theologisches Literaturblatt*, p. 325.

[12] Bachmann, "Der Römerbrief verdeutscht und vergegenwärtigt," p. 518.

[13] Rudolf Bultmann, "Ethische und mystische Religion im Urchristentum" [II], *Die Christliche Welt* 34 (1920), pp.738-743.

[14] Emil Brunner, "'Der Römerbrief' von Karl Barth: eine zeitgemäß-unmoderne Paraphrase," *Kirchenblatt für die reformierte Schweiz* 34 (1919), pp. 29-32.

[15] Steinmetz, *Theologisches Literaturblatt* p. 323. See also Epprecht, Mennicke, Wernle.

[16] Adriaan van Veldhuizen, *Nieuwe theologische studiën: praktisch maandschrift voor godgeleerdheid*, 2 (1919), p. 109. See also Jülicher, *Anfänge*, p. 90; ET p. 74 and George Merz's review in *Christentum und Gegenwart: evangelisches Monatsblatt* 11:3 (1920), p. 48.

[17] Wilhelm Wuhrmann, *Schweizerische theologische Zeitschrift* 37 (1920), pp. 59-60. See also Steinmetz, p. 323.

[18] Wernle, "Der Römerbrief in neuer Beleuchtung," p. 169.

which is eternal in [Paul's] message." But to do so, Wernle said, "I must distinguish and choose."[19] And this, he charged, is precisely what Barth had refused to do. For example, "When Paul writes: 'our salvation is nearer than when we first believed,' Barth does not have the slightest feeling of unease that almost nineteen centuries have passed and the hoped for salvation has not yet come; on the contrary, Barth manages to carry readers – without their knowledge – happily beyond this cliff. Everything between Paul and his exegete remains in harmony."[20] "There is absolutely no point in the thought of Paul that he finds disagreeable ... not even the most modest remnant conditioned by the history of the times is left over."[21]

The most consistently elaborated charge against Barth, however, was that his exegesis had not done justice to the actual content of Paul's *Epistle to the Romans*. As powerful, illuminating, and insightful as much of it was, most said it had been done at the expense of the real, historical Paul. Several spoke of the "violence" Barth had done to Paul.[22] Wernle said, "If Barth had not so contemptuously ignored the historical background of *Romans* he would not have gone so thoroughly wrong."[23] Jülicher, in probably his most repeated charge, claimed the reason for this was because Barth was "a sworn enemy of historical-criticism."[24] He warned: "He who despises the past because only he who is alive is right cannot gain anything from the past. He who in holy egoism thinks only of his own problems and chides the dead, who can no longer answer him, can surely not demand that a product of the past – as the *Letter to the Romans* most surely is – should become alive for him."[25] The problem, as Carl Mennicke described it, was that Barth did not make "the least attempt to deal with the difficulties of modern consciousness." "These difficulties," he said, "do not concern him at all."[26] Wilhelm Loew said the problem with

---

[19] Wernle, "Der Römerbrief in neuer Beleuchtung," p. 168

[20] Wernle, "Der Römerbrief in neuer Beleuchtung," p. 169.

[21] Wernle, "Der Römerbrief in neuer Beleuchtung," p. 169. Barth repeats the phrase "disagreeable points" ("ungemütliche Punkte") several times throughout his preface to the second edition of his *Römerbrief* and once in his preface to the third edition. For Barth, as we shall see, it was a representative phrase which expressed the attitude of many of his contemporaries.

[22] Jülicher, *Anfänge*, p. 93; ET p. 76. See also Martin Werner's review in *Evangelisches Schulblatt: Organ des Evangelischen Schulvereins der Schweiz* 54 (1919), p. 400 and Loew, "Noch einmal Barths Römerbrief," p. 586.

[23] Wernle, "Der Römerbrief in neuer Beleuchtung," p. 167

[24] Jülicher, *Anfänge*, p.90; ET pp. 74-75.

[25] Jülicher, *Anfänge*, p. 98; ET p. 81. Friedrich Gogarten, then an apparent ally, defended Barth against Jülicher's charge of "holy egoism" in his brief essay, "Vom heiligen Egoismus des Christen: eine Antwort auf Jülichers Aufsatz in Nr.29 'Ein moderner Paulausleger,'" *Die Christliche Welt* 34 (1920), pp. 546-550. Also in Moltmann, *Anfänge*, pp. 99-104; ET "The Holy Egoism of The Christian: An Answer to Jülicher's Essay: 'A Modern Interpreter of Paul," *The Beginnings of Dialectical Theology*, pp. 82-87.

[26] Mennicke, "Auseinandersetzung mit Karl Barth," p. 6.

Barth's approach was that one has "intensive experience without any feeling of distance."²⁷ The broad and overwhelming consensus among reviewers of Rom I was that Barth had simply read too much of the present, too much of his own situation, into the text.²⁸ Many concluded that Barth's commentary on Paul's *Epistle to the Romans* actually said more about Barth than it did about Paul.²⁹

Though Barth had not elaborated any substantive explanation of his views regarding the exegetical task in his brief, final preface, he did make a few comments which drew considerable fire. Probably his most provocative statement was: "If I had to choose between it [the critical historical method] and the old doctrine of inspiration, I would resolutely choose the latter." He also said with respect to the question of distance between the modern reader and Paul: "The difference between then and now, there and here, must be considered. But the purpose of this consideration can only be the recognition that these differences have no significance for what really matters," and then added: "What was once a serious matter is still serious today, and what today is serious, and not just arbitrariness and whim, stands also in direct relation to what was formerly serious. Our questions, if we understand ourselves aright, are the questions of Paul, and Paul's answers, if their light illumines us, must be our answers."³⁰ In retrospect, given the hermeneutical assumptions of the day, it should come as no surprise that reviewers criticized Barth's preface more so than any other part of Rom I.³¹ Karl Fueter referred to it as "proud."³² Jülicher called it "presumptuous" and found it so offensive that he recommended readers ignore it. (Ironically, Jülicher himself spent most of his review refuting statements made in the preface). Many thought Barth's concluding line, "this book has time to – wait," was arrogant – as if the author already knew that he had written something important.³³ But the line that drew even more fire was

---

[27] Loew, "Noch einmal Barths Römerbrief," p. 586.

[28] Epprecht, "Der Römerbrief von Karl Barth," p. 2; Karl Fueter, "Allerlei Theologisches," *Neue Züricher Zeitung und schweizerisches Handelsblatt* 140:2008 (21.12.1919); Hadorn, *Berner Tagblatt*, p. 2; Loew, "Noch einmal Barths Römerbrief," p. 586; Steinmetz, *Theologisches Literaturblatt*, p. 323.

[29] Hans Baur, *Schweizerisches Protestantenblatt* 42 (1919), p. 128; Ernst Gerber, "Ein neues Buch über den Römerbrief," *Brosamen: Evangelisches Volksblatt* 32:17 (27.4.1919), pp. 2-3; Hadorn, *Berner Tagblatt*, p. 2; Jülicher, *Anfänge*, passim; Loew, "Noch einmal Barths Römerbrief," p. 587; Steinmetz, *Theologisches Literaturblatt*, p. 325; Paul Wernle, "Der Römerbrief in neuer Beleuchtung," passim.

[30] Rom I, p. v.

[31] Most reviewers of Rom I refer explicitly to and cite directly from the preface: Brunner, Fueter, Gogarten, Hadorn, Jülicher, Loew, Karl Müller, Steinmetz, Windisch.

[32] Karl Fueter, "Allerlei Theologisches."

[33] Barth said in the opening lines of his preface to Rom II: "In the preface to the first edition I called this a 'preliminary work.' If this allusion has attracted as much attention as that almost notorious last sentence ('This book can wait ...'), I do not need to justify myself today when I present the book in a new revision." Rom II, p. vi.

the one in which he claimed he had written his commentary in "the joy of discovery."[34] Barth later admitted that he had said this perhaps "somewhat romantically,"[35] but at the time the phrase only reinforced the suspicion of many that Karl Barth was a thoroughgoing "pneumatic."

Barth read the reviews of Rom I with great interest. He makes comments about many of them in his letters to Thurneysen.[36] For example, on May 11, 1919 he sent along a copy of Brunner's review and wrote: "Everything he says suggests he misses the point, ... but I can't exactly pin down what is really missing."[37] On July 14, 1920, he reported, "Yesterday afternoon Jülicher's long-heralded 42-centimeter shell landed here. Help me to take the measurements of the shell-hole and dig out from all the rubble. Yet it is not really so bad, more a gentle evening rain that moistens everything than a terrible thunderstorm."[38] On September 18, 1920, he wrote, "I thought [Wilhelm Loew's] review was clever, but not without the odor of death. ... For a moment I thought I should write [a] letter to him publicly (in the *'Christliche Welt'*), but I refrained from it. Let them all present their smart objections. Another time it will be *our* turn again."[39] Though other reviews evoked a similar response, apart from his correspondence with Thurneysen, a few personal letters to a few of his reviewers,[40] and one lengthy letter written in response to Paul Wernle's review,[41] Barth remained silent in face of his critics' charges throughout 1919 and 1920.[42]

---

[34]Reviewers who cite or allude to the phrase "joy of discovery" include Hans Baur, "Selbstkritik oder Selbstzerfleischung?" *Schweizerisches Protestantenblatt* 43 (1920), pp. 275-277; Brunner, "'Der Römerbrief' von Karl Barth: eine zeitgemäß-unmoderne Paraphrase"; Gerber, "Ein neues Buch über den Römerbrief"; Jülicher, *Anfänge*, p. 104; George Merz, *Christentum und Gegenwart: evangelisches Monatsblatt* 11:3 (1920), p. 48; Ernst Miescher, *Christlicher Volksfreund: Blätter zur Förderung christlichen Glaubens und Lebens* 45:6 (8.2.1919), p. 71; Emil Müller, "Der Römerbrief," *Monatsblatt für das reformierte Volk des Aargaus* 29:7 (1919), pp. 51-54; Alexander Münch, *Das neue Werk: Der Christ im Volksstaat* 1 (1919), pp. 487-488.

[35] Rom II, p. xvii.

[36] Karl Barth to Eduard Thurneysen, *Karl Barth-Eduard Thurneysen Briefwechsel, 1913-1921* (Zürich: Theologischer Verlag Zürich, 1973): Epprecht, 3 Feb. 1919, p. 316; Gerber, 21 May, 1919, p. 328; Münch, 28 Oct., 1919, p. 349; Fueter, 26 Dec., 1919, p. 363; Mennicke, 3 May, 1920, p. 386; J. Müller, 21 May, 1920, p. 390; et al. Hereafter cited *B-Th. Br. I*.

[37] Karl Barth to Eduard Thurneysen, 11 May, 1919, *B-Th. Br. I*, p. 326.

[38] Karl Barth to Eduard Thurneysen, 14 July, 1920, *B-Th. Br. I*, p. 410.

[39] Karl Barth to Eduard Thurneysen, 18 September, 1920, *B-Th. Br. I*, pp. 423-4. Barth continued: "It is amazing that such a clever man ... is not able to let you know anywhere that he does not dare to take the decisive jump. His review, I would almost say, has something 'unconverted' about it."

[40] Robert Epprecht, Carl Mennicke (*B-Th Br. I*, p. 386).

[41] Karl Barth, "Karl Barths Brief an Paul Wernle" (24 October, 1919), Rom I, pp. 638-646.

[42] Barth's essay, "Biblische Fragen, Einsichten und Ausblicke" (1920), *Das Wort Gottes und die Theologie* (Munich: Christian Kaiser Verlag, 1925), treats several hermeneutical and

But in September of 1921 when it came time to draft a preface for the second edition of his *Römerbrief*, Barth chose to hold his silence no longer. He recognized that he needed to respond to his critics and provide an explanation for his particular exegetical approach. When he did, he pulled no punches. His critics described his preface to Rom II as "angry," "arrogant," "hateful," "embarrassing." Jülicher was again scandalized by the "outrageous self-confidence" of the preface, but this time said he saw in it "evidence of a disturbed disposition."[43] Even Barth himself described it as "pugnacious"[44] and in a letter to Thurneysen on Dec.11, 1921, said:

> In part I quite understand your scruples concerning the preface to *Romans* – It belongs naturally on the level of Dempsey vs. Carpentier, especially in the parts that were directed against Wernle, which you perhaps have especially in view. It is to be conceived as an attempt at a *knockout* blow which positively had to be made this once on account of his excessively burdensome and contrary interference with me. If there is no way of making him be quiet, this may at least impel him to stop making *those* foolish statements. ... In comparison with those verses in [Rom.]16:17-20 my preface is really quite irenic, although directed against the same front. Or are my feelings in this whole matter perhaps too hardened and cynical when I think of this preface in line with your own earlier interpretation of it, as a hearty battle cry full of Homeric invective, a vestibule as it were in which the wanderer is first eyed and growled at by the house dog lying there on the carpet and then addressed as "Jacob!" by a parrot on its perch, before he enters the first proper room where men live? That must be as it is because of the earthly aspect of the matter, and it is perhaps useful at least in a propaedeutic fashion for some who will not understand the rest. I see now quite a number of types of people with whom one must deal in some such way as this in order to win their attention. A few words thrown in on 'method' or of 'self-interpretation' (there are certainly not many of them in the preface) often have a pacifying effect in moments when for the time being any greater alarm would not be good.[45]

This portion of Barth's letter was written in part to console Thurneysen, who, after having previously given it his "unconditional approval," had begun to have misgivings about the preface to Rom II. He had told Barth that it perhaps sounded a bit too much like "self-interpretation," that it might only serve to "stiffen" the positions of his critics, and that perhaps the best thing to do would be to "omit the preface entirely."[46] This time, however, Barth decided he

---

exegetical issues, but only indirectly responds to the kinds of criticisms raised against Rom I. Hereafter cited as "Biblische Fragen, Einsichten und Ausblicke."

[43] Adolf Jülicher, "Der Römerbrief" in *Theologische Literaturzeitung* 47:25 (1922), pp. 539-540.

[44] Barth, "Nachwort," p. 295; ET p. 265.

[45] Karl Barth to Eduard Thurneysen, 11 December, 1921, *Karl Barth-Eduard Thurneysen Briefwechsel, 1921-1930* (Zürich: Theologischer Verlag Zürich, 1974), pp. 21-22. Hereafter cited as *B-Th. Br. II*.

[46] "Think of this – and this is also the reason I was so long silent – I had a, how shall I say, serious temptation in regard to your preface (to Rom II). When I looked at it again weeks later, it suddenly seemed to me to be somehow not quite right, and I reproached myself that I had done you no good deed with my unconditional approval. It seemed to me to be, on the one

would stick to his guns and publish the preface as written. The last time Thurneysen had warned Barth about the dangers of writing his preface as a means of "self-interpretation," as a means of explaining why and how he had written what he had written, Barth decided he would supply only a very brief preface to his work instead of one of the longer, more polemical ones he had prepared.[47] He recognized that he could not afford to take this route again. Behind Thurneysen's concern about self-interpretation, of course, was his concern that readers would focus on the book's method rather than its content. Barth shared this concern. But Barth also realized, as apparently Thurneysen did not, that the topic of method could not go completely unaddressed. This is why in his preface he insisted that a few words about method be "thrown in." Not only might they serve to "win the attention" of quite a number of people who might not otherwise be reached, they might even be "useful at least in propaedeutic fashion for some who [would] not understand the rest."

But there is another reason why Barth insisted on throwing in a few words about method. Now more was at stake. Now it was not only a matter of being understood. It was a matter of not being *mis*understood. Barth felt he had no choice but to respond to his critics. Many he cited and called by name. Others he responded to but did not name, which is evident from examining reviews of Rom I. But even though he had anticipated many of his reviewers' criticisms (as we now know from his preface drafts to Rom I), Barth said he had learned something from them. In his preface to Rom II he said that one of the reasons for his "further development and advance" beyond Rom I was due to his "close following of the reception which was given my first edition."[48] While several reviews had actually been positive and constructively critical, the majority had not been. Barth's preface to Rom II represents an attempt to respond to those criticisms which, from his perspective, had not only most seriously misunderstood his work, but had subjected it to the most distortion and caricature. Barth was not able to respond to all the criticisms put to Rom I, but he did address the one issue his reviewers had most vigorously attacked, namely, his exegetical method. This is what was at issue when, after listing four reasons for his ad-

---

hand, like a self-interpretation which in relation to the following book was as superfluous as, for instance, an artist's self-interpretation concerning his work. On the other hand, the *specific* description of the idols that were to be overthrown, it seemed to me, would only strengthen and stiffen their positions since there are always people who at once take sides when a sharp attack is made; at any rate it would forever barricade the doors for those on the outside. ... To take account of these considerations it would have been necessary for you to omit the preface *entirely* – for a time it seemed to me really that *that* was the thing to do! But then I realized suddenly that *that* was simply too clever and calculating." Eduard Thurneysen to Karl Barth, 2 Dec., 1921, *B-Th Br. II*, pp. 16-18.

[47] Appendix 1, "The Historical Background of The Preface to The First Edition of Barth's *Römerbrief*."

[48] Rom II, p. vii.

vance beyond Rom I, Barth stated at the outset of his preface to Rom II: "More important for me are certain basic matters that concern both editions."[49] More than anything else, the preface to Rom II represents a defense of Barth's exegetical method. As such it became the most famous – certainly the most quoted – part of Rom II; and though it had anything but a "pacifying effect," it did indeed, as Barth predicted, "win the attention" of a number of his contemporaries.

Ironically, however, for all its fiery polemic and all the attention it received both immediately after its publication and throughout succeeding years, the preface to Rom II *did not* accomplish its author's purpose. It did not change the minds of his critics. It did not significantly alter the majority opinion among biblical scholars that when it came to biblical exegesis Barth was still a "declared enemy of historical-criticism." To them, he was still a "Pneumatiker," an "Alexandrian," a "gnostic," a "Marcionite," a "Biblicist," etc. Nor did it satisfy the methodological questions of his critics. These remained central. In fact, like Rom I, not only was it the preface of Rom II more than anything else that drew the most fire from reviewers, it was again Barth's exegetical method which appeared to them as the main target. Ironically, all Barth's attempts to defend himself against the specific charges of his critics in his preface to Rom II seem only to have deepened their suspicions. For various reasons, it was simply too late. From an exegetical standpoint, doubt had been cast on the entire enterprise. Prejudices had been formed. Trenches had been dug. Despite all his denials, the labels with which he had been vilified by reviewers of Rom I had stuck.

Barth's decision not to discuss his own understanding of the exegetical task in any substantive way from the outset had been a gamble. Rather than distracting his readers, Barth had hoped, following Thurneysen's advice, that his exegesis of Paul's *Epistle to the Romans* would itself provide sufficient explanation of his understanding of the exegetical task. Knowing how deeply preoccupied his contemporaries – and practically the entire theological enterprise of the foregoing century – had been with respect to questions of method, he did not wish for strategic reasons to open up this particular can of worms. After all, this is precisely what he had attacked in his commentary. Moreover, he knew that in this regard, nothing he could say in any preface would ever fully satisfy his critics. This is not, of course, to suggest, as we shall see, that Barth did not have deep hermeneutical convictions from the beginning. But it is an interesting question whether or not in retrospect Barth would have been better off had he provided some kind of explanation of his exegetical method in his preface to Rom I. Would his approach to the task of exegesis have been taken any more seriously by his contemporaries had he said something more about his hermeneutical principles from the start? Would it have helped his cause if,

---

[49] Rom II, p. viii.

rather than being put on the defensive, rather than being forced to give answers to questions he had not framed, he could have preempted his critics by offering a preliminary word of explanation? Whether or not, in the long run, this would have made any significant difference, we will never know. But one thing is certain: Karl Barth has never really been acquitted of the charges made against him by reviewers of Rom I. The same charges made then have been repeated throughout the twentieth century and loom over his theological legacy to this day.

B. Karl Barth's Commitment to Theological Exegesis

It is more than merely a tribute to Karl Barth's fortitude that he continued to pursue biblical exegesis after the torrent of criticism he received at the hands of reviewers of Rom I and II. It is an indication of how important he saw the task of biblical exegesis to be. Throughout his career Barth claimed that biblical exegesis remained the presupposition and goal of all his work. And so it was from the beginning, according to Thurneysen, who in 1956, said in his essay, "Die Anfänge":

> Karl Barth stands before us already in this early period as a reader and expositor of Scripture. The tablets of Holy Scripture are erected before him and the books of the expositors from Calvin through the biblicists and all the way to the modern critical biblical interpretation lie open in his hands. Both then and now this has been the source from which his whole theology has come. It has grown out of the work of preaching, and it serves the proclamation of the church. And so it has remained. That the springs of the Bible should flow afresh in our time is the great concern that here is central, and indeed the sole concern. Barth is no abstract thinker, as will be very clear from these beginnings, and abstract here would mean liberated from the Scriptures. He does not project theological speculations out of his own mind; he is not concerned about a system; he is and he remains a student and teacher of Holy Scriptures. Whoever tries to understand him as other than this will not understand him at all.[50]

Barth himself was steadfast throughout his career in affirming this as well. In 1963, with the republication of Rom I, he reminded readers that it was chiefly because of the interest in biblical exegesis shown in this work that he had been appointed to his first teaching post.[51] And it is significant that though he was

---

[50] Eduard Thurneysen, "Die Anfänge," *Antwort: Karl Barth zum siebzigsten Geburtstag.* Eds. Rudolf Frey, et al. (Zürich: Evangelischer Verlag Zürich, 1956), p. 832; ET *Revolutionary Theology in The Making*, trans. James D. Smart (Richmond: John Knox Press, 1964), pp. 12f.

[51] "I owe my invitation to a chair at Göttingen (which I received as early as the beginning of 1921) and hence my elevation to 'proper academic theology' not to the famous second edition of Romans, but to the first, which afterwards faded into oblivion. (The chair for Reformed Theology was a new one, founded with the help of American Presbyterians). One might well ask how this book made the group of individuals who at that time counted for anything in the German Reformed Church think that I was suited to the task. Given its content and style, no

appointed to an honorary chair at Göttingen to teach "introduction to the Reformed confession, Reformed doctrine and Reformed church life,"[52] nearly half the courses he taught there were courses in biblical exegesis. While he almost always gave priority to his courses in historical or dogmatic theology (typically three or four hours per week),[53] every semester until the summer of 1925, he taught a one-hour course in New Testament exegesis, for example, on *Ephesians, Colossians, I Corinthians*,[54] *Philippians*,[55] *James, I John*, and the Sermon on the Mount. The only exception to this was in the summer semester of 1922 when after having already announced and made preparations for a three hour course on *The Epistle to the Hebrews* he was forced to cancel it due to the degree to which he found himself absorbed in preparation for his course on the theology of Calvin.[56] But it was not only his courses in historical and dogmatic theology that absorbed him. Throughout these years Barth often expressed in his letters to Thurneysen more interest and enthusiasm for his courses in biblical exegesis than his courses in theology and regretted that he had not arranged more time for them.[57] On May 18, 1924, for example, only two weeks into the new semester, Barth reported to Thurneysen: "What delights *me* most is the

---

one will be surprised to hear that at first I found it a novel experience to be addressed in so compelling a way in my capacity as a Reformed theologian. First of all I had to accustom myself to the function that I was supposed to have. In fact the second edition of Romans which I had produced in the meanwhile made it easier for me: one will hardly find the first edition distinguished by a particular Calvinistic content. What moved a man like Professor Karl Müller in Erlangen (who was foremost in recommending me) or the retired pastor Adam Heilman in Göttingen (who was most energetic in getting things going) to invite me there was surely the form of the book. It suggested that I was passionately concerned with Holy Scripture." See Karl Barth, preface to German reprint of Rom I (Zürich: Evangelischer Verlag Zürich, 1963).

[52] Eberhard Busch, *Karl Barths Lebenslauf* (Munich: Christian Kaiser Verlag, 1975), pp. 141-142; ET *Karl Barth: His Life From Letters and Autobiographical Texts*, trans. John Bowden (Philadelphia: Fortress Press, 1976), pp. 128-9. Hereafter cited as *Lebenslauf*.

[53] For a listing of the courses Barth taught at Göttingen and Münster, see *B-Th. Br. II*, pp. 741-743.

[54] Karl Barth, *Die Auferstehung der Toten. Eine akademische Vorlesung über I. Kor. 15* (Munich: Christian Kaiser Verlag, 1924) ET *The Resurrection of the Dead*, trans. H.J. Stenning (New York: Hodder & F.H. Revell Company, 1933).

[55] Karl Barth, *Erklärung des Philipperbriefes* (Munich: Christian Kaiser Verlag, 1927); ET *The Epistle To The Philippians*, trans. James W. Leitch (Richmond: John Knox Press, 1962).

[56] Karl Barth to Eduard Thurneysen, 22 January, 1922, *B-Th Br. II*, p.29 and 2 April, 1922, p. 65. *Die Theologie Calvins, 1922*, ed. Hans Scholl (Zürich: Theologischer Verlag Zürich, 1993); ET *The Theology of John Calvin*, trans. Geoffrey Bromiley (Grand Rapids: William B. Eerdmans, 1995).

[57] Barth later said: "Nowadays I tear my hair in amazement that I could dare to announce that I would lecture on Ephesians for only one hour a week. Of course I hardly got as far as the second chapter." See Busch, *Lebenslauf*, p. 142; ET p. 129.

course on *The Epistle to the Philippians* on Wednesdays. ... Paul! That's what it is! Next to him all dogmatics is slime, and ethics too."[58]

No official at Göttingen apparently ever asked Barth to teach exegesis courses. He did so by his own initiative. It was, at the time, what he knew best and felt most qualified to teach. The foundation for several of his exegesis courses had been already laid by the intense studies he had undertaken as a pastor in Safenwil after 1915. The insights he had gained in these years often provided the groundwork for these courses.[59] Though as an honorary professor of Reformed theology there was no compulsion for students to go to his classes, Barth's courses were very popular and his exegesis courses were often, if not always, more popular than his courses in dogmatic and historical theology. In his first semester at Göttingen his course on *The Epistle to the Ephesians* had between fifty and sixty students whereas in his course on the Heidelberg Catechism there were only about fifteen.[60] During the winter semester of 1923/24 his course on the theology of Schleiermacher[61] had some thirty students whereas his course on *I John* had ninety.[62] Such popularity did not, of course, endear him to his colleagues and the fact that it arose in part because of his "*Bibelstunden*" probably only reinforced his colleagues' opinion that he was more of a preacher than a scholar.[63] But it is clear that Barth "did more than *just empty* their lecture halls" because of his appeal as a preacher.[64]

---

[58] Karl Barth to Eduard Thurneysen, 18 May, 1924, *B-Th Br. II*, pp. 252-253. See also, e.g., 28 Feb., 1923, pp. 149-152.

[59] For example, in January of 1919 Barth began to study I Corinthians. He eventually wrote a "mini-commentary" on chapter 15: "Yesterday and today I sat over I Corinthians 15, but I came to a dead stop in the earliest stages as I started to work through it thoroughly. ... The chapter is the key to the entire letter with its remarkably profound disclosures on this and that, which have their source in ultimate wisdom. Some of them have struck us recently like shocks from an electric eel" Karl Barth to Eduard Thurneysen, 11 November, 1919, *B-Th Br. I*, p. 350. This study became the basis of his lecture course on I Corinthians. Busch states that in 1919 Barth "was particularly preoccupied with Ephesians, which he had read through cursorily the previous year for hours on end with his confirmation candidates. ... In the summer of 1919, he gave a series of sermons on the book which during the following winter he then reshaped as a short commentary. The next summer he looked at the epistle again during a Bible class. The provisional results of Barth's biblical studies can be seen in a lecture which he gave at a conference of the Student Christian Movement in Aarburg on 9 June on 'Christian Life'" *Lebenslauf*, pp. 121-122; ET pp. 108-9. In 1920, in addition to his intense study of *Romans* while rewriting his commentary, Barth studied Colossians and II Corinthians.

[60] Karl Barth to Eduard Thurneysen, 18 Nov., 1921, *B-Th Br. II*, p. 9.

[61] Barth, *Die Theologie Schleiermachers*.

[62] Karl Barth to Eduard Thurneysen, 20 Dec., 1923, *B-Th Br. II*, p. 209. However, part of the reason why Barth's exegesis courses were so popular may have been that they were only one-hour courses.

[63] Barth gained a reputation for giving "first-rate *Bibelstunden* for the educated." Eduard Thurneysen to Karl Barth, 21 June, 1923, *B-Th Br. II*, p. 177 (see p. 178n.2). There is a difference however between the one-hour lecture courses on exegesis that Barth offered at the uni-

Barth approached his exegesis courses with the same seriousness as his courses in dogmatic and historical theology. In his next book after Rom II, *Die Auferstehung der Toten* (1924), which in terms of its exegetical approach he saw in basic continuity with the approach he had taken in his exegesis of *Romans*,[65] Barth said that he saw it as his task to "uphold and continue the attempt of a *theological* exegesis," not at the expense of – much less in opposition to – historical questions and concerns, but as a "necessary *corrective*." He said that given "the decisive historical orientation of the appointed New Testament scholars of today," he recognized it was no doubt considered a "scandal and outrage" that the problems which interested them "seem to be of little or no interest to me at all." Yet he said the scandal and outrage were certainly "mutual because my questions and concerns do not seem to trouble them much either."[66]

Obviously not everyone at the time lacked interest in the kinds of questions and concerns Barth had focused on in his exegesis, for on July 22, 1925 he received an invitation to become Professor of Dogmatics *and* New Testament Exegesis at Münster.

At Münster, having *ordinarius* and not merely *extraordinarius* professorship status, Barth continued to teach courses in New Testament exegesis alongside courses in historical and dogmatic theology. In his first semester, in addition to a seminar on Calvin's *Institutes* and a one-hour lecture course on Eschatology, he taught a four-hour lecture course on *The Gospel of John*.[67] It was about this time, in the mid-twenties in Germany, that a vigorous discussion focusing on "pneumatic exegesis" began to emerge. This became a wide-ranging discussion that included participants from a variety of disciplines (not only biblical scholars and dogmaticians, but practical theologians and psychologists of religion as well), and it lasted throughout the rest of the decade until other matters in Germany began to take center stage.[68] Many involved in it recognized that it

---

versity and what is generally known as '*Bibelstunden*,' the latter having often an *unwissenschaftlich*, even pietistic connotation. Whether Hirsch deemed Barth as "unwissenschaftlich" because of his '*Bibelstunden*' is unclear. But given the substance of some of their conversations at the time, as Barth later recalled (see p. 107 below), Barth's approach in such courses may well have contributed to Hirsch's charge. Karl Barth to Eduard Thurneysen, 2 April 1922, *B-Th Br. II*, p. 64. At any rate, Barth later remarked about his Göttingen colleagues, "the faculty even tormented me a bit: they wanted to keep me under. ... On the black notice board where announcements of lectures were pinned they put mine next to the lessons of the teacher who showed students how to play the harmonium." See Busch, *Lebenslauf*, p. 146; ET p. 133.

[64] Eduard Thurneysen to Karl Barth, 30 July 1925, *B-Th Br. II*, p. 364.

[65] Barth, *Die Auferstehung der Toten*, preface p. v.

[66] Barth, *Die Auferstehung der Toten*, preface p. v.

[67] Karl Barth, *Erklärung des Johannes-Evangeliums 1-8: Vorlesung, Münster, Wintersemester 1925/26*, ed. Walther Fürst (Zürich: Theologischer Verlag Zürich, 1976).

[68] Paul Althaus, "Paulus und sein neuester Ausleger," *Christentum und Wissenschaft*, 1 (1925), pp. 20-30, 97-102; Philipp Bachmann, "Der Römerbrief und Barths Auslegung dessel-

had been largely initiated by Barth's *Römerbrief* and that in its wake a general reassessment of the presuppositions of the reigning exegetical method was long overdue. In describing the pneumatic exegesis discussion of the 1920s, James M. Robinson said "it took on proportions explainable only in terms of the hermeneutical embarrassment scholarly circles sensed in trying to cope with Barth's *Romans*."[69] Rudolf Bultmann referred to pneumatic exegesis as a "detestable expression" which was "only likely to pervert a true understanding of

---

ben," *Allgemeine evangelisch-lutherische Kirchenzeitung: Organ der Allgemeinen Evangelisch-lutherischen Konferenz* 59 (1926), pp. 434-440, 458-463, 484-492.; Johannes Behm, *Pneumatische Exegese? Ein Wort zur Methode der Schriftauslegung* (Schwerin: Fr. Bahn, 1926); Karl Buschbeck, "Der Römerbrief," *Evangelisches Kirchenblatt für Schlesien* 25:45 (1922), pp. 335-337; Oscar Cullmann, "Les problèmes poses par la methode exegetique de l'ecole de Karl Barth," *Revue d'histoire et de philosophie religieuses* 8 (1928), pp. 70-83; Ernst von Dobschütz, "Die Pneumatische Exegese, Wissenschaft und Praxis," *Vom Auslegen des Neuen Testamentes* (Göttingen: Vandenhoeck & Ruprecht, 1927), pp. 49-64; Erich Fascher, *Vom Verstehen des Neuen Testaments: Ein Beitrag zur Grundlegung einer zeitgemäßen Hermeneutik* (Gießen: Alfred Töpelmann, 1930), pp. 25-35; Heinrich Frick, *Wissenschaftliches und Pneumatisches Verständnis der Bibel* (Tübingen: J.C.B. Mohr [Paul Siebeck], 1927); Karl Girgensohn, *Die Inspiration der heiligen Schrift* (Dresden: C.L. Ungelenk,1925); Robert Jelke, "Historisch-kritische und theologische-dogmatische Schriftauslegung" in *Das Erbe Martin Luthers, Festschrift für Ihmels* (Leipzig: Dörffling & Franke, 1928) pp. 215-235. Adolf Jülicher, *Theologische Literaturzeitung* 47 (1922), pp. 537-542; Wilhelm Koepp, *Die gegenwärtig Geisteslage und die 'dialektische' Theologie: eine Einführung* (Tübingen: J.C.B. Mohr [Paul Siebeck], 1930), p. 82, 104; Gerhard Krüger, "Dialektische Methode und theologische Exegese. Logische Bemerkungen zu Barths 'Römerbrief,'" *Zwischen den Zeiten*, 5:2 (1927), pp. 116-157; Waldemar Macholz, "Pneumatische Exegese – eine berechtigte theologische Forderung," *Pastoralblätter* (69), pp. 70ff. Artur Neuberg, Rezension von: Barths Römerbrief, 2.Aufl in neuer Bearbeitung. *Pastoralblätter für Predigt, Seelsorge und kirchliche Unterweisung* 64 (1921), pp. 497-504; O. Procksch, "Über pneumatische Exegese," *Christentum und Wissenschaft* I (1925), pp. 145-158; Erich Schaeder, "Die Geistesfrage in der neueren Theologie der Gegenwart," *Zeitschrift für systematische Theologie* 3 (1925), pp. 424-460. See esp. pp. 448ff; Johannes Schneider, "Historische und pneumatische Exegese," *Neue Kirchliche Zeitschrift* 42:12 (1931), pp. 711-733; Roland Schütz, "Kritisches zur Theologie der Krisis," *Theologische Studien und Kritiken: Beiträge zur Theologie und Religionswissenschaft*, 1925, pp. 263-288; Erich Seeberg, "Zum Problem der pneumatischen Exegese," in *Sellin-Festschrift* (Leipzig: Deichert, 1927), pp. 127-137. "Das Problem der pneumatischen Exegese" in *Menschwerdung und Geschichte* (Stuttgart: W. Kohlhammer Verlag, 1938), pp. 138-148; Reinhold Seeberg, "Zur Frage nach dem Sinn und Recht einer pneumatischen Schriftauslegung," *Zeitschrift für systematische Theologie*, 1927, pp. 3-59; Frederik Torm, *Hermeneutik des Neuen Testaments* (Göttingen: Vandenhoeck und Ruprecht, 1930), pp. 18f.; Friedrich Traub, "Wort Gottes und pneumatische Schriftauslegung," *Zeitschrift für Theologie und Kirche* 8 (1927), pp. 83-111. Georg Wobbermin, "Pneumatische oder religionspsychologische Methode der systematischen Theologie?," *Zeitschrift für Theologie und Kirche* 8 (1927), pp. 53-62.

[69] James M. Robinson, "Hermeneutics After Barth," in *The New Hermeneutic*, ed. James M. Robinson (New York: Harper & Row, 1964), p. 17. Robinson characterizes the pneumatic exegesis discussion of mid-1920s as a "dismal affair ... for it was Bultmann who had something better to say" (pp. 28-29).

the problem."[70] Bultmann said: "Nothing is involved which is in the least analogous to some mysterious entity, the Spirit (*pneuma*) acting as interpreter and whispering the meaning of a text to me." "The statement that the prerequisite for a proper exegesis is prayer is as true and as false as that prayer is a prerequisite for every good work." "I hope all talk of 'pneumatic exegesis' will soon cease. Either it is relevant, in which case it is the duty of every exegete to announce himself as 'spiritual' or to forego exegesis, or it is nonsense. I cannot believe that pastors will permit pneumatic exegesis to be assigned to them as their domain and taken out of the hands of 'scientific' exegetes."[71]

Barth, on the other hand, was not so quick to dismiss the pneumatic exegesis discussion. In his preface to his commentary on *Philippians* (1927), he said: "I do not propose to enter here into the dispute concerning pneumatic exegesis. Although, if I am not mistaken, I am one of those who occasioned it, yet this unpleasant catch-word at all events is not of my coining."[72] Barth claimed that he had been unable to bring much to bear on the dispute – "because so many of the shots aimed at me, which were all too numerous and not without caricature, have been wide of the mark, but above all because it appears to me to have unfortunately bogged down in the sphere of methodological discussions, in which a decision is scarcely to be expected" – and that *as such* it could hardly be fruitfully continued. Nevertheless, he said that the "concretely proposed aim" need not be entirely rejected *if* those pursuing it would "resolve to provide their own examples of an exposition that takes account of the aim in question, and thus show equally concretely how they conceive of this better way."[73] In other words, as he said thirty-five years later to the students and faculty of Princeton Seminary regarding those engaged in contemporary hermeneutical discussions:

---

[70] Rudolf Bultmann, "Die Bedeutung der 'dialektischen Theologie' für die neutestamentliche Wissenschaft," *Glauben und Verstehen* I (Tübingen: J.C.B. Mohr [Paul Siebeck], 1933), pp. 127f.; ET "The Significance of 'Dialectical Theology'" in *Faith and Understanding*, trans. Louise Pettibone Smith (Philadelphia: Fortress Press, 1987), pp. 158f. Hereafter cited as *Glauben und Verstehen*.

[71] Bultmann, *Glauben und Verstehen*, p. 128 n. 12; ET p. 159 n.12 [translation revised].

[72] Barth, *Erklärung des Philipperbriefes*, preface. Barth also used the phrase "die pneumatische Bibelexegese" in his 1925 essay, "Kirche und Theologie" in idem, *Die Theologie und die Kirche* (Munich: Christian Kaiser Verlag, 1928), p. 302; ET "Church and Theology," in *Theology and Church*, trans. Louise Pettibone Smith (New York: Harper & Row, 1962), p. 286.

[73] Barth, *Erklärung des Philipperbriefes*, preface. Moreover, as Barth said in his preface to the English edition of his Römerbrief drafted in 1932: "I ask readers not to say to me too quickly (as a few in Germany have said to me all too quickly), that I am not an exegete or rather: that I am a 'pneumatic' exegete. The reproach which is implied in the word 'pneumatic' may well fall back heavily on those who so easily raise it." Karl Barth, "Vorwort zur englischen Ausgabe der Römerbriefauslegung" in *Zwischen den Zeiten* (1932), pp. 480; ET *The Epistle To The Romans*, trans. Edwyn C. Hoskyns (Oxford: University Press, 1933), p. ix [translation revised].

if such deliberations were to be of any real significance, beyond merely discussing methods and techniques, sooner or later they would have to "jump in the water to see if they are able to swim!"

Barth himself continued to "swim" throughout his years at Münster and later at Bonn, where, having been offered a post as early as Oct. 26, 1929, he moved in March of 1930. At Bonn he continued to teach New Testament exegesis courses alongside courses in dogmatic and historical theology,[74] but by this time the task of a major dogmatic work was well under way and clearly the focus of his thought.[75] The importance of Barth's development throughout this period as a dogmatic and distinctively Reformed theologian can hardly be overstated.[76] Yet it was precisely *as* a dogmatic and distinctively Reformed theologian that Barth continued throughout this period to emphasize the importance of biblical exegesis. Nowhere do we find a better illustration of this than in Barth's farewell speech to a group of students of the Confessing Church (mostly his own, from Bonn) which he made on a retreat led by Hans Asmus-

---

[74] In the summer semester of 1930, he taught a course on *The Epistle to James* alongside a course in Ethics I and a seminar on Anselm's *Cur Deus Homo*? In the winter semester of 1930/31, he taught a course on *The Epistle to the Philippians* alongside Ethics II and a seminar on The Reformation Doctrine of Sanctification. In the summer semester of 1933, alongside his course on Theology of the Nineteenth Century (part II), he taught a course on *The Gospel of John* and in the winter semester of 1933/34, taught alongside his course on Prolegomena to Dogmatics (KD I/2), another seminar on the Doctrine of Sanctification, and an exegesis course on the Sermon on the Mount.

[75] Actually, already at Göttingen as early as 1924, Barth had begun to lay plans for such a work and it is now clear that many of the major features of this work were already in place. For the most important analysis of the genesis and development of Barth's dogmatics, see McCormack's *Karl Barth's Critically Realistic Dialectical Theology: Its Genesis and Development 1909-1936*.

[76] The fact is that Barth was a dogmatic and in many ways Reformed theologian long before he knew or wished to acknowledge himself as such. Only after his appointment to teach at Münster could he say: "I can now admit [after having accepted a newly established honorary professorship of Reformed theology at Göttingen in 1921] . . . that at that time I did not even own a copy of the Reformed confessions, and I had certainly not read them – not to mention all the other horrendous gaps in my knowledge. ... Fortunately it turned out that my theology, such as it was, had been more Reformed, more Calvinistic than I had known." See Karl Barth, "Autobiographische Skizze Karl Barths aus dem Fakultätsalbum der Ev.-Theol. Fakultät in Münster," *Karl Barth-Rudolf Bultmann Briefwechsel, 1911-1966*, ed. Bernd Jaspert (Zürich: Theologischer Verlag Zürich, 1994), p. 299; ET *Karl Barth-Rudolf Bultmann Letters, 1922-1966*, trans. Geoffrey Bromiley (Grand Rapids: William B. Eerdmans, 1981), p. 156. Hereafter cited as *B-B Br*. He later added, "In fact it was only at Göttingen that I again familiarized myself with the mysteries of specifically Reformed theology, burning the midnight oil in my struggle over it." See Busch, *Lebenslauf*, p. 142; ET p. 129. Becoming a Reformed theologian, Barth realized, would be a long and difficult journey. For an analysis of this journey, see Matthias Freundenberg's *Karl Barth und die reformierte Theologie. Die Auseinandersetzungen mit Calvin, Zwingli und den reformierten Bekenntnisschriften während seiner Göttinger Lehrtätigkeit* (Neukirchen-Vluyn: Neukirchener Verlag, 1996).

sen on the evening of Feb. 10, 1935 before his official dismissal from his teaching post at Bonn for, among other things, refusing to take an unqualified oath of allegiance to Adolf Hitler,[77] which was required of all teachers at all German schools and universities:

> Dear friends, who have listened to me, the main thing you have heard from me is dogmatics. Dogmatics is a high and steep art. I do not want to deny that, humanly as well, I strive after it with a certain love and desire. And I dare say that I have noticed that many of you have been excited about this subject matter as well. If this now for the moment has come to an end, accept this as a signal for you to temporarily begin anew your studies at a different place. Take now my last piece of advice: Exegesis, Exegesis, and once more, Exegesis! If I have become a dogmatician, it is because I long before have endeavored to carry on exegesis. Let the systematic art, which can also make one mad, rest a little and hold on to the Word, to the Scriptures, which is given to us and become perhaps less systematic and more biblical theologians. For then the systematic and dogmatic tasks will certainly be taken care of as well. That is what I wanted to say to you and in this way I wish to bid you farewell.[78]

Though suspended from all his official teaching responsibilities, Barth did not leave Bonn immediately. For eight consecutive weekends, from Feb. 8 until the end of March, he traveled back and forth from Bonn to Utrecht, Holland, where he delivered a series of sixteen lectures published that same year under the title *Credo: Die Hauptprobleme der Dogmatik dargestellt im Anschluß an das apostolische Glaubensbekenntnis.*[79] On April 5-6, he concluded this lecture series with a question and answer period. Of the ten questions put to him (or at least of the ten he choose to respond to), two had specifically to do with his exegetical method. In his attempts to advance *theological* exegesis, Barth found that he still had to clarify his relationship to "*pneumatic* exegesis" and his understanding of the relationship between theological exegesis and the science of history.[80] More shall be said about his response to these questions

---

[77] Barth refers to this particular incident in his letter of Dec.22, 1935 to Rudolf Bultmann when he says "you quietly took the oath over which I 'stumbled' ..." Karl Barth to Rudolf Bultmann, *B-B Br.,* p. 163; ET p. 84.

[78] Karl Barth, "Das Evangelium in der Gegenwart" in *Theologische Existenz heute* 25 (1935), p. 17. The passage continues: "I was glad to be among you, I enjoyed working with you, and will fondly remember this time. In view of this, but much more in view of the Word which called us and held us together and which we once again have heard in this hour I would now like to conclude very encouragingly with the word Jonathan said to David: 'And as for the matter about which you and I have spoken, behold, the Lord is between you and me for ever.'"

[79] Karl Barth, *Credo: Die Hauptprobleme der Dogmatik dargestellt im Anschluß an das apostolische Glaubensbekenntnis* (Munich: Christian Kaiser Verlag, 1935); ET *Credo: A Presentation of the Chief Problems of Dogmatics with Reference to The Apostles' Creed,* trans. J. Strathearn McNab (New York: Charles Scribner's Sons, 1936). Hereafter cited as *Credo.*

[80] Barth, *Credo,* appendix, Question II, pp. 153-154, Question V, pp. 160-164; ET pp. 177-179, pp. 186-191.

later, but the point is that suspicion regarding his theological approach to exegesis continued to follow him.[81]

Barth left Germany at the end of May 1935 and accepted a teaching post at Basel, where he remained for the rest of his life producing one volume after another of his *Church Dogmatics*. Deeply involved as he was throughout the rest of his career in producing his *magnum opus*, his interest in theological exegesis by no means diminished. In fact, it has been shown that the later volumes of the *Church Dogmatics* contain even more exegesis than the earlier ones and that overall there is almost twice as much exegesis in each volume produced after the war than there is in each written before or during the war.[82]

C. The Post-War Appraisal of Barth's Hermeneutic

On the hermeneutical front, the only major development throughout the years leading up to and immediately following the Second World War was Rudolf Bultmann's demythologization campaign which he launched on April 21, 1941.[83] While Bultmann and his students continued after the war to work out problems related to this program, Barth continued to produce one exegesis-filled volume after another of his *Church Dogmatics*. But as Barth continued to swim along, as it were, Bultmann and his students became increasingly interested in hermeneutics as a subject in its own right. In 1950, Bultmann published his essay on "The Problem of Hermeneutics" in which he outlined why the discipline of hermeneutics was so important.[84] It was important because the great problem of the day, as Bultmann saw it, was the problem of under-

---

[81] And Barth is still referred to as a *Pneumatiker*. See, for example, H. Jackson Forstman, *Word and Spirit: Calvin's Doctrine of Biblical Authority* (Stanford: University Press, 1962), pp. 146-7; Helmut Thielicke, *Modern Faith & Thought*, trans. Geoffrey Bromiley (Grand Rapids: William B. Eerdmans, 1990), p. 17.

[82] Christina Baxter, "Barth – A Truly Biblical Theologian?" in *Tyndale Bulletin* 38 (1987), pp. 6f. Baxter's statistical analysis is elaborated in her unpublished Ph.D. thesis "The Movement from Exegesis to Dogmatics in the Theology of Karl Barth" (Durham, England, 1981), pp. 445-65.

[83] Rudolf Bultmann, "Neues Testament und Mythologie. Das Problem der Entmythologisierung der neutestamentlichen Verkündigung," *Kerygma und Mythos*, ed. Hans Werner Bartch (Hamburg: Herbert Reich-Evangelischer Verlag, 1951), pp. 15-48; ET "New Testament and Mythology: The Problem of Demythologizing The New Testament Proclamation," *New Testament and Mythology and Other Basic Writings*, trans. Schubert M. Ogden (Philadelphia: Fortress Press, 1984), pp. 1-44.

[84] Rudolf Bultmann, "Das Problem der Hermeneutik," *Zeitschrift für Theologie und Kirche* 47 (1950), pp. 47-69. Also in *Glauben und Verstehen II* (Tübingen: J.C.B. Mohr [Paul Siebeck], 1952), pp. 211-35; ET "The Problem of Hermeneutics," *New Testament and Mythology and Other Basic Writings*, trans. Schubert M. Ogden (Philadelphia: Fortress Press, 1984), pp. 69-94.

standing. Schleiermacher had recognized this problem long ago, which is why he defined hermeneutics as "the art of understanding."[85] Wilhelm Dilthey and Martin Heidegger had also contributed significantly to the development of hermeneutics as a means of addressing the problem of understanding, and Bultmann saw himself advancing in a similar trajectory, as did his students. Interest in hermeneutics and the problem of understanding became so acute among Bultmann's students that later in the 1950s a movement called the "New Hermeneutic" was born. The central question of the New Hermeneutic was, as Ernst Fuchs put it, "How do I come to understand?"[86] Starting in 1959 with the enthusiastic reception of Heinz Kimmerle's republication of Schleiermacher's *Hermeneutics*, including the previously unpublished handwritten manuscripts,[87] leaders of the New Hermeneutic looked to Schleiermacher, "the father of modern hermeneutics," for support. James M. Robinson claimed Schleiermacher as "materially a precursor of the new hermeneutic."[88] Gerhard Ebeling credited him as its "pioneer."[89] But proponents of the New Hermeneutic were looking to the past only as a means to the future. Many saw themselves as standing on the brink of a new era.[90] Bultmann – following Dilthey's

---

[85] F.D.E. Schleiermacher, *Hermeneutik*, ed. Heinz Kimmerle (Heidelberg: Carl Winter Universitätsverlag, 1959), p. 79; ET *Hermeneutics: The Handwritten Manuscripts*, trans. James Duke and Jack Forstman (Atlanta: Scholars Press, 1977), p. 96. Hereafter cited *Hermeneutik*.

[86] Ernst Fuchs, "Das Neue Testament und das hermeneutische Problem," *Zeitschrift für Theologie und Kirche* 58 (1961), p. 219; ET "The New Testament and The Hermeneutical Problem," *The New Hermeneutic*, trans. and ed. James M. Robinson (New York: Harper & Row, 1964), p. 136.

[87] Friedrich Lücke did not originally publish Schleiermacher's so-called "handwritten manuscripts," viz., lecture drafts, notes, etc., due apparently to their fragmentary nature. Wilhelm Dilthey, Schleiermacher's biographer and greatest proponent of his hermeneutic throughout the nineteenth and early twentieth century, was unfamiliar (it is assumed) with these handwritten manuscripts which, according to some, emphasize more strongly the importance of grammatical interpretation in Schleiermacher's hermeneutic. Much has been made of this. Some suggest this corrects a "one-sided psychological emphasis" which Dilthey gave Schleiermacher's hermeneutics. Others, such as Martin Reddeker, suggest it does not. In addition to Heinz Kimmerle's discussion of this issue in his "Introduction" and "Afterword of 1968," see James Duke, "Translator's Introduction," *Hermeneutics: The Handwritten Manuscripts*, pp. 1-18; Hans-Georg Gadamer, "The Problem of Language in Schleiermacher's Hermeneutic," *Schleiermacher As Contemporary*, ed. Robert W. Funk (New York: Herder & Herder, 1970), pp. 68-95.

[88] James M. Robinson, "Hermeneutics After Barth," *The New Hermeneutic*, ed. James M. Robinson (New York: Harper & Row, 1964), p. 71.

[89] Gerhard Ebeling, "Wort Gottes und Hermeneutik," *Wort und Glaube* (Tübingen: J.C.B. Mohr [Paul Siebeck], 1960), p. 331; ET "Word of God and Hermeneutic," *Word and Faith*, trans. James W. Leitch (Philadelphia: Fortress Press, 1963), p. 317. Hereafter cited as "Wort Gottes und Hermeneutik."

[90] For example, in his essay, "Colloquium on Hermeneutics," *Theology Today* 23 (Oct. 1964), Robert Funk expressed the enthusiasm of many: "It is as if, all of a sudden, the things our theological tradition took for granted can no longer be taken for granted. Reality as the

suggestion – wondered if the kind of questions being raised did not indicate that "a great historical movement" was under way.[91] So enthusiastic were many over the prospects of the New Hermeneutic that Ebeling declared: "the development from Schleiermacher via Dilthey to Heidegger shows that the idea of a theory of understanding is on the move towards laying the foundation of the humanities [and] that hermeneutics now takes the place of the classical epistemological theory, and indeed that fundamental ontology appears as hermeneutics."[92]

There was, however, one figure conspicuously absent from these discussions, which disturbed proponents of the New Hermeneutic. That figure was Karl Barth. Bultmann had sought repeatedly to engage Barth in formal discussion of hermeneutics after the war as did several of Bultmann's students, but Barth repeatedly refused. That Barth did not seem to recognize the significance of the kind of hermeneutical questions they were asking and that he could continue to swim along, as it were, as if such questions did not matter, only reinforced what many had suspected all along: Barth was hermeneutically naïve. To some it suggested he was simply cavalier, going his own 'pneumatic' way as he had from the beginning. To others, such as James M. Robinson, as he stated in his programmatic essay entitled "Hermeneutics After Barth," introducing the New Hermeneutic to the English-speaking world, Barth's silence on these matters was simply indicative of the fact that the fruitful limits of his theology had been reached.[93] Though well aware and deeply appreciative of Barth's contribution, Ernst Fuchs accused Barth of having "very unjustly trivialized the hermeneutical problem."[94] Gerhard Ebeling, also deeply indebted to Barth, made the very same charge.[95]

While it is true that Barth tended, at least privately, to be dismissive of these discussions and thought (mistakenly) that all such talk about hermeneutics would be "short-lived," he did claim to follow these discussions "attentively,"

---

post-war generation experiences it does not permit the easy affirmation of some traditional starting point, in relation to which the theological enterprise can be newly ordered; rather, it senses the necessity to take nothing as the presupposition (least of all God or faith) of its theological endeavor. In this connection it should be observed that there is a new and radically open dialogue with secular philosophy, literature, and the arts. Camus is taken to be a more pertinent dialogical partner than Calvin, Wittgenstein than Luther, Nietzsche, Heidegger, and Whitehead than Thomas, Barth, and Tillich" (p. 287).

[91] Bultmann, "Das Problem der Hermeneutik," p. 47; ET "The Problem of Hermeneutics," p. 69.

[92] Ebeling, "Wort Gottes und Hermeneutik," pp. 332-333; ET p. 317.

[93] James M. Robinson, "Hermeneutics After Barth," pp. 31f.

[94] Ernst Fuchs, *Marburger Hermeneutik* (Tübingen: J.C.B. Mohr [Paul Siebeck], 1968), p. 29.

[95] Ebeling, "Wort Gottes und Hermeneutik," p. 324; ET p. 309.

even though he refused to participate in them.⁹⁶ From the very beginning of his *Römerbrief* period, Barth had recognized that no theological or exegetical method could lead to God.⁹⁷ Not only had he made this point in his *Römerbrief* period, he had stated unambiguously in the first half-volume of his *Church Dogmatics*, "There is no method by which revelation can be made revelation that is actually received, no method of scriptural exegesis which is truly pneumatic, i.e. which articulates the witness to revelation in the Bible and to that degree really introduces the Pneuma."⁹⁸ The majority of Barth's contemporaries, however, still did not understand why he refused to talk with them about hermeneutics. Granted, there was not and would never be a perfect theological or exegetical method, but surely some were better than others. Surely one could not afford to be simply indifferent about the question of hermeneutics. But if Barth was not indifferent, why was he so reticent to discuss the topic?

Once again – and it would not be the last time – Ebeling wrote Barth in early 1953, inviting him to attend a conference on theological method. Once again, Barth refused. He responded that "it would be of no use entering this discussion once again," for he had already elaborated his concerns in detail on such matters and had come to the conclusion that "the question of the right hermeneutics cannot be decided in a discussion of exegetical *method*, but only in exegesis itself." He added: "And I think that I can see that discussion of the question of method *per se* now threatens to run out into nothingness." ⁹⁹ Why was Barth so adamant on this point? Why did he think that discussion of the question of method *per se* threatened to run out into nothingness? His reasons go back to the very origins of his theological revolution.

---

⁹⁶ Busch, *Lebenslauf*, p. 483; ET p. 466. Barth made this comment in a letter to his son Christoph on March 13, 1964. Busch states: "he mocked the 'short-lived talk about hermeneutics' and felt free to be 'deeply offended or even considerably amused at hearing the fortunes of the "language event" on the theological market, which I follow attentively (I am inclined to call its most vociferous promoters either the troop of Korah or the international union of garden gnomes)'" (p. 483; ET p. 466).

⁹⁷ Rom II, pp. 57, 110, 137.

⁹⁸ KD I/1:190; CD I/1:183.

⁹⁹ Busch, *Lebenslauf*, p. 404; ET pp. 389-390. Eberhard Busch has said that in the early 1960s Ebeling devoted an entire seminar to Barth's *Römerbrief* prefaces, and that upon hearing about it, Barth was not at all pleased and insisted that if Ebeling and his disciples really wanted to understand him they would study – alongside the *Römerbrief* prefaces – the actual commentary itself, better yet, the *Church Dogmatics*! Conversation with Busch, June 16, 1999.

D. Karl Barth's Problem with "The Hermeneutical Problem"

Karl Barth's theological revolution began sometime after the summer of 1915 when he and Eduard Thurneysen began to study the Old and New Testaments again.[100] "And behold," Barth said, "they began to speak to us – very differently than we had supposed we were obliged to hear them speak in the school of what was then called 'modern' theology."[101] What was so different? The short answer is: God Himself, they believed, began to speak to them through the Scriptures. As never before Barth recognized he was confronted "not by human standpoints, but by the standpoint of God." This changed everything. Barth discovered that "it is not the right human thoughts about God which form the content of the Bible, but the right divine thoughts about men. The Bible tells us not how we should talk with God but what he says to us; not how we find the way to him, but how he has sought and found the way to us."[102] Barth's great discovery, the discovery upon which his entire theological revolution was based, was that the reality of God precedes the possibility of God, that the being of God *precedes* all human questioning.

> When we come to the Bible with our questions – How shall I think of God and the universe? How shall I arrive at the divine? How shall I present myself? it answers us, as it were, "My dear sir, these are *your* problems: you must not ask *me*! ... If you do not care to enter upon my questions, you may, to be sure, find in me all sorts of arguments and quasi-arguments for one or another standpoint, but you will not then find what is really here." [103]

What Barth discovered to be the real content, subject matter, and theme of the Bible was the Word of God. He discovered the God who speaks for Himself. He discovered that the being of God precedes all human questioning.

That the being of God *precedes* all human questioning may not at first seem like a very provocative claim. In fact, *given* the notion that there is a "God," with a few added metaphysical compliments such as Creator, Sustainer, etc., to claim that such a being logically precedes human questioning may even seem self-evident. But the claim that the being of God precedes all human questioning in this case would mean merely that the being of God is something which can be somehow presupposed, such as a given term in an axiomatic equation or

---

[100] Although Barth did not begin his in-depth study of Romans until July 1916 (see Barth to Thurneysen, 19 July, 1916, *B-Th Br. I*, pp. 146-147), it is difficult to say exactly when his 'turn to the Bible' occurred (he was, after all, even prior to his break from liberalism, preaching from the Bible each week). Whether it came because of his turn to the Bible or as a consequence, Barth's break from liberalism, in my judgment, can hardly be assessed apart from his turn to the Bible, whether such a turn began in the summer of 1915 or shortly thereafter.

[101] Barth, "Nachwort," p. 294; ET p. 264.

[102] Barth, "Die neue Welt in der Bibel," in idem, *Das Wort Gottes und die Theologie* (Munich: Christian Kaiser Verlag, 1925), pp. 27-28. Hereafter as cited "Die neue Welt in der Bibel."

[103] Barth, "Die neue Welt in der Bibel," pp. 27-28.

syllogism. This is *not* what Barth saw at issue in his discovery that the being of God *precedes* all human questioning. What was at issue for him was something quite different. It had first to do not with an order of knowing, but with an order of being which in turn enforces its own corresponding order of knowing. It was the discovery that the being of God is not something which can be presupposed, not something which arises in any way, shape, or form from human questioning, not something which can be deduced or inferred axiomatically or in terms of a postulate or syllogism. It is not something which can in any sense be considered "given." That the being of God precedes all human questioning meant to Barth that God is not self-evidently *the object* of human investigation, nor is He *the answer* to the human question, the human dilemma, the human crisis. That the being of God precedes all human questioning meant essentially one thing above all else to Barth. It meant, first and last, that God is free.

Yet this is precisely what he believed the prevailing Protestant theology of the last two hundred years had denied. To whatever extent it continued in theory to acknowledge that the being of God precedes human questioning, it consistently betrayed the implications of this claim in practice. Time and again it reversed this order. Sometimes it did so out of a concern to provide a supposedly firmer, more 'objective,' more 'scientific' foundation for theology. Sometimes it did so for apologetic reasons. Other times it did so simply because this seemed intuitively the most obvious place to begin. But for whatever reason, whether because of modernity's "turn to the subject" or because of Neo-Protestantism's "bad conscience" regarding the Word of God written, the result was that gradually, with ever increasing forcefulness, the human question, the human situation, the human condition became – as a matter of principle – the starting point of theology, the basis and presupposition for discussing the being of God. "In the Protestant theology which has prevailed since about 1700," Barth said,

> It has actually become a fundamental presupposition. The basic difference between this theology and the theology of older Protestantism is that from some source or other, some general knowledge of God and man, it is known beforehand, known *a priori*, what revelation must be, may be, and ought to be. In these conditions and by using such a standard of measurement, a definite attitude to the reality of revelation can be taken up *a posteriori*.[104]

Such a reversal, however, Barth is quick to add, "need not necessarily mean criticism or even negation of this reality." On the contrary,

> Pious, even inspired recognition of this reality is perfectly possible. It should be noted that theological Neo-Protestantism in its beginnings (J.F. Buddeus and C.M. Pfaff among the Lutherans; S. Werenfels, J.F. Osterwald, J.A. Turrettini among the Reformed, and in C. Wolff and the theologians of his school, also in its later forms) could deal with the Bible and dogma in a thoroughly conservative way.

---

[104] KD I/2:5; CD I/2:4.

"Nevertheless," Barth said, "even in these conservative forms it means misconstruction, nay, denial of revelation. Only by happy inconsistencies, only by occasional abandonment of the basic presupposition, only by contradicting itself, can it ever be anything else."[105]

It was Kant who exposed the "happy inconsistencies" of many of these *a priori-a posteriori* procedures. Driving a wedge between all things phenomenal and noumenal, Kant cut off the well-worn paths of theological reflection from below to above. So strict were his standards for discussing any future metaphysic he reduced almost an entire generation of rationalist and speculative theologians to silence with respect to the being of God. But in the aftermath of Kant's *Critiques* and Lessing's "ugly ditch," there was one theologian who was not reduced to silence with respect to the being of God.[106] That theologian was Friedrich Schleiermacher. In contrast to all his rationalist and speculative theological predecessors, Schleiermacher dared to speak of the being of God – not on the basis of any *via causalitatis, via negativa,* or *via eminentiae* – but on the basis of "the pious self-consciousness," specifically, the pious self-consciousness as mediated by "the feeling of absolute dependence." The feeling of absolute dependence was not, of course, just *any* feeling. It was a kind of depth experience, an experience occurring at the deepest level of one's being, beneath the organizing categories of our understanding at a level beyond all knowing and doing.[107] Nor was it just *any* state of pious self-consciousness. It was a state of *Christian* pious self-consciousness. As Barth summarized it, Schleiermacher proceded as follows: "From intellectual reflection upon pious *self*-consciousness there emerge the statements concerning the pious state of mind as such and in itself. From reflection upon pious self-*consciousness* there emerge the statements about the world. From reflections upon *pious* self-consciousness emerge statements about God."[108]

So brilliant, so original was Schleiermacher's contribution that Barth said of him: "He did not found a school, but an era."[109] Schleiermacher was often called "the church father of the nineteenth century," and Barth wondered if –

---

[105] KD I/2:5; CD I/2:4.

[106] Faced with these options, Barth said, "only Schleiermacher could be the savior." *Die protestantische Theologie im 19. Jahrhundert* (Zürich: Evangelischer Verlag Zürich, 1947), p. 380; ET *Protestant Theology in the Nineteenth Century*, trans. Brian Cozens (Valley Forge: Judson Press, 1972), p. 307. However, Barth hastens to add: "Whether the century understood itself rightly in thinking it heard the liberating word from Schleiermacher, whether it might not have been possible to gain further insights of an entirely different kind from all the points which Schleiermacher had touched upon – that is a different question" (p. 381; ET p. 309). Hereafter cited as *Die protestantische Theologie im 19. Jahrhundert*.

[107] F.D.E. Schleiermacher, *Die Glaubenslehre* (Berlin: Walter de Gruyter, 1960), §3, pp. 14f.; ET *The Christian Faith*, trans. H.R. Mackintosh (Edinburgh: T&T Clark, 1928), pp. 5f.

[108] Barth, *Die protestantische Theologie im 19. Jahrhundert*, p. 408; ET p. 337.

[109] Barth, *Die protestantische Theologie im 19. Jahrhundert*, p. 379; ET p. 306.

given that "he was studied, honored, and made fruitful much more in 1910 than in 1830" – he would be regarded as the church father of the twentieth century as well. As one who himself once knew "how to swear no higher than by the man, Friedrich Daniel Ernst Schleiermacher," even Barth later admitted, "Nobody can say today whether we have really overcome his influence, or whether we are still at heart children of his age."[110] Schleiermacher's great achievement had been that he found a way to speak about the being of God in an age when at least among many intellectuals and "cultured despisers" of religion, this was thought to be impossible. Unlike many of his predecessors, he had not spoken about the being of God on the basis of speculation. He had not approached the task of theology as if the being of God were somehow *given* in any immediate sense. Nor had he, like so many of his predecessors and contemporaries, reduced the content of theology to history. Nevertheless, because talk about the being of God was something posited in human self-consciousness, albeit *pious* self-consciousness, and because 'God' was presupposed as 'the whence' of the feeling of absolute dependence, and because this specific 'feeling' served as a point of contact, a material and not merely formal condition for the possibility for talk about the being of God, Schleiermacher's program still followed, according to Barth, the *a priori-a posteriori* procedure of Neo-Protestantism. To be sure, his was vastly different than the *a priori-a posteriori* procedures of his predecessors, particularly since his starting-point was not just any *a priori* but a profoundly religious *a priori*. Nevertheless, it was still the starting-point of an *a priori–a posteriori* procedure.

Thus, as brilliant and intellectually formidable as Schleiermacher's system was, that it had at its starting-point an *a priori–a posteriori* procedure, that it posited talk about the being of God on the basis of the pious self-consciousness, could ultimately mean only one thing to Karl Barth after 1915. It meant that Schleiermacher's system could not acknowledge, could not really honor or do justice to, the fact that the being of God precedes human questioning. It could not because it claimed to know something in advance, even if only formally, about what the being of God must be, may be, and ought to be, prior to any self-revelation of God's being. It claimed that the specific form which absolute dependence has as an original human possession and possibility corresponds to the content which the being of God is and *vice versa*. This is why Schleiermacher's system could not do justice to the fact that the being of God precedes human questioning. As Barth later said in describing his problems with this approach, "[it appears to begin with] a *general* reality whose nature and meaning have already been derived and established in advance, so that on that basis only secondary attention is paid to its particular, concrete, determinable, and determinate form."[111] That the being of God could ever over-

---

[110] Barth, *Die protestantische Theologie im 19. Jahrhundert*, p. 380; ET p. 307.
[111] Barth, "Nachwort," p. 308; ET p. 276.

come its original determination as a *general* reality in this system, such that *primary* and not merely *secondary* attention could be paid to its *particular*, concrete, determinable, and determinate form, is something Barth could simply no longer entertain after his break with liberalism. This is not to say that Barth did not leave open and even later hope for "the possibility of a theology of the third article, in other words, a theology predominantly and decisively of the Holy Spirit."[112] Barth was even prepared to reckon with the possibility, "interpreting everything and everyone *in optimam partem*," that such a theology of the Holy Spirit – "a theology of which Schleiermacher was scarcely conscious" – might even have been "the legitimate concern dominating his theological activity" all along. But even if this had been the legitimate concern dominating his theological activity all along, it was far from clear that this had been its result.

The result had been, in Barth's view, the wholesale anthropologization of theology. The result had been that after Schleiermacher, theologians began to focus upon the human question, the human situation, the human condition as never before. Man increasingly became the subject of theology and God his predicate. Despite Schleiermacher's better intentions and despite the efforts of his better advocates throughout the rest of the nineteenth century, his system proved it could not keep the person and work of the Holy Spirit "from being confused with a mode of human cognition."[113] It could not prevent the collapse of theology into anthropology, pneumatology into psychology, which a host of secular prophets, such as Feuerbach, Nietzsche, Freud, *et al*, were all too eager to announce. But it was not merely that his approach paved the way for the *psychologizing* of theology. According to Barth, and this is something that has received relatively little attention, Schleiermacher's approach also paved the way for the *historicizing* of theology.[114] Yet it was more with respect to his legacy as a 'theologian of culture' that the first serious misgivings about Schleiermacher's influence on twentieth century theology began to emerge in Barth. This occurred during October of 1914 when he discovered that ninety-three German intellectuals had signed a manifesto identifying them-

---

[112] Barth adds: "Everything which needs to be said, considered, and believed about God the Father and God the Son in an understanding of the first and second articles might be shown and illuminated in its foundations through God the Holy Spirit, the *vinculum pacis inter Patrem et Filium."* See Barth, "Nachwort," p. 311; ET p. 278.

[113] Barth, *Die protestantische Theologie im 19. Jahrhundert,* p. 414; ET pp. 343-344.

[114] On Nov.1, 1923, in his opening lecture on Schleiermacher, Barth said: "All the official tendencies of the Christian present emanate from him like rays: church life, experiential piety, historicism, psychologism, and ethicism." *Die Theologie Schleiermachers,* p. 5; ET p. xv. Barth later repeated with reference to Schleiermacher's *Glaubenslehre*: "It raises a most urgent question whether with these very dogmatics theology was not consigned to a branch of the general science of the mind, so that the historicizing of theology was most thoroughly prepared for." Barth, *Die protestantische Theologie im 19. Jahrhundert*, pp. 384-5; ET pp. 311-12.

selves with the war policy of Kaiser Wilhelm II and that among them were nearly all his former teachers. So cataclysmic was this discovery that Barth said: "An entire world of theological exegesis, ethics, dogmatics, and preaching, which up to that point I had accepted as basically credible, was thereby shaken to the foundations, and with it everything which flowed at that time from the pens of the German theologians." While Barth was convinced that Schleiermacher himself would never have signed such a document, "it was still the case," he believed, "that the entire theology which had unmasked itself in that manifesto, and everything which followed after it (even in the *Christliche Welt*), was grounded, determined, and influenced decisively by him."[115]

Yet this was not the last time Barth claimed to recognize the direct influence of Schleiermacher, *en masse,* upon his contemporaries. The last time was in the 1950s and 60s when students of Bultmann began to rise up and proclaim the virtue and necessity of a "New Hermeneutic." "The common denominator" of this movement, Barth said, "was and is indeed Schleiermacher – not the very image of him, but certainly a new form which accommodated itself to the 'contemporary spiritual situation' or 'linguistic situation' and to the contemporary (or rather one contemporary) vocabulary."[116] "What connects them with him, and with each other," Barth insisted, "is the consciously and consistently executed anthropological starting point which is evident as the focus of their thought and utterances. And that was and is precisely a clear recurrence of Schleiermacher."[117] And the chief means of establishing this common anthropological starting point to an increasing number was by hermeneutics. To repeat Ebeling's lapidary claim, "the development from Schleiermacher *via* Dilthey to Heidegger shows that the idea of a theory of understanding is on the move towards laying the foundation of the humanities [and] that hermeneutics now takes the place of the classical epistemological theory, and indeed that fundamental ontology appears as hermeneutics."[118] Given their starting point, Bultmann's students were not wrong in looking to Schleiermacher, "the father of modern hermeneutics," as "the precursor of the new hermeneutic." But the consequence, as Barth saw it, was that another generation would once again become preoccupied with the question of method. This is why, with all such talk about "the problem of understanding hermeneutics," "the problem of understanding," etc., Barth claimed he saw in it nothing but "a return to the situation we thought we had left behind in 1920."[119]

The situation Barth thought he had left behind in 1920 was one dominated by the question of method. Barth himself, as a young liberal, as we shall see in

---

[115] Barth, "Nachwort," pp. 293-294; ET pp. 263-264.
[116] Barth, "Nachwort," p. 300; ET p. 269.
[117] Barth, "Nachwort," p. 302; ET pp. 270-271.
[118] Ebeling, "Wort Gottes und Hermeneutik," pp. 332-333; ET p. 317.
[119] Busch, *Lebenslauf*, p. 483; ET p. 466 [translation revised].

his first two published essays, was thoroughly preoccupied with the problem of method.[120] But in Rom I (and with equal vigor in Rom II), Barth attacks "the methods of this age," "the methods of the world," "the methods of the old, fading world," etc.[121] He asks his contemporaries: "Are we not finally aware that through each religious method ... we are being led like Israel in the desert?"[122] He warns: "Only by rejecting the *methods* of the existing world, will you serve toward its real, radical revolutionization. ... But *your method* is solidarity with the 'enemy.'"[123] He challenges those "lording" their methods over others to own up to it[124] and proclaims, "Death lurks wherever there is life, but especially in all dogmas, statutes, methods, systems, standpoints, programs, and snail shells in which men again and again want to lock away the dear God in order to dispense with the One Thing necessary."[125] The One Thing necessary, Barth insists, is that "which *is*," and that which is, he had discovered, was the being of God – the Being who speaks for Himself – and no method or hermeneutic could ever substitute for that. This is why Barth refused to engage Bultmann and his pupils regarding "the problem of hermeneutics" throughout the 1950s and 60s. As far as he was concerned there was really nothing *new* about the "New Hermeneutic." Its proponents were merely seeking to establish better grounds for the old *a priori–a posteriori procedure* of Neo-Protestantism.

In retrospect, it may be that Barth was sometimes a bit too dismissive of these discussions. He was certainly mistaken to suggest they would be "short-lived." But proponents of the "New Hermeneutic" were even more mistaken to claim that Barth "very unjustly trivialized the hermeneutical problem." The fact is: Barth did not trivialize the hermeneutical problem. He took it more seriously than they did. The difference was they saw the hermeneutical problem as having fundamentally to do with the problem of human understanding. Barth saw the hermeneutical problem as having fundamentally to do with the being of God.

E. The Being of God Is the Hermeneutical Problem: Background to Barth's Discovery

To summarize: Karl Barth's discovery that the being of God precedes human questioning had many implications, not least of all, hermeneutical ones. Barth

---

[120] I shall discuss these essays in detail in Chapter 5.
[121] Rom I, pp. 469, 498, 513, 524, 528.
[122] Rom I, p. 277.
[123] Rom I, p. 498.
[124] Rom I, p. 510.
[125] Rom I, p. 576.

realized that because the reality of God's being precedes all human attempts to inquire as to its nature, no method or hermeneutic could be set up in advance to understand this reality adequately. The reason no method or hermeneutic could be set up in advance is that this would be to presuppose *a priori* knowledge about God's being or (which is the same thing) how God's being could or should be revealed. To presuppose such knowledge, Barth discovered, was *ipso facto* to deny the freedom of God's being, and the freedom of God's being is what he had discovered as a result of hearing God speak through the Scriptures. Barth discovered that God is not only free before His revelation, but after and in the moment of His revelation as well. That is, God is free and cannot be directly identified with the medium of revelation even in the event of revelation itself. There is no knowledge of God's being which human beings have as an *a priori* or an *a posteriori* possession or deposit. Knowledge of God's being is always, first and last, a gift. Therefore no method is adequate – not a dogmatic, not a critical, nor even a dialectical method – unless God speaks, unless it is God Himself who speaks when He is spoken of. God is not bound to or bound by any method or hermeneutical technique. He freely determines the what, when, where, and how of His revelation. This is why the being of God or more precisely, the fact that the being of God precedes human questioning, is the hermeneutical problem.[126]

However, Barth's contemporaries, those both before and after the situation he thought he had left behind in 1920, did not generally recognize this as *the* hermeneutical problem. They were preoccupied with other hermeneutical problems. This is one reason why Rom I fell as it was once famously described like "a bombshell which exploded on the playground of theologians."[127] James M. Robinson claimed in 1964 that the reason why it made such an impact hermeneutically was because the period leading up to it had been a period of "hermeneutical sterility" and that "part of the shock caused by

---

[126] The phrase "God's being is the hermeneutical problem" I owe to Eberhard Jüngel, who introduces his book, *Gottes Sein ist im Werden* (Tübingen: J.C.B. Mohr [Paul Siebeck], 1965): "In the following pages an attempt will be made to elucidate what it means that the being of God proceeds, and thus precedes all human questioning. In this attempt we confront the hermeneutical problem in its most concentrated form while we turn our thought to the doctrine of God. The being of God is the hermeneutical problem of theology. More exactly: the fact that the being of God proceeds is precisely the hermeneutical problem. For only because the being of God proceeds is there an encounter between God and man" p. 10; ET *The Doctrine of the Trinity: The Being of God is in Becoming*, trans. Horton Harris (Grand Rapids: William B. Eerdmans, 1976), pp. xx-xxi.

[127] Karl Adam, "Die Theologie der Krisis," *Hochland: Monatsschrift für alle Gebiete des Wissens, der Literatur und Kunst*, 23 (1926/27), pp. 271-286. Also: *Gesammelte Aufsätze zur Dogmengeschichte und Theologie der Gegenwart* (Augsburg: Literar. Institut P. Haas & CIE., K-G., 1936), pp. 319-337. "Barths Römerbrief schlug gleich bei seinem ersten Erscheinen (August 1918 [sic!]) wie eine Bombe auf dem Spielplatz der Theologen ein . . .," p. 325.

Barth's *Romans* is due to this vacuum into which it exploded."[128] Closer analysis of the situation before 1920, however, suggests something quite different. Far from being a period of "hermeneutical sterility," it was a period of burgeoning interest in hermeneutics. This is reflected not only by the many works on biblical and theological hermeneutics that appeared in Germany between the end of the 19th and early part of the 20th centuries, but also by the rise of interest in hermeneutics among certain philosophical movements such as among phenomenologists, e.g., Edmund Husserl and Martin Heidegger,[129] and former students of Neo-Kantian philosopher, Hermann Cohen: Ernst Cassirer, Ferdinand Ebner, Paul Natorp, Franz Rosenzweig, Eugen Rosenstock-Huessy, *et al*.[130] But the most obvious reason why the period leading up to Barth's *Römerbrief* was such an intense period of hermeneutical discussion was because of Wilhelm Dilthey.

Dilthey's contribution played a very significant role in the period leading up to and immediately following Rom I.[131] Having held Hegel's former chair in philosophy at the University of Berlin from 1882 until his death in 1911, Dilthey was considered by many of his contemporaries to be Germany's lead-

---

[128] Robinson, "Hermeneutics After Barth," pp. 17-19.

[129] Phenomenology was not, however, well-known to Barth at this time. In a *"Rundbrief"* to Thurneysen, Barth wrote, "I have the remarkable fortune that my procedure appears intelligible to the people from the standpoint of phenomenology (although I have never read Husserl, etc.)." See Karl Barth to Eduard Thurneysen, 7 June, 1925, *B-Th. Br. II*, p. 329. Interestingly enough, Ernst Fuchs says with reference to this period: "Heidegger himself at the time took great interest in the development being introduced in theology by Karl Barth." See Fuchs, "The New Testament and the Hermeneutical Problem," p. 112.

[130] Franz Rosenzweig and Eugen Rosenstock-Huessy were members of the "Patmos Circle," a group much interested in hermeneutical issues. Graham Ward, in *Barth, Derrida and The Language of Theology*, has made much of Barth's relationship to this group, suggesting he was significantly influenced by it, but there is little to support this claim. For a more precise historical assessment of Barth's relationship to this group and its significance, see Bruce McCormack's article review, "Graham Ward's *Barth, Derrida And The Language of Theology*," *Scottish Journal of Theology*, 49:1 (1996), pp. 97-109.

[131] In his Schaffer Lectures at Yale University Divinity School in October, 1951, Rudolf Bultmann stated: "Reflection on the art of hermeneutics has been increasingly neglected, at least in German theology, since Schleiermacher, who himself was interested in it and wrote important treatises on it. Only since the first World War has the interest in hermeneutics revived, when the work of the great German philosopher Wilhelm Dilthey became effective." See Bultmann, *Jesus Christ and Mythology* (New York: Scribners, 1958), pp. 45-46. Though there is no evidence that Barth heard Dilthey while a student in Berlin in the fall of 1906 (his exclusive interest at the time, he claimed, was Adolf von Harnack – see Busch, *Lebenslauf*, p. 50; ET p. 39), Barth did know Dilthey's massive biographical work first published in 1870, *Leben Schleiermachers* (Berlin: Walter de Gruyter, 1922, 2nd ed.) which he refers to in his 1923/24 Göttingen lectures on Schleiermacher as "basic." See Barth, *Die Theologie Schleiermachers*, p. 2; ET p. xiii. Barth could not, therefore, have been unaware of Dilthey's interest in or the significance he attributed to Schleiermacher's hermeneutics, given the attention this topic receives in this volume.

ing philosopher of the last half of the nineteenth century as well as of the early decades of the twentieth.[132] In *Sein und Zeit* (1927), Heidegger said that his entire generation was indebted to Dilthey not only for relativizing the study of history to hermeneutics but for raising the question of hermeneutics to a fundamental level of importance.[133] Dilthey had argued in probably his most influential essay, "*Die Entstehung der Hermeneutik*" (1900), that hermeneutics was *the* foundational discipline of all human sciences (*Geisteswissenschaften*).[134] The reason was because at the heart of all human sciences lies the task of understanding other people, and this depends on our ability "to re-experience [*Nachfühlen*] alien states of mind."[135] It also depends on the degree to which our "recomprehension [*Nachverständnis*] of individual existence can be raised to objective validity." Moreover, because "the existence of other people is given to us only from the outside, in sensory events, gestures, words, and actions," Dilthey said, it is "only through a process of reconstruction [*Nachbildung*] that we complete this sense of perception, which initially takes the form of isolated signs. We are thus obliged to translate everything – the raw material, the structure, the most individual traits of such a completion – out of our own sense of life."[136] Hermeneutics is important therefore because it analyzes each of these moments in the process of understanding and because it analyzes the problem of understanding in general and from it derives universally valid rules of interpretation.

There are at least two major reasons why Barth and his contemporaries could not ignore the rise of hermeneutics which Dilthey and many others began to call attention to at the turn of the century. First, Barth's generation had inherited a heightened historical consciousness. Dilthey, Nietzsche, Ranke, and others in the latter nineteenth century had contributed significantly to its development. Barth's generation recognized as perhaps no generation before the complexity of historical understanding and the inherent problems of historiography. Theologians of the previous century had been preoccupied with the question of the relationship of faith and history above all others. Barth himself

---

[132] Dozens of books and dissertations on Dilthey's contribution immediately followed his death in 1911. For a list, see H.A. Hodges bibliography in *Wilhelm Dilthey: An Introduction* (New York: Oxford University Press, 1944).

[133] Martin Heidegger, *Being and Time*, trans. John Macquarrie & Edward Robinson (New York: Harper & Brothers, 1962), pp. 449f.

[134] Wilhelm Dilthey, "Die Entstehung der Hermeneutik" in *Gesammelte Schriften* (Leipzig and Berlin, 1914-1936, V, pp. 317-331; ET "The Rise of Hermeneutics," trans. Fredric Jameson, *New Literary History*, 3 (1972), pp. 229-244. Hereafter cited as "Die Entstehung der Hermeneutik."

[135] Dilthey, "Die Entstehung der Hermeneutik," p. 317; ET pp. 230-231.

[136] Dilthey, "Die Entstehung der Hermeneutik," p. 318; ET p. 231.

in his early years had been deeply preoccupied with this question as well.[137] Hermeneutics as discussed by many at the time was seen as the only means available for bridging Lessing's still very "wide, ugly ditch." "Thus hermeneutics," Gadamer says, became "the foundation for the study of history."[138] If one of the major problems was as Dilthey stated: "how can one quite individually structured consciousness [e.g., that of a modern reader's] bring an alien individuality of a completely different type [e.g., an ancient author's] to objective knowledge through reconstruction?,"[139] what other discipline could address this kind of problem? How else but by analyzing the problem of understanding itself? How else but by analyzing its component parts, viz., *Nachfühlung, Nacherleben, Nachbildung, Nachverständnis*, etc.? How else but by a discipline which integrates and reflects critically upon not only the grammatical and historical sides of interpretation but upon the psychological and intuitive sides as well, that is, not only about skills such as philology required to decode a foreign language, but skills such as empathy needed in order to come to terms with the "alien individuality" or "mind" of an author? It was Schleiermacher whom Dilthey rightly credited with having pioneered this approach to interpretation. It was he who sought originally to broaden the scope of interpretation to include not only grammatical but psychological interpretation (interpretation involving the psychological aspects of an author's life as a whole as well as the moment of composition) and not only comparative or historical interpretation but divinatory interpretation (interpretation requiring empathetic identification with an author by means of a creative or intuitive leap of the imagination).[140] Schleiermacher was not, of course, the first to recognize these aspects of interpretation,[141] but he was the first to integrate them into a more systematic, "general hermeneutic," which suggests a second reason why Barth and his contemporaries could not ignore the hermeneutical discussions of the early decades of the twentieth century.

---

[137] Karl Barth, "Der christliche Glaube und die Geschichte" (1910), *Vorträge und kleinere Arbeiten, 1909-1914*, ed. Hans-Anton Drewes and Hinrich Stoevesandt (Zürich: Theologischer Verlag Zürich, 1993), pp. 155-212. This essay was first published in *Schweizerische theologische Zeitschrift* 29 (1912), pp. 1-18, 49-72. Hereafter cited as "Der christliche Glaube und die Geschichte."

[138] Gadamer, *Wahrheit und Methode*, p. 203; ET p. 199.

[139] Dilthey, "Die Entstehung der Hermeneutik," p. 318; ET p. 231.

[140] Biblical interpreters such as Ernesti and Buddaeus were, for Schleiermacher, exemplary of those who had too narrowly focused on grammatical interpretation. Others, such as those of the emerging "Tübingen School," he believed, were focusing too narrowly on historical interpretation. For important background to Schleiermacher's hermeneutic, see Hans Frei's *The Eclipse of Biblical Narrative* (New Haven: Yale Universtiy Press, 1974), chapters 10-15. Also, Harald Schnur's *Schleiermacher's Hermeneutik und ihre Vorgeschichte im 18.Jahrhundert* (Stuttgart: Verlag J.B. Metzler, 1994).

[141] So did his Romantic predecessors and contemporaries: Herder, Novalis, Schelling, Schlegel, *et al.*

The second reason why hermeneutics could not be ignored was because of the increased scientific demands placed upon the discipline of theology by an increasingly secular academy. Theology had been considered a science for centuries, in the sense that, like all other human sciences, it sought to follow a self-consistent path of knowledge with respect to a definite object and in the sense that it sought to give an account of this path to itself and to all others capable of concern for its object. Since the Enlightenment, however, the claim that theology was a science had been increasingly challenged. Following a self-consistent path of knowledge with respect to a definite object was not enough. This alone would not qualify theology as a science. Modern universities insisted that if theology was really a science, its status would have to be assessed as such on the basis of "a general concept of science," that is, on the basis of standards valid for other sciences. There were many theologians engaged in discussing theology's status as a science in the early decades of the twentieth century, including Karl Barth.[142] But as important as this discussion was to theologians, the concern to meet the scientific standards of the day was probably felt as intensely among biblical exegetes. Faced with the concrete task of exegeting the Bible in a modern university context, biblical scholars sought to apply rigorously scientific standards to it and to avoid giving it any special treatment. No more privileged reading of the Bible would be allowed. Biblical exegesis would follow only strict, objective rules of interpretation. The goal, which arose early in the eighteenth century and remains a maxim to this day, was "to read the Bible like any other book."[143]

But how does one go about reading the Bible like any other book? Where does one begin? And how can one be sure that one is doing so properly? The answer Dilthey and others were giving at the turn of the century was hermeneutics. As "epistemology imported by the humanities, the first science of the human sciences," as it has been defined in our day,[144] hermeneutics was seen as important because it could arbitrate the terms of theology's status as a sci-

---

[142] See p. 52f. below. Discussing theology's relationship to the sciences however was never a topic of major interest to Barth, even though his interest in it was significantly deepened by his friendship with Heinrich Scholz in the late 1920s, which is reflected in the opening pages of the *Church Dogmatics*.

[143] One of the first persons to articulate this view was Jean Alphonse Turrettini, who said: "At the very outset, we observe that, in general, there is no method of interpreting Scripture other than that of other books" *De Sacrae Scripturae interpretandae methodo tractatus bipartitus*, 1728, p. 196. Johann August Ernesti promulgated a similar view in *Institutio interpretis Novi Testamenti*, 1761. Hans Frei provides a fascinating account of the circumstances which gave rise to such a view in *The Eclipse of Biblical Narrative*, pp. 55f.

[144] Jeffrey Stout, *Ethics After Babel: The Languages of Morals and Their Discontents*, (Boston: Beacon Press, 1988), p. 298. This is Stout's "bad sense" definition of hermeneutics yet a definition Dilthey himself could have written. Stout's "good sense" definition is: "The art of enriching our language in conversation with others; also, reflection designed to raise this art to consciousness without reducing it to a set of rules."

ence. After all, as an undeniably *human* science, how else could it be assessed?

Yet it was not just any hermeneutic, a hermeneutic related to any particular subject matter or field, that Dilthey and others had in mind when they discussed hermeneutics. It was a comprehensive, 'general hermeneutic.' Here again, Dilthey and his contemporaries acknowledged, it was Schleiermacher who had led the way. It was Schleiermacher who first set out to establish a comprehensive, general hermeneutic. The major impetus for elaborating his *Hermeneutik* had arisen from his dissatisfaction with prior attempts and because of his concern that "At present there is no general hermeneutics as the art of understanding, but only a variety of specialized hermeneutics."[145] The problem with past efforts, such as those established with biblical, classical, or juridical hermeneutics in view, was that they had become overly specialized and had neglected the problems of understanding in general. Because "special hermeneutics" as then practiced, he said, "degenerates into a collection of observations ... at the expense of its scientific character and so, too, of its certainty," Schleiermacher sought to construct "special hermeneutics as *only* an abbreviated procedure which must be governed by general rules."[146] These "general rules" were established with the aim of transcending particular applications in a more comprehensive and systematic way than had his contemporaries, Friedrich Wolf and Friedrich Ast. Dilthey and his many followers at the turn of the century saw themselves as advancing Schleiermacher's project. But more than simply building on his edifice, they were determined to expand it and work out the unresolved problems of a general theory of understanding. Joachim Wach's three-volume work, *Das Verstehen: Grundzüge einer Geschichte der hermeneutischen Theorie im 19. Jahrhundert,* represents one of the most important examples of this.[147] Wach's account, whose central figure is Schleiermacher, traces the development of this quest to establish a general hermeneutical theory of understanding from the late eighteenth century to the early decades of the twentieth. Wach's volumes are significant both because of their analysis of this development and their contribution to it.[148] Yet they are also significant because they demonstrate how deeply influential the hermeneutical tradition of Schleiermacher to Dilthey was throughout the early decades of the twentieth century.

---

[145] Schleiermacher, *Hermeneutik*, p. 147; ET p. 95.

[146] Schleiermacher, *Hermeneutik*, p. 93; ET p. 122. Italics mine.

[147] Joachim Wach, *Das Verstehen: Grundzüge einer Geschichte der hermeneutischen Theorie im 19. Jahrhundert* I-III (Tübingen: J.C.B. Mohr [Paul Siebeck], 1926-1933). Frei states: "After the turn of the century, the influence of Dilthey and then Heidegger in philosophy, and that of the early Barth and the later Bultmann in theological biblical-exegesis, reawakened interest in Schleiermacher's hermeneutics." *The Eclipse of Biblical Narrative*, p. 285.

[148] See Charles M. Wood, "Theory and Religious Understanding: A Critique of the Hermeneutics of Joachim Wach," unpublished Ph.D. dissertation, Yale University, 1972.

But there is another way in which the hermeneutical tradition of Schleiermacher and Dilthey exercised an influence in the early decades of the twentieth century. I pointed out earlier that many involved in the so-called 'pneumatic exegesis' discussion of the 1920s and '30s recognized that the chief impetus behind it had been Barth's *Römerbrief* and that even Barth himself, at least in terms of its substance, had taken credit for having initiated it. Not everyone was in total agreement about this, however. While almost everyone agreed that Barth had something to do with initiating the 'pneumatic exegesis' discussion, some claimed there was another more important reason which had given rise to it. Several, such as Wach, Erich Fascher, Johannes Schneider, and others, suggested that Barth's *Römerbrief* and the 'pneumatic exegesis' discussion which followed it were merely symptomatic of a much larger movement, that these were only products – not the source – of a much greater development, namely a theory of understanding which had emerged out of the hermeneutical tradition of Schleiermacher and Dilthey. Wach made this point in the introduction to his first volume of *Das Verstehen* in 1926.[149] Though later, in his second volume in 1929, he acknowledged that the 'hermeneutical instruction' of Rom I had been, in its own limited way, significant,[150] Wach and others still regarded Barth's contribution as only a single point in the trajectory of the development of a theory of understanding which had its origins in the hermeneutical tradition of Schleiermacher and Dilthey. The implication which was drawn well beyond the 1920s and 30s was that – whether Barth and his followers had understood it this way or not – his *Römerbrief* was actually not so much the product of a *theological* revolution as it was the product of a *hermeneutical* revolution. Gerhard Ebeling suggested as much when in 1959 he described Barth's *Römerbrief* as a "critical advance." "This critical advance," he said, "seemed indeed to have purely theological motives, but fitted completely into the general contemporary movement of the hermeneutical problem."[151]

That Karl Barth's *Römerbrief* had been a 'critical advance' in the development of a theory of understanding in the trajectory of the hermeneutical tradition of Schleiermacher and Dilthey was not an uncommon view among proponents of the New Hermeneutic. Not until 1965 when Hans-Georg Gadamer referred to Rom I as "a virtual hermeneutical manifesto" did some begin to surmise that perhaps Barth had been saying something quite different all along, and that his *Römerbrief* was not to be understood in terms of *continuity*, but rather in terms of *discontinuity* with the hermeneutical tradition of Schleiermacher and Dilthey. Because Gadamer never elaborated his claim about Rom I being a virtual hermeneutical manifesto, this has never been clear. But the fact that he referred to Rom I as hermeneutical manifesto meant that he saw it

---

[149] Wach, *Das Verstehen*, I, p. 23 n. 2.
[150] Wach, *Das Verstehen*, II, pp. 59-60.
[151] Ebeling, "Wort Gottes und Hermeneutik," p. 324; ET p. 309.

standing over against a prevailing hermeneutical hegemony, and the only possible candidate for that is the hermeneutical tradition of Schleiermacher and Dilthey, which brings us once again to the thesis of the present study.

The thesis of this study announced in Chapter 1 may be usefully expanded as follows: that one of the major reasons why Barth's *Römerbrief* fell like a bombshell was *not* because it fell into a so-called hermeneutical 'vacuum,' but because it challenged the most influential hermeneutical tradition of the nineteenth and twentieth centuries, the hermeneutical tradition of Schleiermacher and Dilthey. The basis of this challenge, as I have suggested, arose out of Barth's *theological* discovery that the being of God precedes all human questioning, all human attempts to inquire as to its nature. It arose out of Barth's conviction that the being of God is the fundamental hermeneutical problem, not the problem of human understanding. The reason why the fact that the being of God precedes human questioning posed such a problem, Barth came to realize, was because it challenged the assumption of those who had striven since Schleiermacher to establish a general hermeneutic, viz., that general rules could and should be applied when attempting to understand any text – and therefore the subject matter of any text – even prior to experience of the subject matter of the text in question. It challenged, in short, the attempt of Schleiermacher, Dilthey, and others to "derive universally valid rules of interpretation"[152] prior to interpretation itself, because it is not actuality that follows possibility but rather possibility that follows actuality with respect to knowledge of God, and if this is so with respect to knowledge of God why not with respect to knowledge acquired elsewhere?

In his discovery that the being of God precedes human questioning, Barth discovered a God who was free (This is essentially what is at issue in Barth's discovery of a God who is 'wholly other'). Because God is free, he believed, any attempt to bind or contain Him or any attempt to force Him to conform to any method or hermeneutic came down not simply to a matter of inadequacy, but to a matter of reduction and distortion. And if this was the case with respect to the being of God, what about other free, or at least relatively free, subjects? If the nature of the object to be known determines the way taken in knowing, as Barth believed he had discovered in light of the revelation of God's being, what does this say about how we should approach other objects? This suggests something important about Barth's reluctance to discuss the question of hermeneutics *in abstracto*. It suggests something important about why he refused to separate the question of method from actual exegesis: to do so was to risk reduction and distortion. This is what he believed had happened to the content of the Bible. Historicism and psychologism, the two great tools of reductionism throughout the nineteenth and twentieth centuries, which he later claimed had been "thoroughly prepared for" by Schleiermacher, had at-

---

[152] Dilthey, "Die Entstehung der Hermeneutik," p. 320; ET p. 234.

tempted to reduce the content of the Bible to its historical antecedents and/or to general psychological processes within the minds of its authors.[153] Such reductionism posed the most serious threat to the discipline of theology in modern times. But given the hermeneutical preoccupations of Barth's contemporaries at the turn of century, perhaps as great a threat was that talk about *how* to explicate the Bible would replace explication itself.[154] Barth's attempt to expose these threats to the discipline of theology is one reason why Rom I was considered so revolutionary.

F. From Special Hermeneutics to General Hermeneutics

Karl Barth was not content merely to repudiate the dominant hermeneutical tradition of his day, however. He was determined to overcome it. His early conviction regarding the priority of actual exegesis over hermeneutics should not therefore be understood as an attempt on his part to avoid discussing hermeneutics. Nor does it represent some kind of pragmatic penchant in his theology. Neither does it imply, as certain post-modern readers suggest, that Barth saw the task of interpretation as essentially a matter of applying "ad hoc hermeneutical principles." Barth was never so naive as to think that exegetes could simply set aside hermeneutical issues in favor of a pure or presuppositionless kind of exegesis. Nor did he ever suggest that the question of hermeneutics or method was simply arbitrary or inconsequential. The fact is that Barth was never indifferent about method. His method, from beginning to end, was dialectical. However, he recognized that adopting an appropriate method was not enough. No hermeneutic, no method, not even a dialectical method, was adequate in itself. So given his recognition of the inadequacy of hermeneutics on the one hand and his recognition on the other that hermeneutics could hardly be avoided relative to the discipline of theology, what was Barth's alternative to the hermeneutical hegemony of the tradition of Schleiermacher and Dilthey, that is, the general hermeneutics tradition?

The dilemma which is evident from the beginning of the *Römerbrief* period was that he recognized on the one hand the legitimate scientific concern of general hermeneutics, viz., the concern to avoid arbitrary, idiosyncratic, privileged interpretation of the Bible, specifically, Paul's *Romans*; yet he also recognized on the other hand that the general hermeneutical rules applied by his contemporaries had not and could not do justice to the unique subject matter of Paul's Epistle. He recognized, in other words, the importance of reading the Bible "like any other book," yet he also recognized that the Bible – because of

---

[153] Barth, *Die protestantische Theologie im 19. Jahrhundert*, p. 384; ET p. 312.

[154] Appendix 2, Preface Draft IA, p. 278 (p. 583), Preface Draft II, p.283 (p. 589). Those page numbers cited in parentheses are from the *Gesamtausgabe* edition of Rom I.

its special subject matter – is not like any other book. Barth's solution, the solution which launched his hermeneutical revolution, was to move from what he would later call "special hermeneutics" to general hermeneutics.[155] Instead of making a special hermeneutic, such as biblical hermeneutics, subordinate to or a sub-discipline of a general hermeneutic, or regarding special hermeneutics – as Schleiermacher did – "as only an abbreviated procedure which must be governed by general rules," Barth recognized it was necessary to move in the opposite direction, that is, to move from special hermeneutics to general hermeneutics. He referred to this approach to the task of interpretation as "special hermeneutics" because he sought by means of it to honor the freedom and uniqueness of any particular subject matter of any text in light of how he had learned to honor the sovereign freedom and uniqueness of the particular subject matter of the Bible. The upshot of this was that instead of giving priority to reading the Bible like any other book, Barth determined he would try to read any other book like the Bible. "Biblical hermeneutics," therefore, became for Barth, "not so much a specific application of general hermeneutics, but the pattern and measure of all others."[156] As such, Barth said, there are specific "principles of exposition" we can learn from the Bible which "are valid for the exposition of every human word, and can therefore lay claim to universal recognition."[157] And the reason why, he said, was because: "It is not at all that the word of man in the Bible has an abnormal significance and function. We see from the Bible what its normal significance and function is. It is from the word of man in the Bible that we must learn what has to be learned concerning the word of man in general."[158]

Karl Barth's move from special hermeneutics to general hermeneutics indicates an important yet heretofore unexamined part of his attempt to overcome the theological legacy of Friedrich Schleiermacher. It is analogous to the move he refers to in his famous debate with his teacher, Adolf von Harnack. In September 1923, Harnack published an open letter in *Die Christliche Welt* entitled, "Fifteen Questions to Those Among the Theologians Who Are Contemptuous of Scientific Theology," in which he suggested Barth was a "fanatical subjectivist." In Question #15, Harnack asked: "Granted that there are inertness, short-sightedness and numerous ills, yet is there any other theology than that

---

[155] Barth introduces the theme of "special hermeneutics" in KD I/2:514f.; CD I/2:464f..

[156] Karl Barth, *Rudolf Bultmann: ein Versuch, ihn zu verstehen* (Zürich: Evangelischer Verlag Zürich, 1952), p. 58; ET "Rudolf Bultmann – An Attempt to Understand Him," *Kerygma and Myth*, II, trans. Reginald H. Fuller (London: SPCK, 1962), p. 125. Hereafter cited as *Ein Versuch, ihn zu verstehen*. This does not contradict Barth's statement: "There is no such thing as a special biblical hermeneutic." See KD I/2:515; CD I/2:466. What Barth means in this context is that there is no such thing as a special biblical hermeneutic constructed under the hegemony of a general hermeneutic.

[157] KD 1/2:515; CD I/2:466.

[158] KD 1/2:515; CD I/2:466.

which has a firm connection and is in blood-relationship to *science in general?*"¹⁵⁹ In reply Barth stated: "If theology were to regain the courage to face up to concrete objectivity (*Sachlichkeit*), the courage to bear witness to the *Word* of revelation, of judgment and of *God's* love, the outcome might well be that 'science in general' would have to seek 'strong ties and a blood-relationship' with theology instead of the other way around."¹⁶⁰ Actually, Barth had already said as much in Rom II,¹⁶¹ but he later elaborated his view of theology as science in *CD* I/1: "If theology allows itself to be called, or calls itself, a science, it cannot in doing so accept the obligation of submission to standards valid for other sciences."¹⁶² "If it is ranked as a science, and lays claim to such ranking, it must not be disturbed or hampered in its own task by regard for what is described as science elsewhere. On the contrary, to the discharge of its own task it must absolutely subordinate and if necessary sacrifice all concern for what is called science elsewhere."¹⁶³ Indeed, if theology is to be called a science, Barth insisted, it must make a "necessary protest against a general concept of science."¹⁶⁴ It is this same "necessary protest" that special hermeneutics makes against general hermeneutics. And it must do so for the same reasons: for the sake of the freedom of the subject matter.

It is necessary to point out, however, that giving priority to special hermeneutics never meant for Barth the end of general hermeneutics. "Biblical hermeneutics must be guarded against the totalitarian claim of a general herme-

---

[159] The 1923 correspondence-debate between Barth and Harnack is also contained in Jürgen Moltmann, ed., "Ein Briefwechsel zwischen Karl Barth Und Adolf Von Harnack," *Anfänge der dialektischen Theologie I*, (Munich: Christian Kaiser, Verlag, 1966, 2ⁿᵈ ed.), pp. 323-347 (cited above, p. 325); ET "The Debate on the Critical Historical Method: Correspondence Between Adolf von Harnack and Karl Barth," *The Beginnings of Dialectical Theology*, trans. Keith R. Crim, ed. James M. Robinson, (Richmond, VA: John Knox Press, 1968), pp. 165-187 (cited above, p.166, translation slightly altered). See also H. Martin Rumscheidt, *Revelation and Theology: An analysis of the Barth-Harnack correspondence of 1923* (Cambridge: University Press, 1972). Hereafter cited as *Anfänge*.

[160] Barth, *Anfänge*, p. 329; ET p. 170 [translation slightly revised].

[161] "[Theology] owes its historical existence and its place in the *universitas litterarum* to its essence as ultimate risk which must necessarily be dared, as the extraordinary, irregular, revolutionary attack . ... Wissenschaftlichkeit means Sachlichkeit. Sachlichkeit in theology is unconditional respect before the uniqueness of the theme which is here chosen. ... Scientific theology is repentance, rethinking, 'renewed thinking.' ... It is the question mark and the exclamation point on the most extreme margin of the university." See Rom II, p. 515.

[162] KD I/1:8; CD I/1:10.

[163] KD I/1:6; CD I/1:8.

[164] Whether or not theology is called a science, Barth states: "This question is not a vital one for theology. There is no necessity of principle, nor are there any internal reasons, why it should claim to belong to this genus . ... [and] it would make not the slightest difference to its real business if it had to rank as something other than science" (KD I/1:5-6; CD I/1:7-8). Nevertheless, Barth elaborates "three practical reasons why we should quietly insist on describing theology as a science" in KD 1/1:9f.; CD I/1:11f.

neutics." Nevertheless, "It is a special hermeneutics only because general hermeneutics has been so mortally sick for so long that it has not let the special problem of biblical hermeneutics force its attention upon its own problem. For the sake of better general hermeneutics it must therefore dare to be this special hermeneutics."[165] Biblical hermeneutics, in other words, must be special hermeneutics only because general hermeneutics as such has failed to honor the particularity of the Bible's subject matter. Yet for Barth this never meant a rejection of the primary *goal* of general hermeneutics, namely, the concern to avoid arbitrary, idiosyncratic, privileged interpretation of the Bible. On the contrary,

> It will include the methods of observation used in general hermeneutics. It will have considered all the questions, without exception, which arise from that point of view in forming its general picture of the text. Therefore it will not have to fear any inquiry in respect of historical orientation and criticism. On the other hand, it will not tolerate any restrictions. It will allow the text to speak for itself in the sense that it will give full scope to its controlling object. It will not seek to conceal its ultimate determination for the sake of any preconceived notion of what is possible. It will not distort the text by trying to obscure and level down and render innocuous its real object. It will allow the text to say what, controlled by its object, it does actually say in its historical contingence. In doing this and to this extent, in so far as it can happen in fulfilment of the human task posed, it will explain, unfold and affirm its real historical sense, and thus make it possible to follow the sense of the text itself, what it does actually say.[166]

Barth's attempt to overcome the hermeneutical tradition of Schleiermacher and Dilthey was, to repeat, never a matter of simply negating general hermeneutics. From the beginning, Barth never tolerated any narrowing of the scope of interpretation. He insisted that "all the questions, without exception" general hermeneutics might raise should be considered. He insisted on "using all the crowbars and wrecking tools needed to achieve *relevant* treatment of the text."[167] Nevertheless, he also refused to "tolerate any restrictions" or any leveling down of a text which might occur because of preconceived notions about what is possible. *It was not therefore because of its attempt to broaden the scope of interpretation, rather it was because of its tendency to narrow or limit the scope of interpretation, to restrict and distort what a text might actually say in light of its controlling object, that Barth tried to overcome general hermeneutics.* This is something most of Barth's contemporaries at the time of Rom I and II did not understand. As a result, neither did they understand that he was talking about an approach to interpretation which was not less rigorous or less critical, but more rigorous, "more critical."[168]

---

[165] KD I/2:523; CD I/2:472.
[166] KD I/2:814-815; CD I/2:726.
[167] Rom II, p. xii.
[168] Rom II, p. xii.

Thus, contrary to what many have suggested in recent years, Barth did not simply reject or dismiss the hermeneutical tradition of Schleiermacher.[169] He sought to overcome it and not by simply negating it but in the manner of an *Aufhebung* by actually engaging and affirming it (at least, for instance, in terms of its goal), negating it, and then reconstituting it entirely on a higher plane. This is what is at issue in Barth's assertion: "For the sake of better general hermeneutics, hermeneutics must be this special hermeneutics."[170] Nor is this to suggest that there are not important points of continuity between Barth and Schleiermacher's hermeneutic. Barth agreed with Schleiermacher, for instance, that the scope of interpretation should always be as comprehensive as possible. He agreed with Schleiermacher that interpretation should always be scientific and not arbitrary or privileged. Both recognized the importance of a hermeneutic which could be generally applied (as Jüngel has said: "The most important thing about Barth's hermeneutic is its universality").[171] But the means by which such a hermeneutic is established marks a very significant difference between Barth and the hermeneutical tradition of Schleiermacher, and this difference has not been well understood or appreciated.[172]

---

[169] Werner Jeanrond, for example, states that Barth too hastily "rejected" Schleiermacher's hermeneutics "because it misses the theological axioms which he, Barth, insists must be accepted before good interpretation could begin ... and fails to appreciate Schleiermacher's penetrating insights into the process of human communication and into the conditions of understanding." See "Karl Barth's Hermeneutics," in *Reckoning with Barth*, ed. Nigel Biggar (Oxford: Mowbray, 1988), p. 94. Thomas Provence asks: "Why did [Barth] find the hermeneutical model of Schleiermacher and his intellectual heirs so bankrupt that he felt compelled to develop his own hermeneutical philosophy?" in *The Hermeneutics of Karl Barth* (Ann Arbor, MI: UMI, 1980), p. 11. John Thiel elaborates the thesis that "Barth's early hermeneutical encounter with Schleiermacher took the form of a monologue" in "Barth's Early Interpretation of Schleiermacher," *Barth and Schleiermacher: Beyond the Impasse?*, ed. James Duke and Robert Streetman (Philadelphia: Fortress Press, 1988), pp. 11f.

[170] KD I/2:523; CD I/2:472.

[171] Eberhard Jüngel, "Theologie als Metakritik. Zur Hermeneutik theologischer Exegese," *Barth-Studien* (Zürich-Köln: Benziger Verlag, 1982), p. 88; ET *Karl Barth: A Theological Legacy*, trans. Garrett E. Paul (Philadelphia: Westminster Press, 1986), p. 74. Hereafter cited as *Barth-Studien*.

[172] G.C. Berkouwer, for instance, recognizes the problem of submitting Scripture to general hermeneutics (as did, he claims, Abraham Kuyper). He also sees the problem of arbitrariness with regard to those who speak of special theological hermeneutics. But he does not recognize Barth's move from special to general hermeneutics or the implications of it, *De Heilige Schrift*, I (Kampen, Netherlands: J.H. Kok N.V., 1966), pp. 147-151; ET *Studies in Dogmatics: Holy Scripture*, trans. Jack B. Rogers (Grand Rapids, William B. Eerdmans, 1975), pp. 112-113. Nor, apparently, does his student, Jack Rogers, who writes: "[Barth] agreed with the view of J.A. Ernesti (1707-1781), who, in 1732, argued that the Bible should be studied like any other human document. Barth said: 'It can lay no a priori dogmatic claim to special attention.' Yet on the other hand, in practice, Barth challenged the adequacy of this principle." See Jack Rogers and Donald McKim, *The Authority and Interpretation of the Bible* (San Francisco: Harper and Row, 1979), p. 424. Kornelis H. Miskotte, however, is one who *did* understand

I have stated that Barth's move from special to general hermeneutics is evident in his *Römerbrief* period. But his first attempt to elaborate this hermeneutical move is found in the middle of his Göttingen lectures on dogmatics of 1924/25. In his attempt to articulate his understanding of the Reformed Scripture Principle, he remarked:

> A professor of theology once told me that he had learned much more from his devout mother than from the whole Bible. To this our reply must be that recognition of the special dignity of the biblical witnesses is not a matter of one experience among others. It is all very well to realize, perhaps, that one may learn more from all kinds of greater or lesser prophets or apostles of a later period, or even of our own time, than from reading the Bible. Yet the issue is not where we learn most, but where we learn the one thing, the truth. It is not a matter of arguing that the Bible is the finest book, but that it is the standard of all fine books. Our learning or experience is in any case indirect, and so are the sources on which we draw. Let us presuppose that it really is Jesus Christ or revelation that is mediated to us; the question then arises how we know this, how we are to recognize it. The question is that of a norm or rule which is indubitably above me but also above my closest authorities. The real question is not the question of what impresses me most sharply but the question of what is the truth, what is revelation, in that which impresses me.[173]

Barth never disputed the fact that as human readers we read the Bible – whether we seek to or not – like any other book. The question for him was: How *do* we read other books? What is the standard by which we read other books? What is the truth by which all other truths are judged? And how are we to recognize it? Barth had come to the conclusion that the subject matter of the Bible was the standard by which he was to read all other books, and the way he came to recognize it as such, he claimed, was by the Holy Spirit. But that Barth had a standard to assess other books is not something he arrived at only in 1924/25. It is clear that Barth had a specific standard and a specific means of applying it (that is, a specific method) as early as his *Römerbrief* period. Jülicher had charged that he was a "pneumatic," that he had offered an arbitrary, idiosyncratic, privileged interpretation of Paul's *Romans* when he should have acted as a "scientific exegete" and dealt "with the books of the Bible just as with those of Marcion, Augustine, or Luther."[174] Barth responded in his preface to Rom II by saying that he would have tried to approach the task of interpreting Goethe or Lao-Tzu in the same way had it been his task to interpret

---

Barth's move from special to general hermeneutic but not necessarily in light of Barth's attempt to overcome the hermeneutical legacy of Schleiermacher. See *Als De Goden Zwijgen* (Amsterdam: Uitgeversmaatschappij, 1956), pp. 122-124; ET *When The Gods Are Silent*, trans. John W. Doberstein (New York: Harper & Row, 1967), pp. 146-149.

[173] Karl Barth, *'Unterricht in der christlichen Religion' 1924/25, I*, ed. Hannelotte Reiffen (Zürich: Theologischer Verlag Zürich, 1985), p. 260; ET *The Göttingen Dogmatics: Instruction in the Christian Religion I*, trans. Geoffrey Bromiley (Grand Rapids: William B. Eerdmans, 1991), pp. 213-4. Otherwise known as the "Göttingen Dogmatics." Hereafter cited as *Unterricht*.

[174] Jülicher, p. 98; ET p. 81.

Goethe or Lao-Tzu.[175] Even earlier, in his letter to Paul Wernle on Oct. 24, 1919, Barth said he would have tried to approach Plato in exactly the same way had it been his task to interpret Plato.[176] The question we must now ask is: What was this way? What was this special approach to interpretation Barth was willing to apply not only to *Romans* but to other texts as well?

G. The School of the Holy Spirit

Though Karl Barth plainly stated in his preface to Rom II that he did not hide the fact that he had employed a specific exegetical method, his remarks about it, as such, are rather opaque. At one point he suggests that his exegetical method might best be summarized by the simple formula: "Think deliberately!" or "Consider well!" (*Besinn dich!*).[177] Of course, because there are many ways of thinking deliberately or considering well, this hardly tells us much about Barth's exegetical approach. Fortunately, there are other phrases in his *Römerbrief* prefaces which are a bit more descriptive.

1. *Pneumatic*. While Barth said in his preface to Rom II, "I am no 'pneumatic,' as [Jülicher] has called me," he never actually denied that his approach was, in some sense, a "pneumatic" one. In fact, Barth not only claimed credit for having initiated the pneumatic exegesis discussion of the 1920s (as I pointed out earlier), but throughout his career – even as late as 1962 – he defended the concept of a 'pneumatic' exegesis.[178] In doing so, however, he tried – in his *Christian Dogmatics*, his *Church Dogmatics*, and elsewhere – to qualify what he meant and did not mean by it.[179] He repeatedly, for example, emphasized that such an approach could never "dispose over the Scriptures on the basis of some imagined spiritual power that it possesses" and always

---

[175] Rom II, pp. xv-xvi.

[176] Karl Barth, "Karl Barths Brief an Paul Wernle" (24 October, 1919), Rom I, p. 644.

[177] Rom II, p. xv.

[178] Barth, *Einführung in die evangelische Theologie* (Zürich: Evangelischer Verlag Zürich, 1962), p. 193f.; ET *Evangelical Theology: An Introduction*, trans. Grover Foley (New York: Holt, Rinehart, and Winston, 1963), p. 178.

[179] Karl Barth, *Die christliche Dogmatik im Entwurf I. Die Lehre vom Worte Gottes: Prolegomena zur christlichen Dogmatik 1927*, ed. Gerhard Sauter (Zürich: Theologischer Verlag Zürich, 1982), pp. 516-518. Sauter provides an important editorial comment regarding the origins of "pneumatic exegesis" in Barth's thought: "The term 'pneumatic exegesis' goes back to J.T. Beck, *Einleitung in das System der Christlichen Lehre oder Propädeutische Entwicklung der Christlichen Lehrwissenschaft* (Stuttgart [1838] 1870). On p. 236, Beck speaks about the 'pneumatic standpoint' and treats the pneumatic exegesis of Scripture as equivalent to 'theological exegesis' (p. 255) and defines it as follows: 'the theological, i.e., not merely the believing but the *believing scientific exegesis* [*gläubig wissenschaftliche Auslegung*] must develop the meaning of the whole and the particulars of the text in the spirit of faith or pneumatically with hermeneutical thoroughness reproducing certainty of thought' (p. 255)," pp. 516-517 n. 11. Hereafter cited as *Die christliche Dogmatik*.

basis of some imagined spiritual power that it possesses" and always insisted that "there is no method by which revelation can be made revelation that is actually received, no method of scriptural exegesis which is truly pneumatic, i.e., which articulates the witness to revelation in the Bible and to that degree really introduces the Pneuma."[180] Such a method did not, in other words, refer to a "method of actualization" (*Verwirklichungsmethode*), that is, a method which determines, much less guarantees, any particular result.[181] Rather, "it may be called 'pneumatic,'" he claimed, "to the extent that it uses the freedom, founded ultimately upon the Scriptures themselves, to address to them seriously, ultimately, and definitively a strict question about the Spirit's own testimony heard in them."[182]

2. *Biblicist.* Another term that had been applied to Barth pejoratively which he tried to baptize was the term "biblicist." He said, "The position that I have adopted towards the text has been called 'biblicist.' For this some have blamed and some have praised me. The word is not mine, but I accept it, provided I am allowed to explain what I mean by 'biblicism.'"[183] Barth did not go into much detail about what he meant by it in his preface to Rom II, only that "Taken precisely, all the 'biblicism' which I can be shown to have consists in my having the prejudice that the Bible is a good book, and that it is worthwhile to take its thoughts at least as seriously as one takes one's own." But like the concept of "pneumatic exegesis," Barth persisted in defending a certain kind of "biblicism" throughout his career. In his *Göttingen Dogmatics* he described "biblicism" or what he called a "second-degree biblicism" in terms of a "biblical attitude."[184] "The biblical attitude, that of the prophets and apostles," he said, "is the attitude of witnesses, the attitude that put the scriptures in the

---

[180] KD I/1:190; CD I/1:183.

[181] KD I/1:278; CD I/1:263. Barth states: "We do not refer to a method of actualization that is placed in our hands or anyone else's hands along with the Bible when we for our part point to this sign, to this pointer that is given to us. ... [even] interpretation itself can be only a pointer, not the discovery of the Holy Spirit or the Christian principle in the Bible, nor the mediation of the Word of God in it."

[182] Barth, *Einführung in die evangelische Theologie*, p. 194; ET p. 177.

[183] Rom II, p. xv.

[184] Barth elaborates on this "specific human attitude" which corresponds to the experience of faith in KD I/2:912-919; CD I/2:816-822 and there refers to it as a "biblical attitude": "We call it 'biblical' because it has its prototype and exemplar in the attitude of the biblical witnesses themselves, because it consists in the regard for and imitation of this prototype, that is, in the institution of a kinship between the outlook, approach and method of the biblical writers." KD I/2:912; CD I/2:816. It is "a specific type of thinking which is not necessarily bound up with faith and the experience of faith, but which even on the basis of this faith we have to learn as a distinctive thing, although on this basis we can learn it with instruction and practice, just as we learn anything else." See KD I/2:917; CD I/2:820. Barth's discussion of this "biblical attitude" remained virtually unchanged from his *Göttingen Dogmatics* to his *Christian Dogmatics* to his *Church Dogmatics*.

canon and called their text holy, the attitude not of spectators or reporters or thinkers, but of people who come down from the absolute presupposition, the *Deus dixit*, with all the irresistible momentum of a boulder rolling down a mountain side." Barth describes such biblicism as a "formal," "relative," yet "formative principle": "It is a human attitude which we can learn and exercise and study, which we can grow accustomed to, in which the more or less of any human attitude will always play a part. Biblicism is not identical with faith and obedience. It is a rule of thought [*Denkregel*] resulting from them."[185] But Barth distinguishes in both his *Göttingen* and *Christian Dogmatics* between "material" and "formal biblicism."[186] Formal biblicism such as the Reformers practiced is an attitude, a posture, a way of human thinking shaped by the Bible, a way in which those cultivated by its "rule of thought" learn to think its thoughts and hear its message again and again, whereas material biblicism, such as practiced by later Protestantism, is a way which has nothing necessarily to do with *hearing* the Bible, but consists of applying (*via* proof-texting) what one thinks one has already heard from it simply by repeating its words. Material biblicism, in other words, because it is content merely to recapitulate the Bible's words, presumes to have direct and immediate access to what the Bible really says and for this reason it makes no real effort to hear the Bible's message at all, but instead, "makes bold to master it or to posit it itself."[187]

3. *Nachdenken*. One of the most important terms Barth uses to describe his exegetical method was *Nachdenken*, i.e., to 'think along,' 'think after,' or 're-think.' In one of the more quoted statements from his preface to Rom II, Barth says:

> Compare Jülicher, for example, with Calvin. How energetically the latter goes to work after he has conscientiously established 'what is there' to rethink the thoughts of the text after it, that is, to come to terms with it until the wall between the first and the sixteenth century becomes transparent, until Paul speaks there and the man of the sixteenth century hears here, until the conversation between document and reader is concentrated entirely on the *matter* (which cannot be different here and there!).[188]

---

[185] Barth, *Unterricht*, pp. 352-353; ET pp. 291-292.

[186] Barth refers to this in his *Church Dogmatics* as "modern biblicism." In contrast to "the biblicism of the Reformers," it is the biblicism of J.T. Beck, J.C.K. Hofmann, Gottfried Menken and other Neo-Protestants. Barth asks: "Are we not dealing [here] with a pious, but in its audacity no less explicitly modern leap into direct immediacy, with a laying hold of revelation, which, involving as it does a jettisoning of the fathers, although it purports to be a laying hold of the Bible, is perhaps something very different from the obedience of faith which only occurs when revelation lays hold of us by the word of the Bible." See KD I/2:678-680; CD I/2:607-609. This follows Barth's thesis that Neo-Protestantism sought to be the *ecclesia docens* (the teaching church) before and at the expense of being the *ecclesia audiens* (the hearing church).

[187] Barth, *Unterricht*, p. 353; ET p. 292.

[188] Rom II, p. xi.

At a time when *Nachbildung, Nacherleben, Nachfühlung, Nachverständnis*, and other such technical hermeneutical terms and concepts were being used to describe the exegetical task, Barth's choice of the term *Nachdenken* (used three times in the preface to Rom II) could hardly have been an arbitrary one. More comprehensive than these other terms that ostensibly describe distinct stages in the overall process of *Verstehen*, it implies that exegesis follows a certain logic, a certain procedure. Yet unlike these other *nach*-prefix terms it never had for Barth the same psychological connotation it did for the hermeneutical tradition of Schleiermacher and Dilthey. That is, rather than reconstructing thoughts in the mind of an author or retracing genetically the path of the creative process which gave rise to an author's words, it meant accompanying with one's own thoughts the thoughts of an author along a particular path – not necessarily the genetically reconstructed thoughts – but the thoughts of the author as stated and with reference to a particular subject matter. Simply put, Barth said: "to think *after* means to think *with*."[189] And to think *with* an author, whether it is Homer or Goethe or the prophets and apostles, meant for Barth – in the strictest sense – to think *with* them, not *about* them. The significance of this difference will become more apparent in the course of this study, but suffice it to say, Barth was not interested in just any form of *Nachdenken*.

Each of the above terms (pneumatic, biblicist, *Nachdenken*) is important because each comes out of Barth's *Römerbrief* period and represents a hermeneutical concept he defended throughout his career. Yet there is another phrase that perhaps better describes what is really at issue in the hermeneutic of Barth's *Römerbrief* period, although it does not come out of this period. In 1952, Barth wrote an essay entitled "Rudolf Bultmann – An Attempt to Understand Him." In this essay he sought to come to terms with the contribution of him whose name in the twentieth century "is inseparably linked with the idea of 'understanding.'"[190] Barth said he found it ironic that for all Bultmann's talk about understanding he was "not at all easy to understand." But one of the chief reasons why he found Bultmann so difficult to understand was because of his preoccupation with the process of understanding itself and because of his requirement that to understand the New Testament truly, one must approach it with a particular self-understanding, i.e., an existentialist self-understanding. Barth referred to this as an "anthropological straight jacket" because it set *a priori* limits on our understanding and said:

> It is impossible to understand any other person unless we are ready to let him tell us something we did not know before, something we could not find out for ourselves, something we have hitherto been prejudiced against, perhaps with much justification. We shall never understand him if we are sure we know beforehand the limits of our understanding. We shall never understand him if we lay down these limits before we have given him a chance to

---

[189] *Unterricht*, p. 309; ET p. 253.
[190] Barth, *Ein Versuch, ihn zu verstehen*, p. 9; ET p. 83.

speak for himself. These limits, it is true, are found in all personal relationships. They are signs of real narrow-mindedness. Thus it is certain that even if we manage to be completely open-minded, it will take us a long time to reach a perfect understanding. No doubt from time to time we shall be jolted out of our narrow-mindedness and widen our sights for a moment. But it is quite another thing to regard as our sacred duty and an iron law to confine ourselves within our narrow-mindedness and refuse to budge an inch.[191]

This clearly suggests Barth's problem with the so-called "hermeneutics of understanding" tradition which Bultmann and, later, proponents of the "New Hermeneutic" claimed to follow. But it is in the subsequent lines of this essay that Barth states not only his problem with this approach but his response to it:

> To understand another I shall have to overcome this unwilling attitude, and cease to maintain it as a matter of principle. Such willingness, or its absence, can never be taken for granted, whether towards others or towards a text. It can never be guaranteed or contrived artificially by our own strength, any more than we can contrive it in our relation to God. For genuine understanding between man and man, however, incomplete, *the school of the Holy Spirit* will undoubtedly be necessary. For it is only through the Holy Spirit that the Old and New Testaments can be appreciated as a testimony to the Word of God. Not even myths or persons like Goethe for instance can be understood without this initial willingness, that is, without something such as *the school of the Holy Spirit*. The erection of this doctrine of the prior understanding as the norm, which lies at the root of Bultmann's hermeneutic, would seem to be the death of all right and genuine understanding. For it appears to compete with the Holy Spirit and unduly to restrict his operation.[192]

Karl Barth's answer to the problem of hermeneutics was, in short, "*die Schule des Heiligen Geistes*" (the school of the Holy Spirit).[193] This was his answer not only to the hermeneutical problem Bultmann and his students were discussing throughout the 1950s and 1960s, it was also his answer to the dominant hermeneutical tradition of the nineteenth and twentieth centuries. Though the phrase "the school of the Holy Spirit" never appears in Barth's *Römerbrief* period, that he associated something like it in this period with his attempt to overcome the hermeneutical tradition of Schleiermacher and Dilthey and the concept of "understanding in general" is indicated by the fact that immediately after the paragraph above he makes the following reflection:

---

[191] Barth, *Ein Versuch, ihn zu verstehen*, pp. 45, 58-59; ET pp. 114, 126.

[192] Barth, *Ein Versuch, ihn zu verstehen*, pp. 59-60; ET pp. 126-7 [translation revised]. Emphasis mine.

[193] Barth does not provide a reference for it, but the phrase "school of the Holy Spirit" comes from Calvin. With respect to the doctrine of predestination, for example, Calvin states: "For Scripture is the school of the Holy Spirit, in which, as nothing is omitted that is both necessary and useful to know, so nothing is taught but what is expedient to know. Therefore we must guard against depriving believers of anything disclosed about predestination in Scripture, lest we seem either wickedly to defraud them of the blessing of their God or to accuse and scoff at the Holy Spirit for having published what it is in any way profitable to suppress." See John Calvin, *Institutes* III.xxi.3, Ford Lewis Battles trans. (Philadelphia: Westminster Press, 1960) p. 924. See also *Institutes* IV.xvii.36.

Thirty years ago when we launched the new movement in theology our aim – at least mine – was to *reverse* the current concept of 'understanding' of the New (and the Old) Testament; and of understanding in general. The basis of man's knowledge, as we saw it, depended on his being known by the object of his knowledge. We were concerned with the Word, God's (gift and) message to man. We felt that the Word of God also throws light on the words people address to one another. Our aim was to emancipate understanding, both of the Bible and, for this reason, of things in general, from the Egyptian bondage in which one philosophy after another had tried to take control and teach us what the Holy Spirit was allowed to say as the Word of God and of man in order to be understandable. Although we did not know the word, we were seeking to 'demythologize' the belief that man was the measure of his own understanding and of all other understanding. It turned out to be a long and arduous path with many differences and separations. We stumbled upon many obstacles, sometimes alone, sometimes in company with our colleagues. There were many by-paths and false turnings, and we had to be constantly recalling ourselves and our colleagues to the main road. I am far from thinking we have reached the end of the road. But we were quite sure this was the right road. Now, as I see it, Bultmann has forsaken our road and gone back to the old one again. He has gone back to the old idea of understanding which we had abandoned.[194]

Why was Barth so convinced in 1952 that Bultmann had forsaken their original road and gone back to the old one again? Given their many longstanding disagreements, why had Barth not said so – at least as clearly – before? The reason seems to have something to do with Bultmann's 1950 essay, "The Problem of Hermeneutics." In this essay, as I mentioned, Bultmann did not merely look back to the hermeneutical tradition of Schleiermacher and Dilthey. He also placed his own project directly in its trajectory.[195] This is why Barth said: "Now, as I see it, Bultmann has forsaken our road and gone back to the old one again. He has gone back to the old idea of understanding which we had abandoned." This is why he saw Bultmann and his students return not simply to hermeneutics but to the hermeneutical tradition of Schleiermacher and Dilthey as but a "lusting after the fleshpots of Egypt."[196]

Karl Barth's theological revolution had to do from the beginning not only with a reversal of the current understanding of the Bible, but with 'understanding in general,' that is, with the way he and his contemporaries went about understanding not only the Bible but other books as well. This is what is at stake in Barth's move from special hermeneutics to general hermeneutics and this is what is at stake in his claim: "Our aim was to emancipate understanding, both

---

[194] Barth, *Ein Versuch, ihn zu verstehen*, p. 60; ET p. 127 [translation revised].

[195] Bultmann concludes his essay: "The same holds good, finally, of the kind of understanding to which Schleiermacher and Dilthey orient their hermeneutical theory and which can be said to be understanding of historical phenomena in the ultimate and highest sense, namely, the interpretation that questions texts about the possibilities of human existence as one's own." It is on this basis that he then says, "Interpretation of the biblical writings is not subject to different conditions of understanding from those applying to any other literature." See Bultmann "Das Problem der Hermeneutik," p. 231; ET pp. 85-86.

[196] Barth, *Ein Versuch, ihn zu verstehen*, p. 61; ET p. 128.

of the Bible and of things in general, from the Egyptian bondage in which one philosophy after another had tried to take control and teach us what the Holy Spirit was allowed to say as the Word of God and of man in order to be open to understanding." From the beginning, Barth was convinced "that the Word of God also throws light on the words people address to one another." From the beginning, he believed that the way we come to understand not only the Bible but the words people address to one another was by the Holy Spirit.[197] This is not to say, as I have emphasized, that Barth was unaware of or uninterested in hermeneutics or hermeneutical problems. Nor is it to say that he did not recognize that our hearing was also always a thoroughly human experience involving thoroughly human factors such as varying degrees of 'willingness' or 'unwillingness,' 'open-mindedness' or 'narrow-mindedness,' etc. To say that the way we come to understand both the Bible and the words people address to one another is by the Holy Spirit, never meant for Barth that we as interpreters could ignore what he referred to as "the relative conditions of hearing."[198] It never meant that having an appropriate or inappropriate 'human attitude' was not a factor in our attempt to hear the Word of God or the words people address to one another. As Barth said at the end of §5, "The Nature of the Word of God" in CD I/1:

> ... the hearing and receiving of the Word of God by a man can be known by him and others only in faith. We are saying the same thing when we say, in the Holy Spirit. Faith, of course, is also a human experience. A specific human attitude corresponds to this experience, and this human attitude finds its expression, too, in specific human thoughts. But whether or not this experience is the experience, this attitude the attitude, and these thoughts the thoughts of the faith that has heard the Word of God, is decided spiritually, i.e., not by faith, but by the Word believed.[199]

---

[197] This presupposes that the knowledge the Holy Spirit bears witness to in Holy Scripture is of a very special kind: "What does the Bible offer us toward an understanding of the meaning of the world? ... The immediate answer to our question is, of course, that the Bible offers us a knowledge of God: we look to it not so much to give us knowledge about this particular or that, as to indicate to us the beginning and the end, the origin and the limit, the creative unity and the last problem of all knowledge. ... It is not a meaning apart from other meanings, for in it all others – the meanings of natural science, of history, of aesthetics, and of religion – are at once included and concluded; and this meaning in the last analysis will be found to be identical with that of philosophy, so far as philosophy understands itself ... all the knowledge that we possess takes its start from the knowledge of God." See Barth, "*Biblische Fragen, Einsichten und Ausblicke,*" pp. 70-71. More shall be said about this throughout the course of this study, but at this point it is sufficient merely to point out that Barth had a rather 'high bar' definition of understanding which made him reluctant to say that he had understood anything until he had understood it in light of the revelation of God in Jesus Christ and therefore by way of the Holy Spirit.

[198] Barth, *Unterricht*, pp. 317f.; ET p. 261f.; see also *Die christliche Dogmatik*, pp. 408f.

[199] KD I/1:190; CD I/1:183.

This statement clearly shows where the emphasis for Barth lies. While hearing is an experience both human and divine, whether or not we hear is decided not humanly, but divinely, that is, not by any human factor, but by the Word of God. Yet to say that our hearing is decided by the Word of God is not to say that human factors (experiences, attitudes, thoughts, etc.) are insignificant. Barth fully recognizes that such factors play a very significant role in our hearing. Still, such factors do not ultimately determine whether or not we hear, nor do they constitute in and of themselves what might be called *the subjective possibility* of hearing, as if the objective possibility of hearing lies with the Word of God and the subjective possibility with the human hearer. By no means. Even the subjective side of hearing, according to Barth, which includes all human factors, is directly supervised and superintended by the Holy Spirit, which is to say, by the Word of God. The Word of God, in other words, creates its own hearer and creates its own hearer by the Holy Spirit who not only imparts and enlivens faith but shapes and instills in the life of the individual believer a "specific human attitude" which corresponds to the experience of faith. It is this "specific human attitude" that Barth refers to as a "biblical attitude" and it is this specific attitude that is formed and shaped in "the school of the Holy Spirit."

The specific attitude which is formed and shaped in the school of the Holy Spirit is, to repeat, a specifically *human* attitude, that is, "It is a human attitude which we can learn and exercise and study, which we can grow accustomed to, in which the more or less of any human attitude will always play a part."[200] But it has nothing to do with any "aptitude," such as any "genius" quality as in the case of Schleiermacher, nor does it have to do with any inherent competence or capacity within the life of an individual believer such as a "linguistic competence" or "a capacity for words." Neither is it a prerequisite of or identical with faith and obedience. Rather, Barth says, "It is a rule of thought resulting from them." It is a rule of thought which informs and governs the individual believer's approach to the task of interpretation, and not only one's approach to interpreting the Bible, but every human word. Yet it is a rule of thought one cannot learn on one's own. It is something one must be taught. This is why the school of the Holy Spirit is so important. The school of the Holy Spirit is where we learn to think according to the Bible's own rule of thought. It is where we learn to think after the thoughts of the prophets and apostles and, on that basis — in so far as it is possible — after the thoughts of others as well. It is where we are trained and inculcated into a specific human attitude which Barth calls a "biblical attitude."

There is more that takes place in the school of the Holy Spirit, however, than the shaping of a specific attitude, disposition, or demeanor. There are specific lessons, specific hermeneutical principles, to be learned. I mentioned

---

[200] Barth, *Unterricht*, pp. 352-353; ET pp. 291-292.

earlier Barth's claim that there were "principles of exposition" to be learned from expositing the Bible which are valid for the exposition of every human word. What are these principles of exposition? To answer this question I believe it is necessary to go to the place where Barth first discussed his exegetical method, namely, his prefaces to Rom I and II. Here Barth discusses an approach to exegesis which he claims he would apply not only to the Bible but to Goethe, Lao-tzu, and even Plato, if it were his task to interpret their works. It is also here that he contrasts his approach to exegesis with that of his contemporaries. This is done in all the *Römerbrief* prefaces, but perhaps more deliberately in his preface drafts to Rom I than anywhere else. In the first line of his very first preface draft to Rom I, Barth states: "The following book is an attempt to read the Bible differently than we were generally taught at universities under the dominance of the theology of the 1890s. Question: in what way different? I wish to answer: more in accordance with its subject matter, content, and substance, entering with more attention and love into the meaning of the Bible itself."[201] Closer examination of the *Römerbrief* prefaces, particularly in light of the hermeneutical tradition he sought to overcome, suggests there is much at stake in Barth's attempt to read the Bible in this way. In fact, there are at least four principles of exposition implicit in Barth's statement here which shall serve as a kind of *Leitsatz* throughout the rest of this study, and it is to these principles that I now turn.

---

[201] Appendix 2, Preface Draft I, p. 277 (p. 582).

Chapter 3

Sachlicher, Inhaltlicher, Wesentlicher

To read the Bible in a way that is "*sachlicher, inhaltlicher, wesentlicher,*" that is, "more in accordance with its subject matter, content, and substance," represents Karl Barth's most important hermeneutical principle. Though unstated in Rom I, it is a principle he strongly emphasizes in his preface drafts to that volume.[1] In fact, it was in these preface drafts that Barth first used the term "*sachlich*" to describe his method after his break with liberalism, and given the fact that Barth's entire theology has been described as an attempt to do theology in a *sachlicher* manner, this is important.[2] To understand this principle it is necessary to understand the specific context out of which it arose. Barth introduced his address at Leutwil on February 6, 1917 entitled, *"Die neue Welt in der Bibel,"* with a single question: "*Was steht in der Bibel?*"[3] His attempt throughout this address and throughout his *Römerbrief* period to answer this question suggests much not only about the specific context out of which this principle arose, but also about the single most important issue that distinguishes his approach to the task of exegesis from that of his contemporaries.

A. Karl Barth's "Turn to the Bible"

Was steht in der Bibel? Barth's preliminary answer in 1917 was: "*History!* The history of a remarkable, even unique, people; the history of powerful, intellectually vigorous personalities; the history of Christianity in its beginnings."[4] "The Bible is full of history." Yet the problem with this answer is that one quickly discovers it is a rather odd sort of history, certainly not the sort one reads about in schoolbooks or the kind one would expect to find in the newspaper. It is, rather, a history which at all its decisive turns leaves us asking – as we would with respect to all that is elsewhere called history – "How did it all come about? How is it that one event followed another?"[5] But to

---

[1] Appendix 2, Preface Drafts I, Ia, II, and III, passim.
[2] There is at least one instance of Barth using the word "*sachlich*" prior to this time but not with reference to his theological method. Karl Barth to Eduard Thurneysen, 10 Sept., 1915, *B-Th Br.* I, p. 80.
[3] Barth, "Die neue Welt in der Bibel," p. 18.
[4] Barth, "Die neue Welt in der Bibel," p. 22.
[5] Barth, "Die neue Welt in der Bibel," p. 23.

such questions, Barth says, the Bible answers, if not "with silences quite unparalleled," then with explanations such as: "God created" or "God spoke" or "God provided," explanations which, however plausible or implausible, simply do not fit within the causal nexus or canons of explanation assumed by most historians. Of course, "history" is not *all* that the Bible contains. The Bible also contains "morality." "It is a collection of illustrations and teachings of virtue and human greatness."⁶ Yet, ironically, so many of its "heroes" e.g., Samson, David, Amos, Peter, *etc.*, hardly make worthy exemplars for "the good, efficient, industrious, publicly educated, average citizen of Switzerland." Even more problematic is the fact that "at certain crucial points the Bible amazes us by its remarkable indifference to our conception of good and evil."⁷ History and morality seem, thus, rather inadequate answers to the question "*Was steht in der Bibel?*" And the same must be said of religion and piety. Here again: Of course the Bible contains religion and piety! In fact, Barth says, "All religions may be found in the Bible, if one will have it so." But no serious reader of the Bible can stop with this answer. Why? Because

> there is a spirit in the Bible that allows us to stop awhile and play among secondary things as is our custom – but soon after it begins to drive us on ... on to the main subject [*die Hauptsache*], whether we want to or not. There is a river in the Bible that carries us away, once we have entrusted our destiny to it – away from ourselves to the sea. Holy Scripture interprets itself in spite of all our human limitations. We need only dare to follow this drive, this spirit, this river, to grow out beyond ourselves toward the highest answer.⁸

What is this "highest answer"? What is this "main subject" to which we are so ineluctably driven? Barth says it is God. The Bible, of course, contains history, morality, religion, and piety as well. But none of these constitute the real "content of the contents." None of these really tell us what the Bible is *about*. The Bible, Barth says, is *about* God. "'God' is the content [*der Inhalt*] of the Bible."⁹

There is no record of Barth ever saying anything like this about the Bible before his break with liberalism. As a young liberal, Barth believed that the Bible had to do primarily with religion, with piety, with the pious thoughts and experiences of those who had been filled, more or less, with what he called "Christian certainty" [*christliche Gewißheit*].¹⁰ He introduced his 1909 con-

---

⁶ Barth, "Die neue Welt in der Bibel," p. 24.

⁷ Barth, "Die neue Welt in der Bibel," p. 25; e.g., "In how many aspects of morality the Bible is grievously wanting! How little fundamental information it offers in regard to the difficult questions of business life, marriage, civilization, and statecraft, with which we have to struggle."

⁸ Barth, "Die neue Welt in der Bibel," p. 22.

⁹ Barth, "Die neue Welt in der Bibel," p. 29.

¹⁰ *Gewißheit* or "certainty" is a theme which appears frequently in Barth's writings prior to 1915. In his confirmation lessons of 1910-1911, Barth elaborates his understanding of "*Die christliche Gewißheit.*" See Karl Barth, "Konfirmandenunterricht 1910-1911," in idem, *Kon-*

firmation class to the topic of the Bible, for example, by telling his students: "Christian certainty, and therefore also our instruction, is based on the revelation of God in the Holy Scriptures, especially the New Testament, because it is there that we find the earliest reports and thoughts about Jesus, written down by men who experienced themselves the glory of Christian certainty to the liveliest [*lebhaftesten*] degree."[11] Though Barth referred to the New Testament as "indispensable" for this reason, he said the Old Testament was also "important" because it teaches us about "the religion from which Jesus emerged." He hastened to add, however, "With the conclusion of the Bible, God did not close the book of revelation. Everything that is Jesus-like in people, can be revelation, a message from God. People, poets, art, nature, strong impressions."[12] Still, one of the major thoughts he seems to have tried to drive home to his students was that "We call the Bible *holy* Scripture, not because of its letters or because its particular thoughts have a special holiness, but because it talks about him who is holy."[13] Thus, even as a liberal, Barth never wished to deny but rather wished positively to affirm that the Bible was – to whatever limited extent it could express the pious expressions of its individual authors – about God. But even if this is why it was ultimately important, it was still for him *primarily* about religion, about piety, about "people who *experienced* God and who now communicate these experiences."[14] And even if it was about something more or less or other than this, how else could it possibly be scientifically studied except as a "document of piety"? This, in short, was Barth's view of the Bible before his break with liberalism.[15]

There came a time, however, when this view would no longer suffice for Barth as a description of the Bible's primary content. While Barth's theological conversion seems to have come about as the result of a coalescence of more than one crisis, it is clear that beyond his disappointment with his German teachers who had signed that "horrible manifesto" supporting the war policy of Kaiser Wilhelm II, one of the major reasons for his break with liberalism came, he said, as a result of the fact that "the textual basis of my sermons, the Bible,

---

firmandenunterricht, 1909-1921, ed. Jürgen Fangmeier (Zürich: Theologischer Verlag Zürich, 1987), pp. 60-61. Hereafter cited as *Konfirmandenunterricht, 1909-1921*.

[11] Barth, *Konfirmandenunterricht, 1909-1921*, p. 67.
[12] Barth, *Konfirmandenunterricht, 1909-1921*, p. 69.
[13] Barth, *Konfirmandenunterricht, 1909-1921*, p. 67.
[14] Barth, *Konfirmandenunterricht, 1909-1921*, p. 69.
[15] What Barth later said about the position of Heinrich Weinel, Professor of New Testament at Jena, in a letter to Thurneysen applies equally to Barth himself before his break with liberalism: "that prophets and laymen alike make a mistake if they think 'God' is the subject matter of theology. No, theologians must be 'scientific investigators of piety'; that alone is possible." See Karl Barth to Eduard Thurneysen, 7 Oct., 1922, *B-Th Br. II*, p. 104. More shall be said about the young, liberal Barth in chapter five.

which hitherto I had taken for granted, became more and more of a problem."[16] It is also clear that whatever his problem with the Bible was, it was precisely this notion of the Bible as primarily a "document of piety" that he attacked shortly after his break in his "*Die neue Welt der Bibel*" essay:

> The content of the Bible is not at all formed by the right human thoughts about God but by the right divine thoughts about men. The Bible tells us not how we should talk with God but what he says to us; not how we find our way to him, but how he has sought and found the way to us; not the right relation in which we must place ourselves to him, but the covenant which he has made with all who are Abraham's children by faith and which he has sealed once and for all in Jesus Christ. It is this which is within the Bible. The word of God is within the Bible. Our grandfathers were right after all when they so passionately defended the fact that revelation is in the Bible and not only religion, and when they would not allow the subject matter to be turned upside down for them by so pious and clever a man as Schleiermacher. And our fathers were right when they guarded warily against being drawn out upon the shaky ground of the religious personality cult. The more candidly we search for piety in Scripture, the more certainly we come sooner or later to the answer: What is piety? – "It is that which bears witness to *me*!"[17]

This statement is significant for two reasons: first, because it elaborates a distinction which had obviously become very important to Barth: "The content of the Bible is not at all formed by the right human thoughts about God but by the right divine thoughts about men ..."; and secondly, because it represents Barth's first public criticism of Schleiermacher (the only theologian mentioned in the address). Taken as a whole it suggests that whatever it was that brought Barth and Thurneysen to the point of saying aloud that they "could no longer share the faith of Schleiermacher,"[18] it had fundamentally to do with the fact that Barth had discovered the content of the Bible to be something other than what Schleiermacher claimed it was. For all Schleiermacher had meant to him, for all the years he had spent studying him since his "Eureka!" experience in 1906 when he first read the *Speeches*,[19] Barth had come to the conclusion that Schleiermacher had made a fundamental mistake. He had tried to turn the subject matter of the Bible upside down. He tried to claim that the Bible was not primarily about God, but about us. So simple yet utterly profound was this discovery that it shook Barth to his foundations and forced him to relearn his theological ABCs and rethink his theological identity. Barth's forefathers, he recalled, had been among the few who had not followed but had opposed this reversal. They had stood against the attempt of their contemporaries to turn the subject matter of the Bible upside down. This, Barth claimed, was *his* true

---

[16] Karl Barth, "Autobiographische Skizze Karl Barths aus dem Fakultätsalbum der Ev.-Theol. Fakultät in Münster," *Karl Barth-Rudolf Bultmann Briefwechsel*, 1911-1966, p. 296.

[17] Barth, "Die neue Welt in der Bibel," p. 28.

[18] Eduard Thurneysen to Karl Barth, 6 Oct. 1921, *B-Th Br.* I, p. 525.

[19] Barth, "Nachwort," p. 291; ET p. 262.

theological heritage, and now he would set about sorting it out, even if sorting it out meant – at least, initially – publicly declaring in no uncertain terms that his "ancestral line" did not include Schleiermacher.[20]

Reclaiming his theological heritage apart from Schleiermacher, however, would be easier said than done.[21] It is true that both Barth's grandfathers had taken positions which were generally opposed to Schleiermacher. Franz Albert Barth (1816-79), Barth's paternal grandfather, had been one of J.T. Beck's first students in Basel. Karl Achilles Sartorius (1824-93), his maternal grandfather, had begun his career "following a strictly orthodox, Reformed line," but late in the 1840s had studied in Berlin with Schelling and then in Heidelberg with Richard Rothe and "as a result, came to some degree under the influence of Schleiermacher, but subsequently ... went over to a somewhat primitive theological conservatism, tempered slightly by the gentle pietism of my good grandmother."[22] Barth's own father, Fritz Barth (1856-1912), was probably even more self-consciously opposed to Schleiermacher than Franz Barth. As a professor of New Testament and Church History at Bern, he had, as the younger Barth described it, "a (moderately) 'positive' theological attitude and direction."[23] But as firm as these personal and spiritual ties were and as abiding as their influence remained, Barth could never deny that – even while the Bible's subject matter had been turned upside down – he had experienced something extraordinary during his years of university training under teachers

---

[20] It is because of this crisis that Barth appealed to "an ancestral line which runs back through Kierkegaard to Luther and Calvin, and so to Paul and Jeremiah" because they recognized that *God* speaks. At the same time, Barth wishes to "explicitly point out that this ancestral line ... does not include Schleiermacher. With all due respect to the genius shown in his work, I can not consider him a good teacher in the realm of theology because, so far as I can see, he is disastrously dim-sighted in regard to the fact that ... one can not speak of God simply by speaking of man in a loud voice." See Karl Barth, "Das Wort Gottes als Aufgabe der Theologie," in idem, *Das Wort Gottes und die Theologie* (Munich: Christian Kaiser Verlag, 1925), pp. 164f.

[21] As Barth later said about his *Römerbrief* period: "It is certain that in what I thought, said, and wrote from that year [1916] on, I simply did without [Schleiermacher], and that his spectacles were not sitting on my nose as I was expounding the *Epistle to the Romans*. He was no longer a 'church father' for me. It is further certain, however, that this 'without him' implied a rather sharp 'against him.' On occasion, I intentionally made that explicit. Yet I really did not do it – since 'old love never fades' – without a deep inner regret that it could not be otherwise." See Barth, "Nachwort," pp. 295-296; ET pp. 265-266.

[22] Barth, "Nachwort," p. 292; ET p. 263. Barth inherited his grandfather Sartorius's Schleiermacher books and said: "He had indeed purchased Schleiermacher (good for me that he did!), but had hardly read him seriously, and judging from a few biting notes in the margins, had not loved him."

[23] Barth, "Nachwort," p. 290; ET p. 261.

"decisively influenced" by Schleiermacher, and especially under one he later referred to as "*the* theological teacher of my student years."[24]

B. Wilhelm Herrmann: A *Sachlicher* Approach

Wilhelm Herrmann (1846-1922) was Barth's most revered theological teacher; yet it was he, with ninety-two other German intellectuals, who had so profoundly disappointed Barth in 1914 by signing the manifesto supporting the war policy of Kaiser Wilhelm II. This singular event, as previously mentioned, symbolized for Barth the spiritual and moral bankruptcy not only of an entire generation of theologians, but of the theological enterprise of an entire era. And all this was even more devastating to Barth because of how deeply indebted he felt toward Herrmann. It was, after all, because of him, Barth said, "that my own deep interest in theology began."[25] But as devastating as this was to him personally, Barth could never forget what Herrmann had taught him. Unlike his other teachers, Herrmann had been a truly independent thinker. Though a qualified Ritschlian, he had not been an unquestioning follower of the Ritschlian school which dominated the last quarter of the nineteenth century. Nor could he countenance the rising 'history of religions' school led by Ernst Troeltsch, but instead was among its sharpest critics. Herrmann's opposition to the various theological programs of his contemporaries was based on his very distinctive understanding of religious knowledge, which he identified with the knowledge of faith. The knowledge of faith, he argued, is a very special kind of knowledge which cannot be reduced to or identified with any other form of knowledge such as historical knowledge or scientific knowledge. As one who began to study Kant from his youth, Herrmann well understood the concerns of his neo-Kantian colleagues at Marburg. He understood, and taught Barth to understand, that the object of religious knowledge is something entirely different than anything that can be perceived in the phenomenal world, that it is unique and on an entirely different plane. He taught Barth that the reality known by faith is beyond all sense perception and that one must vigilantly guard against confusing it with something else or domesticating it in any way. He taught Barth, in short, to be suspicious of metaphysics, apologetics, and natural theology, to be wary of positivism, historicism, psychologism, and other forms of theological reductionism.

---

[24] Karl Barth, "Die dogmatische Prinzipienlehre bei Wilhelm Herrmann," in idem, *Vorträge und kleinere Arbeiten, 1922-1925*, ed. Holger Finze (Zürich: Theologischer Verlag Zürich, 1990), p. 551. Hereafter cited as "Die dogmatische Prinzipienlehre bei Wilhelm Herrmann"; ET "The Principels of Dogmatics According to Wilhelm Herrmann," in *Theology and Church*, trans. Louise Pettibone Smith (New York: Harper & Row, 1962), p. 238.

[25] Barth, "Die dogmatische Prinzipienlehre bei Wilhelm Herrmann," p. 551; ET p. 238.

But Herrmann instilled in Barth more than simply a vigilance for theological reductionism. In 1925, Barth reflected on his teacher's legacy in an essay entitled, "The Principles of Dogmatics According to Wilhelm Herrmann" in which he set out to describe the "basic thing" Herrmann had taught him.[26] Barth concludes this essay by saying that if one considered the deeper lying concerns of Herrmann's theology, his life's contribution might be understood quite differently than most had understood it and even quite differently than Herrmann himself had understood it. Given his concern for "the Immediate" and for the independence of the reality known by faith, his deeper concern could have been for

> ... the sovereignty of the *Word*, of the divine Word himself over all human words. His fight against 'doctrinal legalism' could be understood positively as an appeal to pay attention to the Speaker *and* Hearer who is above all that we say and hear. It could be understood as a reminder of the meaning of the demand which the Church with its doctrine makes upon men by pointing to the immediate event on the higher plane which the Church can only serve. It could be understood as a warning against all forced conformity, as a protest against every divergence by which that event is *not* served, as a thundering summons to the subject matter itself, to the true theme, to him about whom everything centers in the Bible, in dogma, in preaching. ... And would it then not be understandable that dogmatics, that theology must be *wholly* free as well as *wholly* bound, free and bound through its object, through its task?[27]

Whether this was ever really Herrmann's deeper concern, the "basic thing" Barth seems to have learned from him had to do with his "thundering summons to the subject matter itself." Herrmann taught Barth to fix his focus on the subject matter, to not be distracted from it, and to follow through with it at all costs. To this extent, Herrmann's approach to theology had been, in its way, "*sachlich*" (*sachlicher*, at least, than his historicizing and psychologizing contemporaries). Granted, Barth eventually discovered that the subject matter in the Bible, in dogma, in preaching was different than Herrmann thought it was. Granted, Herrmann's notion of the subject matter seemed in the final analysis to have had more to do with the faith of the individual believer than with God. Indeed, so formal, so individualistic was his definition of faith that it not only risked losing faith's objective moment, it risked reducing God to an idea, to an idealistic concept which served only to ground the human experience of faith.[28]

---

[26] Barth, "Die dogmatische Prinzipienlehre bei Wilhelm Herrmann," p. 552; ET p. 239.

[27] Barth, "Die dogmatische Prinzipienlehre bei Wilhelm Herrmann," pp. 602-603; ET p. 271.

[28] Herrmann talked a great deal about faith, but because of his lifelong animus against reducing faith to mere intellectual assent and his wariness of doctrine as a *Lehrgesetz*, a law to which faith must subscribe, his definition of faith – contrary to the classical, three-fold understanding of faith which includes *notitia* of the object of faith, *assensus* to its truth, and *fiducia* as saving trust in it – did not include *assensus*. To insist upon faith as assent to any particular cognitive content betrayed, according to Herrmann, *sola fide*. Herrmann's was, as Hans Frei suggested, a one-sided understanding of faith as *fides qua creditur* at the expense of *fides quae*

Granted all these differences and more, Herrmann taught Barth something very important. He taught Barth to keep his eye on the subject matter and to follow through with it to the end without confusing it with or reducing it to something else. One might even say that it was Herrmann who first taught Barth to do theology in a *"sachlicher, inhaltlicher, wesentlicher"* way.

Yet it would be a serious mistake to suggest that it was really Herrmann who taught Barth to do theology in the *sachlicher, inhaltlicher, wesentlicher* way he did beginning in his *Römerbrief* period, as if, after 1915, Barth could have simply adopted Herrmann's method only with reference to a different subject matter or a subject matter that had been turned right side up, having more to do with God than with the individual believer instead of one that had more to do with the individual believer than with God. There are at least two reasons why. First, because there is nothing that suggests that Barth ever recognized that it was a *sachlicher, inhaltlicher, wesentlicher* approach to theology that Herrmann was striving for until *after* he discovered that God, the Word of God, was the real subject matter, content, and theme of the Bible. Only after this, and even then only after a decade, was Barth able to suggest that such an approach to the Bible, to dogma, and to preaching may have been what Herrmann was really striving after. Only after this, and even then only in light of a very generous and hopeful reading of what *may* have been his teacher's better intentions, did Barth entertain the possibility that he and Herrmann may have been chewing on the opposite ends of the same bone (that is, the objective and subjective sides of revelation). But even if it were the same bone (and there were several reasons why he thought it might not be), interpretation of it could not, he came to realize, begin from Herrmann's starting-point,[29] which suggests the second reason why Barth could not have adopted Herrmann's method as such.

Barth had recognized and always deeply appreciated the fact that a "breath of freedom blew through [Herrmann's] lecture hall."[30] But there is no indication that he ever thought that this breath of freedom had to do with the Word of God until he discovered the Word of God itself (or understood himself to have been discovered by it). He knew that the subject matter of theology had, under

---

creditur. See Hans Frei, "The Doctrine of Revelation in the Thought of Karl Barth, 1909 to 1922," unpublished Ph.D. dissertation, Yale University, 1956, pp. 329-361. For another nuanced discussion of not only Herrmann's understanding of faith, but of his relationship to Barth, see McCormack's *Karl Barth's Critically Realistic Dialectical Theology*, pp. 49-68.

[29] Bruce McCormack, using Michael Beintker's phrase, has identified this starting-point as as "'ethical-anthropological pre-understanding" which would only allow for an idealistic conception of God." See McCormack, *Karl Barth's Critically Realistic Dialectical Theology*, p. 66. See also Beintker's *Die Gottesfrage in der Theologie Wilhelm Herrmanns* (Berlin: Evangelische Verlagsanstalt, 1976), p. 117.

[30] Barth, "Die dogmatische Prinzipienlehre bei Wilhelm Herrmann," p. 597; ET p. 267.

Herrmann, to do with something radical and free.[31] But, again, he did not know how radical or how free the subject matter of theology truly was until he discovered that the real subject matter of the Bible was God, the Word of God. When he did he discovered that what was at issue was not merely a difference of degree but of kind, not merely a quantitative but a qualitative distinction, an infinite qualitative distinction. What was at issue was not merely the freedom of faith as experienced in the life of the individual believer, but the sovereign freedom of God, the Word of God, the true subject matter of the Bible and theology. This is what seems to be at stake in Barth's claim: "I let Herrmann say something basic to me, which, followed out to its consequences, later forced me to say almost everything else quite differently and finally led me even to an interpretation of the basic thing itself which was entirely different from his."[32] This "basic thing" Barth claims he let Herrmann tell him had to do with the freedom of the subject matter, the freedom, for example, of faith as experienced in the life of the individual believer. But having followed this "basic thing" out to its consequences, having honored its freedom by not confusing it with or reducing it to something else, Barth discovered that this "basic thing" was not *the* basic thing after all, and an interpretation of "the basic thing itself" was needed "which was entirely different than his." In other words, what was needed was a thundering summons to the subject matter which was truly about the subject matter itself. What was needed was an interpretation of the subject matter itself which was even *sachlicher, inhaltlicher, wesentlicher* than Herrmann's, for in light of the true subject matter of the Bible, even his interpretation – which was certainly *sachlich* in its way – was not *sachlich* enough.

The purpose of the foregoing discussion has been to emphasize the fact that Barth's talk of a more *sachliche* approach to theology arises out of a specific context and that to discuss what Barth means by a more *sachliche* approach to theology apart from this specific context is to risk misunderstanding something very important about his theology and his theological conversion. Contrary to what some have suggested, Barth did not come to an understanding of theology's true subject matter as a result of abstract thinking or as a consequence of any philosophical inquiry. He did not arrive at it by means of Idealism nor was it the product of anything he learned from neo-Kantianism. It came from reading the Bible. As important as Herrmann, neo-Kantianism, and other influences were in providing Barth with critical tools to articulate the *Sachlichkeit*

---

[31] Reflecting on his student days under Herrmann, Barth said: "Our rebellious minds, repudiating all authority, there found satisfaction. We listened gladly when traditionalism on the right, rationalism on the left, mysticism in the rear were thrown to the trash heap, and when finally 'positive and liberal dogmatics' were together hurled into the same pit." See Barth, "Die dogmatische Prinzipienlehre bei Wilhelm Herrmann," p. 597; ET p. 267.

[32] Barth, "Die dogmatische Prinzipienlehre bei Wilhelm Herrmann," p. 552; ET p. 239.

of the biblical *Sache*, none of these were ultimately decisive.[33] What was decisive was Barth's discovery that God, revelation, was the subject matter of the Bible.

C. What Exactly Is *Die Sache* of the Bible?

As important as it is to emphasize *where* Barth made the discovery which led to his theological conversion, it is also important to clarify *what* it was he actually discovered. Barth's theological conversion, for example, has often been described in terms of his discovery of "a [strange] new world within the Bible."[34] Such a description, however, while not wrong, has more to do with the title of his 1917 essay than its actual substance. The fact is, according to this essay as well as his preface drafts to Rom I, the impetus behind Barth's conversion was never so much the discovery of a "new world" within the Bible as it was the discovery of God, of God's Word. The tendency in more recent years to characterize it as the former has been unfortunate, not only because this has focused attention away from the objective content at issue in Barth's discovery, but also because it has – especially given the kind of "text as world" talk many constructivists, narrativists, intratextualists, *et al*, have sought to associate with Barth – called into question what many have long regarded as Barth's greatest strength, *viz.*, his commitment to biblical realism. In other words, in addition to leaving ambiguous what Barth actually discovered, it has left ambiguous whether the Bible really depicts for Barth *the* one real world.[35] Without pursuing this latter issue further, I should emphasize that the real impetus behind Barth's theological conversion was not so much his discovery of a "new world," a new perspective, *Weltanschauung*, or way-of-being-in-the-

---

[33] This is still obviously not clear to those who continue to speak, for example, of "Barth's Idealistic heritage" as basically determinative of his doctrine of God, e.g., Jürgen Moltmann, *The Trinity and the Kingdom*, trans. Margaret Kohl (New York: Harper & Row, 1981), pp.139-144, et al.

[34] The word "strange" (*fremd, seltsam*, etc.) appears neither in the German title nor the text of this essay.

[35] In his essay, "Barth and Textuality," *Theology Today* 43 (October 1986), pp.361-76, George Lindbeck, for example, refers to "the strange new world" of the Bible more than half-a-dozen times without once raising the question as to Barth's understanding of the Bible's real referent. While I do not suggest that Lindbeck reads Barth as a pure constructivist, the question is by no means clear with respect to Stephen H. Webb, *Re-figuring Theology: The Rhetoric of Karl Barth* (Albany, NY: State University of New York Press), 1991; Mark Wallace, *The Second Naiveté: Barth, Ricoeur, and the New Yale Theology* (Macon, GA: Mercer University Press, 1990; Graham Ward, *Barth, Derrida and the Language of Theology* (Cambridge: University Press), 1995, et al. For a more sober discussion of Barth's realism, see Ingolf U. Dalferth's essay, "Karl Barth's Eschatological Realism" in Stephen W. Sykes, ed., *Karl Barth: Centenary Essays* (Cambridge: University Press, 1989), pp.14-45.

world within the Bible as it was his discovery that the Bible's central subject matter, content, and theme was God. It was this discovery and the implications flowing from it which Barth saw as distinguishing his approach to the task of exegesis from that of his contemporaries and it is this that stands behind his insistence upon a reading of the Bible which is "more in accordance with its subject matter, content, and substance." But the question which must now be asked is: how is it, exactly, that "God" is the *Sache* of the Bible according to Barth?

Discussing Barth's understanding of the Bible's *Sache* is complicated for at least two reasons. First of all, not only is there in English no equivalent adjectival form of the German word *sachlich*, neither is there an equivalent noun for the word *Sache*. The latter can be translated 'object' or 'subject' or 'subject matter,' depending on the context, but even when the context is known its meaning is still sometimes ambiguous. Secondly, the *Sache* at issue in the Bible is no ordinary *Sache*. Thus, while it is clear that by using the term *Sache* to describe the Bible's content Barth wishes to indicate 'something' which is objectively real, it is also clear he is not referring to an empirical object, a *datum*. God is the 'object' of the Bible only to the extent that He is a Subject who must give Himself to us as object if He is to be known. The *Sache* of the Bible is not therefore an object which gives itself to us without reservation or qualification such that it is ever "at our disposal" as it were. He is an object which always remains Subject even as He gives Himself as object.

Yet Barth's reference to God as the *Sache*, *Hauptsache*, or *Inhalt* of the Bible requires further qualification, for as such it is still somewhat ambiguous. Even in the essay, "*Die neue Welt in der Bibel*," it is apparent that Barth was not entirely content to refer to the *Sache* of the Bible as 'God.' Such an answer, he realized, was simply too bald. While in one sense it said everything, more needed to be said. Besides, such an answer only raised the question: "Who then is God?" which is the question Barth asks and tries briefly to answer in Trinitarian terms at the conclusion of this essay.[36] Barth's struggle to articulate what or who it was he had discovered in the pages of the Bible is further evidenced by the fact that at the conclusion of this essay he admits: "It is because of our unbelief that even now I can only stutter, hint at, and make promises about that which would be opened to us if the Bible could speak to us unhindered, in the full flow of its revelations."[37] And Barth's struggle to articulate what he had discovered the Bible to be about continued. In his preface

---

[36] Barth, "Die neue Welt in der Bibel," pp.29f. Although Barth's doctrine of God would undergo many significant transformations before KD II/1 and II/2, this early reference to the Trinity (it would appear even an immanent Trinity: "Who then is God? The heavenly Father! Of course. But also the heavenly Father upon the *earth*, and upon the earth also really the *heavenly* Father!" p.31) suggests a radical break from his liberal past.

[37] Barth, "Die neue Welt in der Bibel," p.31.

drafts to Rom I it is interesting that as much as Barth propounds the importance of reading the Bible according to its central subject matter, content, and substance, not once does he actually try to define precisely what the central subject matter, content, and substance of the Bible or *The Epistle to the Romans* is. Instead, one of the most consistent points made throughout the early preface drafts to Rom I is that one either knows what the *Sache* of the Bible or *Romans* is or one does not.[38] Later in his preface to Rom II Barth tried to become a bit more precise in his description of the Bible's *Sache*:

> What do I mean when I say that the inner dialectic of the *Sache* and the recognition of it in the wording of the text is the decisive factor in understanding and interpretation? ... "God is in heaven, and thou on earth." The relationship of *this* God to *this* man, the relationship of *this* man to *this* God, is for me the theme of the Bible and the sum of philosophy in one. The philosophers call this crisis of human knowing the source. At this crossroads the Bible sees Jesus Christ.[39]

Here, more than simply "God," the Bible's *Sache* is described as a dialectical relation between a specific, holy, transcendent God and a specific human creature.[40]

Barth's conception of the biblical *Sache*, it seems fair to say, was emerging throughout his *Römerbrief* period. There seems to have been for him both a determinant and indeterminate sense about what the Bible's central subject matter, content, and theme was. On the one hand, what he experienced in the pages of the Bible had not been some esoteric, pre-thematic, non-cognitive "I-Thou" encounter, for it certainly involved cognition and cognitive concepts. Yet, on the other hand, what he had discovered had not been an idea or a concept. It was not something abstract. It was something alive, yet highly mysterious. As he described it to Thurneysen in his letter of Sept. 27, 1917, "During the work [of exegesis] it was often as though something was blowing on me from afar."[41] Later Barth could summarize all this by simply saying: "Revelation is the theme of the Bible."[42] But by revelation he meant the self-revelation of God in Jesus Christ. More than any abstract dialectical relation, Jesus Christ was, as stated above, already for Barth in his *Römerbrief* period the Bible's

---

[38] Barth states, for example, "The words 'history' and 'understanding' make no sense for me at all without this living context between the past and the present which cannot be achieved through some art of empathy, but is *given* in the subject matter and in which one must *be*." Appendix 2, Preface IA, p. 281 (p. 587), etc. This point shall be elaborated at length in the next two chapters.

[39] Barth, Rom II, p. xiii.

[40] Though there is an "infinite qualitative distinction" between God and humanity, at the "crossroads" between these two realms which do not intersect, stands – like a single "mathematical point" – Jesus Christ.

[41] Karl Barth to Eduard Thurneysen, 27 Sept., 1917, *B-Th. Br. I*, p. 236.

[42] KD I/2:534: "... die Offenbarung ist der Gegenstand des biblischen Zeugnisses" CD I/2:492.

central subject matter, content, and theme.[43] But whether identifying the Bible's *Hauptsache* as God, as revelation, or as Jesus Christ, fixing it exclusively to any one of these seems not for him to have been the important thing. Rather, what seems to have been important was his discovery that Holy Scripture taken as a *whole* "interprets itself" – beyond our human weaknesses and limitations – *and* when it does it speaks about something *whole*. This is the substance of the question he asks in the essay "*Die neue Welt in der Bibel*": "What is the significance of the remarkable line from Abraham to Christ? What of the chorus of prophets and apostles? and what is the burden of their song? What is the *one thing* that these voices evidently all desire to announce, each in its own tone, each in its own way?"[44]

Barth's turn to the Bible, in other words, clearly had to do with his discovery that the whole Bible bears a unified witness.[45] Indeed, the most overlooked feature of "*Die neue Welt in der Bibel*" – perhaps only because it is so apparent – is the fact that Barth speaks over fifty times about the Bible as if it were a whole, as if it bore a unified witness, as if, to borrow his image, all its voices were singing the same song (e.g., "the Bible says," "the Bible proclaims," "the Bible presents," etc.). Such a view is simply not seen in Barth before his break with liberalism in 1915.[46] Even so, this is still not the most revolutionary feature of Barth's turn to the Bible.

The most revolutionary feature was in fact not about the Bible at all, but about *what* or rather *who* the Bible bore witness to. Barth discovered that the

---

[43] In his preface to the third edition, Barth refers explicitly to "the Spirit of Christ" as the Bible's subject matter. Rom II, third edition, p. xx.

[44] Barth, "Die neue Welt in der Bibel," p. 20.

[45] This discovery, it must be emphasized, in no way diminished Barth's lifelong appreciation for or interest in the rich diversity and complexity of the biblical witness.

[46] Notwithstanding what was earlier said about Barth's claim, "We call the Bible *holy* Scripture, not because of its letters or because its particular thoughts [*einzelnen Gedanken*] have a special holiness, but because it talks about him who is holy," Barth can hardly be described as a champion of the unified witness of the whole Bible in this period because it is the diversity and individuality of the parts of the Bible that he takes pains to emphasize, rather than its unity. Such is the case when, against 'biblicism' and in the name of Luther, Barth insisted *only* where the Bible furthers Christ ("*Christum treibt*") does it become a "source of revelation." See Barth, "*Der christliche Glaube und die Geschichte*," pp. 165-166, 204-205. Despite points of continuity, this clearly represents a different position than the one later articulated in his preface to the third edition of his *Römerbrief* where, in response to Bultmann, he said: "My conclusion is that in no case can it be a question of playing off the Spirit of Christ, the 'subject matter,' in such a way against 'other spirits,' that in the name of the former certain passages are praised, but certain others, where Paul is not speaking 'from the subject matter' are belittled. Rather it is a question of seeing and making clear how the 'Spirit of Christ' is the crisis in which the *whole* [*das Ganze*] finds itself. *Everything* is *litera*, the voice of 'other' spirits, and whether and in what respect *everything* can be understood also in the context of the 'subject matter' as the voice of the *spiritus* (of Christ) is the question by which the *litera* must be studied." More shall be said about this particular passage in chaper five.

Bible bore witness to God and the reason why this was so revolutionary was because the God he discovered there was "wholly other." Barth's discovery of God's "wholly otherness" is well known. Less well known, yet equally decisive in terms of its hermeneutical implications, was his concomitant discovery of God's *wholeness*, His utter simplicity. God's simplicity, the notion of God as *"etwas Ganzes,"* is a major theme which runs throughout Barth's writings from 1916 to 1920.[47] That Barth concludes his *"Die neue Welt in der Bibel"* address stating, "The whole Bible authoritatively proclaims that God must be *all in all*," suggests something of the importance of this theme.[48] It suggests that even more significant than his discovery that *the whole Bible* bears a unified witness was his discovery that the whole Bible bears unified witness to a *whole*, to a *single subject matter*, to *one thing*. It is this "one thing that these voices evidently all desire to announce" in the Bible that revolutionized Barth's approach to interpreting Holy Scripture, and the following suggests why.

D. The Whole in Light of Its Parts and the Parts in Light of the Whole

In claiming that "the whole Bible authoritatively proclaims that God must be *all in all*," Barth was making more than simply a dogmatic point about the Bible's central subject matter, content, and theme. He was also making a hermeneutical point, or better yet, a dogmatic point which had very significant hermeneutical implications. If God is the *Sache* of the Bible and God must be understood as something whole, then the *Sache* of the Bible must be understood as something whole as well. This is the basis of Barth's belief that the whole of the Bible must be interpreted in light of its parts and that its parts must be interpreted in light of the whole. This is a hermeneutical principle that is not only stated in the preface drafts to Rom I and applied throughout Rom I, it is something Barth saw deriving again and again from *The Epistle to the Romans* itself.[49]

---

[47] "Die Gerechtigkeit Gottes" (1916), p. 5; "Der Christ in der Gesellschaft" (1919), pp. 36f.; and "Biblische Fragen, Einsichten und Ausblicke" (1920), *passim*, in idem, *Das Wort Gottes und die Theologie* (Munich: Christian Kaiser Verlag, 1925) and Rom I, pp. 171, 480, 491, etc.

[48] Barth, "Die neue Welt in der Bibel," p.32.

[49] For example, in his exposition of Romans 11:25-26 regarding the hardening which "has come upon part of Israel, until the full number of the Gentiles come in," Barth states: "Divine thinking starts fundamentally on the inside. ... It does not look at any particular [*das Einzelne*] only by itself, but looks at all particulars in the trajectory of the whole [*das Ganze*] and finally it also sees this whole never as a sum of particulars, but sees it as the principle which penetrates and organizes all particulars." See Rom I, p. 452. This whole/parts dialectic is found throughout Rom I, e.g. pp.156, 222, 300, 305, 309, 324-325, 356-363, 451-459, 491, 559-565, etc.

The first, most obvious implication of this principle is that to interpret the Bible one must have a sense of what the whole of the Bible is about. One must have an acquaintance with its central subject matter, content, and theme. Without this sense of the whole, without this acquaintance with (*and* participation in, as I shall elaborate in the next chapter) its central subject matter, content, and theme, interpretation of the Bible is, according to Barth, impossible. Similar to the point Schleiermacher made in his lectures on *Hermeneutics* nearly a century before,[50] Barth insisted that to interpret not only the Bible but *any text* one must have a sense of what the whole is about. As he said in his preface to Rom II and as is already implied in his preface drafts to Rom I, this is how he would seek to approach the texts of Goethe and Lao-tzu as well.[51] One could, of course, he recognized, do otherwise. One could, for instance, interpret a novel like *Moby Dick* as if it were really about whales if one wanted to, but in Barth's view this would hardly do justice to the actual subject matter of *Moby Dick*.

Interpreting a text according to its subject matter, content, and theme, that is, according to the whole and not merely the parts, is essentially what Barth later referred to in his *Church Dogmatics* as "the universal rule of interpretation."[52] Barth states it simply: "a text can be read and understood and expounded only with reference to and in the light of its theme." Reading, understanding, and expounding a text *only* with reference to and in the light of its theme means that interpretation occurs only when a specific theme or subject matter is consistently maintained as such throughout. There are two implications of this rule which are clearly operative in Barth's preface drafts to Rom I and his preface to Rom II. First, any attempt to interpret a text beside or apart from its subject matter, content, and theme is actually no interpretation at all

---

[50] "Grammatical interpretation is mainly concerned with the elements which characterize the central subject matter. Technical interpretation is mainly concerned with the over-all coherence and with its relation to general laws for combining thoughts. At the very beginning, therefore, one must immediately grasp the over-all coherence. The only way to do this is by a cursory reading [*cursorische Lection*] of the whole text." See Schleiermacher's *Hermeneutik*, p.56. This initial act of grasping an overall coherence, this "sensing of the whole" (*Ahnung des Ganzen*) is what Schleiermacher describes as "divinatory interpretation." It is on this basis that he sought to interpret the whole (*das Ganze*) in light of the parts (*die Einzelheiten*) and the parts in light of the whole. Barth highlights this point in his treatment of Schleiermacher's hermeneutics in his 1923/24 lectures on Schleiermacher and describes it, i.e., divinatory interpretation, as "the new thing" Schleiermacher was proposing over and against his contemporaries, e.g. Wolf and Ast, who also stressed this principle. Barth, *Die Theologie Schleiermachers*, pp.323f. Whether Barth himself appropriated the principle of reading the whole of a text in light of its parts and the parts in light of the whole from Schleiermacher (it actually goes back long before him), the similarity between them on this point is unmistakable.

[51] Rom II, p. xv.
[52] KDI/2:546; CD I/2:493.

(that is, as such it does not yet qualify as interpretation).[53] Secondly, those who *do* actually interpret a given text (legitimately or illegitimately is not the question here) do so always – whether they acknowledge it or not – with a sense of what the whole of the text is about. Obviously there was never such a thing for Barth as unprejudiced or presuppositionless exegesis; and for him it was never simply the case that we as interpreters bring only general prejudices to a given text.

Barth's specific interpretive presupposition regarding the Bible was that it was about God. What this meant for him was that any interpretation of the Bible which did not reckon with the fact that God, that Jesus Christ, that revelation is its central subject matter, content, and theme, was *not yet* an interpretation of the Bible. It is at just this point, however, at the point where Barth might seem most dogmatic (in the negative, narrow-minded sense), one finds him arguably the most open, for he does not insist that this is the *only* way to read the Bible. There is, of course, no denying that the self-revelation of God in Jesus Christ was for Barth the Bible's subject matter, content, and theme and that of this he was thoroughly convinced. Nevertheless, it is also significant that he claimed in his *Römerbrief* prefaces that he was perfectly willing to entertain the possibility that the Bible might be better explained in other terms, by another subject matter, content, or theme. As he stated in his preface to Rom II:

> Whether [my] presuppositions can be maintained can be shown, as with all presuppositions, only in using them, that is, in this case, in the exact investigation and consideration of the text verse by verse. Naturally this verification can be only a relative, more or less certain verification, and of course my presupposition also is subject to this rule. If I now proceed provisionally on the assumption that in *Romans* Paul was really speaking of Jesus Christ and not of something else, it is to begin with an assumption as good or as bad as any of the provisional assumptions of the historians. The exposition alone can decide whether and to what extent I have succeeded in carrying through my assumption. If it is false, and Paul has really spoken of something other than the permanent crisis of time and eternity, why then in the course of dealing with the text I myself will carry it *ad absurdum*. If someone should ask me further, on what ground I approach *The Epistle to the Romans* with just this assumption, I would answer with the counter question of whether an earnest man can approach a text which is not patently frivolous with any other assumption than this – that God is God? And if anyone should persist in complaining about what violence I do to Paul with this assumption, then I raise the countercomplaint that it is doing violence to Paul to let him speak apparently of Jesus Christ but in reality of a truly anthroposophic chaos of absolute relativities and relative absolutes, of precisely the chaos for which in all his letters he has

---

[53] Rom II, p. x. "I do not reproach [my critics] for their historical criticism, the justification and necessity for which I to the contrary do specifically recognize, but for their contentment with an interpretation of the text which I cannot regard as any interpretation at all, but only as the first primitive attempt at one."

only expressions of the most angry disgust. Even though I can by no means claim to have explained everything satisfactorily, I have found no reason to abandon my assumption.[54]

Barth's assumption here should be taken seriously, for it suggests something important. As an interpreter of *The Epistle to the Romans*, Barth saw it as his task to speak about "the same subject matter as Paul," but that he had actually done so, he realized, could never, at any point, be simply assumed or taken for granted.[55] It was not something that could be subjected to independent corroboration or extrinsic verification. Apart from "the inner testimony of the Holy Spirit" – a very important concept at the heart of Calvin's doctrine of inspiration which Barth mentions in his prefaces to both Rom I and II – interpretation is always a matter of approximation. It is always a matter of beginning with a provisional assumption, and as Barth says, "exposition alone can decide whether and to what extent I have succeeded in carrying through my assumption." But even when one has come to a firm conviction as to what the content, subject matter, and theme of a book is – to the point where one can say with Barth, "I have found no reason to abandon my assumption" – openness is still crucial. For beyond reckoning with the relativity of all human words and phrases, interpreters must reckon with the alterity of the subject matter itself which, with respect to the subject matter of the Bible, means being open every morning to "a fresh, new hearing of the Word of God." And if with respect to the subject matter of the Bible, why not a fresh, new hearing of the subject matter of other books as well?

But if Barth's openness in this regard is to be taken seriously, so also should his claim that all presuppositions – including his own – be tested by use be taken seriously, since he obviously had something more concrete and objective in mind than those characterizing his hermeneutic as basically "*ad hoc*" seem to suggest. The first criterion, as stated in both his preface drafts to Rom I and in his preface to Rom II, is whether or not a text's proposed subject matter and theme has been understood *in light of its parts*. The proposed subject matter or theme that makes the most sense out of the most parts is more likely to be the actual subject matter and theme of a text than the proposed subject matter or theme that does not. This is something Barth thought in most cases could be more or less demonstrably measured. The point is: whatever presuppositions we might entertain as to what a given text is about, we are obliged to understand the whole of a text in light of its parts. But in saying in light of its parts Barth meant and was quite serious about not just some of its parts but *all* of its parts! In his preface drafts to Rom I as well as in his preface to Rom II he repeatedly expresses regret on the one hand that he has not "explained everything satisfactorily" in Paul's *Romans*, yet utter astonishment on the other that so many claim they have interpreted *Romans* while leaving so many of its parts

---

[54] Rom II, p. xiv.
[55] Appendix 2, Draft Preface IA, p. 279 (p. 584) and Preface Draft II, pp. 283-284 (p. 590).

"left over." This was one of the major reasons, as I pointed out in chapter two, Paul Wernle accused Barth of being a "biblicist." The following represents Barth's response to this charge:

> With a certain bitterness Wernle writes, "There is absolutely no point in the thought of Paul that he finds disagreeable ... not even the most modest remnant conditioned by the history of the times is left over," and then he lists what should have been "left over" as "disagreeable points" and "remnants conditioned by the history of the times," namely: the Pauline "trivializing" of the earthly lifework of Jesus, Christ as the Son of God, reconciliation through the blood of Christ, Christ and Adam, Pauline scriptural proofs, the so-called "baptism sacramentalism," double predestination, and Paul's relation to the magistrate. Let us imagine a commentary on *Romans* in which these eight little points remain unexplained, that is, are declared to be "disagreeable points" which are "left over" in this interlaced work of contemporary parallels! How could that be called a "commentary"? In contrast to this agreeable ignoring of disagreeable points, my Biblicism consists in my having thought through these "offenses to the modern consciousness" until I thought that I had in part discovered in them the most excellent insights; and in any case was able to speak of them and explain them to some extent. To what extent I have explained them correctly is a question in itself. Now as before, there are passages in *Romans* that are also hard for me to explain. I could go even further and admit to Wernle that my calculation does not come out even in any single verse, that I (and the attentive reader with me) sense more or less clearly in the background a 'remnant' that is not understood and not explained and which awaits working out. But it awaits *working out* – not being left over. The view that unexplained historical crumbs should in themselves be the seal of true research is something that I as a so-called "Biblicist" and Alexandrian cannot get through my head.[56]

This point should not be overlooked because it demonstrates that whatever Barth's understanding of the exegetical task, it was not something he perceived as less rigorous or demanding than his contemporaries understood it to be, but something more rigorous, more demanding. Moreover, it demonstrates that however open Barth may have been to being disabused of his presuppositions regarding the subject matter of the Bible, such openness must be understood in light of the fact that his minimum criterion for disabusal was neither vague nor subjective, but highly concrete and objective, viz., has the text as a whole really been understood in light of its parts?[57]

Yet if we are to understand the whole of a text in light of its parts, then it was also important for Barth that we understand the parts of a text *in light of its whole*. Modern historical-critical exegesis, Barth freely acknowledged, had made a significant contribution toward our understanding of various parts of the Bible. In all his preface drafts to Rom I, as in his preface to Rom II, Barth

---

[56] Rom II, pp. xiv-xv. These comments are very similar to those Barth made to Wernle in his letter of Oct. 24, 1919 included in the *Gesamtausgabe* edition of Rom I, pp.638-646.

[57] Barth's hermeneutic can hardly be described as *"ad hoc"* at this point. However open to a fresh, new hearing of the Word one might be, it did not mean for Barth that one had to feign amnesia regarding what one had once heard or act as though, *prima facie*, any interpretation is as good as the next.

expressed gratitude for historical criticism and admitted that in terms of "antiquarian" interest one could find better things than he could ever write in such giants of the biblical studies guild as Weiß, Godet, Lipsius, Jülicher, Lietzmann and Zahn. Nevertheless, one of Barth's greatest conflicts with members of the biblical scholars' guild was over the fact that for all their interest in the parts, for all the "attention and love" they manifested in focusing upon historical details, most seemed either to misunderstand or be entirely oblivious to the question of the Bible's whole. They seemed never to get beyond the level of preliminary investigation (which Barth referred to as "the first primitive attempt at establishing 'what is there'")[58] to a consideration of the Bible's central subject matter, content, and theme. Many had either forgotten, lost sight of, or had become ambivalent as to what the Bible as whole was about. Their preoccupation with the parts gradually eclipsed what had attracted most of them to the Bible in the first place. Barth claimed that he too was concerned about the parts and said in his preface drafts to Rom I with respect to his own exegesis of *Romans*, "The informed reader will not fail to recognize in this matter, that I have considered these as well."[59] By contrast, however, Barth insisted – and insisted by referring to it as a "rule" – that the parts be interpreted not independently or by some abstract criteria but in light of the whole: "If the whole which I intended to present is substantiated in itself, then it also substantiates the particular, despite all differences of opinion, whereas more than one stunning book about Paul serves to warn us that a thousand correct particulars certainly do not always make an intelligible and well-founded whole."[60]

This is a very telling remark which says a great deal about Barth's hermeneutics. First, interpretation for Barth has both *first and last* to do with interpreting the whole of a text and not merely its parts. The key thought here is: the whole either substantiates itself or it is not substantiated at all. Secondly, it is not the parts that substantiate the whole (though the whole cannot be known without the parts), rather it is the whole that substantiates the parts. And thirdly, not only are the parts substantiated by the whole, there is no possibility of even interpreting the parts apart from an interpretation of the whole. This is what the dominant science of biblical exegesis had generally failed to understand, in Barth's view. Instead it tried to pile up more and more information about the parts, more and more historical data, as if this could suffice as an interpretation of the whole or as if this could "replace explication itself."[61] The

---

[58] Rom II, p. x. Barth made this same point in his very first preface draft to Rom I. With reference to the contribution of historical criticism, Barth said: "What can be said in this regard about the Bible has been brilliantly and impressively stated in today's theology. We are sincerely thankful for it. It had to be said and had to be heard. We *have* heard it, but we cannot stop with it now." See Appendix 2, Preface Draft I, p. 277.

[59] Appendix 2, Preface Draft IA, p. 279 (p. 584) and Preface Draft II, p. 283 (p.590).

[60] Appendix 2, Preface Draft IA, p. 279 (p. 584) and Preface Draft II, pp. 283 (p. 590).

[61] Appendix 2, Preface Draft IA, p. 278 (p. 583) and Preface Draft II, p. 283 (p. 589).

presupposition behind this approach, of course, was that interpretation could proceed from the parts to the whole without any prior consideration of the whole. Indeed, for the sake of "objectivity," it was held that exegesis *must not* proceed on the basis of any prior consideration of the whole for that would be to prejudice one's exegetical 'results.' On the contrary, what first had to happen was an independent, impartial evaluation of the parts according to the most rigorous standards of historical criticism and then, and only then, at a second stage, after the results were in, on the basis of all the 'facts,' could one draw conclusions about the whole. What advocates of this approach failed to recognize was that they had already drawn conclusions as to what the whole was about. They had already approached the Bible as if it were basically *about* piety or history or some other form or combination of both.[62] Beginning with the presupposition that the Bible was about something other than this, in Barth's view, would have made a significant difference in the way they interpreted the parts.

E. The Challenge of Interpreting "What is There" Dialectically

This is not by any means to suggest that for many biblical scholars the piety or history at issue in the Bible had nothing whatsoever to do with God. On the contrary, many if not most (in Barth's *Römerbrief* period at least) believed that the Bible had *something* to do with God. The problem, however, as Barth saw it, was that they tended either to see the Bible as having only *partly* to do with God or they approached the "what is there" question of the Bible as if it could be answered in basically two different ways, first according to its grammatical, literary, and historical sense and then according to its theological sense. Barth, of course, realized that the "what is there" question of the Bible could be answered in two different ways as well. However, because he believed the *Sache* at issue in the Bible was to be understood dialectically, he realized that the "what is there" question of the Bible was much more complicated than most exegetes of his day were prepared to acknowledge, and this is clearly why each of the five times he uses the phrase "*was da steht*" in his preface to Rom II it is in quotation marks.[63] The difference was this: whereas most exegetes, including Barth, believed that the "second" sense (the theological sense) could not be determined independently of the "first" sense (the historical, grammatical, literary sense), Barth believed, unlike most biblical exegetes, that neither could the first sense be interpreted independently of the second. In other words,

---

[62] This was a piety and history, I might add, which more often than not, according to the standards of the history of religions school, was to be understood as basically similar or at least comparable to the piety and historical forms of other religions.

[63] Rom II, pp. x-xii.

whereas they, for example, could rightly insist that Jesus Christ be understood in light of the context (i.e., his historically reconstructed field or horizon), Barth whole-heartedly agreed, but insisted further that the context be understood, *first and last*, in light of Jesus Christ. Thus, in addition to his repeated insistence upon a historical understanding of the Bible, Barth consistently denies in his preface drafts to Rom I, in his preface to Rom II, as well as in his *Church Dogmatics*, that a 'historical' understanding of the Bible is any understanding at all, but represents, at best, only a provisional preparation to understand.[64] Strictly speaking, for Barth, there was no such thing as a genuine theological understanding of the Bible apart from a historical understanding, just as apart from a theological understanding there was nothing but the most trivial, banal sort of historical understanding of the Bible.[65]

Why was there no such thing as a genuine theological understanding of the Bible apart from a historical understanding, just as apart from a theological understanding there was nothing but the most trivial, banal sort of historical understanding of the Bible? The reason is because what was fundamentally at issue in the Bible for Barth was *one* thing, not two. For him, already in his *Römerbrief* period, there was only *one* central subject matter, content, and theme at issue in the Bible. As he later said in his *Church Dogmatics*: "In exegesis, too – and especially in exegesis – there is only one truth."[66] Proceeding as if there were basically two truths, two subject matters, contents, and themes at issue in the Bible represented a violation of Barth's "universal rule of interpretation," viz., that "a text can be read and understood and expounded only with reference to and in the light of its theme."

The other problem with this bifurcated, two-stage, dualistic, "double-entry bookkeeping" approach to the Bible, as Barth called it,[67] was that it tended to lead exegetes to read the Bible as if rather than a *witness,* it were primarily a *source* or a *repository* of historical, cultural, psychological content on the one

---

[64] KD I/2:513f; CD I/2:464f.

[65] The 'positive' significance of a historical understanding of the Bible for Barth shall be discussed in chapter six, "The Meaning of The Bible Itself."

[66] KD I/2:520; CD I/2:470. Barth adds: "In face of it, the unfortunate possibility that the matter of which the word speaks may be alien to us does not excuse us. Nor does it permit us, instead of proceeding from the substance to the word, to go first to the word, i.e., to the humanity of the speakers as such."

[67] "We contrive for a little to be satisfied to have our knowledge split into a thousand parts, each man clinging with jealous eagerness to his own fragment, the spiritual bond being cast to the winds – you take your biology! you take your history! I have my religion! you in your small corner and I in mine! ... we feel we must oppose a special truth about the world to a special truth about God; but this is to establish a system of double-entry bookkeeping [*eine doppelte Buchführung einzurichten*] which converts the knowledge of God offered in the Bible into what it is not. For the fear of the Lord which is offered us in the Bible is not something apart from other things: it is the beginning of wisdom." See Barth, "Biblische Fragen, Einsichten und Ausblicke," p.74.

hand and theological content on the other. As a consequence, not only was it widely assumed that it fell primarily to biblical critics to distinguish between the human and divine parts of the Bible, that is, to distill and establish for the purposes of subsequent theological reflection the so-called exegetical 'results' (a term, with respect to biblical exegesis, Barth almost always uses ironically, placing it in italics or in quotations marks), it assumed something about the Bible's *Sache* which Barth found deeply problematic. It assumed that the *Sache* at issue in the Bible could somehow – at some point – be divided and then parcelled out. It assumed that the Bible's *Sache* was something one could somehow work or build up to; that on the basis of historical-critical judgments, it could be deduced, inferred and then be added on to as if the former were somehow determinative of the latter, rather than vice versa. In short, it assumed that the *Sache* of the Bible was something other than a whole. And the reason why this posed such a problem for Barth is because, as he stated in his Tambach lecture of September 25th, 1919, "The Divine is something whole, complete in itself ... It does not permit of being applied, stuck on, and fitted in. It does not permit of being divided or distributed ... It does not passively permit itself to be used: it overthrows and builds and it wills. It is complete or it is nothing."[68]

To understand Karl Barth's hermeneutics it is necessary to understand him at this fundamental point. To claim that God, that Jesus Christ, or that divine revelation is the *Sache* of the Bible meant for Barth that the *Sache* of the Bible is a single, indivisible whole. The fact that the *Sache* of the Bible is a single, indivisible whole, that it could not, as such, be divided, distributed, used, applied, stuck, or added on to, etc., meant that it could only be recognized and acknowledged as such from the beginning. That it could only be recognized and acknowledged as such from the beginning did not mean that many interesting observations *about* the Bible could not be made prior to maintaining this presupposition, but only that such observations could not yet *as such* qualify as interpretation of the Bible until they could be related to or be seen in light of the Bible's central subject matter, content, and theme. Anything less would violate what Barth later called the "universal rule of interpretation," namely, that "a text can be read and understood and expounded only with reference to and in the light of its theme."

F. Truth and Memory

But how does one attain this or any other presupposition about the Bible apart from reading the Bible itself? This is where many have misunderstood Barth

---

[68] Barth, "Der Christ in der Gesellschaft," p.36.

and have accused him of imposing a dogmatic *a priori* on the Bible.[69] The fact is that Barth never said one must have this or any other presupposition about the Bible before reading the Bible, only that the actual task of its interpretation does not begin until the Bible's subject matter, content, and theme has been taken into account as such. Until then, one's relationship to the Bible, he believed, could only be a matter of a *preparation* to hear, to understand, and to expound.[70] Readers should not, he insisted, confuse the task of preparation with the task of interpretation itself. Interpretation begins only when a determination about a text's subject matter, content, and theme has been made. No one can interpret any text without having some presupposition, however provisional, about what the subject matter of the text is. Barth's presupposition was that the Bible was about the self-revelation of God in Jesus Christ. He believed this – and believed dogmatically, such being appropriate to the subject matter itself – because this is what he believed the Bible *itself* bore witness to. Those who accuse Barth of imposing a dogmatic *a priori* on the Bible are wrong, therefore, not because he does not read the Bible with dogmatic presuppositions, but because his dogmatic presuppositions, at least as he saw it, were established not in *a priori* but in an *a posteriori* fashion.

But the question remains: How do we as readers know that the self-revelation of God in Jesus Christ is really what the Bible as a whole is about, that *this* is its central subject matter, content, and theme? Barth's answer is simple: until the subject matter of the Bible makes itself known, we don't. Were it not for the fact that *Deus dixit*, that "God has spoken" and continues to speak through the words of the Bible, we would not know that the Bible's subject matter is the self-revelation of God in Jesus Christ. Why? Because "it is only by revelation that revelation can be spoken in the Bible and that it can be heard as the subject matter of the Bible. If it is to be witness at all, and to be apprehended as such, the biblical witness must itself be attested by what it at-

---

[69] This is something Barth explicitly denied. "The Bible is the literary monument of an ancient racial religion and of a Hellenistic cultus religion of the Near East. A human document like any other, it can lay no *a priori* dogmatic claim to special attention and consideration." See Barth, "Biblische Fragen, Einsichten und Ausblicke," p.76.

[70] "If we ask ourselves, and as readers of Holy Scripture we have to ask ourselves, what is meant by hearing and understanding and expounding when we presuppose that that which is described or intended by the word of man is the revelation of God, the answer we have given forces itself upon us. Hearing undoubtedly means perceiving revelation by the word of man – understanding, investigating the humanly concrete word in the light of revelation – expounding, clarifying the word in its relation to revelation" KD I/2:515; CD I/2:466. Moreover, Barth says, "The understanding of it cannot consist merely in discovering on what presuppositions, in what situation, in what linguistic sense and with what intention, in what actual context, and in this sense with what meaning the other has said this or that." KD I/2:513; CD I/2:464.

tests."[71] This is indeed, as Barth later freely admitted, a hermeneutical circle.[72] But it is a circle, he insisted, which exists between two very definite poles.

> Theological exegesis is an exegesis which is carried out under a quite definite presupposition. This is, firstly, that the reader of the Old and New Testaments remembers that in this book the Church has up to now heard God's Word; and secondly, that this reader or investigator reads in the expectation that he himself will also for his time hear God's Word. The place of theological exegesis lies right between this remembrance [*Erinnerung*] and this expectation [*Erwartung*], corresponding to the time of the Church between Christ's Ascension and Second Coming.[73]

Though vastly different in content than expressed here in 1935, memory does seem to have played some sort of role in Barth's hermeneutic from the very beginning of the *Römerbrief* period.[74] In his preface drafts to Rom I, for example, he responds to his own question, "What kind of reader did I have in mind as I wrote? I say, the same as Paul himself had in mind, namely, everyone who is in any way moved by the same matter which *The Epistle to the Romans* is all about. For everyone who is able to have the need and the joy to allow the truth that it declares to be called to their 'memory' (Rom.15:15)."[75]

From the beginning Barth realized that not every interpreter would recognize the Bible's true subject matter, content, and theme. He realized that this was contingent upon two things: first, being *moved* by it (i.e., participation in the subject matter) and secondly, *remembering* it. Both, he acknowledged, were actions dependent on the Holy Spirit. Only by the inner testimony of the Holy Spirit can interpreters really understand what the true subject matter of the Bible is. But in addition to being convinced by the Holy Spirit's witness as to what the true subject matter of the Bible is, it is also necessary that readers be reminded again and again throughout the process of interpretation that it is *God* who is the subject matter of the Bible and it is *He* who has spoken and continues to speak through it. Remembering that God is the subject matter of the Bible and that it is He who has spoken and continues to speak through it, readers learn to read the Bible in *expectation* that He will speak there again.

Though it is with reference to Rom.15:15 that Barth speaks about readers allowing "the truth that it declares to be called to their 'memory,'" there is a distinctly Johannine ring to these words, which resonates well not only with how one identifies the Bible's central subject matter, content, and theme, according to Barth, but also with how one moves from special to general hermeneutics. It is the Holy Spirit, "the Spirit of truth," according to John 14, who brings the

---

[71] KD I/2:519; CD I/2:469.

[72] See, for instance, John D. Godsey's *Karl Barth's Table Talk* (Richmond: John Knox Press, 1962), p.54.

[73] Barth, *Credo*, p.153; ET p. 77.

[74] I am not suggesting here that Barth had a notion of ecclesial memory in mind or that it plays any role whatsoever in his Römerbrief period.

[75] Appendix 2, Preface 1A, p. 279 (pp.584-585); Preface II, p. 285 (p.592).

Lord's words to "remembrance" and bears witness to the truth. And it is in bringing His words to remembrance and bearing witness to the truth that the Spirit teaches believers the truth of "all things" or, as it says in John 16:13, guides them into "all the truth." It would appear, if I may infer from what Barth later said about the school of the Holy Spirit, that this is how the move from special to general hermeneutics is made. The Holy Spirit guides believers into the truth of "all things" by instilling within them a specific kind of attitude, an attitude which Barth refers to as a "biblical attitude." This attitude, which is a specifically human attitude, as I discussed in chapter one, is an attitude characterized by remembrance and expectation. Having heard God speak through the Bible and remembering, according to His promise, that He will do so again, believers learn to read the Bible with an attitude of expectation – and not only the Bible, but other books as well. This is what Barth means when he says: "It is from the word of man in the Bible that we must learn what has to be learned concerning the word of man in general."[76] Since the words of the Bible have borne witness to the truth, believers learn to read the words of others, for example, Goethe or Lao-tzu, in expectation that they too, in their own way, may bear witness to the truth. Jesus Christ is the truth. Truth is not therefore something one can ultimately talk about *in abstracto*. Yet truth is one. And even though there is no truth which is true outside or apart from Jesus Christ, there may be words found outside of the Bible which also bear witness to the truth. Nevertheless the basis and standard for knowing that there are words *outside* of the Bible which bear witness to the truth, according to Barth, is the truth which the words *inside* the Bible bear witness to, namely, Jesus Christ. In other words, although we approach the Bible, or any other text for that matter, every new morning with the expectation that it might speak to us afresh, we do not do so as if God's Word had never been spoken or as if we had gone to the school of the Holy Spirit in vain.[77]

While much of this goes beyond what Barth actually says in his *Römerbrief* period, the fact that he said in his preface to Rom II and even earlier that he would be willing to apply the same method he had applied to Paul's *Romans* to the works of other authors indicates, as Barth himself later claimed, that the move from special to general hermeneutics was already on its way.[78] Yet the idea to move from special to general hermeneutics came, it would appear, as the result of Barth's discovery of a more basic hermeneutical principle,

---

[76] KD I/2:515; CD I/2:466.

[77] Not going to school "in vain," whether it be "the school of dogma" or "the school of divine command" (KD II/2:718.f; CD II/2:645f.) is a phrase Barth uses at various points throughout the *Church Dogmatics*, and it refers to the fact that dogmatic thinking does not ignore but builds on, at least provisionally, knowledge once learned.

[78] I am referring here to what was discussed at the end of chapter two, viz., Barth's claim that his original "aim was to emancipate understanding, both of the Bible and of things in general . . ." See pp. 61-62 above.

namely, that to understand a text, any text, one must understand it in light of its central subject matter, content, and theme. To understand the Bible in light of its subject matter, content, and theme meant that the parts of the Bible had to be understood in light of the whole and the whole in light of its parts. But to understand the parts of the Bible in light of the whole and the whole in light of its parts meant one thing more. It meant the question of truth could not be avoided. It meant that there was a level of resolution, a higher court, as it were, beyond the parts and the whole, namely, *the truth*.

Truth is a topic which has yet to be discussed, though it has been mentioned. In chapter one, I related Barth's response to a professor of theology who had once told him that he had learned much more from his devout mother than from the whole Bible: "It is all very well to realize, perhaps, that one may learn more from all kinds of greater or lesser prophets or apostles of a later period, or even of our own time than from reading the Bible. Yet the issue is not where we learn the most, but where we learn the *one thing*, the *truth*."[79] This is a comment Barth made in the summer of 1924, but it reflects a conviction he clearly held much earlier than this. Truth, while mentioned rarely in Barth's writings before 1915, is a major theme throughout Barth's *Römerbrief* period. In Rom I there are few concepts mentioned more often. It is cited even more often than 'grace' or 'revelation,' though it is a word he repeatedly associates with them. In his exegesis of Rom.1:16-17, under the rubric "Die Sache," Barth identifies "the truth" with God's "very own being," with the "reality" of His being, which precedes our knowledge of it.[80] And because God's being has to do with – indeed, is itself – "the truth," the truth the Gospel announces is "not a general truth."[81] It is not, Barth insists throughout Rom I, a truth among other truths. "It is not *a* truth, rather *the* truth."[82] It is not a truth that is a "necessarily supplementable truth beside other truths, but rather a whole, singular truth which shines in its own light."[83] It is this truth which calls into question all other truths. It is this truth which stands in judgment over all our attempts to "assert" or "vindicate other truths next to this one unique truth."[84] "This greater, other truth will and must supercede and convert the smaller, merely spiritual-historical 'truths.'"[85] Besides this truth, Barth says, "all other *so-called* truths, namely the merely historical and psychological ones, can only be considered as preliminary, supplementary circumstances and side-effects.

---

[79] Barth, *Unterricht*, p.65.

[80] Rom I, pp.18-24, esp. p.23.

[81] Rom I, p.23.

[82] Rom I, p.19.

[83] Rom I, p.205.

[84] Rom I, p.347.

[85] Rom I, p.167. The word "supercede" translating *aufheben* here fails to capture the negative, nullifying, neutralizing significance of this very rich term.

These certainly need to be observed as symptoms, but the eye that has become wise will *no* longer seek orientation from them."[86]

Barth did not seek to take his orientation from such truths, and he saw this as one of the great differences between his approach to exegesis and that of his contemporaries. In his view, their approach simply ignored the question of truth. "It receives *Romans* and carefully dissects the living whole [*das lebendige Ganze*] into individual, dead pieces [*einzelne tote Stücke*], the truth into the truths [*die Wahrheit in Wahrheiten*], and builds it up again as 'doctrines of faith and ethics.'"[87] Instead of dissecting "the truth into the truths," Barth sought, by contrast, to interpret the truths in light of *the truth*. He discovered that *truth* in all its uniqueness, wholeness, and indivisibility was something that could not be ignored: "Thirty years from now let us talk about simplicity, but now let us talk about the truth!"[88] "*Die Wahrheitsfrage*" was paramount to Barth, as Hermann Strathmann pointed out in his review of 1923.[89] Throughout his exegesis of *Romans* the question of truth takes precedence again and again over method, which is precisely why Gadamer refers in *Truth and Method* to Rom I as "a hermeneutical manifesto." Truth – a word, interestingly enough, one searches for in vain throughout Schleiermacher's *Hermeneutik* – is the issue Barth saw himself inescapably confronted by in reading the Bible and it is this we see him wrestling with already in 1917, in his "*Die neue Welt in der Bibel*" address. Even then the issue had become not the various "truths" of the Bible, but "*the* truth."[90] This is why interpretation, as he said in 1924, "means that I have not merely to think the thoughts of Scripture after it, to think with these thoughts, to think them for myself, but that I have also to think them as *truth*. The formula that the subjective possibility of receiving revelation is primarily an acceptance of it as true has clearly been scorned in modern theology. Yet I do not see how we can avoid it."[91]

Karl Barth's theological revolution was, in sum, born of his discovery of *the truth*, specifically, that the being of God is the truth and that the being of God precedes all human questioning. This discovery, Barth seems to have realized very early on, had revolutionary hermeneutical implications, not least of which

---

[86] Rom I, p.166.

[87] Rom I, p.420.

[88] Rom II, p. ix. Barth adds: "Anyone who in this situation is concerned with *the truth* must now muster the courage for once *not* to be simple."

[89] Hermann Strathmann, *Die Theologie der Gegenwart* 17 (1923), pp.261-262.

[90] Barth, "Die neue Welt in der Bibel," p.30.

[91] Barth, *Unterricht*, p.309; ET p.254. Barth adds: "We are not dealing merely with ideas and narratives and concepts and images. These are simply the means by which the prophets and apostles gave their witness. We are dealing with the thoughts of the witness itself that I am invited to think after, to think with, to think for myself. Perhaps I can do no better than think with the help of the ideas, even though they are remote and strange to me as such. We best think certain things by saying Yes and Amen to what is there."

was that truths, even so-called biblical truths, must be interpreted in light of *the truth*. The reason this was so revolutionary was that, as Barth stated in his letter to Paul Wernle on Oct.24, 1919, all he and his generation had been offered as students at the university in the name of scientific exegesis of the Bible, was little more than "a *gestaltlos* rubble heap of individual, relative truths."[92] When he discovered that God was the truth, the *Hauptsache* of the Bible, and that "the whole Bible authoritatively proclaims that God must be *all in all*," he knew that his approach to interpreting the Bible would never be the same. To measure everything in light of the Bible's central subject matter, content, and theme, the whole in light of its parts and the parts in light of the whole, meant that the question of truth, sooner or later, had to be reckoned with. And this, Barth realized, implied a vastly different approach to the task of exegesis than that generally practiced by his contemporaries.[93]

Barth was not alone, however, in recognizing how far-reaching the implications of this approach to the task of exegesis were. Rudolf Bultmann, already recognized in 1922 as a rising star among his peers, spoke highly in his review of Barth's second edition of his *Römerbrief* and enthusiastically praised – with one reservation – Barth's exegetical approach of measuring everything in light of the subject matter.[94] And despite Barth's rather pointed rebuttal of Bultmann in his preface to the third edition of his *Römerbrief,* which suggested that Bultmann still did not recognize some of the deeper implications of interpreting the Bible in light of the subject matter, Bultmann's estimation of the significance of Barth's *sachlicher* approach to exegesis grew throughout the 1920s. In fact, by 1926, at the conclusion of his review of *Die Auferstehung der Toten*, Bultmann was even comparing the significance of Barth's accom-

---

[92] See Barth's letter of Oct. 24, 1919 to Professor Paul Wernle, which is included in Rom I, pp. 638-646.

[93] *Die christliche Dogmatik*, pp. 515f.

[94] Rudolf Bultmann, "Karl Barths 'Römerbrief' in zweiter Auflage," *Die christliche Welt* 36 (1922), pp. 320-323; 330-334; 358-361; 369-373. Also contained in *Anfänge der dialektischen Theologie* I (Munich: Christian Kaiser Verlag, 1962), pp.119-142; ET "Karl Barth's Epistle To The Romans In Its Second Edition," trans. Keith R. Crim, in idem, *The Beginnings of Dialectic Theology* I, ed. James Robinson (Richmond: John Knox Press, 1968), pp.100-120. "In the understanding of the task of interpreting the text as Barth develops it in the preface, I am quite in agreement with him." Yet on the other hand, Bultmann added: "But I must reproach Barth for having let this ideal become a schema by means of which he does violence to the Letter to the Romans and to Paul." "One must measure by the subject matter to what extent in all the words and sentences of the text the subject matter has really found adequate expression, for what else can be meant by 'measuring'? In Barth, however, I find nothing of such measuring and of the radical criticism based on it. It is impossible to assume that everywhere in *The Epistle to the Romans* the subject matter must have found adequate expression, unless one intends to establish a modern dogma of inspiration, and something like this seems to stand behind Barth's exegesis – to the detriment of the clarity of the subject matter itself" (pp.140-141; ET pp.118-120).

plishment in the field of theological exegesis to that of F.C. Baur's in the field of historical exegesis.[95] Baur's contribution had tended to eclipse the significance of theological exegesis, "but precisely at this point," Bultmann announced, "Barth has shown a new direction." Because of Barth's contribution to our understanding of the exegetical task, Bultmann declared: "we stand at a new beginning." Whether Barth saw it as a new beginning or as a return to a more ancient or classical approach, he said in his early preface drafts to Rom I, "This longing for a *sachlicher, inhaltlicher, wesentlicher* understanding of the Bible has been in us all for a long time."[96]

---

[95] Rudolf Bultmann, "K. Barths 'Die Auferstehung der Toten,'" *Theologische Blätter* 5 (1926), pp. 12f. See also *Glauben und Verstehen* 1 (Tübingen: J.C.B. Mohr [Paul Siebeck], 1933), pp. 63f.; ET "Karl Barth, The Resurrection Of The Dead" trans. Louise Pettibone Smith, in *Faith and Understanding* (Philadelphia: Fortress Press, 1987), p.92f.

[96] Appendix 2, Preface Draft IA, p. 280 (p.585) and Preface Draft II, p. 286 (p.593).

Chapter 4

Entering into the Meaning of the Bible

Interpreting a text according to its subject matter, content, and substance constitutes Karl Barth's most important hermeneutical principle. Yet it is only one hermeneutical principle mentioned in his *Römerbrief* period. Beyond interpreting the Bible "more in accordance with its subject matter, content, and substance," Barth insists that interpreting the Bible, or any text for that matter, is a matter of "entering into" its meaning.[1] It is a matter not only of identifying its subject matter, content, and substance, but of participating in it. So important is this principle of participation to Barth that he describes it as "the chasm which separates me from the method of today's dominant science of biblical exegesis."[2] To appreciate the significance of this claim, one must consider the following statement:

> Here I am forced to indicate with a few sentences the chasm which separates me from the method of today's dominant science of biblical exegesis. To understand an author means for me mainly to *stand with him*, to take each of his words in earnest, so long as it is not proven that he does not deserve this trust, to participate with him in the subject matter, in order to interpret him from the inside out. But today's theology does not stand with the prophets and the apostles; it does not side with them but rather with the modern reader and his prejudices; it does not take the prophets and apostles in earnest, but while it stands smiling sympathetically beside them or above them, it takes up a cool and indifferent distance from them; it critically or merrily examines the historical-psychological surface and misses its meaning. That is what I have against it. When I speak about "standing with an author" I mean beginning with the presupposition that what once was a serious problem, is still one today and that, conversely, the problems with which we are concerned today, if they are really serious problems and not merely fads, must be the same as those with which notable people of all times have wrestled. The decisive prerequisite for the interpretation of a text for me therefore is participation in its *subject matter*. No historical meticulousness and no art of empathy and no trip to the Orient can offer even the slightest substitute for this participation. Without this living context of the past and present which is given within the *subject matter*, the words "history" and "understanding" have no meaning at all: history then remains a chaos and the willingness to understand, a fiddling about with empty forms. Mixed into this lively context of the subject matter, the understanding of history is a continuous, ever more honest dialogue between the truth which *was*, which *comes*, and which is *one* and *the same*. And the art of history will have to consist precisely in suspending from this dialogue the insignificant differences of former and present ways of thought and sensibilities, rather than ignoring what is important and developing with loving interest that

---

[1] Appendix 2, Preface Draft I, p. 277 (p. 582).
[2] Appendix 2, Preface Draft IA, p. 281 (p. 587) and Preface Draft II, p. 284 (p. 591).

which is paltry. Whoever does not continually "read in" because he participates in the subject matter, cannot "read out" either.[3]

These are some of the most important lines in Barth's preface drafts to Rom I, and the sentence which stands out among them is: "The decisive prerequisite for the interpretation of a text for me therefore is participation in its *subject matter.*" What is the significance of this claim?

A. A Scientific Approach to Exegesis

In order for one to understand why Barth spoke of participation as "the chasm which separates me from the method of today's dominant science of biblical exegesis," some background is necessary. As I mentioned earlier, Barth was already in his *Römerbrief* period at odds with his contemporaries' understanding of theology as a science.[4] For the majority of Barth's contemporaries, to be "scientific" was to be objective, and to be objective meant, above all, to face a given object of investigation as an unbiased observer. Unbiased interpretation meant allowing "facts to speak for themselves," as it were, and only by impartial analysis was this thought to be possible. In short, the "non-participatory, distancing of oneself" was thought to be a condition for the possibility of genuinely scientific interpretation. In the period immediately preceding Rom I, this was a widely held presupposition among biblical scholars such as Jülicher, for example;[5] yet it is one of the major hermeneutical presuppositions Barth was seeking to overcome. Still contending with the presupposition of a presuppositionless exegesis in the 1930s, he said:

> There is a notion that complete impartiality is the most fitting and indeed the normal disposition for true exegesis, because it guarantees a complete absence of prejudice. For a short time, around 1910, this idea threatened to achieve almost canonical status in Protestant theology. But now we can quite calmly describe it as merely comical.[6]

It is not exactly clear why Barth designated 1910 as the height of popularity of the idea of impartial exegesis,[7] but it is clear that the persistence of this idea

---

[3] Appendix 2, Preface Draft II, pp. 284-285 (pp. 591-592). A statement almost identical to this appears in Preface Draft IA, p. 281 (p. 587).

[4] See pp. 46f. above.

[5] Jülicher, *Anfänge*, p.80.

[6] KD I/2:519; CD I/2:469.

[7] It is likely that this date has to do with the rise of Ernst Troeltsch's program. Barth twice associated the year 1910 with Troeltsch. In his essay "Unerledigte Anfragen an die heutige Theologie" (1920), Barth said he "listened to [Troeltsch] in 1910, with dark foreboding," having realized "that it had become impossible to advance any further down the dead-end street we were strolling along with relative ease." In *Die Theologie und die Kirche*, p. 4; ET "Unsettled Questions for Theology Today" in *Theology and Church*, pp. 60-61 [translation revised]. In his famous "Concluding Unscientific Postscript on Schleiermacher," Barth said: "One thing,

among biblical scholars continued to be a source of amazement to him throughout his career.[8]

As suggested earlier, scientific objectivity as a result of his discovery of the Bible's subject matter, content, and theme, had come to mean something different to Barth than it did to the majority of his contemporaries. They understood scientific objectivity in terms of impartiality and unprejudiced observation; he understood it in terms of being faithful to the object of investigation. To be scientific to him meant fidelity to the object.[9] And such fidelity meant participation. It also meant, with respect to the interpretation of a book, for example, a certain fidelity to the author which I shall discuss at length in the next chapter. But what disturbed Barth about the dominant science of biblical exegesis was that "the *mistrust* one has, the Unwillingness-To-Understand, the non-participatory, distancing of oneself, has simply been made into a scientific principle."[10] The fact that mistrust, and not simply a critical-minded sobriety, had been elevated to a scientific principle by the dominant science of biblical exegesis indicated to Barth just how impossible the situation had become. Not only had his contemporaries convinced themselves of their own impartiality, they had convinced themselves that approaching texts with mistrust was a matter of impartiality, a matter of merely exercising pure and unprejudiced scientific judgment, all the while siding "with the modern reader and his prejudices."[11] This pretense of objectivity is something Barth ridicules throughout his *Römerbrief* prefaces and he does so not only because he perceived such pretense as false,[12] but because it precluded the one thing necessary for truly

---

however, is certain, that even before 1910 I was a stranger in my innermost being to the bourgeois world of Ritschl and his pupils. ... Even the 'historicism' by which Ernst Troeltsch and the historians of religion of that time thought they could outbid the Ritschlians ... struck me as being too sterile, and at any rate not what I was looking for." See Barth, "Nachwort," p. 291. Barth later wrote about being in Marburg shortly before 1910 among students who were ridiculing Herrmann's work as naive "at a time when the star of *Troeltsch* with his world-wide programmes and perspectives was nearing its zenith!" Barth, "Die dogmatische Prinzipienlehre bei Wilhelm Herrmann" (1925), p. 586.

[8] In 1948, Barth said of his "colleagues in Old and New Testament studies" in his preface to KD III/2, vii; CD III/2, ix: "so many still seem to pride themselves on being utterly unconcerned as to the dogmatic presuppositions and consequences of their notions, while unwittingly reading them into the picture." Actually, it was a long time before any major figure in the biblical studies' guild openly challenged the presupposition of a presuppositionless exegesis, e.g. Rudolf Bultmann, "Ist voraussetzungslose Exegese möglich?" *Theologische Zeitschrift* 13, (1957), pp. 409-17, ET "Is Exegesis Without Presuppositions Possible?," *Existence and Faith*, trans. Schubert Ogden (New York: Meridian Books, 1960), pp. 289-296.

[9] Rom II, p. 515.

[10] Appendix 2, Preface Draft III, p. 288 (p. 596). Italics added.

[11] Appendix 2, Preface Draft IA p. 281 (p. 587) and Preface Draft II, p. 284 (p. 591).

[12] To the sentence, "If we would only once again take our place, standing in attention before the rich treasures of *the* one and only *Römerbrief* (the real one, not the theologically worked-over one) as our predecessors at the time of the Reformation," Barth added in Preface

scientific interpretation, namely, participation, which brings us to the following topic.

As previously cited, in each of his *Römerbrief* prefaces, including all his preface drafts to Rom I with the exception of the first, Barth refers to "the doctrine of inspiration" and twice to "the doctrine of verbal inspiration." Speaking favorably of this doctrine he realized would be controversial since even before David Friedrich Strauss referred to it as "the Achilles' heel of the Protestant system" in 1840,[13] many Protestant theologians and biblical scholars had long since rejected it. They tended to see the ancient doctrine of *theopneustia* as a superstitiously mechanistic belief, one of the last relics of medieval faith the Reformation had failed to overcome. Others, like Barth before his break with liberalism, regarded it as a "product of the post-Reformation."[14] He defined it rather dismissively in his notes for his 1910-1911 confirmation class as follows:

> On the the grounds of II Tim.3:16, the claim that the books of the Bible have been written by God's Spirit, the authors are only tools, slate pencils. The Bible's author is God. This opinion is not yet present in the ancient church (Origen). Certainly not in Luther (position to *The Epistle of James* and *Revelation*). But then really in Protestantism, the doctrine of *verbal inspiration* (Buxtorf, except for the vowel points!). Expression of high regard for the Bible, understandable in those days of conflict. But *untenable*: Why so many personal matters? Different styles? Variants? Lost materials? Inaccuracies? Contradictions?[15]

In his essay of 1910, "*Der christliche Glaube und die Geschichte*," which I shall discuss in more detail in chapter five, Barth claimed that to the extent that Calvin had a doctrine of inspiration at all, it was surely *not* a doctrine of "*Verbal inspiration*"![16] This is ironic, of course, because it is Calvin's doctrine of *verbal* inspiration that he specifically commends in his preface to the third edition of his *Römerbrief*: "... from the first edition on I have not denied the certain analogy between my procedure and the old teaching of verbal inspiration. ... This doctrine, in the form in which *Calvin* presented it, seems to me at least very ingenious and worthy of discussion."[17] Indeed, these remarks are fascinating because it is probably Barth, more so than anyone else, who is responsible for reintroducing the doctrine of biblical inspiration to the twentieth century

---

Draft IA, "instead of today placing ourselves beside it with our terrible historical-psychological 'objectivity' (which is not)!" p. 280 n.8.

[13] David Friedrich Strauss, *Der christliche Glaube* 1 (Tübingen: C.F. Osiander, 1840), p. 136.

[14] Karl Barth, "Zwinglis '67 Schlussreden' auf das erste Religionsgespräch zu Zürich 1523" (1906), *Vorträge und kleinere Arbeiten, 1905-1909*, ed. Hans-Anton Drewes and Hinrich Stoevesandt (Zürich: Theologischer Verlag Zürich, 1992), p. 113.

[15] Barth, *Konfirmandenunterricht, 1909-1921*, pp. 68-69.

[16] Barth, "*Der christliche Glaube und die Geschichte*," pp. 167f.

[17] Rom II, pp. xxi-xxii.

continental theological discussion, contrary to the opinion of many who have insisted that he rejected it.[18]

Yet it is important to note why Barth introduced the doctrine of inspiration in his *Römerbrief* prefaces in the first place. He said in one preface draft that compared to the so-called "scientific principle" of mistrust, the non-participatory, distancing of oneself required by the dominant science of biblical exegesis, he had found "the doctrine of verbal inspiration more fruitful. It at least contains the wise challenge of stubbornly occupying readers with a biblical text until it is brought forth to significant speech, until it stands before us not as a dead relic of Jewish or near-eastern nonsense, but as a living link in a movement which should move us as well."[19] Though Barth said in his final preface to Rom I, "I am happy that I do not have to choose between the two," that is, between "the critical historical method of biblical research" and "the

---

[18] In the 1950s, for example, there were many, both 'conservative' and 'liberal,' who flatly denied that Barth held a doctrine of verbal inspiration: R. A. Finlayson, "Contemporary Ideas of Inspiration," in idem, *Revelation and the Bible*, ed. Carl F. H. Henry, (Grand Rapids: Baker, 1958), p. 228; Frederick Herzog, *The Possibility of Theological Understanding: An Inquiry into the Presuppositions of Hermeneutics in Theology*, Princeton Theological Seminary, 1953, Th.D. DSS, p. 251. Such a view persists among many to this day, e.g. Nigel Biggar, *The Hastening that Waits: Karl Barth's Ethics* (Oxford: Clarendon Press, 1993), p. 101. Ironically, Barth's two volumes on "The Doctrine of The Word of God" may be among the most carefully nuanced elaborations of the doctrine of verbal inspiration in the twentieth century. See KD I/2:523-598; CD I/2:473-537. Barth states, "If inspiration is co-ordinated into that circle of God's manifestation by the Spirit only for our illumination by the same Spirit, the inspiration of the biblical witnesses which is the link between the two, between God and us, can and must be regarded quite definitely not merely as real but as verbal inspiration." KD I/2:575; CD I/2:518. Yet he also says: "Verbal inspiration does not mean the infallibility of the biblical word in its linguistic, historical and theological character as a human word. It means that the fallible and faulty human word is as such used by God and has to be received and heard in spite of its human fallibility." KD I/2:592; CD I/2:533. See also *Unterricht*, pp. 265-276; ET pp. 217-226. Barth's understanding of verbal inspiration, in short, has to do not with any particular *property* of the words themselves, nor with any particular *experience* of their human authors, nor with any particular *use* as David H. Kelsey and other functionalists would have it. See *The Uses of Scripture in Recent Theology* (London: SCM, 1975), pp. 211-212. Rather, it has to do with God's *promise* which goes with the particular words of the Bible, which, as Barth later claimed, is analogous to God's promise to the children of Israel. Like the children of Israel, the words of the Bible are special not because they are necessarily superior or in any way better than others. They are special because they were 'chosen.' These words, from specific times and places, were chosen as "The source and norm of our knowledge and speech about God." They were "chosen" among others and perhaps, one might add, in the spirit of Romans 9-11, chosen that others might be blessed. What then is special about these 'chosen' words is that through them there is a promise made by the Spirit on their behalf. Like "the pillar of cloud by day and the pillar of fire by night," Barth refers to this as "the promise which is the traveling portion given to our undertaking to know God if it is an obedient undertaking." KD II/1:267; CD II/1:236.

[19] Appendix 2, Preface Draft III, p. 288 (p. 596).

old doctrine of inspiration," to claim that he did not suggested to his contemporaries that he had, *ipso facto*, already chosen *against* the former (something Barth was never willing to concede).[20] Nevertheless, Barth's point – which was never made in the final, published preface to Rom I – was that reading the Bible according to the doctrine of verbal inspiration required participation or at least a posture open to participation, unlike "the non-participatory, distancing of oneself" required by the dominant science of biblical exegesis. In this sense, therefore, reading the Bible according to "the old doctrine of inspiration" was more scientific than the so-called "critical historical method of biblical research."

Thus, contrary to Jülicher who claimed that Barth had "forced" him straightaway to make a decision between "practical exegesis" and "strictly scientific exegesis,"[21] Barth insisted that truly scientific exegesis would tolerate no separation, bifurcation, or "double-entry bookkeeping" approach, as if the task of interpreting the Bible could be so easily divided or compartmentalized. In short, the decisive difference between Barth's approach to interpretation and his contemporaries', as he saw it, was participation in the subject matter: whereas he sought it, they sought, in the name of scientific objectivity, to avoid it. Barth realized that participation in the subject matter of the Bible (and the subject matter of many other books as well) was not something he as an interpreter could produce of himself or attain on the basis of his own resources or ability. Nor was it something that came about as a result of adopting any particular attitude or posture. Yet participating in the Bible's subject matter did teach Barth that there were some postures and attitudes more appropriate to interpretation than others. The specific attitude or posture involved in being stubbornly occupied by a biblical text *"until* it is brought forth to significant speech ... *until* it stands ... as a living link in a movement that should move us as well" is one I shall consider more closely in a moment. But before I do it is necessary to point out something Barth *did* see as a condition for the possibility of participation in the subject matter of a text.

B. A Living Context

As I mentioned in chapter one, the most frequent charge made against Barth by critics of both Rom I and II was that he failed to interpret *Romans* adequately in light of its actual context. This is a charge often made by modern biblical scholars against theologians, and perhaps against Barth as much as any theologian in the twentieth century. But I believe the charge arises, in the case of Barth at least, because of a fundamental misunderstanding about what the true

---

[20] Eberhard Jüngel makes this point in *Barth-Studien*, p. 85.
[21] Jülicher, *Anfänge*, p. 88; ET p. 73.

context of the Bible is. Certainly the Bible must be understood in light of its context. But for many modern biblical scholars, understanding the Bible in light of its context has meant understanding the Bible primarily, if not exclusively, in light of its historical context, that is, in light of its anthropological, cultural, sociological, political, and religious milieu, whereas for Barth – at least from the beginning of his *Römerbrief* period – understanding the Bible in light of its context meant something significantly more than this. For him the context was infinitely wider. The fact that "the whole Bible authoritatively proclaims that God must be *all in all*" meant that God Himself, that revelation, was the actual context in which the Bible was to be understood.[22] Such a context Barth describes in the quotation cited at the beginning of this chapter as a "living context" which is to be found "within the *subject matter*" of the Bible. And "without this living context of the past and present which is given within the *subject matter*," he claimed, "the words 'history' and 'understanding' have no meaning at all."[23]

What is this "living context of the past and present which is given within the *subject matter*" of the Bible and why did Barth see it as so important? The first thing that must be said about understanding the Bible in light of its living context is that for Barth it did not in any sense absolve interpreters from understanding the Bible in light of its historical context. As earlier stated, for him there was no such thing as a genuine theological understanding of the Bible apart from a historical understanding. Nevertheless, as significant as the historical context was, it was never an independent or autonomous context, but rather only one part of the whole context within which the Bible was to be understood. It, like all other parts, had to be understood in light of the whole. God, for Barth, was the whole; or more precisely, God revealed in Jesus Christ was the whole, the actual horizon or context within which the Bible was to be understood, "for in him all things were created ... and in him all things hold together" (Col.1:16-17).

Barth's claim that apart from this living context "the words 'history' and 'understanding' have no meaning at all" is significant, therefore, because it says something important about his understanding of the relationship between revelation and history. One of the major themes of Rom I and Rom II is that there is an infinite qualitative distinction between time and eternity, between revelation and history. Revelation is not a predicate of history. Revelation is *totaliter aliter*. While it occurs *in* history, it is not *of* history. But to say reve-

---

[22] The discussion of Barth's hermeneutics in terms of 'narrative' which has taken place over the last twenty-five years has tended to eclipse this point. To say that God, that Jesus Christ, the content of revelation, is the context in which the Bible is to be understood means it was not a literary category that established the basic "web of meaning" for Barth; it was a dogmatic one.

[23] Appendix II, Preface Draft II, p. 284 (p. 591).

lation occurs *in* history but is not *of* history still does not say all that needs to be said about Barth's understanding of the relationship between revelation and history. Though it makes plain that revelation is not a product *of* history, it leaves ambiguous how revelation *in* history is to be understood. It leaves ambiguous the question of the context in which revelation is to be understood. To say that revelation occurs *in* but is not *of* history might still suggest, for instance, that even though revelation is not a product of history, history is still the primary, governing context in which revelation is necessarily understood. After all, if revelation is *in* history, how can it be understood other than *as* history? The great danger here is that revelation might still be understood as somehow passing over *into* history, that it might nevertheless be identified with history, be distilled from some universal notion of history or be transformed into some kind of amalgamated, hyphenated form of history, for example, 'salvation-history.' Barth certainly left himself open to this when in the only place he mentioned salvation-history in Rom I he left its relationship to revelation unclear. In fact, he even appears to equate salvation-history with revelation.[24] This is why Barth made it clear in Rom II, repeatedly, that whatever 'salvation-history' might be, it should not be confused with revelation.[25] It was precisely this kind of ambiguity that he was trying to avoid in moving from a so-called "process eschatology" in Rom I to a so-called "consistent eschatology" in Rom

---

[24] "It is neither high spiritedness nor enthusiasm when, in the midst of this serious and painful process of the crucifixion of the old man, as well as in the midst of the defeats of this battle between the Old and New, we are always talking in advance of the glory of the coming world of God, when we refer to the imminent victory, when we neither acknowledge the bad 'reality' as truth nor take it serious, when we do not allow experience to have a word unless it is experience of God, when we do not want to know a thing about any psychology unless it is psychology of grace, and no history that is not *Heils*geschichte." See Rom I, p. 222.

[25] Barth states in Rom II: "Flesh is flesh; and all that takes place within its sphere, every step we undertake towards God, is as such *weak*. Because of the qualitative distinction between God and man, the history of religion, Church History, is *weak* – utterly *weak*. Since religion is human, utterly human history, it is flesh, even though it be draped in the flowing garments of the 'History of Salvation'" (p. 276); "Strangely great and strangely powerful are the connexion and relation between God and the world, between there and here. For when we have clearly perceived that, if divinity be so concretized and humanized in a particular department of history – the history of religion or the history of salvation – God has ceased to be God" (p. 79); "We are no longer permitted either to regard it as a thing in history or to subject it, as though it could be identified with religious experience, to psychological analysis. It is neither a constant factor traceable throughout the evolution of human being and having and doing, nor is it a special department of Church History or of the History of Comparative Religion, nor can it be disclosed in the so-called History of Salvation" (p. 126). For an important perspective on Barth's mature relationship to *Heilsgeschichte*, see Hans-Joachim Kraus' essay, "Das Problem der Heilsgeschichte in der 'Kirchlichen Dogmatik'" in *Antwort: Karl Barth zum siebzigsten Geburtstag*, ed. Rudolf Frey, et al (Zürich: Evangelischer Verlag Zürich, 1956), pp. 69-83.

II. The broader contours of this transition have been discussed elsewhere,[26] but the point is that Barth was seeking to make clear that revelation did not pass over into history – in the sense of a *metabasis eis allo genos* – in any way.

Barth's further attempt to clarify the relationship between revelation and history is seen when various passages in Rom II are compared with Rom I, for example, his exegesis of Rom.4:23-25: "Now it was not written for his sake alone, that it was reckoned unto [Abraham]; but for our sake also, unto whom it shall be reckoned, who believe on him that raised Jesus our Lord from the dead, who was delivered up for our trespasses, and was raised for our justification." In Rom I, under the rubric "Die Historie," Barth interprets these verses:

> What is Abraham's history [*Abrahamsgeschichte*] supposed to mean for us? For what reason are we looking back into the distant past from this present life? Certainly not because of our half-humble, half-arrogant 'interest' in remote heroes and church fathers. The human part in itself is not important, and the undirected preoccupation with it is a pure waste of time and energy. By the mere 'interest' in that which once was, *Geschichte* becomes a confused chaos of meaningless relations and events. Despite all our skill at knot-tying, *Historie* turns into a triumphant unfolding and describing of this chaos, whereby all which *really* was, remains certainly hidden.
>
> Besides this endlessly "interesting" way of *Historie*, a different one is possible. Its nature consists in the fact that it lets *Geschichte* talk to us and us with *Geschichte* about the one and only theme of the kingdom of God. This is the way of the Bible. "*Historia vitae magistra,*" (Calvin). The possibility of such conversation with *Geschichte*, in which a thousand refractions from this same light will again and again shine – the openness for the genius of the Old Testament, the key to the mystery of that which was and will be – all this will be ours to the measure in which we ourselves are participating in *Geschichte*. We *can* participate in Christ, therefore, we *can* also understand *Geschichte*. For in Christ is revealed the meaning of the times hidden within the longitudinal framework of past and future. It is there, it can also be discovered. Only when we have not yet understood ourselves and not yet heard God's Word in Christ for ourselves, could we not then understand or misunderstand Abraham. Otherwise Abraham will immediately become a memory for us of that which is also in us and which we cannot hear and speak enough about as well. We thus stand rank and file with Abraham. His matter is ours, our decisive question of life is his. When we speak about Abraham, we speak about ourselves, we speak about humanity.[27]

However, in Rom II, under the rubric "Vom Nutzen der Historie," Barth interprets these same verses, Rom.4:23-25, as follows:

> "Not for his sake alone, but for ours also." *Historie* can have a use. The past can speak to the present; for in the past and present is a simultaneity which heals the past of its dumbness and the present of its deafness, which can enable the past to speak and the present to

---

[26] Barth's move from a "process eschatology" (Rom I) to a "consistent eschatology" (Rom II) is discussed at length in McCormack's *Karl Barth's Critically Realistic Dialectical Theology*, pp. 129-319. The terms "process eschatology" and "consistent eschatology" are borrowed from Michael Beintker, *Die Dialektik in der 'dialektischen Theologie' Karl Barths*, pp. 45, 110-111.

[27] Rom I, pp. 143-144.

hear. This simultaneity makes possible a soliloquy in which time is at once dissolved and fulfilled, for it proclaims and hears the *Unhistorische, Unanschauliche*, and *Unbegreifliche*, which is the end and the beginning of all *Geschichte*. Genesis' history [*Genesishistorie*] opens its mouth and utters that which is *Unhistorische*, that to Abraham his faith was reckoned as righteousness. In so far as his situation is ours also, our ears can be opened to hear the *Unhistorische*. In such a soliloquy, where the present becomes aware of the *significance* of human events in their *unity*, *Historie* displays the usefulness which is expected of it. On the other hand, apart from the *Unhistorischen*, the past remains dumb and the present deaf. However, the clearest witnesses and documents can say nothing and the sharpest *historische* attentiveness can hear nothing if this soliloquy does not take place contemporaneously in the present. Apart from a glimpse of the *Unhistorischen*, Abraham cannot say anything to us and we cannot hear him. Where apart from the study of the sources, there is not a living awareness of the *significance* of human events in their *unity*, where *Geschichte* is a mere juxtapositioning of cultures or a sequence of epochs, a mere plurality of *different* immediacies, of *different* individuals, times, circumstances, and institutions, where it teems and spins with mere appearances which charge about in all directions, there it is nonsense. To call such nonsense "reality" is not the same as calling it true. To say that it is "interesting" is not the same as saying it is full of meaning. A past looking at us with a host of faces is not yet an intelligible, understood, or recognized past. If *Historie* is unable to offer more than this, it is useless. As a critical collection of material, it is *not* "*Geschichte*," it is photographed and analyzed chaos, despite the degree of antiquarian love and precision, despite the most skilled "empathy" into the mood of ancient days and ways, and despite all incidentally applied, ever so intelligent, points of view. *Geschichte* is a synthetic work of art. *Geschichte* emerges from events and has a single and unified theme. Where this work of art, this event, this one theme is not in the historian from the start, there is *no Geschichte*.[28]

What one sees in comparing Barth's exegesis of Rom.4:23-25 in Rom I and Rom II is an attempt to distinguish more sharply between revelation and history. In both Rom I and Rom II, for example, that which apart from revelation is called "history" is described as "chaos." But in Rom II, this chaos is described as more profound. The crisis of historians, their inability to make sense of past events apart from revelation, is characterized in more severe terms. The fruit of their labor, apart from revelation, is, in Rom II, not even deemed worthy of the name "history." Yet the most significant difference between Rom I and II – and this applies not only to his exegesis of Rom.4:23-25 – is that Barth introduces the term *das Unhistorische* to describe revelation. And he identifies this term with another he uses in Rom II, "primal history" (*Urgeschichte*).[29] Barth uses both of these terms throughout Rom II to make clear that revelation is neither a part nor a predicate of history, nor does it pass over into history, even in the event of revelation itself. For even in the Incarnation, when God entered into history, He was never a part of history, in the sense of being an 'object' of historical investigation. This never meant for Barth that God had not acted *in* human history, only that historians *qua* historians could not know this as an act of *God* apart from revelation. In this sense,

---

[28] Rom II, pp. 121-122.
[29] Rom II, pp. 5, 117f., 149, 219, 231f.

revelation was and always remained for Barth "*unhistorisch.*" But that he had identified revelation itself in Rom II as "*das Unhistorische*" suggested to many that he did not believe that God had acted *in* history at all, that revelation could not encounter history in any way. Barth soon after recognized the danger he had risked in Rom II and later admitted that "readers of it today will not fail to appreciate that in it Jn.1:14 does not have justice done to it."[30] Nevertheless, his talk about revelation as "the Unhistorical" left a lasting impression which remains to this day. And this is unfortunate because it has tended to overshadow other important features of Barth's understanding of the relationship of revelation and history which he consistently maintained both in Rom I and Rom II and throughout his career.

For example, beyond Barth's overall historiographical critique which is reflected in his obviously quite deliberate conflation of the terms "*Geschichte*" and "*Historie,*"[31] the most striking feature in his exegesis of Rom.4:23-25 in

---

[30] "I should like at this stage to utter an express warning against certain passages and contexts in my commentary on Romans, where play was made and even work occasionally done with the idea of a revelation permanently transcending time, merely bounding time and determining it from without. Then, in face of the prevailing historism and psychologism which had ceased to be aware at all of any revelation other than an inner mundane one within common time, the book had a definite antiseptic task and significance. Readers of it today will not fail to appreciate that in it Jn.1:14 does not have justice done to it." See KD I/2:55-56; CD I/2:50.

[31] There are two words for history in German, "*Historie*" and "*Geschichte.*" The latter, *Geschichte*, is the older, more common, and from the perspective of Germanistics, purer term; whereas the former, *Historie*, is more specialized and has its origin in the early nineteenth century, viz., out of an emerging consciousness among scholars that the discipline of history was indeed a *Wissenschaft*. So *wissenschaftlich* had the methods of historical inquiry become – so it was thought – that many scholars believed that a new term was needed to distinguish between history so-established and all else that had been or might otherwise still be called history. This new term was called *Historie* and, for many throughout the nineteenth and twentieth centuries, became associated with the 'facts' or 'what really happened' in contrast to *Geschichte*, the mere 'reports,' 'stories,' or even 'tales' of what may have really happened. The difference, according to Van A. Harvey, is that "*Historie* means that which is public and verifiable according to generally accepted standards of history writing. So understood, it is to be contrasted with *Geschichte* ... which refers to the *significance* of a historical fact and so cannot be made verifiable by historical canons." See *Handbook of Theological Terms* (New York: Macmillan, 1964), p. 121. Whether, as a historiographical question, Barth thought in his *Römerbrief* period that fact and significance could be distinguished clearly enough to warrant two definitions of history, by interchanging the words *Historie* and *Geschichte* in the passages above, Barth was making the point that with respect to understanding the Bible he did not accept the distinction as a very serious one. What was serious for him was precisely the fact that so many of his contemporaries, Harnack, Troeltsch, Wernle, *et al*, did take this distinction seriously, viz., so seriously that faith depended on it. The terms *Historie* and *Geschichte* are juxtaposed throughout the *Church Dogmatics*. The former is often associated with that which is "apprehensible by a neutral observer or apprehended by such an observer." As such it is a notion "totally alien" to the Bible and thus "obviously and utterly inappropriate to the object of its witness. The neutral observer who understood the events recorded in it as revelation would

both Rom I and II is the claim that history has a "unity," that it has "one and only theme" or, as he says in Rom II, "a single and unified theme." In Rom I this theme is described as "the kingdom of God." In Rom II it is more consistently characterized as "the crisis." But the main point in both Rom I and Rom II is that apart from knowledge of this "unity," this "single and unified theme," history makes no sense. This is a point from which Barth never departed.[32] "*Geschichte*," to repeat what he says above, "is a synthetic work of art. *Geschichte* emerges from events and has a single and unified theme. Where this work of art, this event, this one theme is not in the historian from the start, there is *no Geschichte*."

However, claiming that history apart from this single and unified theme is "a confused chaos of meaningless relations and events" which ought not be readily confused with "reality" does not mean that Barth was an historical skeptic. Nor does it mean he was ever, as were a small but growing number of

---

cease thereby to be a neutral observer." Whatever might be established in terms of Historie in the Bible, Barth describes consistently as "trivial" and as having "no significance for the event of revelation." Moreover, "we should be discarding again all that we have said earlier about the mystery in revelation if we were now to describe any of the events of revelation attested in the Bible as 'historisch'" KD I/1:343; CD I/1:325 [translation revised]. See also KD III/1:84f.; CD III/1:78f., KD IV/1:562f.; CD IV/1:505f. Barth later distinguishes the two terms as follows: "'Historie' something that can be proved by general historical science, whereas 'Geschichte' is something that really takes place in time and space, but may or may not be proved. The creation story has to do with 'Geschichte,' for instance. It has to do with something that happened and therefore something historical, but something that is not open to historiographical investigation." See *Karl Barth's Table Talk*, p. 45.

[32] It is interesting to compare what Barth says in his exegesis of Rom.4:23-25 in both Rom I and II with what he later says in the *Church Dogmatics*. For example, in discussing the creation account in Genesis, he says: "Historie, i.e., that which is accessible to man because it is visible, perceptible and understandable Geschichte for him, is *objective* in the sense that it is creaturely Geschichte within the context of other creaturely Geschichte, an event prior to which and side by side with which there are other events of basically the same type with which it can be compared and integrated. And Historie is *subjective* in the sense that the picture of such creaturely events is put into its creaturely context. But it is precisely this context which is missing in the creation story. God the Creator is the only possible context [!]. For precisely this reason it is not Historie and there can be no Historie about it. Therefore it can only be *unhistorische* Geschichte and there can be only *unhistorical* history writing [*unhistorische* Geschichtsschreibung] about it. But we hasten to add: all Geschichte without exception is in this regard always unhistorisch, and can only be reported about as such, because God's creation continues throughout all Geschichte, because the entire Geschichte in all its movements, relations, and appearances, always has an element in which it is immediate to God and is immediately posited by Him. And how can it be ignored that all Geschichte is actually and finally only important and noteworthy to the extent that it has this element, that it is therefore not only historisch but also at the same time unhistorisch? How can it be ignored that all history writing [Geschichtsschreibung] is mindless and unproductive to the extent that that which is only *unhistorisch* and nothing more than *unhistorisch* is talked about." See KD III/1:84f.; CD III/1:78f. [translation revised]. Italics his.

his contemporaries in the early decades of the twentieth century, part of any "anti-historical revolution," as some have alleged.[33] What it does mean is that history was not for him an independent or autonomous sphere. History was not a category which could comprehend, contain, or in any way circumscribe revelation. Nor was history capable of disclosing revelation, no matter how closely examined or how broadly defined. For Barth, it was not that history was disclosive of the meaning of revelation; it was that revelation was disclosive of the meaning of history. It was not that history established or grounded revelation; it was that revelation established and grounded history.[34] Such an approach gave priority not to "religion but reality, not history but truth,"[35] and is illustrated by Barth's later description of his earliest conversations with his Göttingen colleague, Emanuel Hirsch:

> [Hirsch] also came to my lectures and listened a couple of times to what I had to say about the Heidelberg Catechism and the Epistle to the Ephesians. Even now, I can still hear him telling me, before he went off back to his Stelzendorf: "Do you know, Karl Barth, I don't think that things will turn out as you expect. Before we can talk about the Heidelberg Catechism and the Epistle to the Ephesians, we must first know what history is." I asked him, "But how will you discover what history is?" He replied, "First I must tackle Troeltsch, Dilthey, Yorck von Wartenburg and some other great figures from the beginning of the 1920s (he himself had first started from Fichte ... but he broke loose later). Well, first of all we must find a concept of history and only on the basis of that will we be able to read texts like the Heidelberg Catechism and the Epistle to the Ephesians." ... Even then, that is in the winter of 1921-22, I noticed ... that we did not think in the same way. For me it was quite the other way round: first of all I wanted to study the Heidelberg Catechism and the Epistle to the Ephesians. Only then did I want to try to understand what 'history' is. But these were two very different approaches.[36]

The point is that in Rom I and Rom II Barth insists that history *can* be understood. In Rom I, as he states above, "We *can* participate in Christ, therefore, we *can* also understand *Geschichte*. For in Christ is revealed the meaning of the times hidden within the longitudinal framework of past and future." In Rom II, he says, "*Historie* can have a use. The past can speak to the present for in the past and present is a simultaneity which heals the past of its dumbness and the present of its deafness, which can enable the past to speak and the present to hear." The key here, in both Rom I and II, is that there is "a simultaneity" (*ein Gleichzeitiges*) in the past and present which makes the past no longer merely past, which allows the past to address the present and the present to hear. "This simultaneity," Barth claims, "makes possible a soliloquy in which time is at once dissolved and fulfilled," and he identifies this simultane-

---

[33] Bruce McCormack discusses this point in *Karl Barth's Critically Realistic Dialectical Theology*, pp. 233f.
[34] Rom II, p. 118.
[35] Barth, "Biblische Fragen, Einsichten, und Ausblicke," p. 80.
[36] Busch, *Lebenslauf*, p. 148; ET p. 135.

ity with revelation, with that "which is the end and the beginning of all *Geschichte*."[37] Jesus Christ is He in whom this simultaneity is found. In Him is the "unity" of history. He is its "single and unified theme." In Him is a "living context" which allows the past to speak to the present and the present to hear. This is what Barth was presupposing when he said in his opening lines to his preface to Rom I:

> Paul spoke to his contemporaries as a child of his age. But much more important than this truth is the other, that he speaks as a prophet and apostle of the Kingdom of God to all men in all ages. The differences between then and now, there and here, must be considered. But the purpose of this consideration can only be the recognition that these differences have no significance for what really matters.[38]

So important was this point for Barth that he repeated something similar to it in each of his preface drafts to Rom I except his first. He knew that stating that "the differences between then and now, there and here ... have *no* significance for what really matters" would be considered controversial, because for many of his contemporaries the differences between then and now, there and here, *were* significant, and not least of all with respect to things Barth believed really did matter. But as it turned out, the most disturbing thing about Barth's claim for his contemporaries was not so much the claim itself but *how* he could make it. On what basis could he claim that "the differences between then and now, there and here, have *no* significance for what really matters"? How could he speak so confidently, as if Paul were our contemporary? How could he speak so authoritatively in the name of Paul? What had happened to Lessing's "wide, ugly ditch" for Barth? This is what exasperated readers of Rom I and II more than anything else. As Wilhelm Loew said, one has "intensive experience without any feeling of distance."[39] Jülicher said, "Barth knows well that without scholarly equipment no Greek document written 1900 years ago can be properly evaluated."[40]

Barth did indeed know the importance of scholarly equipment for understanding ancient texts, but he realized that more important than scholarly equipment was something even more basic. How could anyone speak in the present about things in the past being significant or insignificant, meaningful or meaningless, apart from a shared context, a living context, which embraces, unites, and in some sense transcends both the past and the present? Dilthey had claimed that "interest" was the key: "Understanding has various degrees. These are determined first of all by interest. If our interest is limited, so also is

---

[37] Barth talks about revelation being the beginning and end of history in Rom I, pp. 68, 374, 565 and in Rom II, pp. 121-123.
[38] Rom I, p. 3.
[39] See pp. 17-18 above.
[40] Jülicher, *Anfänge*, pp. 90-91; ET p. 75.

our understanding."⁴¹ Schleiermacher apparently held a similar view, according to Barth.⁴² But Barth insisted in his exegesis of Rom.4:23-25 in both Rom I and II that "interest" was not enough (the words 'interest' and 'interesting' are put in quotation marks three times in Rom I and once in Rom II in the passages cited above). Interest – no matter how deep – could not substitute for a living context. Nor could 'empathy' (as I shall discuss in detail in the next chapter) or anything else a historian might bring to the task of interpretation.

Barth did not use the phrase "living context" in his final prefaces to Rom I or II, but it is clear that the reason he emphasized it so strongly in his preface drafts to Rom I was because he saw it as a necessary condition for the possibility of historical interpretation: "Without this living context of the past and present which is given within the *subject matter*, the words 'history' and 'understanding' have no meaning at all." By raising it, Barth was seeking to remind his contemporaries that historical interpretation did not take place in a vacuum, *in abstracto*, or from some divine vantage point. Many historians and biblical scholars operated as if the only real, relevant, or living context was their own, or as if they had their own divine vantage point. Many had wittingly or unwittingly adopted a belief in the autonomy of the present which subordinated the past to the present, as if it were primarily *we* in the present who confer meaning upon the past, as if *we* were the primary arbiters of whether something from the past is to be regarded as a "dead relic" or "living link."⁴³ The result of this was that historians and biblical scholars not only tended to forget their own historicity, e.g., the relativity of their own standpoints, perspectives, prejudices, values, etc. but also tended to develop a rather condescending attitude towards the past which is why Barth said that today's theology "does not take the prophets and apostles in earnest, instead, while it stands smiling sympathetically beside them or above them, it takes a cool and indifferent distance from them."⁴⁴ Which brings us back to why acknowledging a living context was so important to Barth.

The reason is that participation presupposes it. Without this living context, this simultaneity, which allows "the past to speak to the present and the present to hear," interpretation is impossible. "The decisive prerequisite for the interpretation of a text for me," Barth said, "is participation in its subject matter" and participation requires openness, e.g., openness to the possibility "that what was once true will always be true" and that "what was once a serious matter is

---

[41] Dilthey, "Die Entstehung der Hermeneutik," p. 319.

[42] Barth, *Die Theologie Schleiermachers*, p. 314; ET p. 175.

[43] Appendix 2, Preface Draft III, p. 288 (p. 596).

[44] Appendix 2, Preface Draft II, p. 284 (p. 591). A similar statement appears in Preface Draft IA, p. 281 (p. 587): "it does not take the prophets and apostles in earnest, but while it stands smiling sympathetically albeit condescendingly beside them, it conceitedly distances itself from them and outwardly examines them historically and psychologically."

still serious today."⁴⁵ This is why acknowledging a living context was so important to Barth. "Without this presupposition," he insisted, "history is chaos."⁴⁶ Entering into the meaning of the Bible means entering into "a continuous, ever more honest dialogue between the truth which *was*, which *comes*, and which is *one* and *the same*."⁴⁷ It means beginning with "the presupposition that what was once a serious problem is still one today and that, conversely, the problems with which we are concerned today, if they are really serious problems and not merely fads, must be the same as those with which the notable people of all times have wrestled."⁴⁸ In his final preface to Rom I Barth related this point specifically to Paul: "What was once a serious matter is still serious today, and what today is serious, and not just arbitrariness and whim, stands also in immediate relation to what was formerly serious. Our questions, if we understand ourselves aright, are the questions of Paul, and Paul's answers, if their light illumines us, must be ours."⁴⁹

---

⁴⁵ Appendix 2, Preface Drafts IA, p. 281 (p. 587), IV, p. 290 (p. 599), V, p. 292 (p. 601), and Rom I, p. 3.

⁴⁶ Appendix 2, Preface Draft IA, p. 281 (p. 587).

⁴⁷ Appendix 2, Preface Draft III, p. 288 (p. 596). See also Preface Draft IA, p. 281 (p. 587). The notion of interpretation as dialogue is important and something I shall return to. It is significant that in Preface Drafts IV and V and his final preface to Rom I Barth said: "Historical understanding is a continuous, more and more honest and penetrating conversation between the wisdom of yesterday and the wisdom of tomorrow, and these are one and the same. With respect and gratitude I remember here my father, Professor Fritz Barth, whose whole lifework has been an application of this insight."

⁴⁸ Appendix 2, Preface Draft II, p. 284 (p. 591).

⁴⁹ Rom I, p. 3. In light of his claim, "Our questions, if we understand ourselves aright, are the questions of Paul," Jüngel states, "[Barth] assumes that there are such things as basic human questions which endure throughout all historical vicissitudes. He shares this premise with liberal theologians. The problem is that he cannot agree with them on just what these basic questions are. He knows of other questions more urgent than theirs. Now a shrewd thinker might reason: If even contemporaries cannot agree on these basic human questions, their identity throughout all historical vicissitudes must be rather tentative. But Barth does not think that these questions are, so to speak, just sitting around, waiting to be asked. Indeed, he added the clear reservation 'if we understand ourselves aright.' Yet we do not always understand ourselves aright. Hence the hermeneutical imperative: Consider well! Consider yourself!" See Jüngel, *Barth-Studien*, p.89. Jüngel is perhaps right that Barth shared with liberal theologians the premise that there are basic human questions which persist through time, but it is important to emphasize, as I shall in the next chapter, that arriving at this premise was, for Barth, not a matter of a shared general anthropology, but of revelation, a matter of beginning with Paul's questions and answers.

C. Active Participation

Acknowledging a living context was important to Barth because participation – "the decisive prerequisite of interpretation" – presupposes it. Participation, however, has yet to be defined. Thus far it has only been described in terms of openness. This is certainly an important aspect of participation. Indeed openness on the part of interpreters is as essential to participation as is a living context. As Barth characterizes it both in his *Römerbrief* period and later, openness implies a kind of surrender. It implies risk, even sacrifice.[50] But openness can also imply passivity and passivity is not at all what Barth meant by participation in the subject matter of a text. On the contrary, it was the "cool and detached" distancing of readers or, as he says in the later preface drafts to Rom I, the posture of "passive detachment" adopted by so many modern biblical interpreters that he felt was so disastrous. By contrast, Barth's notion of participation demanded that readers take a position of "active" or "substantive participation." Entering into the meaning of the Bible meant engaging in "a continuous, ever more honest dialogue" with the past. It implied not only openness, receptivity, etc., but a certain level of self-giving and personal involvement on the part of the reader. It implied coming to the text with one's whole self, with the full depth and weight of one's problems, questions, and concerns, including the fundamental questions of one's existence as Bultmann and his existentializing colleagues would later emphasize.[51] Ultimately, it implied a certain "audacity" or "daring" (*Parrhesia*).[52] "This daring," as Barth insisted in 1917, "is faith: and we read the Bible rightly, not when we do so with false modesty, restraint, and attempted sobriety, for these are passive qualities, but when we read it in faith."[53]

Barth discusses active participation in a variety of ways throughout his *Römerbrief* period. But there are three ways he describes it in his *Römerbrief*

---

[50] "How can we expound it except by surrendering ourselves with them [the biblical witnesses] to the recollection, their recollection, and to the expectation, their expectation? It is only in this surrender – and not in an arbitrary doing of what they omitted to do – that our exposition of that witness will be kept pure and will become our own witness." See KD I/2:536; CD I/2:484. See also Godsey, *Karl Barth's Table Talk*, ed. John Godsey, p. 47. C.S. Lewis speaks in similar terms in *An Experiment in Criticism* (Cambridge: University Press, 1961), p. 19. "We sit down before the picture in order to have something done to us, not that we may do things with it. The first demand any work of art makes upon us is surrender. Look. Listen. Receive. Get yourself out of the way (There is no good asking first whether the work before you deserves such a surrender for until you have surrendered, you cannot possibly find out."

[51] This is already evident in Bultmann's second review of Rom II.

[52] Jüngel provides an extensive gloss on the concept of *Verwegenheit* ("audacity" or "daring") relative to Barth's beginnings in *Barth-Studien*, pp. 62f.

[53] Barth, "Die neue Welt in der Bibel," p. 34.

prefaces which stand out among the rest. The first way is in terms of *einlegen* or "reading in."

1. No Reading Out Without Reading In

One of the most radical statements of Barth's preface drafts to Rom I is: "Whoever does not continually 'read in' because he participates in the subject matter, cannot 'read out' either." [54] This maxim is repeated in preface drafts IA, II, and III, and it is clear that Barth knew how provocative his advocacy of it would be. He said: "I have consciously raised again the method which has long since been repudiated in theology of 'reading in' our own problems into the thought world of the Bible."[55] "In fact," he said, for this very reason "I know that this book is already scientifically done for even before it appears."[56] Among the reasons he cites for having done so is: "It could not be otherwise ... I from the beginning felt I was participating in it [the subject matter] much too strongly," and "heard Paul speaking directly *to us* so clearly." Barth claimed he simply had no alternative: "One can only *understand* that for which one *stands.*"[57] This is why he remarked in anticipation of his critics' scorn: "I, on the contrary, will readily accept the reproach that I have 'read in' *too little.*"[58] Later, in his preface to Rom II, he responded to the critics of Rom I: "The suspicion that here more is read in than is read out is really the most relevant thing they can say about my whole undertaking."[59]

Barth defended the practice of "reading in," or what is otherwise known as eisegesis, throughout his career.[60] But it should be underscored that in stating,

---

[54] Appendix 2, Preface Draft III, p. 288 (p. 596). See also Preface Drafts IA, p. 281 (p. 587) and II, p. 285 (p. 592).

[55] Appendix 2, Preface Draft III, p. 287 (p. 595).

[56] Appendix 2, Preface Draft III, pp. 287-288 (p. 595).

[57] Appendix 2, Preface Draft III, p. 288 (p. 596). "*Verstehen* kann man aber nur das, wozu man *steht.*"

[58] Appendix 2, Preface Draft IA, p. 282 (p. 588). See also Preface Draft II, p. 285 (p. 592).

[59] Rom II, p. xiii.

[60] "Exegesis is always a combination of taking and giving, of reading out and reading in. Thus exegesis, without which the norm cannot assert itself as a norm, entails the constant danger that the Bible will be taken prisoner by the Church, that its own life will be absorbed into the life of the Church, that its free power will be transformed into the authority of the Church, in short, that it will lose its character as a norm magisterially confronting the Church. All exegesis can become predominantly reading in rather than reading out and to that degree it can fall back into the Church's dialogue with itself. Nor will one banish the danger, but only conjure it up properly and make it acute, by making correct exposition dependent on the judgment of a definitive and decisive teaching office in the Church or on the judgment of a historico-critical scholarship which comports itself with equal infallibility. If we assume that one or other of these authorities is worthy of the Church's highest confidence, then either way the Church goes astray in respect of the Bible by thinking that in one way or the other it can and should control correct exposition, and thereby set up a norm over the norm, and thereby capture the true norm for itself. The exegesis of the Bible should rather be left open on all sides, not for the sake of

"Whoever does not continually 'read in' because he participates in the subject matter, cannot 'read out' either," Barth was neither endorsing "reading in" as the goal of exposition, nor was he suggesting, as some post-modernists, that *only* "reading in" is possible. He was simply stating the fact: "Exegesis is always a combination of taking and giving, of reading out and reading in."[61] As he later explained, "Our supposed listening is in truth a strange mixture of hearing and our own speaking, and, in accordance with the usual rule, it is most likely that our own speaking will be the really decisive event."[62] This is not to suggest that we never experience exceptions to this rule. On the contrary, despite all our eisegesis, despite all our hermeneutical devices to make a text speak, despite all our efforts to tell ourselves what we are to hear, there are occasions when, beyond all our attempts to grip, to subdue, and to master, we find *ourselves* really gripped, subdued, and mastered by a text's subject matter, though not by virtue of anything we might bring or do to the text, but by virtue of the fact that it makes itself heard beyond the mixture of our hearing, speaking, and interrupting. This is certainly so with respect to the Bible, and if with respect to the Bible, why not other texts as well?[63]

By emphasizing the role of *einlegen* in his *Römerbrief* period, Barth was seeking to call attention to the significance of our presuppositions. Even though by grace the reading in of our presuppositions may not always be the decisive event in our efforts to exegete a text, our exegesis is nevertheless always conditioned by them. As exegetes we ought to be aware of this. This is why acknowledging reading in as a legitimate and even necessary part of exegesis was so important to Barth. How else do we critique our presuppositions

---

free thought, as Liberalism would demand, but for the sake of a free Bible. Here as everywhere else the defense against possible violence to the text must be left to the text itself, which in fact has always succeeded in doing something a purely spiritual and oral tradition cannot do, namely, maintaining its own life against the encroachments of individual or total periods and tendencies in the Church, victoriously asserting this life in ever new developments, and thus creating recognition for itself as a norm." KD I/1:108-9; CD I/1:106.

[61] KD I/1:109; CD I/1:106. In the preface to the English edition of his *Römerbrief* Barth said: "No one can, of course, read anything out of a text without at the same time reading something into it. Moreover, no interpreter is rid of the danger of reading in more than he reads out. I neither was nor am free from this danger." Karl Barth, "Vorwort zur englischen Ausgabe der Römerbriefauslegung," in *Zwischen den Zeiten* (1932), p. 480; ET *The Epistle To The Romans*, trans. Edwyn C. Hoskyns (Oxford: University Press, 1933), p. ix [translation revised]. Hereafter cited "Vorwort zur englischen Ausgabe."

[62] KD I/2:520; CD I/2:470.

[63] This goes to the heart of Barth's theology of the Word and his understanding of the move from "special" to "general hermeneutics." There is not only a "Word within the words" of Scripture, but all words are mysteriously related to the Word, which means that apart from grace, apart from the fact that all words are contained and find their ultimate significance in the Word made flesh, all our exegesis is nothing but eisegesis. More shall be said about this in the following chapters. See especially KD I/2:521-522; CD I/2:471-472, cited on pp. 237-238.

apart from acknowledging them as such? More shall be said about this in the next two chapters. But this is not the primary reason why reading in was so important to Barth. The primary reason he "consciously raised again the method which has long since been repudiated in theology of 'reading in' our own problems into the thought world of the Bible" is because active participation requires it. However, this did not mean for Barth that interpreters may simply read in any presupposition or problem they please, which is why he later was very careful to stipulate that we must avoid "the sickness of an insolent and arbitrary reading in."[64] This brings us to a second way in which Barth describes active participation.

2. Like Through Like

In his preface drafts to Rom I, as well as in his exegesis of Rom.4:23-25 in Rom II (immediately following in the same paragraph cited earlier on pp.103-104), Barth quotes from Friedrich Nietzsche's essay, *"The Use and Abuse of History"*:

> You may only interpret the past out of the highest power of the present: only in the strongest efforts of your noblest qualities will you divinize what in the past is great, worth knowing and preserving. Like through like! Or else you will pull the past down to yourself! . . . It is the mature and preeminent man who writes history. He that has not passed through some greater and nobler experience than his contemporaries will be incapable of interpreting the greatness and nobility of the past. The voices of the past speak in oracles; and only the master of the present and the architect of the future can hope to decipher their meaning.[65]

In citing Nietzsche's claim that one "may only interpret the past out of the highest power of the present . . .," Barth was merely saying in others words what he had said in his *"Die neue Welt in der Bibel"* essay of 1917: "The Bible gives to everyone and every age only such answers to their questions as they deserve: high and divine content if it is high and divine content that they seek; transitory and 'historical' content, if it is transitory and 'historical' content that they seek – nothing whatsoever if it is nothing whatsoever that they seek."[66] Barth agreed with Nietzsche that only in the highest vitalities and most fervent passions of the present can one hope to recognize "what in the past is great,

---

[64] KD I/2:521; CD I/2:470.

[65] Friedrich Nietzsche, Unzeitgemäße Betrachtungen, II. Vom Nutzen und Nachteil der Historie, in: *Werk* I (München: Carl Hanser Verlag, 1954), p. 250. Appendix 2, Preface Drafts IA, pp. 281-282 and II, p. 285. As it turned out, however, rather than these, Barth chose instead to include the milder, less provocative lines of Goethe: "Since long ago the True was found/ a group of noble men it bound/ Hold fast then – that ancient Truth!" The impression made upon readers by the latter quotation was, apparently, so innocuous that its lines are among the few from the final preface that go entirely unmentioned by reviewers. It is difficult to imagine that this would have been the case *had* Barth cited these lines from Nietzsche.

[66] Barth, "Die neue Welt in der Bibel," p. 20.

worth knowing and preserving." He agreed with Nietzsche that history is something done in the present, not in the past. It is only in the strength of one's most intense experiences and affections, only out of the deepest convictions and insights of the present, that one can hope to recognize the significance of the past. The difference, for Barth, was that God was "the highest power of the present." Only in God, only in faith, only in the power of the Holy Spirit can one know what is truly great and worth knowing in the Bible. Another book may require different vitalities, different passions, but the hermeneutical principle remains the same: "Like through like!" One can only take from a book that which one is ready to receive. One can only hear that for which one has "ears to hear."[67] In his review of Rom I, Jülicher accused Barth of having a privileged hermeneutic, that "the understanding of the Bible is restricted to the citizens of a new world."[68] Barth responded in his preface to Rom II: "I consider the view that today the most important thing is ... to think, and above all to say and write, something anyone can understand to be a thoroughly hysterical and rash view."[69] Actually, as suggested earlier, Barth had already anticipated this criticism, which is why he asked rhetorically in his preface drafts to Rom I: "What kind of reader did I have in mind as I wrote? I say, the same as Paul himself had in mind, namely, everyone who is in any way moved by the same matter which the *Römerbrief* is all about."[70]

Thus for Barth understanding the Bible or any other text has to do with bringing the right presuppositions to the task of interpretation, that is, presuppositions appropriate to the text's subject matter. It is dependent on a "living context which ... is *given* in the subject matter and in which one must *be*."[71] Far from any unprejudiced approach of a spectator it is only in the power of a participant's prejudice that one can know what is important in the past.[72] Far from any non-participatory distancing of oneself, interpretation requires the most intense form of participation and personal engagement. Far from taking up a position of disinterested neutrality or non-partisanship, it requires quite the

---

[67] "He who has ears to hear, let him hear!" is how Barth understands Nietzsche's phrase, "Like through like!" Appendix 2, Preface Drafts IA, p. 282 (p. 588) and III, p. 290 (p. 598).

[68] Jülicher, *Anfänge*, p. 94; ET p. 78.

[69] Rom II, p. ix.

[70] Appendix 2, Preface Draft IA, p. 279 (p. 584) and Preface Draft II, p. 285 (p. 592).

[71] Appendix 2, Preface Draft IA, p. 281 (p. 587).

[72] This is not to equate prejudice with faith. The point is that we can never fully transcend our prejudices or think they are unimportant. Barth is clearly aware of this in his Römerbrief period. But the importance of 'productive' (my word, not his) prejudices or authorities in Barth's thought seems to have grown as his hermeneutical circle widened after his Römerbrief period to include the church, viz., the church's confessions and fathers. As he later said: "No one has ever read the Bible only with his own eyes and no one ever should. The only question is what interpreters we allow and in what order we let them speak." KD I/2:728; CD I/2:649. See also Karl Barth, *Die christliche Dogmatik*, pp. 522-525 and *Unterricht*, pp. 288f.; ET pp. 237f.; pp. 314f. ET pp. 257f.

opposite. As Barth later said, "Neutrality is really a decision of unbelief."[73] This is what the dominant science of biblical exegesis had failed in his view to understand. It had approached the task of interpretation in general and historical interpretation in particular as a 'science' in the sense of a procedure requiring the cool and detached objectivity of an observer. It demanded that interpreters gain 'critical distance.' Barth rejected this demand.[74] So did Nietzsche, which is one reason why, throughout his essay, "The Use and Abuse of History," he scorns the notion of history as a science. Barth echoes some of the same concerns throughout his *Römerbrief* period, though he never goes so far as to reject the notion of history as a science. Instead throughout this period he repeatedly refers to the interpretation of history, as well as to the task of interpretation as a whole, as an "art."[75] In one preface draft he says: "The same relationship stands between a book and its reader as between a work of art and its beholder [*Beschauer*]: it is not only what the author is able and wants to make it, but just as much so what the reader is able and wants to take from it."[76] In making this claim Barth was not granting any autonomy or privilege to readers of the present nor was he saying that we can make the Bible say anything we want. He was merely pointing out the fact that what we as readers bring to a text is significant. There is no reading out without reading in. What we bring to a text has a great deal to do with what we get out of it. "Like through like!" This is so not only with respect to the Bible, but all great literature. We find in it only what we seek.

Those committed to the dominant science of biblical exegesis, in Barth's view, had seldom sought very much from the Bible; therefore it was hardly surprising that they rarely found much. What they typically found in Barth's

---

[73] Karl Barth, "Die Souveränität des Wortes Gottes und die Entscheidung des Glaubens," *Theologische Studien* 5, Zollikon-Zürich (1939), p. 18.

[74] This is one reason why Barth's hermeneutic can hardly be described in terms of a "second naiveté" (See Mark I. Wallace, *The Second Naiveté: Barth, Ricoeur, and the New Yale Theology* [Macon, GA: Mercer University Press, 1990].) It is not a *second* naiveté (as distinguished from a first) because it does not follow upon any "critical distance" (Ricoeur) or process of "distanciation," (David Tracy, *The Analogical Imagination* (New York: Crossroad, 1991), pp.127f.) achieved by the interpreter. Barth says nothing of an intermediate stage or moment of objectifying detachment or disengagement with respect to the Bible's subject matter. Rather than a "second naiveté" (Ricoeur) or even "new naiveté" (Jüngel), Barth refers to his own approach in terms of a "tested, critical naiveté!" (*geprüfter, kritischer Naivität!*) (KD IV/2:542; CD IV/2:479). This specific phrase maintains the dialectic between "the Word and the words" which these and other phrases such as 'pre-critical' or 'post-critical' do not. See Rudolf Smend, "Nachkritische Schriftauslegung," *Parrhesia* (Zürich: Evangelischer Verlag Zürich, 1966), pp. 215f. More shall be said about the critical aspect of Barth's hermeneutic in chapter five.

[75] Appendix 2, Preface Draft II, pp. 284-285 (p. 591) and Preface Draft III, p. 288 (p. 596).

[76] Appendix 2, Preface Draft II, p. 286 (p. 594). Regarding his own book, Barth adds: "The worth or worthlessness of this book will depend on them as well."

estimation was relatively trivial. While they saw themselves as penetrating deeply into the text – into its deep 'historical' marrow – to Barth they were still preoccupied merely with matters of the surface. The problem as he saw it was that they refused to participate in the subject matter of the Bible, or at least what they considered to be participation was passive not active participation. They were content merely to take up the position of a *Zuschauer*, i.e., an observer, a spectator, or bystander, rather than a *Beschauer*, i.e., a beholder. To approach the task of interpretation as a *Beschauer* rather than as a *Zuschauer*, Barth realized, required a much deeper level of involvement than the dominant science of biblical exegesis was prepared to offer. Dilthey had realized this as well, which is why he reminded his contemporaries, as previously cited: "Understanding has various degrees. These are determined first of all by interest. If our interest is limited, so also is our understanding." Both Schleiermacher and Dilthey had long since realized the limits of historical interest as well as the vast complexity of historical understanding. They realized how naive so many of their contemporaries were in claiming to approach texts like the Bible in the name of "pure" historical interest. Mere grammatical and historical interest they recognized simply could not do justice to most ancient texts, not least of all, the Bible. More was required. This is why Dilthey and Schleiermacher had been so deeply committed to broadening the field of interpretation beyond grammatical and comparative (historical) interpretation. They recognized that psychological and divinatory interpretation was also needed. But whether a *balanced* psychological and grammatical, comparative and divinatory approach was sufficient in Barth's view to interpret the Bible (and many other texts, for that matter) is the question we shall consider in the next chapter. But first it is necessary to consider Barth's most famous description of active participation.

3. Until I Almost Forget That I Am Not the Author . . .

The most provocative hermeneutical statement in all Barth's *Römerbrief* prefaces is undoubtedly the one made in his preface to Rom II. To appreciate its significance, some background is necessary. Barth, as I have said, had been severely scolded by reviewers of Rom I for not having taken the actual context of Paul's *Epistle to the Romans* seriously enough. They claimed he had not done justice to the real, historical Paul. Instead he had "read in" his own situation such that many concluded Barth's commentary said more about him than it did about Paul. No one argued this point more vigorously than Jülicher. He accused Barth of having the "holy egoism" of one who "thinks only of his own problems" and added: "He believes he has placed himself on the side of Paul, while we others are content merely to observe him. He does not want to notice that he often enough places himself ahead of Paul. ..."[77] Jülicher claimed Barth

---

[77] Jülicher, *Anfänge*, p. 97; ET p. 80

had approached the exegesis of Paul exactly as Marcion had: "[Marcion] proceeded with the same sovereign arbitrariness and assurance of victory, with the same one-sided dualistic approach of enmity to all that comes from the world, culture, or tradition, and never tired of tossing a few pet ideas in front of us. And this has the same effect – that when we give ourselves to these tones without interruption we finally hear only them and nothing else."[78]

It is hardly surprising therefore that among all his critics Barth saved some of his sharpest words of rebuttal for Jülicher, though already in one preface draft to Rom I, Barth had said that he was forced to "directly advance the assertion that the 'uncritical' works of a Calvin or J.T. Beck are more *concerned with the subject matter [sachgemäßer]* than, for example, those of Jülicher or Lietzmann."[79] Jülicher had twice commented on Barth's reliance on Calvin in his review of Rom I. So Barth responded in his preface to Rom II by juxtaposing Jülicher's approach to exegesis with Calvin's:

> Compare Jülicher, for example, with Calvin. How energetically the latter goes to work after he has conscientiously established "what is there" to think the thoughts of the text after it, that is, to come to terms with it until the wall between the first and sixteenth centuries becomes transparent, until Paul speaks there and the man of the sixteenth century hears here, until the conversation between document and reader is concentrated entirely on the *subject matter* (which *cannot* be different here and there!). Truly, anyone who thinks he can eliminate Calvin's method with the cliché, now so well worn, about the "restriction of the doctrine of inspiration," proves only that in *this* direction he has not yet really *worked* at all. Conversely, how near Jülicher (I mention him only as an example!) stays to the runic symbols of the words, as little understood afterward as before; how quickly he is ready to credit to some singular view and teaching of Paul this and that exegetical raw material, scarcely touched by any scholarly reflection as to the meaning; how quickly ready, by means of a few rather banal categories of his own religious thought (feeling, experience, conscience, conviction), to have *already* understood and explained him then and there; but how quickly he is ready, if all this cannot be done in the twinkling of an eye, to save himself from the Pauline ship with a clever leap, and to ascribe responsibility for the meaning of the text to the "personality" of Paul, to the "Damascus experience" (which evidently can explain the most incredible things), to Late Judaism, to Hellenism, to the ancient world in general, and to some other demigods.[80]

This is a significant passage and one to which I shall soon return, but for now the main thing is to note the contrast Barth draws between these two approaches. Calvin's approach is characterized in terms of patience, whereas Jülicher's is characterized in terms of haste. Three times Barth speaks of Calvin waiting "until ...": "until the wall between first and sixteenth centuries becomes transparent, until Paul speaks there and the man of the sixteenth century hears here, until the conversation between document and reader is concentrated entirely on the *subject matter* ..." whereas three times Barth says of Jülicher:

---

[78] Jülicher, *Anfänge*, p. 95; ET p. 78.
[79] Appendix 2, Preface III, p. 288 (p. 596).
[80] Rom II, p. xi.

"how quickly ready" he is to do otherwise. Calvin works "energetically" to really think the thoughts of the text after it, whereas Jülicher shows "he has not yet really *worked* in this direction at all." Calvin is interested in hearing Paul both then and now, here and there, whereas Jülicher seems interested in hearing Paul only then and there. But the main difference Barth suggests is that whereas Calvin seeks conscientiously and painstakingly to focus on the subject matter, Jülicher does not. Whereas Calvin works patiently "until the conversation between document and reader is concentrated entirely on the *subject matter*," Jülicher is easily distracted. Instead of focusing on the subject matter he ends up arbitrarily reducing the meaning of Paul's words to historical or psychological banalities. Instead of following through with the task, instead of being conscientiously committed to thinking the thoughts of the text after, it come what may, he is ready "in the twinkling of an eye, to save himself," to, as it were, abandon "the Pauline ship." This, as Barth saw it, was the major difference between Calvin's approach and Jülicher's, and not merely between their approaches but between his own and that of the dominant science of biblical exegesis.

But Barth was not content merely to point out the differences between his approach and that of the dominant science of exegesis by juxtaposing Calvin and Jülicher. He also realized more needed to be said about his *own* approach. Thus in the next paragraph he stated some of his most important hermeneutical convictions, and among them his most provocative claim in all his *Römerbrief* prefaces:

> In contrast to all this, I intend now for this first primitive attempt at paraphrase and what belongs with it to constitute only the starting point for a dialectic movement as inexorable as it is elastic, using all the crowbars and wrecking tools needed to achieve *relevant* treatment of the text. The historical critics must be *more critical* to suit me! For how "what is there" is to be understood cannot be established by an appreciation of the words and phrases of the text, strewn in from time to time from some fortuitous standpoint of the exegete, but only through an entering, as freely and eagerly as practicable, into the inner tension of the concepts presented by the text with more or less clarity. Krinein[81] means for me, in reference to a historical document, the measuring of all the words and phrases contained in it by the matter of which it, unless everything is deceptive, is clearly speaking, and the relating to the questions it unmistakably poses all the answers given, and relating these again to the cardinal question, which contains all questions, the question of the meaning of everything that it says in the light of "all that can be said," and therefore really "all that is said." As little as possible should be left over of those blocks of merely historical, merely given, merely accidental concepts; as far as possible the connection of the words to the Word in the words must be disclosed. As one who would understand, I must press forward to the point where insofar as possible I confront the riddle of the *subject matter* and no longer merely the riddle of the *document* as such, until I can almost forget that I am not the author, until I have almost understood him so well that I let him speak in my name, and can

---

[81] Though the word 'critical' derives etymologically from the Greek word *krinein*, the latter, Barth no doubt recognized, had a much broader connotation, viz., 'to judge' or 'to discern.'

myself speak in his name. I know that these sentences will bring me another severe reprimand but I cannot help myself. What then do we call "understanding" and "explanation" – has Lietzmann, for example, ever seriously asked himself this question – when one scarcely makes the slightest attempt to at least concern oneself in this direction (I too can do no more than this), but rather, in contrast to so much astonishing diligence in another direction, takes no pains, is content with the most meager results, and sees in this the triumph of a true scientific attitude?[82]

Though echoing many of the very concerns he had raised in his early preface drafts to Rom I, the above paragraph was Barth's first really substantive, public elaboration of his own hermeneutical principles. And apart from the claim, "The historical critics must be *more critical* to suit me!," the sentence which stood out most was: "As one who would understand, I must press forward to the point where insofar as possible I confront the riddle of the *subject matter* and no longer merely the riddle of the *document* as such, until I can almost forget that I am not the author, until I have almost understood him so well that I let him speak in my name, and can myself speak in his name." Of the various ways Barth tried to describe the active participation required of interpreters, this was by far the most radical. Having been roundly criticized for having read into Paul his own thoughts, for having said more about himself than about Paul, Barth apparently decided he would respond to his critics by upping the ante, so to speak, by driving his point about active participation home even deeper. Not only would he admit that he had read his own concerns into Paul's *Epistle to the Romans*, he would claim: "I can almost forget that I am not the author"; not only that he had come to an understanding of Paul, but "I have almost understood him so well that I let him speak in my name, and can myself speak in his name."

It is interesting that Rudolf Bultmann quoted this very sentence at the conclusion of his 1922 review of Rom II which appeared in *Die christliche Welt* and hailed it as "the high point of exegetical understanding"[83] (interesting because in 1920 he had referred to Rom I as the product of "enthusiastic revivalism").[84] Bultmann's endorsement, however, was exceptional, for while he hailed it, the vast majority of reviewers assailed it. They claimed it attained to the heights of hermeneutical "hubris."[85] Barth knew, of course, that it would draw fire. This is why he said: "I know that these sentences will bring me another severe reprimand." But it is difficult to imagine that he could have known how much furor this single statement would ignite.

In his review of Rom II, Jülicher focused in on this sentence and said: "The thing that makes Barth's book so dangerous, in my opinion, ... is the claim

---

[82] Rom II, pp. xi-xii.
[83] Rudolf Bultmann, "Karl Barths 'Römerbrief' in zweiter Auflage" in *Die christliche Welt*, 36:21 (1920), p. 372.
[84] See p. 16 above.
[85] Jülicher, "Der Römerbrief" in *Theologische Literaturzeitung* 47:25 (1922), p. 542.

Entering into the Meaning of the Bible 121

made by its author to speak in Paul's name. ... This combination of pernicious sensitivity and outrageous self-confidence which meets us here, and the host of self-commendations which are poured upon us, has an embarrassing effect. ... [Barth] claims unequivocally to understand the *spirit* of Paul and to make the wall between him and modern people transparent."[86] As he had in his review of Rom I, Jülicher again accused Barth of being a "pneumatic." But this time his verdict was: "In presuming this spiritual possession [*Geistesbesitz*] ... I see the evidence of a disturbed disposition."[87] Other reviewers were not as severe as Jülicher but were similarly disparaging. Julius Boehmer suggested it was merely a homiletical sort of claim.[88] Kurt Deißner, professor of New Testament in Greifswald, said although it sounded very "impressive," Barth's claim about forgetting that he was not the author, speaking in Paul's name, etc. only raised "the fundamental question: how, and in what manner does this wall become 'transparent' so that we modern people can really hear Paul speak to us, so that we can see him and learn to understand him?" Deißner claimed that in his opinion Barth's approach did "not lead us to historical *reality*."[89] As a member of the dominant science of biblical exegesis, he argued instead for a more objective approach. While granting the limitations of such an approach, he insisted:

> I certainly know that it is only an ideal, that it will never work out in our scientific work that we turn off our own voice completely, to the degree that the knowledge we gain is no longer clouded by our subjectivity. But the attempt must nevertheless be made, with all vigor, with all the available means of historical research, of comparative religious studies, of psychology, etc., so that men of faith from the past become so alive that the light comes from *them*. Then they will not merely remain men of 'history' for us, but through the *analogia fidei*, the inner contact will begin by itself.

In the end, Deißner said Barth's stated goal, to "almost forget that I am not the author ...," weighed against its actual results forced him to ask: "Is it truly the light of Paul and his world of thought that shines to us from Barth's *Römerbrief* or is it not much more Barth's own world of faith we come to know here ... such that we actually hear Barth through Paul rather than the true Paul through Barth?"[90] Others echoed this same charge. Hermann Strathmann, professor of New Testament at Erlangen, appreciated Barth's concern to speak in Paul's name (as did others),[91] but the result, he claimed, was as so many reviewers of

---

[86] Jülicher, "Der Römerbrief" in *Theologische Literaturzeitung*, p. 539.
[87] Jülicher, "Der Römerbrief" in *Theologische Literaturzeitung*, pp. 539-540.
[88] Julius Boehmer, *Die Studierstube: kirchlich-theologische Monatsschrift* 20 (1922), pp. 146-149.
[89] Kurt Deißner, *Die Theologie der Gegenwart* 16 (1922), p. 270.
[90] Kurt Deißner, *Die Theologie der Gegenwart*, p. 271.
[91] Konrad Hoffmann, "Karl Barths Römerbrief in zweiter Auflage" in *Kirchlicher Anzeiger für Württemberg: Organ des Evangelischen Pfarrvereins* 31, 1922, pp. 129-130; Joseph Wittig,

Rom I had said: Barth's exegesis has more to do with the interpreter than the one allegedly interpreted, namely, Paul.[92]

Yet it was Adolf Schlatter, the great Tübingen master – Barth's former teacher whom his father had insisted he study under during the winter semester of 1907/8[93] – who focused almost exclusively in his review of Rom II on Barth's way of relating to Paul (or at least his way of *claiming* to relate to Paul). Schlatter began his review questioning whether it was even appropriate for us to think of Paul primarily as an "author" and we his "readers."[94] But his deeper concern was:

> In contrast to those commentaries which offer only preparatory helps to understanding, Barth conceives of the work of the exegete as the responsibility for repeating the word of Paul to himself and his readers in such a way that it becomes a component part of their own inner being. Barth seeks to achieve this by bringing the Pauline word out of the situation in which it arose. The exegete is not to repeat once more a word directed to men who were once alive, but the word should encounter us free from all restrictions of time, and loosed from all historical conditions, "vertically from above" ... Therefore the *Epistle to the Romans* is for Barth a timeless, entirely modern, entirely contemporary word. All that is human, all that is historical, sinks away. What is Rome, what is the early Roman Christian community, what is Paul? Nothing that should keep our eyes from God. ... By this, Barth joins the long list of exegetes of the early church and the Reformation who read the *Epistle to the Romans* under the domination of the then-current theory of inspiration. This theory affirmed that God speaks here; therefore let man sink from sight! Because, however, he cannot entirely disappear, everything that belonged to the history of a New Testament document stood in the old commentaries only in the "introduction," only in the foreword. After such matters are quickly dealt with as mere preparatory knowledge, the real work of the exegete begins; now God speaks to him.

"Neue religiöse Bücher" in *Hochland: Monatsschrift für alle Gebiete des Wissens, der Literatur und Kunst* 21 (1923/24), p. 420, et al.

[92] Hermann Strathmann, "Karl Barths Römerbriefkommentar" in *Die Theologie der Gegenwart* 17 (1923), pp. 261-262.

[93] Fritz Barth had succeeded Schlatter at Bern in 1889. Having been forced to attend Tübingen in the winter semester of 1907/08 "by the stricter compulsion" of his father, Barth the younger later said, he had "listened to Schlatter with fiercest obstinacy." See Barth, "Autobiographische Skizze" (Münster), p. 294.

[94] Schlatter's review begins: "'The author to the readers.' These are the words which Barth placed over Romans 1:1-7. These words repulse anyone who has learned to know Paul. Paul an 'author' who had nothing but 'readers' in mind – but how were things done in those days? ... Does it have no consequences for the reproduction of the letter if the apostle is turned into an 'author' and the community that listens to him into 'readers'?" ... This apparently incidental little heading is a product of Barth's intention which supports his entire undertaking and which created the total material of his extensive book." Adolf Schlatter, "Karl Barths 'Römerbrief'" in *Die Furche* 12 (1922), pp. 228-232. Also contained in Jürgen Moltmann, ed. *Anfänge der dialektischen Theologie* I (Munich: Christian Kaiser, Verlag, 1962), pp. 142-147; ET "Karl Barth's Epistle To The Romans," *The Beginnings of Dialectical Theology*, trans. Keith R. Crim, ed. James M. Robinson, (Richmond, VA: John Knox Press, 1968), pp. 121-125. Hereafter cited as Schlatter, *Anfänge*.

So what then, according to Schlatter, did Barth actually exegete? Schlatter said: "He becomes the exegete of his own life and the interpreter of his own heart; it is done not by placing before us what is his own, for that would be the refutation of the *Epistle to the Romans* ... but it is done by his own life situation and that of his contemporaries providing the content of the Pauline words which would otherwise remain empty."[95] To Schlatter, Barth had become a thoroughgoing subjectivist. Not only did he completely ignore the concerns of the Christian community to which Paul wrote, he believed "The exegete of the divine Word should not be a historian, because the historian allegedly speaks only human words." This was, of course, reprehensible. To Schlatter, "the struggle of Paul with Greeks and Jews belongs to the deepest and most exciting of all human events and forms an achievement that is worthy of our attention in the highest degree." Yet Barth had said nothing about this. "We hear nothing of the Greek religion and its devastating effects, of the synagogue and its religious failure, of the law, which at that time ordered by its very concrete norms the conduct of all who looked to God." Instead, "You, the reader, are the Greek; you are also the Jew; and your sole concern must be that the word of Paul reaches you and shows you the divine wrath, which sinks you with all your piety into nothingness. But are we still hearing Paul when the Greek and the Jew have disappeared from the *Epistle to the Romans*?" Schlatter's answer was emphatically no! With Barth, "the *Epistle to the Romans* ceases to be an epistle to the Romans." Ironically, this was the same Schlatter whose approach, along with that of other more recent exegetes such as J.T. Beck, Godet, and Hoffmann, Barth had praised in his preface to Rom II as exemplary.[96]

Barth's statement – "As one who would understand, I must press forward to the point where insofar as possible I confront the riddle of the *subject matter* and no longer merely the riddle of the *document* as such, until I can almost forget that I am not the author, until I have almost understood him so well that I let him speak in my name, and can myself speak in his name" – made a deep and lasting impression on readers. It was this statement which was repeated again and again not only by reviewers of Rom II, but throughout the pneumatic exegesis movement of the mid to late 1920s.[97] Though many have recognized the significance of this statement,[98] relatively little has been written about it,

---

[95] Schlatter, *Anfänge*, p. 144; ET p. 122.

[96] Rom II, p. xi. As critical as Schlatter was of Rom II, it did not prevent him from maintaining a very warm and cordial correspondence with his former pupil until a year or so before his death on May 19, 1938. See "Adolf Schlatter/Karl Barth: Ein Briefwechsel" in *Theologische Beiträge* 17 (1986), pp. 96-100.

[97] Erich Fascher, *Vom Verstehen des Neuen Testamentes: Ein Beitrag zur Grundlegung einer zeitgemäßen Hermeneutik*, pp. 33f.

[98] Eberhard Jüngel, *Barth-Studien*, p. 91f.; Karl Lehmann, "Der hermeneutische Horizont der historisch-kritischen Exegese" in idem, *Einführung in die Methoden der biblischen Exegese*, ed. Josef Schreiner (Würzburg: Echter Verlag, 1971), p. 50; R.S. Barbour, "Karl Barth:

even though Barth continued to defend it throughout the 1920s and 1930s. Some have suggested that it reflects not only Barth's basic 'pneumatic' orientation, but also his indebtedness to the hermeneutical tradition of Schleiermacher and Dilthey.[99] Even Barth's own student, Georg Eichholz, immediately after quoting this famous line in his essay "Der Ansatz Karl Barths in der Hermeneutik," asked, "Do not such words make Karl Barth into a student of Schleiermacher and Dilthey?"[100]

As far as I am aware, no one in the 1920s except for Rudolf Bultmann[101] tried to make this connection between Barth and the hermeneutical tradition of Schleiermacher and Dilthey, though this is hardly surprising given what Barth had said both directly and indirectly about Schleiermacher in Rom II. (Konrad Hoffmann probably expressed the sentiments of many when he said in his 1922 review of Rom II: "For anyone who comes from the direction of Schleiermacher, this takes one's breath away.")[102] But if Barth was seeking to overcome the hermeneutical tradition of Schleiermacher and Dilthey in his *Römerbrief* period, as I have suggested, it is a very interesting question. Is there a connection between the hermeneutical tradition of Schleiermacher and Dilthey and Barth's hermeneutic? This is a question I shall seek to answer in the next chapter as I elaborate yet another hermeneutical principle of Barth's *Römerbrief* period.

The Epistle to the Romans," *The Expository Times* 88 (1979), p. 267; Michael Lafargue, "Are Texts Determinate?: Derrida, Barth, and the Role of the Biblical Scholar," *The Harvard Theological Review* 81 (1988), pp. 356f. et al.

[99] H. Jackson Forstmann stated in his essay, "Barth, Schleiermacher and *The Christian Faith*" in *Union Seminary Quarterly Review* 21:3, March, 1966, "As heroically as Barth attempts a Diltheyan *Mitleben* he does not finally manage it because of his own fixed ideas about what Christian theology must be" p. 306. Roy A. Harrisville associates Barth's statement with "Dilthey, Schleiermacher, Bengel, Luther," *et al*, in his essay, "Karl Barth and the Römerbrief" in *Dialog: A Journal of Theology* 28 (1989), p. 281.

[100] Georg Eichholz, "Der Ansatz Karl Barths in der Hermeneutik" in *Antwort: Karl Barth zum siebzigsten Geburtstag*, ed. Rudolf Frey, et al (Zürich: Evangelischer Verlag Zürich, 1956), p. 67.

[101] In what appears to be a reference to a prior conversation over Barth's approach, Bultmann states in a letter with respect to the preface to the third edition of the Römerbrief, "But if 'with him' does not mean in psychological empathy with [im Sinn der psychologischen Einfühlung] but under the guidance of the subject matter itself, this might mean not only tacitly or explicitly elongating or shortening the lines drawn in a specific text (p. xxiii) but also correcting them" Rudolf Bultmann-Karl Barth, B-B Br. 31 December, 1922, p. 14; ET p. 4 [translation revised]. See pp. 194-195 below.

[102] Konrad Hoffmann, p. 129.

Chapter 5

With More Attention and Love

In addition to a reading which is "*sachlicher, inhaltlicher, wesentlicher*" and beyond his insistence upon an approach which "enters into" the meaning of the Bible, Barth insists in his first preface draft to Rom I upon a reading which enters into the meaning of the Bible "with more attention and love" (*mit mehr Aufmerksamkeit und Liebe*).[1] At first, the words "more attention and love" might appear only as a passing phrase or simply an off-hand remark expressing a vague or pious sentiment about the way interpretation should be done. Reading on, however, one discovers there is more at stake in this phrase than first meets the eye; for when summarizing the differences between his and the prevailing approach to biblical exegesis, Barth concludes the final sentence of his first preface draft stating that it is, by contrast, the approach taken by "the present, scientific trade of theology which we perceive today as, in the end, *inattentive* and *loveless* with regard to the meaning of the Bible." What was at issue in Barth's call for a more attentive and loving approach to interpretation, and how is it reflected in his *Römerbrief* period? This is the question I shall address in this chapter.

A. *With* or *About* the Author

According to Barth's *Römerbrief* prefaces and especially his early preface drafts to Rom I, the primary difference between a more attentive and loving approach to interpretation and an inattentive and loveless approach is the difference between standing with the author throughout the process of interpretation or not standing with the author. As cited earlier from his preface drafts to Rom I, Barth characterized "the chasm" between his approach to interpretation and that of the dominant science of biblical exegesis of the day as follows:

> Here I am forced to indicate with a few sentences the chasm which separates me from the method of today's dominant science of biblical exegesis. To understand an author means for me mainly to *stand with him*, to take each of his words in earnest, so long as it is not proven otherwise that he does not deserve this trust, to participate with him in the subject matter, in order to interpret him from the inside out. But today's theology does not stand with the prophets and the apostles; it does not side with them but rather with the modern

---

[1] Appendix 2, Preface Draft I, p. 277 (p. 582).

reader and his prejudices; it does not take the prophets and apostles in earnest, but while it stands smiling sympathetically beside them or above them, it takes a cool and indifferent distance from them; it critically or merrily examines the historical-psychological surface and misses its meaning. That is what I have against it.[2]

According to Barth's statement above, standing with an author means, first and foremost, taking "each of his words in earnest." It means not only thinking one's thoughts after the author (*nachdenken*), but thinking one's thoughts with the author (*mitdenken*).[3] It means not merely standing "smiling sympathetically beside" an author, but really standing "on his side" and looking in the direction where his words point. Above all, it means *participating with* the author in the subject matter. In the previous chapter I discussed the importance of active participation in the subject matter. In this chapter it shall be necessary to emphasize that such participation involves a specific kind of relationship with the author, namely, a relationship of love and trust. As participating in the subject matter of a text is not a matter of taking up the detached, passive involvement of a spectator, so participation with an author in the subject matter is not a matter of taking up a "cool and indifferent distance" from the author. It too is a matter of active participation and involvement. Yet active participation and involvement with an author is not a matter of approaching the author as a *source*, but as a *sign*, not as an *object* to be observed for his or her own sake, but as a *witness*. This is a distinction that is crucial for understanding Barth's hermeneutics. More shall be said about it and about what it means to stand with an author and "to take each of his words in earnest, so long as it is not proven that he does not deserve this trust" in a moment. But for now it is important to consider the alternative.

The alternative to standing and thinking *with* an author, as Barth says in his *Römerbrief* prefaces, is to think *about* an author. To think or write *about* an author is to think or write about the author's context, i.e., his historical environment, his sociological, cultural, political milieu, his psychologically reconstructed *Sitz im Leben*. To think or write about an author, in other words, is to think or write about all the various factors and circumstances which may or may not have influenced or shaped the author as a historically conditioned human being. Barth, it must be emphasized, was not opposed as an interpreter to thinking or writing about the author as a historically conditioned human being. On the contrary, he saw it as helpful and even necessary. Nevertheless, his problem with thinking or writing about an author as such was that this was still not to do justice to the author *as an author*. It was still not to think or write in terms of that which actually makes an author an author, namely, the author's

---

[2] Appendix 2, Preface Draft IA, p. 281 (p. 587). A similar statement appears in Preface Draft II, p. 284 (p. 591).

[3] Barth later put it explicitly: "Thinking *after* means thinking *with*." *Unterricht*, p. 309; ET p.253.

words. The primary task of the interpreter, in Barth's view, was not to interpret the *author* but to interpret the author's *words* in light of the subject matter to which they bear witness. That interpreting the former had become a substitute for the latter Barth saw as one of the most serious problems of his day.[4] It represented part of the chasm which separated his approach to exegesis from that of the dominant science of biblical exegesis. This is reflected to a greater or lesser degree in all of Barth's *Römerbief* prefaces, but nowhere more emphatically than in his early preface drafts to Rom I. In Preface Drafts IA and II, Barth states:

> The second request is that one should not seek in this book what is not intentionally stated there – especially all that which I would summarize as '*antiquarian*.' Whoever, for instance, wants to be informed about the little one knows and the great amount one does not know about Paul's 'personality,' about the members and the character of the Roman, Christian church, about Pauline formulas in the context of the history of religions, or about the questions of authenticity which become particularly acute at the end of the letter, will be disappointed here. I have dared confidently to be quiet about these matters, for as interesting as they are, they are not really important questions for understanding the text itself, questions which can be and should be considered, but their discussion should by no means, as has occurred, replace explication itself. ... Whoever insists upon knowing *about* Paul and his letter, will find according to need, direction and taste better things than I could ever write in B. Weiß, Godet, Lipsius, Jülicher, Lietzmann and Th. Zahn. I think I have offered instead a few things *from* Paul which are *not* found in them.[5]

As Barth saw it, his contemporaries had become increasingly interested in writing about *Paul* rather than about *what* Paul wrote about. Again, it must be emphasized, it was not that Barth did not find Paul the man, Paul the historically conditioned, psychologically reconstructed individual, an 'interesting' topic. No, questions about Paul's location and environment, his place in the history of religions, his identity as a religious 'personality,' etc., he said, were "questions which can be and should be considered." Still, these were "not really important questions for understanding the text itself" and "their discussion should by no means, as has occurred, replace explication itself." This is a rather serious charge Barth makes against the state of biblical exegesis of his day; and before going further, it is important to ask whether or to what extent this was really the case. Is it true that members of the dominant science of biblical exegesis were more interested in knowing and writing about *Paul* than about *what* Paul wrote about? Is it true that biblical scholars and theologians tended to be more interested in Paul's identity as a religious personality than in his message as an apostle, and that explication of the former had begun to replace explication of the latter? One need not look far to find evidence that supports Barth's claim.

---

[4] Barth describes part of the crisis of his day in Rom II as one in which "The signpost has become meaningless." Rom II, p. 49. I shall discuss this issue at length in the next chapter.

[5] Appendix 2, Preface Draft II, pp. 282-283 (pp. 589-590).

Paul Wernle, whom I referred to earlier as the "most distinguished Swiss reviewer of Rom I," provides an excellent case in point.

B. The Historical-Psychological Approach of Paul Wernle

Paul Wernle was by far the most influential voice on the Swiss theological scene throughout the first two decades of the twentieth century. Having received his doctorate in 1897 from Basel at the age of twenty-five, he was appointed to its faculty as professor of New Testament in 1900 and as professor of church history and the history of dogma in 1901. Publishing several books in the fields of New Testament, church history, and theology which were regarded as at the vanguard of modern scholarship, he quickly distinguished himself at the turn of the century as both an internationally known scholar and a widely respected churchman. Wernle's greatest work was his massive *Einführung in das theologische Studium* (1908, 1911, and 1921) which was widely used as a textbook in universities throughout Switzerland and Germany.[6] This book is important not only because it introduced the discipline of theology, including Old and New Testament studies, church history, ethics, and practical theology, to literally thousands of students in the early decades of the twentieth century, but also because it provides insight into some of the most pervasive hermeneutical principles in the period immediately preceding Rom I.[7]

---

[6] Paul Wernle, *Einführung in das Theologische Studium* (Tübingen: J.C.B. Mohr [Paul Siebeck], 1908, 1911, 1921). Hereafter cited as *Einführung* (third edition). Though Wernle warns that many parts of it are "not for students in their first semesters, but for the more advanced," he said he wrote it "not for specialists, but for students." To those lacking serious interest in theology he said, "I wanted to show not only how strange the things are they encounter here, but also how substantively and personally important they are, how this science can shake their innermost being." To those more prejudiced, both orthodox and free-thinking, he said he felt he needed "from the start to tell them how narrow and stiff their thoughts were and how broad and rich the subject matter really is!" But the primary reason for writing his book, he said, had been for those who tended "to get lost in the great building of theology because every department head tries to sell his department as the most special and solely important one" (pp. v-ix).

[7] Wernle's six hundred page *Einführung* is divided into three parts. Part I he calls historical theology and is nearly as long as the other two parts combined. It begins with a discussion of "the general study of the history of religion" and moves on to a discussion of "the Israelite-Jewish religion," "the Christian religion," and then to "churches and the history of dogma" including subsections on the ancient church, the church in the Middle Ages, the Reformation, and modernity. Part II he calls systematic theology. It is divided into two sections, the first, "the philosophy of religion and Christian faith" and the second, "philosophical and Christian ethics." Part III comes under the rubric of practical theology and takes up such topics as: "the pastor and the congregation"; "general preparation for the pastorate"; "religious studies and the present" (with a subsection on "the new task: psychology and child psychology"); "the church and the present," etc.

As a champion of the rising history of religions school, Wernle stresses from the outset of his *Einführung* how important criticism has been to the modern scientific study of theology. It has liberated the church from superstition, from narrow-minded orthodoxy as well as shallow-minded liberalism, and if theology is to be truly scientific, it must continue to be critical. Yet for all criticism has done to liberate the church, Wernle admits, its results have sometimes been disturbing. "Indeed it *appears* to lie in the very nature of criticism that there is nothing firm and not only, for example, no firm Wellhausen hypothesis and no firm conclusion about the inauthenticity of John's Gospel, which for many is already strangely unsettling, but also no firm portrait of Jesus, no firm certainty [or] faith in God. And to face the possibility that all of it is nothing but wavering erring human opinion is certainly for no student of theology a joke."[8] But, according to Wernle, though it is necessary that we face the fact that criticism yields no firm certainties, this is no reason to despair.

> With respect to this fact there is no other solution than an ever deeper involvement in the wonderful life and experience of religion itself, this is the other thing I wanted my readers to see. It should not be their priority to 'explain' this life. How can something be explained that has not yet been known or understood? The most important and positive task of the study of theology is the contemplation of religion in its factuality, *primarily in the lives of leading men of God*. This is why the historical disciplines must take priority over all other ones because they alone can give us the illustrative material in all its fullness. One must focus today beyond Christianity. The Holy must be meaningful to us at the most primordial levels. The general study of the history of religion seeks admission in German departments [of theology] today and whoever wishes healing from the deficiencies and dilettantisms of the present must not hinder this. I have left no doubt for my readers about what I consider to be the main task: not the many, but the precious few, *the prophets, Jesus, Paul, Augustine, the Reformers, Kant, Schleiermacher and their kind*. The study that limits itself in strong onesideness upon *these centers of our religion*, in my opinion, is the one best equipped. If we theologians are supposed to be ahead of other faculties, it is not because we are any better or more pious, but – as luck would have it – because we are able to look at the *holiest specimens of humanity* in a richer and deeper way than others. ... And this in my eyes has been the most important thing that has been done for systematic theology and for service to the church.[9]

True to his day, Wernle launches his inquiry with a lengthy section on method, and because the primary means of understanding "the lives of leading men of God" is through their written expressions, no *Hilfswissenschaft* is more important to theology than hermeneutics. And because hermeneutics provides the ground rules for exegesis whether we are reading Plato, Goethe, or any other author, truly scientific investigation demands that we apply, even to the Bible, not a special "biblical hermeneutic, but a general one."[10] "Some of its rules are

---

[8] Wernle, *Einführung*, p. vii. Wernle adds: "For this reason many have already jumped ship, and not the worst ones."
[9] Wernle, *Einführung*, p. vii. Emphasis mine.
[10] Wernle, *Einführung*, p. 32.

familiar and immediately apparent: grammatical-historical exegesis, the strict rejection of all modern, rationalistic, or faith-based inferences, the explanation of an individual passage through parallels of the same author or by one who is a close contemporary, explanation on the basis of the context, the chronological, archaeological, and geographical explanation,"[11] etc. "Yet all this still does not mean that exegesis is trouble-free ... [or that we] arrive at a legitimate reading." Beyond this, Wernle insists:

> Reading should aim at two things: at the understanding of the *person* who writes and at the understanding of the *subject matter* at issue. The first one is a psychological task: from the words, from the signs back into the spirit of the author and then again from the spirit into the words! One must seek to live in an author in such a way that only and entirely *his* time, *his* environment, *his* addressees, *his* circumstances are before one's eyes. Thus growing together with him one experiences within his expressions of his thought the expressions of his heart. ... Yet nothing is to be taken as self-evident. The question must always be: Why did he write this and not that? What is he really wanting to say? And this leads to an important distinction as to which words in a given sentence are stressed and which are not and ought not therefore be pressed, and furthermore, how, psychologically, one thought follows another, or how thoughts in between the lines are conveyed which, though the author did not write, must be supplied. Moving from larger to smaller matters, [one must ask] about the author's disposition, what kind of plan he follows, which ideas dominate his work, and what kind of character, what kind of heart it reveals.[12]

With respect to the Bible, the upshot of this is that "from the four Gospels it is necessary to get acquainted with the four Evangelists, from the Genesis narratives, its narrators, in all their sharply distinguished individuality."[13] Wernle admits this is not easy where the individuality of the author is not so apparent. Nevertheless,

> The goal of all psychological exegesis in the Old Testament is the prophets and in the New Testament, Paul. Other literature has no more glorious task than this; it only takes the same knowledge, art, and love as brought by the researchers of Plato and Goethe to their object. It is to Wilhelm Dilthey's credit as a philosopher to have shown how individuals from the past and their work need to be understood from personal experience.[14]

"But penetrating through to an understanding of the subject matter," Wernle claims, "is different. Here a special sense, a sense for the strange is needed. The reader must be offended by the text, it must accost him at every point ... for this offense, this amazement, is what gives rise to questions and therefore understanding."[15] Yet it is important to observe that even though one's approach to understanding the subject matter is "different" and that "it must be first of all taken hold of as something strange," Wernle says, "in the end, the

---

[11] Wernle, *Einführung*, p. 32.
[12] Wernle, *Einführung*, p. 32.
[13] Wernle, *Einführung*, p. 33.
[14] Wernle, *Einführung*, p. 33.
[15] Wernle, *Einführung*, p. 33.

strange must again be understood according to human nature and by all available means of psychological empathy." In other words, in the end, understanding the subject matter is really not so different from the way we approach understanding the author after all. What we encounter as strange must be "immediately connected and placed in relationship with that which is strange in the context of cultural history, legal history, and religious history: this is the way people were *then*, *this* is the faith, *this* is the custom we meet both now and then. This is the nature of all *Sacherklärung*: introduction to the *Zeitkultur* and thereby the destruction of that which appears to *us* as strange."

Interestingly, the paragraph immediately following this statement begins: "Why is it that reading the Bible has caused so much more difficulty than the reading of any other book, that the history of its exegesis is, like no other book, such a history of foolishness? Is it because the Bible is harder to understand than all other books or because it is to be understood differently than all other books, not in a human way, but in a holy way? God forbid!" "There was a time at first when it was honored as divine but not understood," Wernle recalls, "But then every book of the Bible, even every chapter of the Old and New Testament, had to repeat the same 'truth of salvation.' And so our orthodox ancestors read themselves and their dogma of Christ back into the Bible everywhere."[16] Yet a "great backlash" against this approach to exegesis arose with the Enlightenment, and the Bible was subjected in the name of criticism to "all kinds of hate and contempt." "At this time the Bible could not be understood at all – for one cannot understand that which one does not love." But although the Bible was often used throughout this period merely to "confirm the enlightener's reign of reason or was disdained as an object of superstition," even this ultimately served a good purpose: "Such distancing merely provided possibilities for future understanding." It is here that Wernle makes a claim which is most telling with respect to what has been said up to now about Barth's hermeneutical revolution:

> Only with Herder and Romanticism did the time of free historical understanding begin. It involved neither carrying one's own thoughts back into the past nor sacrificing oneself to the past, but sensitively thinking oneself back into it, listening to its peculiarities, sentiments, expressions, hearing human pleasures and pains from all its foreign sounds, and yet as an honest man of the present. Such understanding of the Bible requires neither a special illumination of the Holy Spirit nor any special faith, but simply an incorruptible sense for the truth which takes an 'a' for an 'a' and a 'b' for a 'b,' a capacity for historical fantasy and love, and the ability to empathize [*einfühlen*] in a lively way into its strange world. Anyone can do this at school just as well with Plato or Sophocles or Homer because read-

---

[16] Wernle, *Einführung*, p. 33. Wernle adds: "Even today this is typical of pious biblical exegesis: one actually *learns* nothing from the Bible; always the same thing is being read in which one already knows even if the exact opposite is being talked about."

ing is exactly the same everywhere. Only once one learns how, one must not forget when it comes to reading the Bible nor sacrifice one's reading of it to any "higher" consideration.[17]

In light of what has been said thus far about Barth's attempt to overcome the hermeneutical tradition of Schleiermacher and Dilthey, general and special hermeneutics, etc., this is a fascinating claim and one I shall later return to. Here it is sufficient simply to point out what it implied to Wernle about understanding the apostle Paul. In the following paragraph Wernle discusses how facts and sources are to be evaluated: "Assessing facts is relatively simple if contemporaneous reports of eyewitnesses who can be trusted as truthful and as having knowledge of the subject matter are present, though it is best if the standpoint, education, and temperament of the reporter is also considered."[18] Still, there is reason to be cautious: "The world war with its battle reports and horror stories written by eyewitnesses, however, has given historians a shocking lesson: What is really true? Whose word can one trust? In time of war the psyche is anything but normal." The best we can hope for then, even under normal circumstances much less under circumstances of stress and trauma, are "probabilities not certainties." Knowing this, however, "puts us in a fortunate position to understand the letters of Paul and the we-passages of *Acts*":

> Eyewitnesses depict experiences sometimes with the most exacting geographical and chronological detail yet especially here Paul's partisanship and temperament must not be overlooked. Now if in such first hand reports we find all sorts of wonderful things, stories of visions, healings, raptures, we must simply accept these as the factual experience and faith of the author while refusing to adapt to the psychology of the day and its implications with respect to questions of worldview. We will thus believe that Paul experienced an apparition of Christ and a rapture into the third heaven, but we will refuse to believe that there are three or more heavens or that Christ was resurrected, etc.[19]

Wernle later discusses Paul at length,[20] but he concludes his chapter on method by discussing the value of other historical disciplines needed for proper scientific investigation: political history, legal, art, and economic history, the history of philosophy and literature, and especially world history, *a la* Ranke, Bezolds, *et al.* "To put it in a nutshell, it is necessary to separate the incomprehensible, the factual, the saga-like, the legendary, the mythical, and the tendentious in spite of the risk that myth and saga might in the end be revealed as the true kernel and the historical merely the husk. But neither the manifold obscurity of the facts nor the transparency of the certain within the uncertain gives us any right to abandon this difficult task."[21]

---

[17] Wernle, *Einführung*, p. 34.
[18] Wernle, *Einführung*, p. 34.
[19] Wernle, *Einführung*, p. 34.
[20] Wernle, *Einführung*, pp. 135-140, 166-170, 186-194.
[21] Wernle, *Einführung*, p. 35.

The reason why we cannot abandon this difficult task is, to repeat, because "The most important and positive task of the study of theology is the contemplation of religion in its factuality." This is Wernle's consistent answer. But it is important to notice that just as consistently, right alongside his talk about the importance of factuality and his claim that "historical criticism is the only way to establish anything factual," he also repeatedly insists that the most reliable information we have is at best "of only hypothetical value." In every case it is always a matter of drawing a general picture.

> After historical criticism has examined and sifted through the traditional material, it is then the task of *critical historical description* to determine a *general picture* with the help of the established facts which, on the one hand, satisfies our need for knowledge of a *causal relation* so far as is allowed, and on the other hand, which clearly and convincingly presents the *ideals and values* of a given time and its particular spiritual life. Such a general picture will have to bear hypothetical character, not merely because oftentimes only the hypothesis can establish the facts, but because in the necessary art of relating and explaining the facts, a very strong and hypothetical moment is added by the historian. Every writer of history tells the course of an event in such a way as it seems probable to him and therefore everyone tells it in a different way. What we earlier said about literature, is true for history as well: *without Miterleben there is no understanding* (Dilthey) and such Miterleben necessarily brings along with it a certain subjectivity.[22]

So here we have something of a paradox. On the one hand, Wernle and others influenced by the history of religions school aimed at "the contemplation of religion in its factuality." On the other hand, their discussion, like Wernle's above, turned again and again back to this "subjective," "hypothetical moment." On one hand, there is an attempt to understand texts "on the basis of the context, the chronological, archaeological, and geographical explanation" and, on the other, an admission that "all this still does not mean that exegesis is trouble free ... [or that we] arrive at a legitimate reading." On one hand, there is an objective science of history, a basically comparative task, and on the other, a subjective art of understanding individual personalities, a basically intuitive psychological task. "*Critical historical description*" on the one hand, "*Miterleben*" on the other. Always "the certain within the uncertain." For Wernle and many like him integrating and balancing these different elements was the great challenge of the day, which is why, immediately after treating the discipline of history, he finally concludes his chapter on method with a lengthy discussion of psychology and its relationship to religious experience.

---

[22] Wernle, *Einführung*, pp. 35-36.

C. Beyond Religious Personality and Experience

Karl Barth was well acquainted with the 'historical-psychological' approach of his contemporaries and with Wernle's approach in particular, which was clearly among the most sophisticated of the day. Barth first encountered Wernle while a student in Bern during the winter semester of 1905/06 when he took a course under Rudolf Steck on "The Synoptic Question" and read Wernle's book, *Die synoptische Frage*.[23] But it was not until 1909, through his friend Thurneysen who was then Wernle's devoted student, that Barth came to know him personally. After making his acquaintance, Barth maintained very close contact with Wernle, exchanging letters and postcards, paying regular visits to him in Basel for several years thereafter. In fact, so prominent was Wernle in Barth's and Thurneysen's discussions that in their correspondence between 1913 and 1921 he is mentioned more often than any of their former teachers, more than twice as many times as Harnack and Herrmann and only slightly fewer times than Kutter and Ragaz. Their letters throughout this period are filled with comments about Wernle's position on a variety of issues and especially his growing concern about their plight.

From 1909 to 1914, Wernle seems to have served as a kind of mentor to both Thurneysen and Barth, sometimes praising, at other times criticizing the insights of the two young pastors.[24] The discussions with them, however, particularly with Barth, became increasingly adversarial.[25] One of Wernle's concerns which he expressed as early as the fall of 1914 was that Thurneysen was allowing himself to be "taken in tow" by Barth.[26] Thurneysen consistently denied this charge yet took a generally more sympathetic position toward his former teacher than Barth. Thurneysen was convinced even after his and Barth's break with liberalism sometime in the summer of 1915 that there was still much to be learned, even in a constructive, positive sense, from Wernle's modern theological orientation. But Barth no longer shared Thurneysen's

---

[23] Paul Wernle, *Die synoptische Frage* (Tübingen: J.C.B. Mohr [Paul Siebeck], 1899). Barth, *Vorträge und kleinere Arbeiten 1905-1909*, ed. Hans-Anton Drewes and Hinrich Stoevesandt (Zürich: Theologischer Verlag Zürich, 1992), p. 46.

[24] Barth-Thurneysen, 5 June 1915, *B-Th. Br.* I, p. 51. See pp. 173-174n.191 below. See also Wernle's comments in response to Barth's article "Nocheinmal: Jesus und die Psychiatrie" (1913), Karl Barth, *Vorträge und kleinere Arbeiten 1909-1914*, pp. 563-4.

[25] Thurneysen-Barth, 11 Jan. 1917, *B-Th. Br.* I, p. 169. Barth and Wernle's clashes were becoming so frequent and intense that at Thurneysen's wedding, to which Wernle had been invited, Barth promised Thurneysen that he would try to keep such "fireworks to a minimum." Barth-Thurneysen, 15 Dec. 1915, *B-Th. Br.* I, p. 118.

[26] Thurneysen-Barth, 27 Oct. 1914, *B-Th. Br.* I, p. 14.

sense of indebtedness to modern theology, particularly that represented by Wernle.[27] On Nov.21, 1915, Barth wrote:

> I have to disagree with you with respect to your gratitude toward modern theology. ... I noticed the following day during a visit with Wernle very strongly that these modern theologians have *nothing* more to offer *me*, except for their contradictions which alert us to our own stupidities and weaknesses, and I am grateful for that. These people, especially with respect to Jesus, have simply misled us with their boring Zeitgeschichte. In particular the Jesus presented by Wernle, inasmuch as I had to encounter him again during these days, is a figure that leaves me completely cold in spite of the excitement (which to me often seems so artificial and overblown) with which he tries to sell it. Did we not get everything that is for us important about Jesus from somewhere else other than from these modern theologians? Yes, obviously we had to go through this school and I would not even think about getting upset at such gentlemen because they did not offer us that which our fathers had, for instance, in J.T. Beck. But it really would be too much now to give them extra gratitude for the detour they caused us to go through and for their continual attempts to make us linger at all kinds of trivialities. I could only agree with your admission regarding such gentlemen if it were entirely in the past perfect sense. I *now* see nothing at all here that would make us move ahead. Even though we are still *very much* in our infancy – it really seems to me that way – I still do not believe that for us there is anything we can take and learn, namely positively, from Wernle and his like.[28]

Barth was not prepared to give up totally on Wernle, however. He still valued contact with him and expressed hope that things might work out for the better.[29] Yet as early as Oct.5, 1915, he had already sensed that a "breakthrough" between them would probably never occur. Even after receiving a letter from Wernle with hopeful signs in it, he wrote:

> Wernle's letter was a true refreshment for me. When I read anything like that by him, I always have to think first: may God preserve this temperament in him! Factually, it is indeed a pity that such an intelligent man is able to shoot past those things that really matter. He is quite a hindrance in his own way. I mean, even more negatively, how much more could we especially have from him if he would just be a little more understanding? Often it seems to me like this: if he could listen quietly for just fifteen minutes to hear how we mean it, he would sense so strongly those common things that unite us so that this noise-making would stop. There is only a thin wall between him and us, I clearly hear him knock on the other side but I no longer believe that the view will be cleared.[30]

It became increasingly evident to Barth how impenetrable this "thin wall" really was. On April 24, 1916, he wrote to Thurneysen: "With Wernle one can either not associate at all or have regular contact, but if so, only with 42-cm artillery."[31] On May 26, 1917, he wrote, ironically: "How could it be that I

---

[27] Barth recalled this early difference between himself and Thurneysen even in his 1968 "Nachwort," p. 293.

[28] Barth-Thurneysen, 21 Nov. 1915, *B-Th. Br.* I, pp. 103-104.

[29] This was the case even after 1919. See Barth-Thurneysen, 28 Jan. 1919, *B-Th. Br.* I, p. 312.

[30] Barth-Thurneysen, 5 Oct. 1915, *B-Th. Br.* I, p. 86.

[31] Barth-Thurneysen, 24 April 1916, *B-Th. Br.* I, p. 130.

was reading these days a few passages from Wernle's *'Einführung'* in which your name is also immortalized?" (Thurneysen had prepared the index to the 1908 and 1911 editions of *Einführung in das theologische Studium* and Wernle had expressed thanks to him in both prefaces). "It never really dawned on me before what a strange work this *'Einführung'* is, particularly with respect to how much we really think and do the opposite of absolutely everything that is written in this compendium of currently valid theology. At one point in the practical theology section which I will show you sometime I was literally laughing so hard it brought me to tears. There are strange things found in this book everywhere you turn."[32]

Barth's relationship with Wernle from this time forth grew even more strained. In 1918, Wernle wrote a review of Barth and Thurneysen's first book, a collection of sermons, entitled, *Suchet Gott, so werdet ihr leben!*[33] which, though critical, Thurneysen and Barth welcomed because of what the association of Wernle's name might do for the book's sale.[34] In 1919, Wernle published his sharply critical review of Rom I.[35] Yet apart from his letter to Wernle of Oct.24, 1919, as previously discussed, Barth kept to his plan and held his fire. But in his preface to Rom II, which he admitted was at least in part "directed against Wernle," Barth finally delivered, as mentioned earlier, what he referred to as "an attempt at a knock out blow which positively had to be made this once on account of his excessively burdensome and contrary interference with me."

Barth's relationship with Wernle is instructive for many reasons, not least of all because it provides insight into one of the most important countervailing influences on Barth throughout his *Römerbrief* period. From the various comments Barth makes in his correspondence with Thurneysen and the number of times he is mentioned in both editions, it is clear that Barth had no contemporary theologian more in view when he wrote Rom I and II than Wernle.[36] Although he could jest in this period with Thurneysen about the influence of "Father Wernle,"[37] the fact is that Wernle's influence on both of them, as we shall see, was significant. Not long after arriving at Göttingen, Barth wrote: "Yes, good heavens, Eduard ... If only we had remained silent at that time when we were so close to becoming harmless and orderly disciples of Wernle. ... But the trouble has been that we have never been *silent* and now we are in for it."[38]

---

[32] Barth-Thurneysen, 26 May 1917, *B-Th. Br.* I, p. 203.
[33] Karl Barth and Eduard Thurneysen, *Suchet Gott, so werdet ihr leben!* (Bern: G.A. Bäschlin, 1917); Paul Wernle, *Kirchenblatt für die reformierte Schweiz*, 33 (1918), pp. 9-11.
[34] Barth-Thurneysen, 19 Jan.1918, *B-Th. Br.* I, p. 257.
[35] Paul Wernle, "Der Römerbrief in neuer Beleuchtung" (See p. 16n.8).
[36] Barth-Thurneysen, 11 Jan. 1918, *B-Th. Br.* I, p. 256; 23 Jan. 1918, *B-Th. Br.* I, pp. 259-260.
[37] Barth-Thurneysen, 18 July 1917, *B-Th. Br.* I, p. 217.
[38] Barth-Thurneysen, 5 Feb. 1924, *B-Th. Br.* II, p. 222.

After Wernle's death in 1939, Barth wrote Karl Ludwig Schmidt that it would be difficult to exaggerate the "degree to which Wernle, through his brilliance in books and articles, held the attention of all Switzerland and influenced it in one way or the other. [He], as *the* representative of modern theology at that time ... meant a great deal to me."[39] Wernle's *Einführung* was a "compendium of currently valid theology" which represented to Barth practically everything he was trying to overcome; and from his preface to Rom II and his letter to Wernle of Oct.24, 1919, it is quite clear that a major part of what he was trying to overcome was Wernle's approach to exegesis. The great weakness of Wernle's exegetical approach, from Barth's point of view, was that it focused primarily on knowing *about* the author. It focused especially on the author's personality and particularly the author's religious personality. For Barth, focus on the concept of religious personality was *the* major feature of Wernle's legacy, which is why, four decades later, Barth recalled:

> There was a time, not far distant, which began in the earlier and later stages of romantic pietism and which culminated in the liberalism of the left-wing Ritschlians and kindred groups, when the concept of the distinguished Christian 'personality' played an enormous role, and under the influence of Carlyle with heroes and hero worship even threatened to become with, for example, Paul Wernle, almost the central concept of Christian thought.[40]

The degree of Paul Wernle's interest in the topic of religious personality was obviously extraordinary, even for his day. But his interest represented not merely the tendency of a few left-wing Ritschlians but of an entire generation which sought to integrate the results of modern psychology, sociology and other human sciences into their study of religion and the Bible.[41] Barth, to be sure, did not oppose the integration of these insights, for example, historical-psychological insights into the life and personality of Paul, but his *Römerbrief* is a *tour de force* against all such attempts to reduce the content of Paul's message to such insights. This is precisely what lies behind Barth's attack on his generation's "cult of personality"[42] and why he refers to the concept of personality as "the idol of the century,"[43] "our god,"[44] "mammon."[45] For most, even those who call themselves believers, he said, "personality" is "the center of the

---

[39] Karl Barth-Karl Ludwig Schmidt, 14 April 1939, cited from Busch, *Lebenslauf*, p. 87; ET p. 75.

[40] KD IV/3:1017; CD IV/3:887.

[41] Ernst Troeltsch, for example, was also deeply interested in the personalities of "the great *bearers of revelation.*" *Glaubenslehre* (Munich: Duncker & Humblot, 1925), p. 44; ET *The Christian Faith*, trans. Garrett Paul (Minneapolis: Fortress Press, 1991), p. 43. See below p. 167.

[42] Rom I, pp. 109, 117, 419, 630.

[43] Rom I, p. 265.

[44] Rom I, pp. 34-35.

[45] Rom I, p. 272.

world and the measure of all things."[46] Barth ridicules the Romantic, pietistic preoccupation with *becoming* a "personality"[47] and saves his sharpest criticism for those who are particularly "eager to become a 'religious personality.'"[48] Such a desire he says is actually "the strongest proof of man's fall."[49] "As long as man lives, as long as he wants and must seek the meaning of his life within his personality (even if it be his religious personality!), the law is still lord over him."[50] "It is none of our business to know whether we are 'religious personalities.'"[51] "Do not be impressed by 'religious personalities'! As if a certain fervor of 'testimony,' a certain spiritual enchantment, a certain loftiness of thoughts, a certain soft, resonating voice of the heart would be the slightest criterion for the truth. All of this is actually *nothing*!"[52] "Among us we should never have to deal with questions like who has the greatest faith, who does the most for God, who has the strongest impact upon others and the world, who is the most important 'religious personality.' Those are the standards of the circus, not of the Kingdom of God."[53] The phrase 'religious personality' is mentioned more than a dozen times in Rom I, and with one exception, always in quotation marks and with biting irony.

Barth also lampoons the practice of referring to the Bible's men of faith as heroes. Abraham's faith had nothing to do with heroism.[54] "The righteousness of the heroes of the Bible is not a historical-psychological advantage within the nature of the flesh, but something based and rooted in a qualitatively other, new nature: not heroism, but being a child of God; not an ever so wonderful unfolding of soul and personality outside of God, but participation in a new history of mankind in God."[55] Again and again, Barth insists, the historical-psychological point of view fails to grasp this. On the contrary, the historical-psychological approach serves only to mask what is really at issue in the Bible and shield readers from its true subject matter, content, and theme.[56] "Only God can think in such a way and pronounce: 'I have made you the father of

---

[46] Rom I, p. 267.
[47] Rom I, pp. 35, 211, 244, 265, 288-289.
[48] Rom I, pp. 251-252.
[49] Rom I, p. 274.
[50] Rom I, p. 274.
[51] Rom I, p. 160.
[52] Rom I, p. 577.
[53] Rom I, p. 475.
[54] "The Bible does not present Abraham as the 'acting one' (even though he *was*!), but as one 'not acting,' not as a hero (even though he *was* one!), but as a member of sinful, suffering humanity, not as a 'friend of God' and 'wonderful soul' (even though he *was*!), but it shows him simply as a believing man" Rom I, pp. 113-114; "... the Bible resists the hubris of personality; it has nothing whatsoever to do with any hero-cult" p. 111. See also pp. 72, 108-110, 115, 117.
[55] Rom I, p. 109.
[56] Rom I, p. 166.

many nations.' This is sheer madness when looked at subjectively and from a historical-psychological perspective."[57] Abraham's faith is "historically and psychologically incomprehensible and irreducible."[58] Therefore, "Hands off you psychologists!"[59]

Many more such statements attacking the historical-psychological point of view are found throughout Rom II.[60] But it is in his address, *"Biblische Fragen, Einsichten und Ausblicke,"* given at the Aarau Student Conference on April 17, 1920, that Barth elaborated his strongest argument against the historical-psychological approach to the Bible. Barth's former teacher, Adolf von Harnack, attended the conference and had addressed the same audience earlier on the question: "What assured knowledge can historians provide for the interpretation of world events?" Barth's address, which he later said led to "a clash with Adolf von Harnack which was of almost historic significance,"[61] began with the following acknowledgment that, to many, could not have been more reassuring: "The Bible is a collection of literary monuments of an ancient tribal religion of the Near East and of a Hellenistic religious cult. Thus as a human document like any other it can lay no *a priori* dogmatic claim to any special attention or consideration." However it is what Barth said immediately after this that undoubtedly raised eyebrows:

> But this insight which is being preached by every tongue and believed in every land we may take for granted today. We need not continue to try to break through this open door. But when we face the actual substance of this insight with serious albeit cool-minded attentiveness, we shall find that we no longer have religious enthusiasm or scientific passion enough to fight against "rigid orthodoxy" or "belief in the dead letter." For it is all too clear that intelligent and fruitful discussion of the Bible begins when we have gotten *beyond* the insight as to its human, historical and psychological character. Would that the teachers of our upper and lower schools, and with them the progressive element among the clergy of our established churches, would quickly resolve to be done with this battle which once had its day but has now truly *had* it! The special *content* of this human document, the remarkable *subject matter* with which the writers of these stories and those who stood behind them were concerned, the biblical *object* – this is the question that occupies and weighs upon us today.[62]

And Barth pushes the point even further. He concedes that he too is fascinated by the religious personalities of the Bible. He too is impressed at how they stand out among their contemporaries and in their *Zeitkultur*: "With the historians and psychologists we are first confronted by the fact that evidently there once lived people of a quite extraordinary mental attitude and perspective.

---

[57] Rom I, p. 136.
[58] Rom I, p. 112.
[59] Rom I, p. 320.
[60] Rom II, passim.
[61] Karl Barth-H. Hag, February 16, 1945. Cited from Busch, *Lebenslauf*, p. 127; ET p. 115.
[62] Barth, "Biblische Fragen, Einsichten und Ausblicke," p. 76.

There are doubtless varying degrees of this peculiarity within the Bible."[63] Furthermore, "The biblical documents have margins and on these margins the different attitudes of other people begin to merge. One cannot fail to recognize therefore a certain striking unity of orientation with specifically *these* people." Yet even though a similar orientation may be found on the margins of the Bible, the fact that this particular "attitude and perspective appear with a frequency, intensity, unified diversity, and diversified unity" in the Bible is "no less remarkable because traces of something similar are found also in Greece, in the wonderland of India, and in the German Middle Ages."[64] But the truly remarkable thing about reading the Bible is that even after all the similarities between it and the ancient world have been taken into account, one is still left asking: "How could anyone be capable of thinking such a chapter as the fifteenth of First Corinthians and putting it down on paper?" "What kind of audience was it that was evidently expected to read such edifying literature the caliber of *Romans* or *Hebrews*?" "What conception of God and of the world was it which made it possible for people to refuse to accept the Old and New Testaments upon the same basis, but to understand one in the light of the other?" This is all very curious indeed. What kind of extraordinary events lie behind it? What could have possibly moved individuals to say and do such peculiar things? "We all know the worry that comes over us when from a window we see the people in the street suddenly stopping and looking up, shading their eyes with their hands and looking straight up into the sky toward something which is hidden from us by the roof. Our worry is unnecessary for it is probably an airplane. But as to the sudden stopping, looking up, and excited attention characteristic of the people of the Bible, we shall not be comforted so easily."[65] It is here that Barth recalls the great turning point of his life:

> This first dawned on me personally with Paul: this man evidently sees and hears something which is beyond comparison, which is absolutely beyond the range of my observation and the measure of my thought. Whatever position I take toward ... that which in mysterious words he claims he sees and hears, I cannot get around the fact that he, Paul, or whoever wrote, for example, the *Epistle to the Ephesians*, is eye and ear in a way that words such as enthusiasm, dismayed, shocked, or overwhelmed simply do not adequately describe. I seem to see behind the banner of such a document a personality who is actually thrown off all ordinary courses and primarily off his own course by seeing and hearing what I for my part do not see and hear – who is, so to speak, precisely as a personality, annihilated [*aufgehoben*] in order to be dragged from land to land as a prisoner to do strange, rash, unpredictable, and yet mysteriously well-planned deeds. And if I ever come to doubt whether I myself am hallucinating, one glance at the profane history of the times, one glance at the widening circle of ripples in the pool of history tells me that there must indeed have been a stone of unusual weight dropped into deep water there somewhere – tells me that among all the hundreds of peripatetic preachers and miracle workers from the Near East who in that

---

[63] Barth, "Biblische Fragen, Einsichten und Ausblicke," p. 76.
[64] Barth, "Biblische Fragen, Einsichten und Ausblicke," p. 77.
[65] Barth, "Biblische Fragen, Einsichten und Ausblicke," p. 77.

day must have gone along the same Appian Way into Imperial Rome, it was specifically this one Paul, with his seeing and hearing, who – if not with all things then at least with respect to the most significant things – really got the ball rolling in that city. And this is only the impact of one named 'Paul.'[66]

Barth goes on to speak of Matthew, Luke, John, and of "a seer and hearer whose simple moral sobriety makes him the more disturbing – James." "And behind these are other figures in Jerusalem and farther back on the shores of the Galilean Sea, whose names and faces may not be distinguished. But always there is the same seeing of the invisible, the same hearing of the inaudible, the same incomprehensible but no less undeniable epidemic of standing still and looking up." Such is what we find in the Old Testament as well. "The people of Israel and Judah were like other people, certainly, but they were people among whom lofty things were being seen and heard continually, a people for whom attention to a Wholly Other seems never to have wholly lapsed."[67] What does this suggest? At a minimum it suggests:

> There were once people who dared. Believe what you will about that around which these seers and hearers moved and which moved them to dare, the movement itself into which they all – the named, the unnamed, and the pseudonymous – were drawn, we can no more deny it than we can deny the rotation of the stellar firmament around an unknown central sun. The fact of this movement meets us in the Bible in an inescapable way. We think of John the Baptist in Grünewald's painting of the crucifixion with his hand pointing in an almost impossible way. It is this hand which is evidenced in the Bible. Yet this phenomenon requires interpretation. By labeling the pointing hand as religion, piety, experience, and so forth, even if we do so with the utmost expertise and love, still nothing is yet accomplished towards its interpretation. Its interpretation rather begins with the fact that the entire process cannot be exhaustively described by the categories of the science of religion, much less that they can contribute anything towards the understanding of the subject matter. There is a decisive element in the biblical experience which cannot be made perceptible by any means of psychological empathy [*psychologischer Einfühlung*] or reconstruction.[68]

Barth spends most of the rest of his "*Biblische Fragen, Einsichten und Ausblicke*" essay attacking the concepts of religion and piety as conceived by the history of religions school *vis à vis* the true subject matter of the Bible. "Biblical piety is not really pious. ... Biblical religious history has the distinction of being in its core, in its deepest essence, neither religion nor history – not religion but reality, not history but truth."[69] The entire study of the history of religions got started not by studying the history of religions but "the untrue religion. *For at the moment when religion becomes conscious of itself as religion, when it becomes a psychologically and historically conceivable quantity in the world, it falls away from its deepest essence, from its truth, to idols. Its truth is*

---

[66] Barth, "Biblische Fragen, Einsichten und Ausblicke," pp. 77-78.
[67] Barth, "Biblische Fragen, Einsichten und Ausblicke," p. 79.
[68] Barth, "Biblische Fragen, Einsichten und Ausblicke," pp. 79-80.
[69] Barth, "Biblische Fragen, Einsichten und Ausblicke," p. 80.

its otherness, its worldliness, its non-historicity."[70] Barth's attack on religion is well-known, as is also his attack on the historical-psychological approach to the Bible, but it is this concept of "psychological empathy" that requires closer attention. Empathy, a term which has been mentioned several times thus far, is, I contend, one of the most important hermeneutical concepts Barth sought to overcome. Indeed, to understand the rise of empathy's significance in the nineteenth and early twentieth centuries is to understand something that stands at the very heart of Barth's hermeneutical revolution.

D. A Short History of the Empathetic Tradition of Interpretation

Few concepts have played a more important role in modern hermeneutics than the concept of *Einfühlung*. The verb *einfühlen* first appeared in the German language in the last quarter of the eighteenth century among Romantic writers, and by all accounts was originally coined to describe the act of projecting oneself or feeling one's way into the spirit of something or someone, particularly the mind or soul of an author or poet.[71] Herder is widely credited as the first to use the term, and it is instructive to consider how it emerged in the larger framework of his thought. Herder's contribution is vast, complex, and difficult to summarize, but of seminal influence. Since Herder was "the inaugurator of typical nineteenth-century theology before its inauguration by Schleiermacher," Barth claimed that "Herder's significance for those theologians who came after him can scarcely be rated highly enough. Without him there would have been no Schleiermacher or de Wette. Nor would there have been the specific pathos of the course of theology in the nineteenth century. Without Herder there would have been no Erlangen or history of religions school. But for Herder there would have been no Troeltsch."[72] Barth held that the roots of modern historicism and psychologism were to be found in Herder, and tracing the development of the concept of *Einfühlung* provides a key insight into how these two main forces of theological reductionism came jointly to exercise such an enormous influence in the nineteenth and twentieth centuries.[73]

---

[70] Barth, "Biblische Fragen, Einsichten und Ausblicke," p. 81.

[71] "*Einfühlung* is a kind of putting of one's self and circumstances (feelings, tendencies) into objects. Aesthetic *Einfühlung* 'loans' a soul to things or allows one to feel the soul of them; ... *Einfühlung* is based upon 'assimilation.' It allows the self to feel in such a way as if it is the other being itself." *Wörterbuch der philosophischen Begriffe: historisch-quellenmässig bearbeitet*, Rudolf Eisler, I (Berlin: E.S. Mittler & Son, 1927), pp. 306-7.

[72] Barth, *Die protestantische Theologie im 19. Jahrhundert*, p. 302; ET p. 223; p. 282, ET p. 200.

[73] Barth, *Die protestantische Theologie im 19. Jahrhundert*, p. 305; ET p. 227. Robert Morgan, "Historicism," *A Dictionary of Biblical Interpretation*, ed. R.J. Coggins & J.L. Houlden (London: SCM, 1990), p. 290. Although historicism did not have the same significance

1. Johann Gottfried von Herder

J.G. Herder (1744-1803) was a ranking leader in Romanticism's reaction against rationalism. "Syllogisms," he said, "can teach me nothing where it is a question of the first entry of truth into the mind, which syllogisms merely develop once it has been received."[74] Long before Schleiermacher it was Herder who sought to save feeling and experience from the Enlightenment's tyranny of reason. "I am not here to think! – To be! To feel! To live! And to rejoice!"[75] But what was so important about feeling and experience for Herder was not so much the *object* of feeling and experience – such as "the Whence" for Schleiermacher – but feeling and experience *itself*. The sheer feeling and experience of being human itself was important because this was for Herder the most direct means possible of participating in God's revelation.[76] Herder believed "so long as I am human I have no knowledge of any truth higher than the human one."[77] "Just as our way of knowing is only human, and must be so if it is right, so our will can only be human too; something which arises from and is full of human feeling. It is humanity which is the noble standard by which we know and act."[78] "Man has no more noble word to describe [God] than man himself, in which the image of the Creator of our earth, as it was possible for him to become visible here, lives reproduced. We have simply to outline his form to arrive at an idea of his noblest duties."[79] We have simply to "work out the analogy of our own nature with the Creator's, our likeness in his image."[80] As Barth says: "Herder thought of this working out of the image of God in ourselves, so to speak, as a passing through a gateway: if we keep our minds and spirits open to the influences of the *world*, which is *God's* world,

---

for Friedrich Meinecke as for Barth, Meinecke makes it clear in his classic, two-volume work on historicism, first published in 1936, *Die Entstehung des Historismus* (Munich: R. Oldenbourg Verlag, 1959), that Herder – and specifically as "creator of a new method, *Einfühlung*, a term he himself invented" – played a central role in the rise of historicism. See pp. 299ff., and especially pp. 355-444.

[74] Barth, *Die protestantische Theologie im 19. Jahrhundert*, p. 284; ET p. 203.
[75] Barth, *Die protestantische Theologie im 19. Jahrhundert*, p. 284; ET p. 203.
[76] "Man's existence, according to Herder, with its historical quality, includes his participation in God's revelation in a manner which is without doubt the most direct possible. With Herder nature in its historical development is the action and speech of the Godhead" Barth, *Die protestantische Theologie im 19. Jahrhundert*, pp. 294-295; ET p. 215. "For Herder's theory does not in fact extend beyond experience as such. He is far from basing theological knowledge upon the object of experience but bases it quite definitely upon experience as such. For the historical objectivity to which he appeals is definitely a *different* one than the objectivity which would, for instance, have to be taken into account in a theology of faith" (pp. 300-301; ET p. 222).
[77] Barth, *Die protestantische Theologie im 19. Jahrhundert*, p. 286; ET p. 205.
[78] Barth, *Die protestantische Theologie im 19. Jahrhundert*, p. 288; ET p. 208.
[79] Barth, *Die protestantische Theologie im 19. Jahrhundert*, p. 288; ET p. 208.
[80] Barth, *Die protestantische Theologie im 19. Jahrhundert*, p. 286; ET p. 205.

then we come to resemble God, as it were, of our own accord."[81]   This is the basis of Herder's claim: "Religion is man's humanity in its highest form."[82] "Religion," he said, "even when looked upon solely as an exercise of the understanding, is the highest humanity, the most sublime flowering of the human soul."[83]   Here is where Herder's link to nineteenth century theology, to Schleiermacher, Troeltsch, the history of religions school, and Wernle is so apparent. "In this connexion," Barth said, "Herder already felt the importance, as the true focal point of revelation, of that feature which, much later, was called the religious 'personality.' ... 'God works upon earth in no other way than through great and chosen men.' 'Religion is dead in a group where it has no living examples; the dead profession of faith, dead customs, pedantic learning and the splitting of hairs, even if it were to perform its work in the original language and upon the lips of the founders, can neither represent nor replace this daughter of heaven, who must be alive in men, or she is no more.'"[84]

But if God works upon earth in no other way than through great and chosen men, through religious personalities, as it were, how is it that dead religion, "the dead profession of faith, dead customs" of the past, can become "alive in men" today? Herder's answer was through history. "Facts form the basis for every divine element in religion, and religion can only be represented in history, indeed it must itself continually become living history."[85] History, which is really about the development of mankind's spirit, the education of the human soul, is actually nothing but a record and commentary of revelation. Standing within history, therefore means in principle standing in the stream of revelation.[86] But beyond studying history Herder held that the most direct means of standing in the stream of revelation was through listening attentively to language and especially to poetry, which he called "the mother tongue of the human race."[87] It is through language and poetry that the human spirit is most immediately expressed. It is through language and poetry that the way of life, the sensibilities, the communal spirit of all peoples, and especially ancient peoples, is most naturally revealed. For Herder, nowhere was this more evident than in the Old Testament, which he deeply admired and celebrated in his book

---

[81] Barth, *Die protestantische Theologie im 19. Jahrhundert*, p. 286; ET p. 206.
[82] Barth, *Die protestantische Theologie im 19. Jahrhundert*, p. 293; ET p. 213.
[83] Barth, *Die protestantische Theologie im 19. Jahrhundert*, p. 293; ET p. 214.
[84] Barth, *Die protestantische Theologie im 19. Jahrhundert*, p. 298; ET pp. 219-220.
[85] Barth, *Die protestantische Theologie im 19. Jahrhundert*, p. 294; p. 214.
[86] Barth, *Die protestantische Theologie im 19. Jahrhundert*, p. 294; p. 214.
[87] Frei, *The Eclipse of Biblical Narrative*, p. 183.

Concerning the Spirit of Hebrew Poetry,[88] a book Barth refers to in his 1924 lectures on dogmatics.[89]

Hans Frei captures the essence of Herder's project when he says, "[Herder] was always concerned with entering the 'spirit' of an age, a man, a people or a work."[90] With a growing number of his romantically inclined contemporaries, Herder believed that this sort of approach was "not only different from but often impeded in principle by technical, categorical investigation." Therefore beyond analyzing a given text merely grammatically, historically, and critically, and classifying it on such basis as 'history' or 'myth' or some other technical category, as so many of his enlightened contemporaries, especially in the field of biblical exegesis, were accustomed to doing, Herder sought something more, something deeper. For him, the essential thing was to understand the human, natural, and communal spirit which had given rise to it. Thus, "It seemed to Herder that understanding an ancient language in its poetic effulgence is a matter of entering imaginatively and empathetically the world of the imagination and culture that produced it."[91] This is how *Einfühlung* emerged as such an important concept.

"Become with shepherds a shepherd," Herder said, "with a people of the sod a man of the land, with the ancients of the Orient an Easterner, if you wish to relish these writings in the atmosphere of their origin; and be on guard especially against abstractions of dull, new academic prisons, and even more against all so-called artistry which our social circles force and press on those sacred archetypes of the most ancient days." But as Frei points out, *Einfühlung* implied for Herder more than simply a total surrender or "submission to the author, his depictions, and the atmosphere out of which they arise."

> Paradoxically, this total surrender, which was the price of entry into the spirit of any specific past to which one was relating himself, was necessarily accompanied by an equally pervasive detachment from it at every other level. The *Einfühlung* into another specific, historical spirit or age, though aesthetically uncritical, was confined solely to the aesthetic mode. No particular manifestation had any more normative claim on one's own religious, philosophical, moral, or even aesthetic positioning of oneself than any other.[92]

The key phrase here is "detachment from it at every other level." As an interpreter, Herder was prepared to surrender himself, at least aesthetically, to "the

---

[88] Frei, *The Eclipse of Biblical Narrative*, p. 184. The Bible as a whole was important to Herder, according to Frei, because it represented "the fullest expression of the one human spirit under the educative guidance of the divine providence."

[89] Barth, *Unterricht*, p. 251; ET p. 206.

[90] Frei, *The Eclipse of Biblical Narrative*, p. 184. It should be said that, according to Frei, the stories of the Bible were important to Herder only "in the broader interpretive context of their place in the history of the human spirit in its various unique and distinctive written self-expressions" (p. 188).

[91] Frei, *The Eclipse of Biblical Narrative*, p. 184.

[92] Frei, *The Eclipse of Biblical Narrative*, p. 185.

spirit of any specific past." But what about at other levels of interpretation, for example, at the level of *Sacherklärung*?

Given his focus on understanding the spirit of an age or author, it might appear that Herder was simply ambivalent regarding other levels of interpretation, such as at the more mundane level of historical fact. But this was not the case, particularly with respect to the Bible. Herder defended many of the main historical fact claims of the Bible and once wrote in his *Letters Concerning the Study of Theology*, "I would very much deplore you, my friend, if, being unconvinced of the historical truth of the earliest Christian history, you were to remain a student of theology" and "whoever turns a Gospel of Christ into a novel has done injury to my heart, even if he has done so with the most beautiful novel in the world."[93] Still, understanding the spirit or outlook that gave rise to the Gospels and other works remained Herder's priority. According to Frei,

> [Herder] can affirm the factual truth of an account or its realistic character as writing, or both, and he can even stress the importance of both; and yet he can remain quite ambiguous as to whether the meaning of the account is the spatiotemporal occurrences to which it refers or the depiction it renders, or whether the meaning is the spirit or outlook that generated such a writing. And in the long run it is the latter that is more important and, if anything, becomes the clue to the former.[94]

Or, to put it another way, "Even when Herder makes an ardent plea for the factual veracity of early Christianity or the simple, realistic quality of a particular biblical writing, his own exegetical point of view has a way of remaining at the aesthetic level, in the sense that the reader's most important task remains neither the reference nor the realism of the account but the direct *Einfühlung* into the spirit whose written expression the account is."[95]

Frei has examined "the well-nigh programmatic indispensability of *Einfühlung*" in Herder's thought in more detail than can be offered here, but there are two presuppositions at issue in Herder's notion of *Einfühlung* which played a very significant role in the development of hermeneutical theory throughout the nineteenth and twentieth centuries, and these need to be highlighted. The first has to do with the emergence of what Frei describes as "an independent, spiritual self-positioning" on the part of the interpreter. In the last chapter I spoke of the tendency among many modern interpreters to subordinate the past to the present, to think that the only real or living context is their own: that it is

---

[93] Barth, *Die protestantische Theologie im 19. Jahrhundert*, p. 298; ET p. 219.

[94] Frei continues: "... in Herder's view it is the spirit of the biblical writings that is to be taken as strongly realistic and as explaining the realism of the writings," p. 191. "One's recapitulative experience of the spirit out of which it arose, sympathetically noting the authenticity and appropriateness of the particular written expression to the original spirit, is the sum total of understanding." Frei, *The Eclipse of Biblical Narrative*, p. 186.

[95] Frei, *The Eclipse of Biblical Narrative,*, p. 189.

primarily *we* in the present who confer meaning upon the past, that it is *we* who are the primary arbiters of whether something from the past is to be regarded as meaningful or meaningless, as a "dead relic" or "living link." Here in Herder is where we find the roots of this tendency which, according to Frei, are the roots of modern historicism.

Herder's concern he said was with "the making contemporary [*Vergegenwärtigung*] of biblical history as the most profound human and religious means of education."[96] The necessary means of making biblical history contemporary was through *Einfühlung*. How else could "the dead profession of faith, dead customs," the dead religious language of the Bible become "alive in men" today but by empathetically recapitulating the experience of the spirit out of which these things arose? But the question this raises is: On what grounds may the professions of faith, customs, and language of the Bible be pronounced dead? From what vantage point may we who are alive in the present pronounce them dead? This is what Frei is referring to when he speaks about the rise of "an independent, spiritual self-positioning" on the part of the interpreter as reflected in Herder. The presupposition at issue in claiming that the professions, customs, and language of the Bible are "dead" is the same presupposition which underlies the claim that every event in the past can be sufficiently explained solely on the basis of its antecedents (i.e., historicism).[97] It is the profoundly spiritual presupposition of a free, autonomous, self-positioning subject, an interpreter who knows himself to be partaking of a specific historical location, that of the present instead of the dead, albeit empathetically retrievable, past. The significance of this move with respect to the history of interpretation Frei says is: "Realistic and figural reading, which had allowed the reader to be incorporated and thus located in the world made accessible by the narration, here gives way to an independent spiritual self-positioning which then locates itself as well as specific past epochs by relating itself to earlier spiritual positionings, locating them in turn by their presently accessible, or spiritually present recapitulation."[98] Whether Herder recognized this as a consequence of adopting this presupposition, the very notion of *Einfühlung*, according to Frei, practically guaranteed it.[99] Thus the great irony of *Einfühlung* was that although it implied "a kind of aesthetic submissiveness to each ancient depiction," a kind of aesthetic surrender to the spirit of an author or age, the presup-

---

[96] Frei, *The Eclipse of Biblical Narrative*, p. 198.

[97] Maurice Mandelbaum defines historicism as "the belief that an adequate understanding of the nature of anything and an adequate assessment of its value are to be gained by considering it in terms of the place it occupied and the role it played within a process of development," in *The Encyclopedia of Philosophy*, 4 (New York: Macmillan, 1967), p. 24.

[98] Frei, *The Eclipse of Biblical Narrative*, p. 199. Frei elaborates how this contributed to the collapse or disillusion of the explicative sense (*explicatio*), what the text says, into the applicative sense (*applicatio*), what the text means, pp. 189f.

[99] Frei, *The Eclipse of Biblical Narrative*, pp. 183-201.

position which governed it was that of a free, autonomous, self-positioning subject who could, in god-like fashion, stand in other ways *above* the spirit of that same author or age.

Frei states at the conclusion of his chapter on Herder:

> It is simply impossible to exaggerate the self-conscious novelty and power of the full-orbed conviction at the end of that century, no matter how far one may see its roots extending into previous history, that a free and self-conscious self-positioning toward the world is an independent and indispensable factor in shaping the depiction of that world with its bearing on the self. It matters little whether this self was the Pietist's self dispositioning itself religiously, that of the Romantic dispositioning itself aesthetically in acute awareness of its own sensibility, that of the philosophical Idealist dispositioning itself in conceptual self-reflexiveness, or that of the budding Existentialist, dispositioning itself in self-committing agency.[100]

This is precisely the kind of freedom Wernle was talking about when he said: "Only with Herder and Romanticism did the time of free historical understanding begin. It involved neither carrying one's own thoughts back into the past nor sacrificing oneself to the past, but sensitively thinking oneself back into it, listening to its peculiarities, sentiments, expressions, hearing human pleasures and pains from all its foreign sounds, and yet as an honest man of the present." To many like Wernle at the beginning of the twentieth century, the "free historical understanding" wrought by Herder and Romanticism meant not only freedom from interpreting the past without prejudice ("neither carrying one's own thoughts back into the past"), it also meant freedom from "sacrificing oneself to the past." Both notions, but especially the latter, typify the sort of perspective which evolved throughout the nineteenth century as a result of the emergence of this free, autonomous, self-positioning subject. Such freedom is apparently the only kind of freedom, "as an honest man of the present," Wernle knew.

A second presupposition at issue in the concept of *Einfühlung* which must be mentioned is that of a common, universally intuitable core of humanity. The condition for the possibility of *Einfühlung*, Herder recognized, was a shared identity or essence intrinsic to all humanity: "The harmony of every creature/ Is one with me, yes, I am they!"[101] In his work, "The Soul," he said:

> Look upon the whole of nature, behold the great analogy of the creation! Everything senses itself and its kind: life intermingles with life. Every string vibrates to its own note, each fiber intertwines with its neighbor, animal feels in harmony with animal; why should man not feel in harmony with man? Our feeling for ourselves should only be the *conditio sine qua non*, the ballast which gives us stability, not an end, but a means to an end – but a necessary means, for it is and must ever be true that we love our neighbor only as we love ourselves. How can we be true to others if we are not true to ourselves? The degree of our

---

[100] Frei, *The Eclipse of Biblical Narrative*, pp. 200-1.
[101] Barth, *Die protestantische Theologie im 19. Jahrhundert*, p. 288: ET p. 208.

sense of self is at the same time the measure of our feeling for others: for it is only our self that we can as it were project [*hineinfühlen*] into the feelings of others.[102]

Herder's supposition that we can "love our neighbor only as we love ourselves" is one I shall return to in a moment, but it is this means of projecting ourselves into others on the basis of a common "sense of self" that needs to be kept in mind as we consider the legacy of *Einfühlung* with respect to Friedrich Schleiermacher, the father of modern hermeneutics.

2. Friedrich Daniel Ernst Schleiermacher

Like Herder, Schleiermacher understood the limitations of grammatical and historical interpretation. Like Herder, he believed it was necessary to enter empathetically into the spirit of an age and author. And like Herder, he too criticized the "one-sided historical interpretation" of his contemporaries, and because of the rising tide of enthusiasm for modern historical-critical investigation, paid a much higher price for doing so.[103] But Friedrich Schleiermacher was a far more sophisticated systematic thinker than Herder and could not therefore be so easily dismissed. F.C. Baur, Christoph Klaiber, and others of the emerging Tübingen school, and later David Friedrich Strauss, accused Schleiermacher of selling history short.[104] For a time such accusations seemed to seal Schleiermacher's fate. But gradually, with his posthumously published lectures on hermeneutics, Dilthey's expository work, and the development of

---

[102] Barth, *Die protestantische Theologie im 19. Jahrhundert*, pp. 288-289; ET p. 208 (The Soul, p. 72).

[103] In his 1819 lectures on hermeneutics, Schleiermacher said: "For example, in the dispute over the historical interpretation of the New Testament there [has] emerged the curious view that there are several different kinds of interpretation. To the contrary, only historical interpretation can do justice to the rootedness of the New Testament authors in their time and place. (Awkward expressions. Concepts of time.) But historical interpretation is wrong when it denies Christianity's power to create new concepts and attempts to explain it in terms of conditions which were already present in the time. It is proper to reject such a one-sided historical interpretation, but it is improper to reject historical interpretation altogether. The crux of the matter, then, lies in the relationship between grammatical and psychological interpretation, since new concepts developed from the distinctive manner in which the authors were affected." *Hermeneutik*, p. 83; ET pp. 103-104. Schleiermacher was also critical of "bogus history" and warns interpreters to be wary of the subtle and sometimes not so subtle prejudices of historians. See, for example, his comments on "an anti-Christian tendency in such a work as Gibbon's" (p. 165; ET p. 225).

[104] The pioneering work of a former generation, viz., the critical labors of Gäbler, Lessing, Reimarus, Semler, with whom Herder had been familiar, had opened the way for an even bolder generation. According to Frei, Schleiermacher's impact on biblical scholarship was almost immediately eclipsed by Strauss's *Life of Jesus*. Strauss, moreover, never tired of saying that "Schleiermacher's christology was an unworkable compromise between traditional ecclesiastical claims and modern historical-critical investigation, and failed to do justice to the integrity of each." Frei, *The Eclipse of Biblical Narrative*, p. 343. On Strauss' impact, see pp. 233f., esp. p. 285.

modern historical consciousness as reflected in figures such as Ranke, Droysen, *et al*, many in the latter decades of the nineteenth century began to recognize the significance of Schleiermacher's approach to interpretation. In chapter two I discussed the impact of Schleiermacher's hermeneutic in the period immediately preceding Barth's *Römerbrief*. Now it is necessary to discuss the specific content of Schleiermacher's hermeneutic in more detail.

Like other Romantic interpreters of his day, Schleiermacher saw interpretation as, among other things, a matter of getting inside the mind or soul of an author by means of aesthetic intuition.[105] "It is essential in interpretation," he said, "that one be able to step out of one's own frame of mind into that of the author."[106] Moreover, with a formula that has been widely repeated ever since, he defined the goal of interpretation as that of trying "to understand an author better than he understood himself."[107] Schleiermacher did not invent this phrase. Herder and others state it much earlier.[108] But it is hardly surprising that Schleiermacher, standing on Herder's shoulders as a second generation free, autonomous, self-positioning subject, developed this as the programmatic goal of interpretation for many subsequent generations. Gadamer claims, "This statement contains the whole problem of hermeneutics" and "in its changing interpretation the whole history of modern hermeneutics can be read."[109] Of course, as one seeks to understand an author better than he understood himself, much hinges on what is meant by *better*. Better in relationship to what? Better awareness of the author's *Sitz im Leben*? Better awareness of grammatical rules the author presupposed? Better awareness of the author's psychological state of mind? Better acquaintance with the subject matter? Understanding an author better than he understood himself has meant many things to many interpreters over the years, but, according to Gadamer, "What it means for Schleiermacher is clear. He sees the act of understanding as the reconstruction of the production. This inevitably renders many things conscious of which the writer may be unconscious. It is obvious that here Schleiermacher is applying the aesthetics of genius to his universal hermeneutics. Creation by artistic genius is the model on which this theory of unconscious production and necessarily conscious reproduction is based."[110] This requires explanation.

One of the major presuppositions behind Schleiermacher's hermeneutic is that interpretation is a matter of tracing the outer speech of an author back to its moment of origination in the inner life or mind of the author. "Speaking being

---

[105] Schleiermacher, *Hermeneutik*, p. 50; ET p. 64.

[106] Schleiermacher, *Hermeneutik*, p. 32; ET p. 42.

[107] Schleiermacher, *Hermeneutik*, p. 50; ET p. 64.

[108] J.G. Herder, Briefe an Theophron, *Sämtliche Werke*, xi, (Berlin, 1879, first ed.; Hildesheim: Georg Olms Verlagsbuchhandlung, 1967) ed. Bernhard Suphan, p. 163.

[109] Gadamer, *Wahrheit und Methode*, p. 196; ET p. 192.

[110] Gadamer, *Wahrheit und Methode*, p. 196; ET p. 192.

only the outer side of thinking," Schleiermacher said, "every act of understanding is the reverse side of an act of speaking, and one must grasp the thinking that underlies a given statement."[111] Therefore interpretation has to do with readers reproducing in their own minds the original experience and thought processes which gave rise to the author's word. It is basically the reverse process of composition, or as Gadamer describes it, a reversal or inversion of the creative process by means of which the interpreter has to make his hermeneutical way back along the creative path, carrying on the process of re-thinking.[112] Therefore, understanding an author better than he understood himself, for Schleiermacher, means becoming more conscious of the various factors and circumstances of which the author was unconscious or perhaps only partially conscious in the process of production. This includes not only becoming more specifically conscious of grammatical rules or literary forms, but also "knowing the inner and outer aspects of the author's life" which may have directly or indirectly influenced the author's thought.[113] It also includes becoming more conscious of the various points in the process of artistic production at which the author, as genius or poet, was unconscious and did not understand himself at all.[114] Of course, understanding an author better than he understood himself in this sense is predicated upon the interpreter's ability to empathize or identify at some psychological level with the author, which is why Schleiermacher is such an important figure in the history of empathetic interpretation.

Schleiermacher may not have used the specific term "*Einfühlung*,"[115] but his hermeneutical program is clearly dependent upon this Romantic concept which is no doubt one reason Barth claimed that without Herder there would have been no Schleiermacher. Schleiermacher stands squarely in the tradition of empathetic interpretation which Herder pioneered, but Schleiermacher was a far more sophisticated systematic thinker than Herder and most of his other Romantic forbearers and contemporaries. Entering empathetically or imaginatively into the mind of an author thus for him was never a matter of sacrificing scientific or systematic considerations to sheer intuitive insights, as it was for many of them. It is important to remember that one of Schleiermacher's primary reasons for constructing a universal hermeneutic was not only because of

---

[111] Schleiermacher, *Hermeneutik*, p. 80; ET p. 97.
[112] Gadamer, *Wahrheit und Methode*, pp. 192-193; ET pp. 188-189.
[113] Schleiermacher, *Hermeneutik*, p. 88; ET p. 113.
[114] Gadamer, *Wahrheit und Methode*, p. 196; ET pp. 192-193.
[115] Though many associate the word *Einfühlung* with Schleiermacher (e.g., Wach, *Das Verstehen* I, p.25, et al.), Frei claims the word may not actually appear in his works. According to *An Historical Dictionary of German Figurative Usage*, ed., Keith Spalding (Oxford: Blackwell, 1967): "although einfühlen can be found in some works of the 2nd half of the 18th c., e.g. Maler Müller, *Adam* I, 19: *'alles, alles so fremd und doch mir einfühlend, ganz mir verwandt,'* it remained rare for a whole century (Sanders in 1860, Grimm in 1862 and even Muret-Sanders in 1899 did not list the word). Psychology gave it wider currency" (p. 872).

the tendency of special hermeneutics to "degenerate into a collection of observations ... at the expense of its scientific character,"[116] but because none of the approaches of his contemporaries, as he saw it, were adequately structured to integrate the various other facets of interpretation. Some (such as Ernesti and Buddaeus among biblical interpreters, for example) focused narrowly on grammatical interpretation, while others more decisively influenced by Romanticism relied so heavily on intuitive insights that they tended toward fanaticism, but none, in Schleiermacher's view, were prepared to approach the task of interpretation in a sufficiently comprehensive, rigorously systematic fashion.

Schleiermacher states at the beginning of his 1819 lectures on hermeneutics that "the success of the art of interpretation depends on one's linguistic competence and one's ability for knowing people."[117] By linguistic competence he means more than simply knowing a foreign language, but "one's command of language, one's sensitivity to its similarities and differences, etc." By knowing people he means more than simply knowing other individuals, but having "knowledge of the subjective element determining the composition of thoughts." The former requires grammatical interpretation, the latter psychological interpretation. "Each side is itself an art. For each side constructs something finite and definite from something infinite and indefinite. Language is indefinite because every element is determinable in a special way by the other elements. This statement also applies to psychological interpretation, for every intuition of a person is itself infinite."[118] Grammatical and psychological interpretation, in other words, have always to do with balancing objective and subjective elements. With respect to grammatical interpretation, for example, there are general language possibilities ("langue") on the one hand and particular language uses ("parole") on the other. With respect to psychological interpretation there are general personality types on the one hand and specific individuals or personalities on the other. "In order to complete the grammatical side of interpretation it would be necessary to have a complete knowledge of the language. In order to complete the psychological side it would be necessary to have a complete knowledge of the person. Since in both cases such complete knowledge is impossible, it is necessary to move back and forth between the grammatical and psychological sides, and no rule can stipulate exactly how to do this."[119] This is why Schleiermacher calls hermeneutics "the art of understanding." "The 'art' lies in knowing when one side should give way to the other."[120] Some texts require a stronger grammatical reading and

---

[116] Schleiermacher, *Hermeneutik*, p. 93; ET p. 122.
[117] Schleiermacher, *Hermeneutik*, p. 82; ET p. 101.
[118] Schleiermacher, *Hermeneutik*, p. 82; ET p. 100.
[119] Schleiermacher, *Hermeneutik*, p. 82; ET p. 100.
[120] Schleiermacher, *Hermeneutik*, p. 32; ET p. 42.

others a stronger psychological reading.[121] The interpreter who emphasizes the grammatical at the expense of the psychological side, Schleiermacher calls a "pedant," while the interpreter who emphasizes the psychological at the expense of the grammatical side, he calls a "nebulist."[122]

Grammatical and psychological interpretation, however, comprise only two polarities in Schleiermacher's system. There are two more: comparative and divinatory interpretation. Divinatory interpretation requires that the interpreter "transform himself, so to speak, into the author in order to gain an immediate comprehension of the author as an individual."[123] It requires that the interpreter empathetically identify with the author, to creatively and imaginatively rethink and relive his or her thoughts and experiences in order to understand in a direct, comprehensive sense the author's work as the creation of an individual mind. Interpretation for Schleiermacher was always a matter of encountering the unique individuality or personality of an author, even if the author of the text in question is anonymous or the text is the product of multiple authors.[124] In fact, it is due to his regard for the individuality of the author that his most "original contribution to hermeneutics" is said to have been made.[125] The categories of prior hermeneutics were simply insufficient to deal with this aspect of interpretation. A deeper, aesthetic dimension was needed, which is what divinatory interpretation brought. Barth describes divinatory interpretation as "the new thing" Schleiermacher contributed to hermeneutics.[126] Yet the act of transforming oneself into the author, reliving his thoughts and experiences, etc., obviously has much in common with what Herder was talking about when he said, "Become with shepherds a shepherd, with a people of the sod a man of the sod." However, divinatory interpretation as such never became for Herder the kind of formal, technical category it did for Schleiermacher. Nor did Herder ever apply it in any systematic or self-consciously critical sense alongside any other interpretive category. Schleiermacher, on the other hand, never applied divinatory interpretation apart from what he called

---

[121] Schleiermacher, *Hermeneutik*, p. 83; ET p. 103.
[122] Schleiermacher, *Hermeneutik*, p. 125, 149; ET pp. 177, 205.
[123] Schleiermacher, *Hermeneutik*, p. 109; ET p. 150.
[124] Schleiermacher, *Hermeneutik*, p. 67, 69; ET pp. 85, 88.
[125] Cornel West, "Schleiermacher's Hermeneutics and The Myth of The Given," *Union Seminary Quarterly Review* 34 (1979), p. 73. Richard R. Niebuhr adds in his essay: "Schleiermacher On Language and Feeling," *Theology Today*, July, 1960, "The most striking contribution of Schleiermacher in his exposition of the problem of interpreting the individuality of the author or speaker [is] through the comparative and divinatory methods, namely the famous section of psychological interpretation" (p. 156).
[126] "The concept of *divinatory*, or, as it is once called, prophetic interpretation was the new thing which Schleiermacher espoused in his addresses, especially against Wolf, but also in careful demarcation from the speculative exegesis of Ast." Barth, *Die Theologie Schleiermachers*, p. 323; ET p. 181.

comparative interpretation. "The comparative method proceeds by subsuming the author under a general type. It then tries to find his distinctive traits by comparing him with others of the same general type."[127] Comparative interpretation thus serves not only to provide a sphere or boundary within which divinatory interpretation can be carried out, but also to corroborate divinatory insights. This is important because divinatory interpretation apart from comparative interpretation, like psychological interpretation apart from grammatical interpretation, tends toward fanaticism. Schleiermacher relates divinatory and comparative interpretation as follows:

> By leading the interpreter to transform himself, so to speak, into the author, the divinatory method seeks to gain an immediate comprehension of the author as an individual. The comparative method proceeds by subsuming the author under a general type. It then tries to find his distinctive traits by comparing him with others of the same general type. Divinatory knowledge is the feminine strength in knowing people; comparative knowledge, the masculine. Each method refers back to the other. The divinatory is based on the assumption that each person is not only a unique individual in his own right, but that he has a receptivity to the uniqueness of every other person. This assumption in turn seems to presuppose that each person contains a minimum of everyone else, and so divination is aroused by comparison with oneself. But how is it possible for the comparative method to subsume a person under a general type? Obviously, either by another act of comparison (and this continues into infinity) or by divination. The two methods should never be separated. Divination becomes certain only when it is corroborated by comparisons. Without this confirmation, it always tends to be fanatical.[128]

This in sum is Schleiermacher's so-called "fourfold expository method." Grammatical and psychological interpretations constitute one set of polarities, comparative and divinatory interpretation the other. Each polarity seeks to balance the other, and it is at the point at which all four polarities intersect that understanding ideally occurs.[129]

However, given this brief description of Schleiermacher's hermeneutic, there are at least two issues which need to be highlighted. The first has to do with the very basis of divinatory interpretation, viz., Schleiermacher's claim that divinatory interpretation "is based on the assumption that each person is not only a unique individual in his own right, but that he has a receptivity [*Empfänglichkeit*] to the uniqueness of every other person. This assumption in turn seems to presuppose that each person contains a minimum of everyone else, and so divination is aroused by comparison with oneself." Having a re-

---

[127] Schleiermacher, *Hermeneutik*, p. 109; ET p. 150.

[128] Schleiermacher, *Hermeneutik*, p. 109; ET p. 150.

[129] "As so often with Schleiermacher," Barth says, "we thus have crosswires." Barth, *Die Theologie Schleiermachers*, p. 324; ET p. 182. He illustrates this as follows:

$$\begin{array}{c} \text{divinatory} \\ \text{grammatical} \;+\; \text{psychological} \\ \text{comparative} \end{array}$$

ceptivity to the uniqueness of every other person or a susceptibility for the experience of others has to do with what Dilthey and others later referred to as a "capacity for empathy" (*Einfühlungsvermögen*). But having a capacity for empathy or receptivity to the uniqueness of every other person presupposes that "each person contains a minimum of everyone else." Schleiermacher does not describe what the content of this "minimum" is, but he does suggest that knowledge of it is based on our self-understanding ("divination is aroused by comparison with oneself"). In other words, it is only in terms of our own self-understanding that we can project ourselves into the mind of an author and rethink and relive his thoughts and experiences, and this is possible only because we share the same human nature. Here we are obviously standing on the same ground as Herder, the ground of a common, universally intuitable core of humanity, the fact that "The harmony of every creature/ Is one with me, yes, I am they!" As for Herder, so for Schleiermacher: "The degree of our sense of self is at the same time the measure of our feeling for others: for it is only our self that we can as it were project [*hineinfühlen*] into the feelings of others."

This brings up a second issue. There is an obvious tension in Schleiermacher's claim on the one hand that "each person is a unique individual in his own right" and on the other hand that each person "has a receptivity to the uniqueness of every other person." The tension is this: If everyone is a unique individual, how unique can an individual be if every person has a receptivity to the uniqueness of every other person? What becomes of individuality, or what are the limits set on individuality, if every individual has an intrinsic receptivity to the individuality of everyone else? This tension is even more apparent in Schleiermacher's statement above that "the divinatory method," on the one hand, "seeks to gain an immediate comprehension of the author as an individual," while on the other hand, "The comparative method proceeds by subsuming the author under a general type." Again, what becomes of individuality if it must be subsumed under a general type? Schleiermacher is obviously aware of this problem, which is why he asks: "But how is it possible for the comparative method to subsume a person under a general type?" Yet his answer to this question seems hardly an entirely satisfactory one given his regard, one might even say reverence, for the mystery of individuality. Schleiermacher suggests that subsuming an author under a general type is not really a problem so long as we recognize that it must be followed by another act of divination and then again by another act of comparison, and that this continues into infinity. And the reason divination must always be followed by another act of comparison is that: "divination becomes certain only when it is corroborated by comparisons. Without this confirmation, it always tends to be fanatical."

That understanding an author's individuality consists of pursuing a movement back and forth between divinatory and comparative interpretation which continues into infinity suggests that Schleiermacher did not see human individuality as something that could ever be simply resolved. This is why he insists that the task of interpretation never ends.[130] For Schleiermacher, individuality remained an enigma, an irreducible and indissoluble mystery always beyond our grasp. Goethe's dictum, "*Individuum est ineffabile*," expresses one of his most passionately held convictions.[131] Dilthey even describes the idea of the creative individual personality as "the very soul of his thought."[132] And this is obviously one of the major reasons why he expressed such antipathy throughout his career for the doctrine of inspiration, which is particularly evident throughout his lectures on hermeneutics. Again and again throughout these lectures Schleiermacher dismisses the doctrine of inspiration as at best unhelpful, unnecessary, and something which "should not influence the work of interpretation," and at worst something which is untenable, which limits our understanding of an author's individual determination of a text and therefore severely distorts the entire process of understanding.[133] It "means that the process of writing is hedged in," making the authors "merely passive tools of the Holy Spirit."[134] Such a theory, he felt, simply denied the free creative process of human production. For him, there were always two basic facts at issue in interpretation: on the one hand, "an author finds himself guided by the power of the subject matter" and on the other, "the author is free."[135] Schleiermacher's fundamental problem with the doctrine of inspiration, in short, was that it denied the latter, that it was reductionistic of human individuality and the "produktive *Geist*" of authors and was therefore to that extent ineluctably docetic. But the question which in turn needs to be raised is: How well does Schleiermacher's own approach fare in this regard? Given that "the comparative method proceeds by subsuming an author under a general type" and that "divination becomes certain only when it is corroborated by comparisons," does his own approach not also risk being reductionistic of an author's individual determination of a text? The following passage (which comes at the conclusion of his second address to the Prussian Academy of Sciences on Oct. 22, 1829 which Lücke published with his other lecture notes on hermeneutics and was originally titled "On the Concept of Hermeneutics, with reference to F.A. Wolf's Instructions and Ast's Textbook") raises important questions in this regard. Schleiermacher states:

---

[130] Schleiermacher, *Hermeneutik*, p. 115; ET p. 164.

[131] "Have I not already written to you, 'Individuum est ineffabile,' from which I derive a whole world?" Goethe to Lavatar, 1780.

[132] See pp. 159-160n.140 below; Dilthey, "Das hermeneutische System Schleiermachers" p. 729; ET p. 168.

[133] Schleiermacher, *Hermeneutik*, p. 84, 159; ET pp. 105-106, 216.

[134] Schleiermacher, *Hermeneutik*, pp. 84-85; ET pp. 106-7.

[135] Schleiermacher, *Hermeneutik*, p. 48; ET p. 62.

> This alone is clear: the explanation of the words and subject matter are not themselves interpretation but only elements of it, and hermeneutics begins with the determination of meaning, although to be sure by means of these elements. Further, no explanation, that is, no determination of meaning, is ever correct unless it is supported by an examination of the spirit of the author and the spirit of classical antiquity. For only a person in a disturbed state of mind speaks or writes against his own spirit, and, were one to insist on an explanation of an ancient writer that stands in clear contradiction to the spirit of antiquity, one would have to prove that the author was a mongrel in his spirit.[136]

It is clear from this statement that Schleiermacher viewed the classical approach of understanding the relationship between words and subject matter, *signa* and *res*, what is written and what is written about, as an important aspect of interpretation. Yet words and subject matter, he claims, "are only elements of it." Something more, something deeper, is needed because "no explanation, that is, no determination of meaning, is ever correct unless it is supported by an examination of the spirit of the author and the spirit of classical antiquity." Here Herder's priority of "entering the 'spirit' of an age, a man, a people, or a work" is clearly echoed. But it is what Schleiermacher says next that raises questions with respect to the freedom of an author's individual determination of a text: "For only a person in a disturbed state of mind speaks or writes against his own spirit, and, were one to insist on an explanation of an ancient writer that stands in clear contradiction to the spirit of antiquity, one would have to prove that the author was a mongrel [*Mischling*] in his spirit." The question this raises particularly in light of what Barth claims he discovered in reading the epistles of the apostle Paul, is: What about Paul? If or to the extent that Paul wrote his *Epistle to the Romans* "against his own spirit," might he not qualify as "a person in a disturbed state of mind"? Is this not what Barth is talking about when he says: "I seem to see behind the banner of such a document a personality who is actually thrown off all ordinary courses and primarily off his own course by seeing and hearing what I for my part do not see and hear – who is, so to speak, precisely as a personality, annihilated in order to be dragged from land to land as a prisoner to do strange, rash, unpredictable, and yet mysteriously well-planned deeds"? Yet even if one were to suggest that Paul did not write against his own spirit when he wrote his *Epistle to the Romans*, it is surely another matter to suggest that he did not write "in clear contradiction to the spirit of antiquity"? Quite apart from the extent to which this would seem to equate the Holy Spirit or the creative spirit of Christianity[137] with the spirit of antiquity, this raises an important question: If Paul did not, indeed, could not, speak or write "in clear contradiction to the spirit of antiq-

---

[136] Schleiermacher, *Hermeneutik*, p. 154; ET pp. 211-212.

[137] Christianity's creative spirit cannot be underestimated, according to Schleiermacher: "Christianity has created language. From its very beginning it has been a potentiating linguistic spirit, and it still is" Schleiermacher, *Hermeneutik*, p. 38; ET p. 50.

uity" lest he be "a mongrel in his spirit," to what extent was he really free as an individual, free as an individual creative genius, to write his epistles?

The question I raise here is essentially the same one I raised earlier. If the comparative method "proceeds by subsuming the author under a general type," what then becomes of individuality, the individuality of an author such as Paul, for example, if it must be subsumed under a general type? Even if divination is relatively successful in identifying the uniqueness of an author's individuality (and how could it be otherwise than relatively successful given that "divination is aroused by comparison with oneself"?), how unique could an author's individuality be if it must be corroborated by comparisons? Until the *truth* of an author's individuality be revealed, will repeated acts of comparison really help? Of course, if stereoscopic vision or the possibility of viewing truth with both eyes open at the same time is ruled out from the beginning, then looking through one eye, the divinatory, and then the other, the comparative, back and forth *ad infinitum*, is obviously better than seeing nothing at all. But is this the only possibility? I shall return to this question in my concluding chapter. Now it is necessary to consider the further trajectory of the empathetic tradition of interpretation into the early twentieth century.

3. Wilhelm Dilthey

Wilhelm Dilthey was Schleiermacher's most influential follower in the nineteenth century and perhaps also in the twentieth. As I said in chapter two, Dilthey held Hegel's former chair in philosophy at Berlin from 1882 until his death in 1911, and was considered by many to be Germany's leading philosopher. Later regarded as the greatest epistemologist of the humanities as well as one of the most insightful historiographical theorists of his era, he was at the time of his death probably best known for having written the definitive biography of Schleiermacher and for having been the greatest champion of hermeneutics of his day.[138] Schleiermacher and the topic of hermeneutics, however, had been of great concern to Dilthey from the very beginning of his career. At age twenty-seven while still a theology student at Berlin, he wrote an essay entitled *Schleiermacher's Hermeneutical System in Relation to Earlier Protestant Hermeneutics,* for which he was awarded a prize in 1860 by the Schleiermacher Society.[139] Though never published in its entirety until 1966, this study

---

[138] As I mentioned in chapter two, praising his "pioneering work," Heidegger stated in *Sein und Zeit* that his entire generation was indebted to Dilthey for having raised the question of hermeneutics to a fundamental level of importance.

[139] Dilthey's so-called *Preisschrift* is divided into three parts: "Hermeneutics Before Schleiermacher"; "The Origins of Schleiermacher's Hermeneutics"; and "Comparison of Schleiermacher's Hermeneutics to the Earlier Systems." Its exact title is "Der eigentümliche Verdienst der Schleiermacherischen Hermeneutik ist durch Vergleichung mit älteren Bearbeitungen dieser Wissenschaft, namentlich von Ernesti und Keil, ins Licht zu setzen." Dilthey, "Das hermeneutische System Schleiermachers in der Auseinandersetzung mit der älteren pro-

is important because of the light it sheds on Schleiermacher's hermeneutics and the rise of the empathetic tradition of interpretation.[140]

---

testantischen Hermeneutik" in *Gesammelte Schriften, II.1. Leben Schleiermachers* (Berlin: Walter de Gruyter, 1966), pp. 595-785; ET *Hermeneutics and the Study of History, Selected Works*, IV, ed. Rudolf Makkreel (Princeton: University Press, 1996), pp. 33-234. Hereafter cited as "Das hermeneutische System Schleiermachers."

[140]Dilthey traces, in the most detailed history of hermeneutics that had been written up to that point in time, the rise of hermeneutics beginning with Matthias Flacius who responded to the Council of Trent's claim that a valid interpretation of Scripture could not be worked out on the basis of Scripture alone. In formulating a method of interpretation on the basis of the unity and coherence of Scripture, Flacius, Dilthey claims, undertook to prove the possibility of universally valid interpretation through hermeneutics and thereby took the first major step to establish the autonomy of hermeneutics. His theory was basically flawed, however, because "while asserting the self-sufficiency of Scripture, it actually subordinated exegesis in practice to the Protestant creeds" (p. 608; ET p. 46). Others such as Salamo Glassius and Wolfgang Franz followed Flacius' lead but were likewise unsuccessful. It was J.A. Turrettini who, in seeking to defend Scripture from mounting criticism, tried to defend the truth of biblical accounts on the basis of reason alone and articulated "for the first time, the principle that hermeneutical rules should possess universal validity." "The supreme rule for him was to explain by appealing to the nature of things themselves. Indeed, he asserts that if a passage contradicts reason, then it must either be given another sense, or, failing that, be rejected as spurious" (pp. 616f.; ET pp. 54-55). But this sort of approach eventually gave rise to a Romantic and Pietistic reaction, viz., "The Hermeneutics of the Affections." "It did not seek doctrines from Scripture, but from a state of the soul. Accordingly, the interpreter was required above all to surrender himself to the state of the soul expressed in Scripture" (p. 619; ET p. 57). This, Dilthey claims, "represents the beginning of psychological interpretation, which would soon, with philosophical encouragement, free itself from its original tendencies." However, pietistic interpreters such as Francke, Wolf, Baumgarten, and Bengel were by and large interested in more than spiritual or psychological aspects of interpretation and actually did much to pave the way for others more adept at grammatical and historical aspects of interpretation, e.g. Semler and Michaelis. With Semler virtually presiding over the dissolution of the unity of the canon, the primary task of exegesis became to understand particular "Scriptures in their local settings," "to pursue the time-bound features of the individual Scriptures" (p. 635; ET pp. 73-74). This practically "destroyed the complicated older method that viewed exegesis as the organ of dogmatics." Ernesti and Keil also contributed to the rise of hermeneutics with their focus on grammatical interpretation which was far more systematic, albeit more mechanical, than the approaches of their contemporaries. But it was "Herder who came closer to true hermeneutics than anyone else before Schleiermacher." "He was the first to direct interpretation to the totality of a work, to its inner spirit, and to the sphere from which it came forth. But he was not able to express this inner spirit except in the form of general aesthetic impressions." Though he never achieved a systematic conception of hermeneutics, the "congenial sensitivity of Herder would become the basis for a sound method of interpretation and a genuinely scientific hermeneutics" (pp. 649-650; ET pp. 89-90). Herder exercised an enormous influence upon Schleiermacher. Dilthey even refers to Schleiermacher as "Herder's disciple" (p. 730; ET p. 170). Other influences include Kant and Fichte. Focus on the "productive I" and the principle of individuality which Fichte advanced led to the development of "the genetic method." As applied by Schlegel, the genetic method became indispensable to the development of Schleiermacher's hermeneutic as also was the work of Schelling, whose "school gave rise to the first

Dilthey spends considerable time recapitulating Schleiermacher's hermeneutical program and its antecedent influences in this early work, but even here it is evident that he was looking beyond it. Interested in more than codifying the history of the hermeneutical tradition culminating in Schleiermacher, his aim, as his later work shows, was to build upon it. Schleiermacher's great achievement had been his focus on understanding itself. What does it mean to understand? How does understanding itself occur? Schleiermacher had done much to begin to answer these questions, but his program had been limited in at least two ways. First, the scope of his program was limited in that he was primarily concerned with understanding human utterances, whereas Dilthey was concerned with the understanding of all human experiences, which is why he sought to establish hermeneutics as the foundational discipline of all human sciences. Secondly, it was limited to the extent that it could provide objective validity in interpretation. Dilthey's aim, therefore, was to broaden the scope of hermeneutics and on the basis of a closer examination of the process of understanding itself, establish for the human sciences the same level of methodological clarity that had theretofore characterized the natural sciences. He wanted to establish a basis for regarding the human sciences which was just as objective as the natural sciences, to develop a neutral theory for understanding all human phenomena which would be accessible to all interpreters, regardless of their particular historical or social location or perspective. In short, he wanted to be able to speak as confidently in terms of general validity and progress in the field of human sciences as others did in the field of natural sciences. In his famous essay of 1900, "*Die Entstehung der Hermeneutik*," the terms "validity" and "general validity" are repeated over and over again. Summarizing the history of hermeneutics he had elaborated forty years before, Dilthey concludes this essay by defining the "*main* task" of hermeneutics as follows:

> To preserve the general validity of interpretation against the inroads of romantic caprice and skeptical subjectivity, and to give a theoretical justification for such validity, upon which all the certainty of historical knowledge is founded. Seen in the context of the theory of knowledge, of logic, and the methodology of the human studies, the theory of interpretation becomes an essential connecting link between philosophy and the historical disciplines, an essential component in the foundation of the human studies themselves.[141]

Nowhere was the need for "the general validity of interpretation against the inroads of romantic caprice and skeptical subjectivity" felt more acutely by

---

the first theory of reconstructive understanding" (p. 657; ET p. 96). In sum, Dilthey states, "... the significance of Schleiermacher's hermeneutics simply cannot be understood, indeed no single aspect of it can be comprehended in its uniqueness, apart from its total relationship to the grand movement that completely transformed historical studies and in whose train we are still caught up today. How fortunate were those men to whom it was granted to establish linguistics, mythology, the history of systems, religious studies, aesthetics, and hermeneutics on the foundation of the great philosophical discovery of the productive I" (p. 657; ET p. 96).

[141] Dilthey, "*Die Entstehung der Hermeneutik*," p. 331; ET p. 244.

Dilthey and his contemporaries than in the field of history. Positivists had striven to secure the general validity of their interpretations, over and against romantic caprice and skeptical subjectivity. But their methods, as Dilthey saw it, were naive. They simply did not understand the complexity of historiography. Nor did they understand history's fundamental dependence upon biography or the unpredictability and irrationality of life, which always places such huge question marks over attempts at historical explanation.[142] Yet on the other hand, with the increasing skepticism of Nietzsche and others of his own day, Dilthey also realized that the very notion of general validity with respect to historical knowledge was being seriously challenged. Schleiermacher had done little conceptually to advance the notion of general validity in historical interpretation. Even though he had many pioneering historical-critical insights into the New Testament, few biblical scholars by the turn of the century believed he had approached the Bible in a seriously historical manner, much less that he had been concerned with the general validity of historical interpretation. Albert Schweitzer said that Schleiermacher's approach had been "not historical, but dialectical."[143] Dilthey believed, nevertheless, that Schleiermacher had begun to develop a tool, hermeneutics that could, properly conceived, eventually establish general validity in interpretation. Thus, standing on Schleiermacher's shoulders, Dilthey announced in his essay, *Plan der Fortsetzung zum Aufbau der geschichtlichen Welt in den Geisteswissenschaften*, "Now we must relate hermeneutics to the epistemological task of showing the possibility of historical knowledge and finding the means for acquiring it ... we must now, starting from the logical forms of understanding, ascertain to what degree it can

---

[142] Like few before him Dilthey was convinced that the key to understanding history was biography. Indeed he saw autobiography as the key to understanding the universe. "So all understanding contains something irrational because life is irrational; it cannot be represented by a logical formula." Wilhelm Dilthey, *Gesammelte Schriften, VII. Der Aufbau der geschichtlichen Welt in den Geisteswissenschaften* (Berlin: B.G. Teubner, 1927), p. 218; ET *The Hermeneutics Reader*, ed. Kurt Mueller-Vollmer (New York: Continuum, 1992), p. 162. Hereafter cited as *Der Aufbau der geschichtlichen Welt*.

[143] Albert Schweitzer, *Geschichte der Leben-Jesu-Forschung*, 2nd ed. (Tübingen: J.C.B. Mohr [Paul Siebeck], 1913), p. 64; ET *The Quest of The Historical Jesus*, trans. W. Montgomery (London: Adam & Charles Black, 1954), p. 63. Schweitzer states: "Schleiermacher is not in search of the historical Jesus, but of the Jesus Christ of his own system of theology; that is to say, of the historic figure which seems to him appropriate to the self-consciousness of the Redeemer as he represents it. For him the empirical has simply no existence. ... He comes to the facts with a ready-made dialectic apparatus and sets his puppets in lively action. Schleiermacher's dialectic is not a dialectic which generates reality, like that of Hegel, of which Strauss availed himself, but merely a dialectic of exposition. In this literary dialectic he is the greatest master that ever lived" (p. 62). Later he speaks of Schleiermacher's "infallible" and "magical dialectic" (p. 63). Schweitzer says later in his book on Paul that Schleiermacher had come to believe that Timothy was not Pauline not because he was a serious historical critic, but because he was an aesthete.

achieve validity."[144] The logical forms of understanding for Dilthey, as I said in chapter two, were *Nachfühlung, Nachverständnis, Nacherleben, Nachbildung*, etc. Part of the task of ascertaining the degree to which historical knowledge could achieve validity was to gain a more precise know-ledge of such processes. In other words, in order to obtain objective validity in historical interpretation, Dilthey saw it necessary to examine the process of genetic reconstruction with more precision. He does so, among other places, in the essay cited above under the rubric "*Hineinversetzen, Nachbilden, Nacherleben*."[145] Here we see how important the concept of empathy was to Dilthey's overall program.[146]

With a technical significance never before seen in the history of interpretation, Dilthey defines empathy as more than simply the act of projecting oneself or feeling one's way into the spirit of something or someone but as "the state of mind" involved in the task of understanding which allows one to discover a "vital connection" in what is given as an object of interpretation, be it a person or text. It is based on "the inner context" of one's own lived experience, and for "higher understanding" to occur it must always be present and ready. Dilthey discusses degrees of empathy but in one of his now more famous passages he describes the role of empathy, in the process of understanding with respect to Luther:

> Life progressively limits a man's inherent potentialities. ... But understanding opens for him a wide realm of possibilities which do not exist within the limitations of real life. The possibility of experiencing religious states in one's own life is narrowly limited for me as for most of my contemporaries. But, when I read through the letters and writings of Luther, the reports of his contemporaries, the records of religious disputes and councils, and those of his dealings with officials, I experience a religious process, in which life and death are at issue, of such eruptive power and energy as is beyond the possibility of direct experience for a man of our time. But I can re-live it. I transpose myself into the circumstances; everything in them makes for an extraordinary development of religious feelings. I observe in the monasteries a technique for dealing with the invisible world which directs the monk's soul constantly towards transcendent matters; theological controversies become matters of inner life. I observe how what is thus formed in the monasteries *is spread* through innumerable channels – sermons, confessions, teaching and writings – to the laity; and then I notice how councils and religious movements *have spread* the doctrine of the invisible church and universal priesthood everywhere and how it comes to be related to the liberation of personality in the secular sphere. ... As Luther leads this movement we can understand his development through the links between common human features, the religious sphere, this historical setting and his personality. Thus this process reveals a religious world in him

---

[144] Dilthey, *Der Aufbau der geschichtlichen Welt*, p. 218; ET p. 162.

[145] Dilthey, *Der Aufbau der geschichtlichen Welt*, pp. 213f; ET pp. 159f.

[146] Rudolf Makkreel claims that many, particularly English readers, have overemphasized the role of *Einfühlung* in Dilthey's thought. *Dilthey: Philosopher of the Human Studies* (Princeton: University Press, 1975), pp. 252-253. The fact is, however, that many German scholars have emphasized it as well.

and his companions of the first period of the Reformation which widens our horizon of the possibilities of human existence. Only in this way do they become accessible to us. Thus the inner-directed man can experience many other existences in his imagination. Limited by circumstances he can yet glimpse alien beauty in the world and areas of life beyond his reach. Put generally: man, tied and limited by the reality of life is liberated not only by art – as has often been explained – but also by historical understanding.[147]

Dilthey's widely acclaimed optimism is clearly evident in this passage. With "the great philosophical discovery of the productive I," the method of empathetic identification, and the overall development of historical consciousness throughout the nineteenth century, Dilthey saw the possibility of understanding alien individuality as greater than ever before. More interested in the inner life of the author than Schleiermacher, Dilthey saw it as now more accessible. Psychology and the study of understanding itself had simply produced more sophisticated tools for grasping the inner life and therewith the alien individuality of authors such as Luther. This is not to say that individuality did not remain a mystery for Dilthey. On the contrary, he refers to it as "the greatest mystery of life."[148] Goethe's dictum, "*Individuum est ineffabile*, from which I derive an entire world," is a belief he held as passionately as Schleiermacher,[149] the major difference being that Dilthey sought on this basis even more passionately to derive that world.[150] But for all his reverence for it, the mystery of individuality was not something entirely insuperable for Dilthey, just as it had not been for Schleiermacher.[151] Because of advances in our understanding of the nature of understanding itself, it too was something that could, with increasing certainty, be assessed in terms of general validity. The basis for this Dilthey suggests in the following passage:

> The possibility of generally valid interpretation can be derived from the nature of understanding. In understanding, the individuality of the exegete and that of the author are not opposed to each other like two incomparable facts. Rather, both have been formed upon the foundation of a general human nature, and it is this which makes possible the commun-

---

[147] Dilthey, *Der Aufbau der geschichtlichen Welt*, pp. 215-216; ET pp. 160-1.

[148] Dilthey, *Der Aufbau der geschichtlichen Welt*, p. 213; ET p. 159.

[149] Dilthey, "Die Entstehung der Hermeneutik," p. 330; ET p. 243.

[150] "We are concerned with the individual," Dilthey said, "not merely as an example of man in general but as a totality in himself" *Der Aufbau der geschichtlichen Welt*, p. 212; ET p. 158. For Dilthey, every individual is a universe unto himself. Practically everything in his system begins and ends with the individual. "The individual constitutes an intrinsic value ... indeed, it is the only intrinsic value we can ascertain without doubt." Dilthey might best be described for this reason as a "metaphysical individualist," a designation I owe to my teacher, the late Victor Preller.

[151] Gadamer claims: "It is true that Schleiermacher saw individuality as a secret that can never be fully unlocked, ... but even this statement needs to be taken only in a relative way: the barrier to reason and understanding that remains here is not in every sense insuperable. It is to be overcome by *feeling* [*das Gefühl*], by an immediate, sympathetic and congenial understanding" *Wahrheit und Methode*, p. 195; ET p. 191.

ion of people with each other in speech. Here the relatively formalistic terminology of Schleiermacher can be further elucidated psychologically. Individual differences are not in the last analysis determined by qualitative differences between people, but rather through a difference in the degree of development of their spiritual processes. Now inasmuch as the exegete tentatively projects his own sense of life into another historical milieu, he is able within that perspective, to strengthen and emphasize certain spiritual processes in himself and to minimize others, thus making possible within himself a re-experiencing of an alien form of life.[152]

Two summary observations about Dilthey's project are now in order. First, it is clear from his statement above that the reason the individuality of the exegete and that of the author are not opposed to each other like two incomparable facts is that both at their core share the same basic human nature. It is "the foundation of a general human nature," Dilthey claims, that "makes possible the communion of people with each other in speech." We have seen, it is important to recall, a common anthropology posited as the basis of hermeneutics before. From Herder we heard that "The harmony of every creature/ Is one with me, yes, I am they!" and from Schleiermacher that "each person contains a minimum of everyone else" and "has a receptivity to the uniqueness of every other person." But here we are told that sharing the same "foundation of a general human nature" means that in the last analysis there really are no "qualitative differences" between peoples, only "a difference in the degree of development of their spiritual processes." What is so striking about this claim is not merely the substance of the claim itself, but the degree of scientific assurance with which it is made.[153] Dilthey begins above by stating that "The possibility of generally valid interpretation can be derived from the nature of understanding." And he makes clear that the objective basis for claiming that the possibility of generally valid interpretation can be derived from the nature of understanding is a common anthropology which can be "elucidated psychologically." Herein lies the basis of objective, generally valid interpretation for Dilthey. Dilthey was confident that psychology was now capable of establishing an objective basis for generally valid interpretation, whereas the "relatively formalistic terminology of Schleiermacher," a reference apparently to divinatory and comparative interpretation, was not. Divinatory interpretation was simply too subjectivistic, which may be why Dilthey consistently minimizes the role of divinatory interpretation in Schleiermacher's hermeneutics in favor of psychological interpretation (this would suggest there is probably some justification in the charge of Heinz Kimmerle and others that Dilthey overemphasized the role of psychological interpretation in recapitulating Schleiermacher's

---

[152] Dilthey, "Die Entstehung der Hermeneutik," pp. 329-330; ET pp. 242-243.

[153] Though the notion that all share the same "foundation of a common human nature" is already implied in Schleiermacher and Herder, neither go so far as to say that this means there are ultimately no "qualitative differences" between peoples, only "a difference in the degree of development of their spiritual processes."

hermeneutic).¹⁵⁴ In any case, in his quest to establish an objective basis for generally valid interpretation derived from the nature of understanding itself, Dilthey sought to safeguard interpretation "against the inroads of romantic caprice and skeptical subjectivity" on the one hand, and against positivism, particularly historical positivism on the other. But there is an irony here which is difficult to miss. Frederic Jameson has perhaps summarized it best: "Dilthey, for all his hostility to positivism, finds himself obliged to come to terms with historical variety through ... a hypothesis which ends up subsuming history as a discipline beneath the newly emergent science of psychology."¹⁵⁵ In other words, in the end, for all his hostility to positivism, Dilthey seems simply to have traded one form of positivism for another.

Finally, an observation about the nature of understanding in Dilthey. I said earlier that Dilthey saw the inner life of the author as more accessible than did Schleiermacher because of the more sophisticated tools produced by psychology and because of our increased knowledge of understanding and its specific moments. In short, because of such advances, the tension between "Ich" and "Du" for Dilthey simply became more relaxed. The upshot of this was that Schleiermacher's goal of understanding an author better than he understood himself – a goal Dilthey enthusiastically embraces and repeats again and again throughout his work – was now from a scientific standpoint more realizable than ever before.¹⁵⁶ But what it meant to understand an author better than he understood himself changed as well. Dilthey, for example, speaks repeatedly about re-experiencing alien forms of life within himself.¹⁵⁷ He even refers to the interpreter's task as that of gathering "the spirits of the past *within* himself."¹⁵⁸ What results from gathering and re-experiencing within oneself such alien forms of life, he says, is an "enlargement" of one's own existence.¹⁵⁹

---

¹⁵⁴ Dilthey, "*Das hermeneutische System Schleiermachers*," pp. 719-720; ET p. 159. In "Die Entstehung der Hermeneutik" he describes Schleiermacher's hermeneutic in considerable detail, yet not once does he mention divinatory interpretation.

¹⁵⁵ Fredric Jameson, Translator's preface to "The Rise of Hermeneutics," p. 230.

¹⁵⁶ "The ultimate goal of the hermeneutic process is to understand an author better than he understood himself. This is an idea which is the necessary consequence of the doctrine of unconscious creation" in "Die Entstehung der Hermeneutik," p. 331; ET p. 244. See also *Der Aufbau der geschichtlichen Welt*, p. 217; ET p. 162.

¹⁵⁷ Wilhelm Dilthey, *Gesammelte Schriften, VIII. Die Typen der Weltanschauung und ihre Ausbildung in dem metaphysischen System* (Berlin: B.G. Teubner, 1931), p. 235. Italics mine.

¹⁵⁸ Dilthey, *Die Typen der Weltanschauung und ihre Ausbildung in dem metaphysischen System*, p. 204.

¹⁵⁹ Wilhelm Dilthey, *Gesammelte Schriften, V. Über vergleichende Psychologie: Beiträge zum Studium der Individualität* (Berlin, B.G. Teubner, 1924), p. 276. "When we join in living through something past by employing the art of historical imagination, we are taught, just as though life itself were our teacher; indeed, our being is *enlarged*, and psychical powers stronger than our own elevate our existence." *Gesammelte Schriften, I, Einleitung in die Geisteswissenschaften* (Berlin: B.G. Teubner, 1922), p. 91.

This notion of understanding as an enlargement of our existence is a very important one for Dilthey. According to Theodore Plantinga,

> Although the understanding of the historian engaged in scholarship involves detachment and reserve, the process of understanding also serves to enlarge our selfhood – if only we will open ourselves to others and the past. Tennyson declared: "I am a part of all that I have met." Dilthey would reverse this by saying that all that I have met and lived has become a part of me, and that I have become a fuller, richer, larger self as a result. Dilthey sees the drive for meaning in life as an effort to reach out to others and make what they have lived part of our own existence. We ingest and digest the other by reliving events of human history, enjoying works of art, and steeping ourselves in other cultures, religions, and societies through the fruits of scholarship.[160]

This notion of understanding as a gathering of alien forms within one's self, as an ingesting and digesting of others, resulting in a richer, larger self, obviously suggests that identifying empathetically with an author meant for Dilthey, as for Herder, entering into a process which ultimately involved far more than surrender. Whatever else it suggests, it is a metaphor for understanding worth remembering as we consider the circumstances leading up to Karl Barth's hermeneutical revolution.

4. Ernst Troeltsch and Georg Wobbermin

The empathetic tradition of interpretation from Herder to Schleiermacher to Dilthey exercised a significant influence on the major theological movements of the early decades of the twentieth century in both Germany and Switzerland. Herder, *Einfühlung*, and the increasing influence of Dilthey played an important role as we have seen in the work of theologians and biblical scholars such as Paul Wernle, a major figure in the history of religions school,[161] as well as in the work of Adolf von Harnack who, in his famous lecture series, *The Essence of Christianity: Sixteen Lectures for Students of All Faculties Delivered in the University of Berlin during the Winter Semester of 1899-1900*, stated that he wanted merely to present Christianity "solely according to its historical meaning," which meant "by the methods of historical science and the experience of life gained by history relived."[162] But where this influence was most apparent was in the history of religions school's most famous representative, Ernst

---

[160] Theodore Plantinga, *Historical Understanding in the Thought of Wilhelm Dilthey* (Toronto: University of Toronto Press, 1980), p. 7. See also p. 62.

[161] Dilthey's name is mentioned several times in Wernle's 1908 and 1911 editions of his *Einführung*, but in the 1921 edition it appears also as shown above in his introductory chapter on method. These references to Dilthey's contribution appear to be the only significant difference between the 1908 and 1921 chapters on method, which, as I alluded to in chapter two, suggests something of the growing influence of Dilthey in the early decades of the twentieth century.

[162] Adolf von Harnack, *Das Wesen des Christentums* (Leipzig: J.C. Hinrichs'sche, 1900), p. 4; ET *What Is Christianity?*, trans. Thomas Bailey Saunders (New York: G.P. Putnam's Sons, 1901), p. 6 [translation revised].

Troeltsch. Actually, according to Gadamer, so important were Dilthey's collected works in the 1920s that they quickly overshadowed Troeltsch's influence.[163] In any case, Troeltsch referred to Dilthey as his teacher, was his colleague at the University of Berlin, and it is to his memory that Troeltsch dedicated his last book, *Der Historismus and seine Probleme*.[164] Indebted to Dilthey's pioneering work on the nature of understanding, Troeltsch discusses the importance of "empathy," "the sympathetic imagination," "the art of sympathy," and "our capacity for sympathy," etc., with respect to historical understanding throughout his work.[165] Historical interpretation, he argued, is fundamentally based upon analogy and correlation.[166] The only means of understanding events, people, places, and things of the past is through our knowledge and experience of events, people, places, and things of the present and of other times and places. Thus understanding an individual such as Paul, for example, is a matter of comparing him with charismatic *Geistestypen* of both the past and present. The basis for drawing such comparisons, Troeltsch insists (again, as we have seen with Herder, Schleiermacher, and Dilthey) is "our common humanity,"[167] the fact that we all share the same basic human nature. Given this basis, Troeltsch is quick to point out: "The creative significance of the personalities [of the past] need not be denied. But," he immediately adds, "the personalities of Judeo-Christian history are neither more nor less irrational than those of Greek and Persian history."[168] In other words, even though the personalities of Judeo-Christian history may differ in various ways, given our common humanity, they are not – indeed they cannot be – in the final analysis so very different than ourselves or those of other times and places. And when asked how he could be so confident about historical judgments made on the basis of our common humanity, Troeltsch says it is based "on the conviction that ultimately the essential uniformity of human nature provides a foundation

---

[163] Gadamer,*Wahrheit und Methode*, p. 479; ET p. 507.

[164] Ernst Troeltsch, *Der Historismus und seine Probleme* (Tübingen: J.C.B. Mohr [Paul Siebeck], 1922).

[165] Troeltsch, p. 516f. "Über historische und dogmatische Methode in der Theologie," *Gesammelte Schriften* 2 (Tübingen: J.C.B. Mohr [Paul Siebeck], 1913), pp. 732f; ET "Historical and Dogmatic Method in Theology" in *Religion in History*, trans. James Luther Adams and Walter E. Bense (Minneapolis: Fortress Press, 1991), pp. 14f. Hereafter cited as "Über historische und dogmatische Methode in der Theologie." See also Troeltsch's article "Historiography," in *Encyclopaedia of Religion and Ethics*, ed. James Hastings (New York: Charles Scribner's Sons, 1925), 6, p. 719.

[166] Troeltsch, "Über historische und dogmatische Methode in der Theologie," p. 731f; ET p. 13f.

[167] Troeltsch, "Über historische und dogmatische Methode in der Theologie," p. 732; ET p. 14.

[168] Troeltsch, "Über historische und dogmatische Methode in der Theologie," p. 736; ET p. 17 [translation revised].

for consensus in recognizing supreme standards of value, and that because of this foundation, the consensus will prevail."[169]

Troeltsch saw his program as being in basic continuity with Schleiermacher's in that he too, like Schleiermacher, was trying to take religion, the phenomenon of religious experience, and religious psychology seriously.[170] But his was not the only school vying for the mantle of Schleiermacher's authority at the turn of the century. Georg Wobbermin, professor of systematic theology and Barth's colleague at Göttingen, insisted that his emerging school of religious psychology was the true heir of Schleiermacher's theological legacy.[171] Like Troeltsch, he too was interested in religion and particularly the psychology of religion. And like Troeltsch, he too relied upon *Einfühlung* and the concept of a general anthropology. Wobbermin even refers to "productive *Einfühlung*" as *the* programmatic concept of his three-volume *Systematische Theologie: nach religionspsychologischer Methode*.[172] This is obviously one reason why Barth saw both Troeltsch and Wobbermin as sharing not only the same father, Schleiermacher, but the same grandfather, Herder. Barth, as I mentioned earlier, claimed that "Herder's significance for those theologians who came after him can scarcely be rated highly enough. Without him there would have been no Schleiermacher. ... But for Herder there would have been no Troeltsch." Though it would be too much to suggest that all of modern theology has been determined by Herder, Barth says, "What does stem from Herder in the newer theology is all that which can be brought under the heading of psychologism and historicism, its methodical point of departure in the

---

[169] Troeltsch, "Über historische und dogmatische Methode in der Theologie," pp. 745-746; ET p. 25.

[170] Claiming to be the true heir of Schleiermacher, Troeltsch argued in his essay of 1908, "*Rückblick auf ein halbes Jahrhundert der theologischen Wissenschaft*" in *Theologie als Wissenschaft*, ed. Gerhard Sauter (Munich: Christian Kaiser Verlag, 1971), pp. 73-104; ET "Half a Century of Theology: A Review" in *Ernst Troeltsch: Writings on Theology and Religion*, ed. Robert Morgan (Atlanta: John Knox Press, 1977), pp. 53-81, that even though "hardly one stone of Schleiermacher's own teaching can remain upon another, his program remains the great program of scientific theology" p. 103; ET p. 80. Barth, at least in 1923, seems to agree that Troeltsch is Schleiermacher's rightful successor and refers to him as Schleiermacher's "most congenial friend in the modern period." *Die Theologie Schleiermachers*, p. 313; ET p. 175.

[171] On Nov.1, 1923, Barth stated in his opening remarks at the beginning of his semester course on Schleiermacher in Göttingen: "That the school of religious psychology, which is in the forefront of interest today, seeks to go back to Schleiermacher and to advance from him (Wobbermin), I may take to be well known in Göttingen." Foreward, *Die Theologie Schleiermachers*, pp. 2-3; ET p. xiv.

[172] Georg Wobbermin, *Systematische Theologie: nach religionspsychologischer Methode*, I-III (Leipzig: J.C. Hinrichs'sche, 1913-1925), II, pp. 7ff. Wobbermin also claims that Troeltsch, "at the height of his expositions," (III, pp.27-28) as well as all "*formgeschichtlichen*" investigaton, is ultimately dependent upon "*produktive Einfühlung*" (III, p. 39). See also III, p. 177n.

correlation 'experience' – 'history.' Georg Wobbermin, for instance, the inventor of the religious-psychological circle, might easily be described as a very schoolmasterly and extremely dull Herder."[173]

5. The Young Karl Barth (Pre-1915)

There is no direct evidence to suggest that Karl Barth was ever decisively influenced by Dilthey, Troeltsch, or Wobbermin, or that he was ever impressed in the least by their programs.[174] But there is evidence of an indirect sort that he was stamped educationally by this tradition. His essay of 1910/12, "The Christian Faith and History," suggests he was preoccupied with the problem of correlating experience and history in the years leading up to his break with liberalism. Given his preoccupation with this problem and the specific means he chose to overcome it, Barth could later testify from his own experience that the theological milieu out of which his revolution was born was one decisively influenced by Herder. Barth's revolution sought to overcome historicism and psychologism. This is well known. Less well known is that in order to overcome historicism and psychologism he had to overcome the legacy of Herder, with "its methodical point of departure in the correlation 'experience' – history.'" This is what he did or at least tried to do. But what is interesting is that he did not do so all at once. Indeed Barth's earliest attempts to overcome historicism reflect the influence of Herder with respect to his "methodical point of departure in the correlation 'experience' – 'history'" and his specific means of correlating experience and history, viz., *Einfühlung*. To understand his connection to Herder and the empathetic tradition of interpretation outlined above it is necessary to consider once again Barth's theological commitments before his break with liberalism.

It is important to recall that Barth was thoroughly grounded in the ways of historical criticism in his first years of theological study at Bern. Though he claimed he was never deeply impressed by historical criticism's so-called 'results' or the moderate positivism of his first teachers, Rudolf Steck, Hermann Lüdemann, Karl Marti, *et al*, he did later express gratitude that these "Bern

---

[173] Barth, *Die protestantische Theologie im 19. Jahrhundert*, p. 305; ET p. 227. Wobbermin states: "The foundation of this [religious-psychological] circle is Einfühlung, but because it manifests itself precisely as creative *Nacherleben* or *Neuerleben*, it must be referred to as *produktive Einfühlung*." *Systematische Theologie: nach religionspsychologischer Methode*, II, p. 8.

[174] I have already discussed Barth's relationship to Dilthey, see p. 43n.131 above. As for Troeltsch, Barth would later observe: "the 'historicism' by which Ernst Troeltsch and the historians of religion of that time (1908-1909) thought they could outbid the Ritschlians (and thus also the teacher whom I still regard so highly, Wilhelm Herrmann) struck me as being too sterile, and at any rate was not what I was looking for. I had just now (not without direct and indirect instruction from Schleiermacher) tasted something of what 'religion' itself was supposed to be." In "Nachwort," p. 291; ET p. 262.

masters" had at least done this for him: "They gave me such a thorough grounding in the earlier form of the 'historical-critical' school that the remarks of their later and contemporary successors could no longer get under my skin, much less touch my heart – they could only get on my nerves, as is only too well known."[175] The little phrase "much less touch my heart" suggests that what was really important to Barth even in this early period was something deeper, more immediate than history, something history itself could not provide, which is exactly what he thought he had discovered in 1906 upon reading Herrmann's *Ethics* and Schleiermacher's *Speeches on Religion to its Cultured Despisers*. The effect of these two books, particularly the latter, was electric: "Eureka! Having apparently sought for 'The Immediate,' I had found it. ... That those *Speeches* were the most important and correct writings to appear since the closing of the New Testament canon was a fact from which I did not allow my great Marburg teacher [Herrmann] to detract."[176] From these remarks it might appear that serious historical critical research was no longer of real interest to Barth after 1906. The fact is, however, that Barth produced a massive historical-critical study on *"Die Missionstätigkeit des Paulus nach der Darstellung der Apostelgeschichte"* for his seminar with Harnack in 1907 and actually maintained, despite what his critics have often alleged, a genuine interest in historical-critical research throughout his life.[177] But what was Barth's main reservation about the historical criticism of his "Bern masters"? What was it in his view that they and other moderate positivists like his father failed to account for?

In his youth, Barth had "intensively" studied Kant's first two *Critiques*.[178] He developed a firm grasp of the difference between things phenomenal and noumenal and an understanding of the limits of reason which not only immunized him from the positivism of his Bern teachers but also cleared the way for him to become an enthusiastic follower of Schleiermacher and Herrmann. Schleiermacher, Barth later said, had stood against his contemporaries' "general flight into history,"[179] and this was appealing to Barth not because Schleiermacher was at all "anti-historical" but because he recognized the rela-

---

[175] Barth, "Nachwort," p. 291; ET p. 262.

[176] Barth, "Nachwort," p. 291; ET p. 262.

[177] Karl Barth, "Die Missionstätigkeit des Paulus nach der Darstellung der Apostelgeschichte," *Vorträge und kleinere Arbeiten 1905-1909*, pp. 148-243.

[178] "There was once a time, so I must begin, in my youthful occupation with theology when – after first having worked through Immanual Kant's *Critique of Practical Reason* several times and (only then, but equally intensively) his *Critique of Pure Reason* – I knew how to swear no higher than by the man, Daniel Ernst Friedrich Schleiermacher." Barth, "Nachwort," p. 290; ET p. 261. Barth's relationship to Kant is of critical importance and has been discussed at length elsewhere, e.g. Simon Fisher, *Revelatory Positivism? Barth's Earliest Theology and the Marburg School* (Oxford: University Press, 1988).

[179] Barth, *Die protestantische Theologie im 19. Jahrhundert*, p. 384; ET p. 311.

tivity of history in light of "the Immediate" which is beyond all history. Schleiermacher, as Barth later characterized it, appealed to a distinctly romantic impulse he found in himself. From his early reading of Schiller, his passion for poetry, to his schoolboy desire to become a playwright, Barth's literary interests and romantic sensibilities, by his own account, played a significant role in his theological development.[180] And it is interesting that in direct connection with his discovery of Schleiermacher and Herrmann, Barth later recalled, "I also loved Eichendorff and was especially fond of Novalis. Was I (am I!) a bit of a romantic myself?"[181] It was this romantic impulse that made him such "a stranger in [his] innermost being to the bourgeois world of Ritschl and his pupils" just as it was this, even before he had read Schleiermacher or Herrmann, that made him so disdainful of the positivistic tendencies of his early teachers. "We can afford to be more romantic than the romantics," Barth claims to have said in 1919.[182] And the reason Barth could afford to be *more romantic* than the romantics is that this is, in many respects, precisely what he himself had been prior to 1915, a romantic, as I think the two most important essays of this period demonstrate.

a. "Modern Theology and Work in the Kingdom of God"

Romantic convictions are clearly expressed, for example, in Barth's first published essay, "Modern Theology and Work in the Kingdom of God," which appeared in 1909.[183] Arising out of a discussion among students as to why, unlike graduates of more conservative theological faculties, so few graduates of more 'modern' theological faculties were entering into foreign missions, Barth argues in this brief essay that there are two basic elements in modern theology which account for this tendency. First, modern theology is characterized by "religious individualism." In modern theology everything relates to the life of the individual. Morality, for instance, which constitutes the very presupposition of religion, is "strictly individual." It has to do not with "norms that approach one from the outside, but with the contemplation and direction of the will upon one truth and authority which is proclaimed within oneself."[184]

---

[180] Karl Barth, "Autobiographische Skizze Karl Barths aus dem Fakultätsalbum der Ev.-Theol. Fakultät in Münster," *Karl Barth-Rudolf Bultmann Briefwechsel, 1911-1966*, pp. 290f.; ET p. 151f.

[181] "Nachwort," p. 291; ET p. 262.

[182] "Nachwort," p. 291; ET p. 262.

[183] Karl Barth, "Moderne Theologie und Reichsgottesarbeit," *Zeitschrift für Theologie und Kirche* 19 (1909), pp. 317-21. Also contained in *Vorträge und kleinere Arbeiten 1905-1909*, ed. Hans-Anton Drewes and Hinrich Stoevesandt (Zürich: Theologischer Verlag Zürich, 1992), pp. 341-347, with introduction, pp. 334-341, followed by responses by Ernst Christian Achelis (pp. 347-351) and Paul Drews (pp. 351-354), and an "Antwort an D. Achelis und D. Drews" by Barth (pp. 354-365). Hereafter cited as "Moderne Theologie und Reichsgottesarbeit."

[184] Barth, "Moderne Theologie und Reichsgottesarbeit," p. 342.

This is why it is so much more difficult for modern students of theology to discuss ethics, the moral life, etc. than it is for more conservative students. The latter need only appeal to outward norms such as those provided by the Bible and dogma, whereas the former have an "incomparably more difficult" task. It is certainly the case that one can come to an understanding that it is impossible to fulfill the moral law and thus experience within the tradition of the Christian Church a power that one must submit to in obedience and trust. But how does this all come about? What specific aspect of the Christian tradition or its expressions in the present become revelation to him? "These are all questions only ... [the individual] can answer for himself; there is no generally valid *ordo salutis*, nor are there any generally valid sources of revelation which one can demonstrate to another."[185] "The Christian who succumbs to that power overcomes the world. ... But the standards of this overcoming of the world must come from his own faith, nobody else can give it to him." The awakening to religious life is an individual matter, as is the revelation upon which the religious life itself is based. "Religion for us is individually expressed experience."[186] In short, the only normative authority in modern theology is the experience of the individual.

The second thing that characterizes modern theology is "historical relativism." History can reveal nothing absolute. Historical judgments, no matter how scientific, are always relative. "This is not the essential thing about [modern] theology as is often claimed by its friends and foes in the heat of battle," rather it is merely one of the more obvious consequences of religious individualism. "Because religion is based upon a personal rather than generally valid reason, it not only considers itself as not being harmed but considers it a law of moral truthfulness to investigate the source of revelation which gives rise to it and causes it to exist by means of generally valid science." Such investigation reflects vital religious interest and is useful not only because of the part it plays in overcoming the world, but also because it brings new stimulus and challenge to life. The modern theologian, therefore, has nothing to lose and everything to gain by embracing historical relativism. The same theologian who owes the strength and peace of his inner life to the New Testament will see in it as well a collection of religious writings like others, with Christianity a religious phenomenon like others, with Jesus a religious founder like others, and will use the same methods in treating its history and development as he does Avesta and Zoroaster.

---

[185] Barth, "Moderne Theologie und Reichsgottesarbeit," p. 343.

[186] Barth, "Moderne Theologie und Reichsgottesarbeit," p. 347. Barth adds "... and we [i.e. modern theologians] see it as our duty to come to grips, clearly and positively with general human cultural awareness of its scientific side. This is for us, when we seek to do the work, in the narrower sense, of the Kingdom of God, both our strength ... and our weakness."

Though religious individualism and historical relativism are undoubtedly the two most important facets of modern theology, Barth acknowledges that there is a temptation for those schooled in modern theology, especially for those who never really took Herrmann and Harnack seriously, simply to ignore these facts when they enter into pastoral ministry. It is far easier simply to fit into the well-established role of being a pastor. But any such "flight into praxis" will have a price, Barth warns, not least of which is one's own personal integrity.[187] Certainly a modern theologian is faced with a much greater challenge in trying to talk with others about religious experience, particularly his own religious experiences. He will often feel "less 'mature' than others who, in honest conviction, have readily at their disposal an entire host of normative ideas and concepts." Indeed, "next to the evangelizing zeal of those in pietistic circles" and others "who manage to talk about their faith in a faster, louder, more authoritative way," he will often feel embarrassed. Still, even though his is a much more difficult path, "it is the most truthful one," and this becomes more apparent the more one reflects upon the reasons for it.[188]

Having received a galley copy of this essay, Fritz Barth wrote his then twenty-three-year-old son on June 17, 1909 telling him he would not have advised him to publish it. He said although open discussion of such problems is certainly to be valued and that "every open confession has its blessing," he feared his son had put himself too "vehemently on the side of the 'moderns'" and that he had done so merely in a "personal way, not by means of any scientific demonstration." He added: "Maybe in a few years you yourself will no longer agree with it. ... Printed things will bind you more in the future; and during your years now, development should happen much more inwardly and not so much on the open market. In principle, it is better to save such explanations for a time of greater maturity. Why start with that which is the most difficult?"[189] Karl responded that he did not consider his article a "confession" but had merely "spoken in the name of a large group of young theologians" and "wanted to show the strength and weakness" of our position. He said he had "nothing to regret and nothing to demonstrate," but simply wanted to describe the present situation as he saw it, that his understanding of religion was as mature as his understanding of the religious work he was about to enter, and, in true romantic fashion, that he himself did not feel bound to anything printed on a piece of paper and that there was no reason why he could not change his mind about such issues in the future, even though he saw this "as not impossible, but unlikely."[190] Oral debate over this essay between father and son continued in private (to the point "that the windows shook"). Paul Wernle seems

---

[187] Barth, "Moderne Theologie und Reichsgottesarbeit," p. 346.
[188] Barth, "Moderne Theologie und Reichsgottesarbeit," p. 347.
[189] Barth, "Moderne Theologie und Reichsgottesarbeit," p. 335.
[190] Barth, "Moderne Theologie und Reichsgottesarbeit," p. 336.

to have reacted against it as strongly as Barth's father.[191] But these debates only foreshadowed a much larger public debate.

Two professors of practical theology, Ernst Christian Achelis of Marburg and Paul Drews of Halle, responded to Barth's essay. Both challenged what they perceived to be Barth's radical individualism and insisted that any such notion must surely be bound to Jesus Christ. Drews stated, "But this religious individualism has its limits. If it still calls itself Christian and should be valid as such, it must feel itself bound to Jesus and the values He has given us."[192] Achelis asked: "Should [Barth's] 'individualism' not rather more correctly be called 'subjectivism'?" and probed further:

> Am I wrong to think that Barth wants to leave it up to individual judgment what the individual wants to acknowledge as liberating revelation in the Christian tradition or in the life-expressions of contemporary religion? Is there, then, an innumerable multitude of possibilities by which revelation frees us and forces us to submit? For evangelical theology and piety, there is only one revelation worthy of *the* name, in which "God has poured out His heart to us," and this revelation is named Jesus Christ. Only *this* side of the Christian tradition and *this* living expression of contemporary religion can help us toward faith and strengthen our faith, in which *the* revelation meets us. Christ alone is the source of revelation which is valid for us All, our faith is simply bound to Him and to the one God who reveals Himself through Him and in Him, and the power we encounter and to which we must wholly submit in obedience and trust is Him, and only Him.[193]

Having said nothing in his essay about Jesus Christ other than that he should be studied like any other founder of religion, Achelis and Drews had essentially pressed Barth into saying whether or not his notion of religious individualism was in any way bound to Jesus Christ. Given the opportunity to reply to his critics, Barth responded as follows: Although glad to agree with Achelis and Drews that religious individualism finds its limit in the fact that it is bound to Jesus Christ, Barth insists this alone does not do justice to his position. His objection to their characterization of his position is that it fails to take into account the specific means by which our relationship to Christ is established. How is it possible to speak meaningfully about Christ as our norm and authority apart from seriously discussing how our relationship to him is established? Is it established merely by means of our assent to doctrines or, as Drews seems to suggest, merely on the basis of our acceptance of "absolutizing historical value-judgments" derived from "a narrowly selected tradition about the historical person of Jesus"?[194] Neither of these means is acceptable. That Drews thinks he can still somehow overcome historical relativism by absolutizing his-

---

[191] Barth, "Moderne Theologie und Reichsgottesarbeit," pp. 337-8. Barth wrote to his friend, Wilhelm Loew, on Sept.4, 1909, that both his father and Paul Wernle had privately – and in no uncertain terms – "put him through the ringer" on account of this essay.

[192] Barth, "Moderne Theologie und Reichsgottesarbeit," p. 352.

[193] Barth, "Moderne Theologie und Reichsgottesarbeit," p. 348-9.

[194] Barth, "Moderne Theologie und Reichsgottesarbeit," p. 360.

torical value-judgments only shows how little he understands historical relativism. As far as establishing a relationship to Christ by means of assent to doctrine is concerned, Barth shows he has as little patience for this as his teacher, Herrmann. But the much larger figure standing behind his objection to such appeals, he makes clear, is Schleiermacher.

Barth claims that assent to doctrine is unacceptable because what is important about doctrine is not its cognitive content, which may be grasped merely at the level of the intellect, but that which gives rise to doctrine and moves one at the deepest level of human consciousness, a level Schleiermacher referred to as the "affections."[195] He reminds his critics that Schleiermacher had said that "the seed of all doctrine" is the "affection" which lies beneath it; and it is only at the level of our affections, there and nowhere else, that our relationship to Jesus Christ is established. Doctrine is merely the attempt to express one's religious affections verbally and at best provides only an occasion for others to come into contact with the affection which gave rise to it. There is nothing pure about doctrine. On the contrary, it is corrupt – as intrinsically corrupt as the language and thought forms that constitute it. Only the affection that lies behind it is pure. Apart from coming into contact with it, doctrine is of no significance to faith whatsoever. The same must be said of all language and thought. Quoting Schleiermacher, Barth says that even the words of Christ himself would not have become Christian truth had they not arisen from his affections and moved their original hearers at the level of their affections. The reason is that (and here Barth cites the basis of Schleiermacher's romantic theory of language) "stepping forth in thought and word is everywhere the vacillating; the innermost which lies back of thought and word is certainly in agreement with itself, the identical but that can never be communicated externally as such ... the effective manifestation of Christ, i.e., that which affects [one] in a certain, definite manner, this is real revelation and the objective factor."[196] In sum, only the underlying affection is of primary significance: "Everything else appearing in thought and word is secondary."[197] By whatever means we may experience Christ, therefore, "the normative, objective, eternal lies only in the 'affection' of this inner experience. Everything which is set forth in thoughts and words belongs itself once again to this relativizing stream of history and is, as that which passes away, only a parable."[198]

From such statements (the last being a paraphrase of Goethe and others, including three quotations from Schiller), it is clear that what stands behind or at least corroboratively alongside Barth's interest in the affections lying beneath all thought and language, and his scorn (reinforced by Herrmann) of mere in-

---

[195] Barth, "Moderne Theologie und Reichsgottesarbeit," pp. 359f.
[196] Barth, "Moderne Theologie und Reichsgottesarbeit," pp. 359f.
[197] Barth, "Moderne Theologie und Reichsgottesarbeit," p. 360.
[198] Barth, "Moderne Theologie und Reichsgottesarbeit," p. 361.

tellectual assent to doctrine itself, is a romantic, expressivist view of language and thought.[199] I shall discuss this view in more detail in the next chapter. Here it is sufficient simply to point out Barth's appeal to romantic figures in defense of it as well as his appeal to Romanticism in defense of his notion of religious individualism. Pressed by Drews as to the exact origins of his concept of religious individualism, Barth says what stands behind the "*principium individuationis*" is that which was "first mightily represented by Romanticism."[200] In sum, Achelis and Drews had charged that Barth's concept of individualism was radically subjectivistic and seemed to have little if anything to do with Jesus Christ. Barth's response was that his concept of individualism was not ultimately subjectivistic and that it was bound to Jesus Christ, but not bound to him by means of mere assent to doctrine or historical investigation. Neither history nor doctrine nor any other outer norm can establish a relationship of faith in Jesus Christ. "No Other but God, and not God as some outer norm but as the individual inner assurance and authority which becomes revelation to him in Christ as he goes through the history of nations and men" can establish such a relationship.[201] The only question is how. Barth had said much about how such a relationship *was not* established, but very little about how it *was* established. This is the question he takes up in the most important essay of his liberal period, and it is here that we see his most important connection to the empathetic tradition of interpretation.

b. "The Christian Faith and History"

Having left Marburg in mid-August 1909, Barth served as a *Hilfsprediger* in the German-speaking Reformed Church in Geneva. There he began an intensive study of Calvin's *Institutes* and continued his study of Schleiermacher. He also continued to reflect upon some of the deeper issues raised in his debate with Achelis and Drews. The result was a lecture he delivered to a group of pastors at Neuchâtel on Oct. 5, 1910.[202] This address, which was later revised and published in the *Schweizerische theologische Zeitschrift* in 1912, actually picks up where his debate with Achelis and Drews left off, in that it seeks to provide a more precise account of the place of Jesus Christ in modern theology and, specifically, *how* a relationship between Him and those living 1900 years later is established. It takes up, in other words, the problem of the relation of faith and history which Barth refers to from the outset as not only "*the* problem of Protestant theology of the present," but "*the* problem of Christian theology

---

[199] Barth, "Moderne Theologie und Reichsgottesarbeit," p. 361.
[200] Barth, "Moderne Theologie und Reichsgottesarbeit," p. 355.
[201] Barth, "Moderne Theologie und Reichsgottesarbeit," p. 363.
[202] Barth, "Der christliche Glaube und die Geschichte" (See p. 45n.137 above). That Paul Drews is a target in this essay is clear from the very beginning (p. 157), but especially from pp. 188f. See also p. 208.

in general."²⁰³ There are many similarities between this and his earlier essay. The major difference is that here Jesus Christ's relationship to faith is stated emphatically: "[He] is the revelation that is the real content of our faith."²⁰⁴ "He Himself is the effectiveness of God."²⁰⁵ "The religious perception of Christ, the viewing of God's effectiveness in Him is [our] justification."²⁰⁶ "As the crucified and therefore risen One, Christ is the salvation-fact of the Christian faith."²⁰⁷ "In every fact of this faith," this one christological salvation-fact is included as its "material" and "central point."²⁰⁸ Still, the question is, How? How is this central salvation-fact of the Christian faith established? How is it related to history?

This is the main problem the two most important movements in theology of the previous forty years, the Ritschlians and the history of religions school, have been preoccupied with, according to Barth. The former tried to resolve it by treating the object of theology as a "historical revelation, specifically in the figure of Christ presented in the Christian community," but they ended up merely identifying this so-called "historical revelation" with an "arbitrary selection of thoughts from the New Testament and the Reformation."²⁰⁹ Members of the history of religions school, however, were more radical. They joined the Ritschlians in their turn to history but sought "history only for the sake of history and as a result missed revelation."²¹⁰ Following strictly scientific methods of historiography, they completely excluded the supernatural, i.e., revelation and miracle. "*God disappeared from history.*" Such an approach, of course, accords with the law of truthfulness which, ever since Kant, should be scientifically self-evident. The historian *qua* historian has no access to revelation or miracle. The historian deals only with relative dimensions, not absolutes, and so does the theologian, provided that he is dealing with facts given or sought after in space and time. "But it is equally certain that as soon as one applies this method one has moved outside the circle of specifically *theological* problems." This is why Troeltsch is able to "make only the vaguest generalizations" about theology's true object.²¹¹ The fact is that historical investigation can demonstrate only that "God, revelation, and miracle ... are scientific non-concepts."²¹² The limitations of such scholarship are not something we can escape nor are they a "calamity" as some suggest. On the contrary, they even

---

²⁰³ Barth, "Der christliche Glaube und die Geschichte," p. 155.
²⁰⁴ Barth, "Der christliche Glaube und die Geschichte," pp. 196-197.
²⁰⁵ Barth, "Der christliche Glaube und die Geschichte," p. 194.
²⁰⁶ Barth, "Der christliche Glaube und die Geschichte," p. 188.
²⁰⁷ Barth, "Der christliche Glaube und die Geschichte," p. 198.
²⁰⁸ Barth, "Der christliche Glaube und die Geschichte," p. 198.
²⁰⁹ Barth, "Der christliche Glaube und die Geschichte," p. 158.
²¹⁰ Barth, "Der christliche Glaube und die Geschichte," p. 159.
²¹¹ Barth, "Der christliche Glaube und die Geschichte," p. 156n.
²¹² Barth, "Der christliche Glaube und die Geschichte," p. 207n.

have the potential of providing a "profane propaedeutic" against false objectifications of the matter.²¹³ Still, it does not get at what is really at issue with respect to theology's true object.

Theology's true object has to do with an inner reality which is made perceptible only by faith. "Faith is the experience of God, an immediate consciousness of the presence and efficacy of the superhuman, supra-worldly and, therefore, absolutely sovereign power of life."²¹⁴ From the perspective of psychology (which provides us with the "raw material for systematic consideration"), the process of faith has supremely to do with "the rise of the individual." But faith is also to be understood "as a social fact." ²¹⁵ What distinguishes "*Christian* faith" is that it is "*somehow* historically conditioned and determined through the personality of Jesus which is made present within human society."²¹⁶ The believer "somehow" intuits Jesus' personality mediated to him in the present and it is this intuiting [*Anschauung*] of Jesus' personality that establishes his relation to reality.²¹⁷ Everything rests, however, on this "somehow."

"Where is this genuine and authoritative view of the person of Christ upon which faith is established to be found? ... *Paul* has given us the first answer to this question. Whether or not he knew 'Christ according to the flesh,' he determines to know him thus 'no longer,' but *to be in Christ* as a new creation (II Cor.5:17)." "The gospel that Paul first proclaimed is not a complex of tradition, [but] his own gospel which he received and learned from no man but through the revelation of Jesus," (Gal.1:12). "Paul bears the basis and authority of his faith in himself."²¹⁸ It lies in his heart. Yet the catholic church "already at the turn of the first and second centuries began to demand more certainty, more visible guarantees, than Paul's inner Christ appeared to offer."²¹⁹ The canon was codified and "history was presented to faith in an all too finished way. The question: where do we find Christ? was no longer a question. Jesus Christ, the same yesterday, today, and in eternity, became a secure, visible, and verifiable fact within the elements of the Church: the New Testament,

---

[213] Barth, "Der christliche Glaube und die Geschichte," p. 161.

[214] Barth, "Der christliche Glaube und die Geschichte," p. 161.

[215] Barth, "Der christliche Glaube und die Geschichte," p. 161. "[Faith] stands heterogeneously over against the cognitive apparatus which assesses validity in logic, ethics, and aesthetics. For here two problems intersect one another which lie on completely different planes ... the problem of the I, of the individual person, of the individual life, and the problem of law-structured consciousness, human culture, and reason." Barth continues: "Through the regulative, heuristic, limit-conceptual moment of faith (which from the beginning belongs to the problem of the individual, not to the problem of reason), the abstract possibility of culture-consciousness is actualized, transformed into concrete reality" (p. 163).

[216] Barth, "Der christliche Glaube und die Geschichte," p. 164.

[217] The word "intuition" (*Anschauung*) is a term used by the early Schleiermacher and one full of many subtle implications for those, like Barth, trained in Kantian thought.

[218] Barth, "Der christliche Glaube und die Geschichte," p. 165.

[219] Barth, "Der christliche Glaube und die Geschichte," p. 166.

the rule of faith, the councils of bishops."[220] But the Reformers "returned to Paul's position. Luther set the authority of Christ Himself against the authority of the tradition. *Not* the authority of the Bible." Instead of "acknowledging the authority of the New Testament at first and then drawing his doctrine from it, he encountered Paul and immersed himself in the thought-world as well as the piety of this witness of faith and then, on the basis of this inner relationship with Paul, he met the one to whom Paul bears witness and He became the foundation and authority of his faith."[221] Regrettably, however, Luther tried to fight against "the authoritarian catholic polemic with the same weapons." So did Calvin, even though his position was more sophisticated. Both reformers, "and even more so their followers, raised the Old and New Testament canon to a formal authority it never had before so that opponents of older Protestantism could say, not unjustly, that here the paper pope took the place of the living one."[222] "Biblicism, thus, fell upon the young Protestant theology like mildew and to this day we still suffer from its consequences."[223]

However, faith and history, which had been presented as united were soon divided by Enlightenment criticism. Lessing claimed that "the accidental truths of history can never become the proof of the necessary truths of reason."[224] Faith, therefore, could no longer be regarded as conditioned by or coinciding with the agreement of any historical teaching authority. Fortunately, it was Schleiermacher who rescued the situation. Standing on the shoulders of Goethe, Schiller, Novalis, *et al*, of the Romantic movement, Schleiermacher (as we observed with Herder) looked to humanity – and particularly religion (which Herder defined as "the highest humanity, the most sublime flowering of the human soul") – as the key to overcoming the separation of faith and history.[225] But Schleiermacher's solution, unlike Herder's, was also specifically christological. In a way strikingly similar to Calvin and Melanchthon,[226] Schleiermacher referred to "'the specifically affecting appearance of Christ,' as the 'true' ... *the Objective*. The Christ of faith is the affecting Christ, for faith as *Anschauung* itself is nothing other than seeing [His] effectiveness as one be-

---

[220] Barth, "Der christliche Glaube und die Geschichte," p. 166.
[221] Barth, "Der christliche Glaube und die Geschichte," p. 166.
[222] Barth, "Der christliche Glaube und die Geschichte," p. 169.
[223] Barth, "Der christliche Glaube und die Geschichte," p. 170.
[224] Barth, "Der christliche Glaube und die Geschichte," p. 178.
[225] "'To perceive the world ... man must encounter humanity; and he can do so only in and through *love* ...' The individual finds in humanity the revelation that is presented in religion. ... Let us therefore approach humanity for it is here that we find the material of religion. That is, the individual finds in humanity the revelation that he perceives and accepts in religion, i.e. within history." Barth, "Der christliche Glaube und die Geschichte," pp. 187-188.
[226] Barth cites Calvin's *Insititutes* III, ii, xxiv and Melanchthon's famous line, "*hoc est Christum cognoscere, beneficia eius cognoscere*." Barth, "Der christliche Glaube und die Geschichte," p. 192.

ing affected [by Him]."[227] It is in seeing Christ's affecting appearance and being affected by Him that the problem of faith and history is overcome. But how exactly does this seeing of Christ's affecting appearance occur? "Where and how are we given a psychologically mediated, justifying and reconciling *Anschauung* of Christ, for it seems we are separated from His person through the entire gap of 1900 years with all the deep differences of thinking, life, and feeling included in it? *What is the psychological-historical vehicle that makes the direct* apprehensio Christi in corde *possible which is present in factual faith?*"[228]

Barth's answer is: *"The historical Jesus becomes the risen, living Christ within the congregation of Christ."*[229] *"It is believing individuals, those who have become alive, who are the rocks upon which and with whom, again and again, the church is being built* (e.g. Mt.16:18).*"*[230] It is only by means of those individuals who have been affected themselves by the affecting appearance of Christ that we today can experience the risen, living Christ.

> This is the type of person we are dealing with in the New Testament. ... The people speaking here, a Paul, a James, the author of First Peter, the many who, with skill and clumsiness, contributed their mite to that which we today have as the synoptic and Johannine tradition, these were people who had experienced for themselves the *apprehensio Christi*. What they left behind for us in reports and thoughts about him is the *witness* of their faith, of their intuition of Christ, which they passed on in the transparency of their words. "We have seen his glory" (John 1:14) and "this we proclaim to you," (I John 1:13). And now when *we* come upon these first historical witnesses of faith it *can* happen to us as well – there is no *must* regarding the rise of life – that we see Christ's glory, that we discover behind the intrinsically transparent word the light that was lit in them. Between us and them, of course, is the *difference* of all kinds of life circumstances, which are expressed in two thoroughly different worlds of imagination. But this is an obstacle that separates us from everyone. Here, the 1900 years, etc., have in principle no meaning. Through the psychological process of *Einfühlung* we are put *beyond* all the things that initially separate us, yet *through* them, into the *soul* of the inspired, i.e., the Christ-inspired, biblical author. We see what he has seen, we experience what he has experienced, we henceforth believe not because of his words, but because we ourselves have heard and recognized that he is truly the Christ, the world's Saviour (e.g. John 4:42).[231]

"Luther's *Einfühlung* into Paul's *Epistle to the Romans* and his *Epistle to the Galatians*," Barth proposes, "offers the classic paradigm" of the sort of approach that is needed. Luther recognized it was neither the New Testament canon as such nor any system of "salvation facts" but the piety of the concrete Paul that was important. This is how Paul's Christ "actually becomes *his*

---

[227] Barth, "Der christliche Glaube und die Geschichte," pp. 192-193.
[228] Barth, "Der christliche Glaube und die Geschichte," p. 203.
[229] Barth, "Der christliche Glaube und die Geschichte," p. 203.
[230] Barth, "Der christliche Glaube und die Geschichte," p. 204.
[231] Barth, "Der christliche Glaube und die Geschichte," p. 204.

own."²³² And Calvin's particular formulation of the doctrine of inspiration helped clarify Luther's position and "open up wider prospects." Calvin "adds alongside the thesis of the *'arcanum testimonium spiritus,'* the inspiredness of the believer."²³³ By doing so, he averted the sort of one-sided view of the inspiration of the biblical canon itself which many of his followers did not. "Thus even though there was already in Calvin's position an approach that could have pointed in a different direction, they escaped neither the synergism nor the intellectualization of the concept of faith that Calvin wanted to avoid." Calvin had described the inner testimony of the Holy Spirit in his *Institutes* (I, 7, 4-5) as follows: "The same Spirit, therefore, who has spoken through the mouths of the prophets must penetrate into our hearts to persuade us that they faithfully proclaimed what had been divinely commanded. ... I speak [here] of nothing other than what each believer experiences within himself." To which Barth adds:

> If one had seriously carried out the first sentence together with the last one, instead of ... concluding from what he says in between [that he taught] a divinity of the letter, [Calvin's] doctrine of the testimonium should have had the effect of dynamite, blowing up the entire house of orthodoxy. Protestant theology would have saved itself the embarrassment of having to be awakened from its dogmatic slumbers by Enlightenment criticism. Then one would have been brought to the insight that the inspiration of the Holy Spirit announced in Scripture must be applied to the biblical *authors* and that between *them* and *us* – but not between their *letter* and *us* – an inner contact and rapport can be established which is the vehicle of the *apprehensio Christi in corde*.²³⁴

Barth concludes this essay arguing that "our *apprehensio in corde* becomes possible and real" not necessarily only by our direct inner contact with biblical authors but "through an entire ancestral line of *mediating* individuals."²³⁵ Here Barth's argument remarkably resembles Paul Wernle's:

---

²³² Barth, "Der christliche Glaube und die Geschichte," p. 205.
²³³ Barth, "Der christliche Glaube und die Geschichte," p. 206.
²³⁴ Barth, "Der christliche Glaube und die Geschichte," pp. 206-207.
²³⁵ Barth, "Der christliche Glaube und die Geschichte," p. 208. "And if it is really true that for most people the revelation-experience is granted to them through the mediation of one or more other individuals, one cannot foresee why the inspiration of history should be limited to biblical authors," (pp.208-209). "Is it possible," Barth asks, "in view of the actual effectiveness of an Augustine or Luther or Schleiermacher to attribute to them, or to the author of *The Epistle of James* or *Jude*, or the *Apocalypse*, a *special* inspiration that is *qualitatively* different than the Christian one?" This is not to say that "the New Testament will not by virtue of its temporal priority always own a strange dignity and effectiveness among other witnesses of faith. But can we therefore give it a higher dignity *in principle*? What can centuries and thousands of years of temporal distance from *Christ according to the flesh* tell us when what we are dealing with is ... *Christ according to the Spirit* who is the same yesterday, today, and in all eternity?" "And this inspiration throughout the history of the Christian religion which is qualitatively similar to the New Testament may by no right be limited to those who *ex professo* have spoken about God and Christ" (p. 209).

The effectiveness of Christ's Spirit, thank God, has still other channels. ... Francis of Assisi and Bodelschwingh with their deeds were sources of revelation [*Offenbarungsquellen*] for their contemporaries just as Paul and Luther and their thoughts were for theirs. The works of a Michelangelo, of a J.S. Bach, of a Mozart and Beethoven are also finally in their deepest content witnesses of faith, transparencies that "portray Christ before our eyes," ... Is it then merely a strange idea ... to claim Schiller as preacher of the cross of Christ? And is not *the effective thing* about Goethe ... the obedientia, the self-denying, loving, obedience of Christ?[236]

Thus, in many respects, Barth's essay ends where it begins: "through the moment of faith, cultural consciousness becomes historical."[237] Faith must be understood as "a social fact." What distinguishes "*Christian* faith" is that it is "*somehow* historically conditioned and determined through the personality of Jesus which is made present within human society." This is the basis of Barth's claim: "The Christ outside us is the Christ in us."[238] Certainly "faith only knows a Christ outside of us," but we cannot know the Christ outside of us apart from the Christ who lives in us, that is, apart from other individuals whose inner lives, having been affected by Him, mediate His "inner life" to us. "Christ outside us = Christ in us, efficacious history = effected faith."[239] This, finally, is how the separation of faith and history is overcome.[240] For those who approach the matter by faith, history and faith are synonymous; but for those who do not, faith and history must simply fall apart into two completely heterogenous categories.

---

[236] Barth, "Der christliche Glaube und die Geschichte," p. 209. This is essentially what Barth had told his 1909 confirmation class: "With the conclusion of the Bible, God did not close the book of revelation. Everything that is Jesus-like in people, can be revelation, a message from God: People, poets, art, nature, strong impressions" *Konfirmandenunterricht, 1909-1921*, p. 69. A significant way in which Barth differs from Wernle, however, is that whereas the latter claims, "the contemplation of religion in its factuality, primarily in the lives of leading men of God," (see p. 129 above), the former claims, "The things being said here are valid not only for the great but all the more for the small, for the countless and unknown ones who are a part of the Christian history of religion as well – members in the middle, mediators of Christ's effectiveness through whom our view of Christ was commanded and formed even before we ourselves were and whose working continues to live in us." Barth, "Der christliche Glaube und die Geschichte," pp. 209-210.

[237] Barth, "Der christliche Glaube und die Geschichte," p. 163.

[238] Barth, "Der christliche Glaube und die Geschichte," p. 193.

[239] Barth, "Der christliche Glaube und die Geschichte," pp. 193; 197; 200.

[240] Barth claims "everything having to do with the truth of the feeling [*Gefühl*] of the justification of one's life has to do with the fact that He is outside us; yet everything having to do with the truth of the intuition [*Anschauung*] of faith has to do with the fact that Christ is inside us. The Christ outside of us is the Christ in us. Effective history is faith being effective. If Julius Kaftan is right with his statement about synergistical controversy, that it is not to be solved but only to be dissolved, this would have hereby taken place with respect to faith and Geschichte." Barth, "Der christliche Glaube und die Geschichte," p. 193.

To summarize, what was important to Karl Barth in his liberal period was not history (at least not history for history's sake), but religion, feeling, piety, and above all, individual experience, i.e. faith. "Religion only knows individual values, *Historie* only generally valid facts."[241] Of utmost importance to Barth was the *direct, immediate* religious experience of God in the life of the individual believer. This is why in his essays of 1909 and 1910/12 Barth expresses nothing but the fiercest antipathy toward "the letter" (a point I shall take up again in the next chapter). Any attempt to identify faith with language (even the language of Jesus Christ himself, much less the language of dogma!) he saw as an "intellectualization of the concept of faith" and therefore a betrayal of it. Faith, he believed, has to do with the immediacy of a relation which lies beyond all attempts at theoretical conceptualization. Yet the problem that obviously bothers Barth in his 1909 essay is the relation between the experience of revelation in the life of the individual believer and its normative conceptualization. Although it is clear that Barth recognizes there is a gap here, it is also clear that he is convinced it can be overcome non-conceptually, i.e., in terms of the mode of appropriation of the revelation of God in Jesus Christ that Schleiermacher had taught, namely, by means of trust. But in Barth's essay of 1910/12, these earlier concerns are taken up and put more pointedly. In discussing the relation of faith and history, Barth asks how Christian faith is related to Jesus Christ. (In many respects, this was simply a more concrete way of relating religious individualism and historical relativism). How can a strictly factual event of the past which is utterly external to the internal experience of an individual become the basis of that individual's internal experience of faith? How can a relative event, then and there, conditioned by space and time, serve to mediate a direct, immediate experience of God here and now? Still fundamentally preoccupied with the problem of *method*,[242] Barth's basic question revolves around how that gap of nearly 1900 years can be bridged between the Jesus of history and the experience of faith in the life of the individual believer living today.

His answer, in short, is through other believing individuals. He had intimated as much in 1909 when he quoted from Schleiermacher's *Speeches*: "There is no evidence in religion, only individuals."[243] But his answer in 1910/12 is much more explicit. The psychological-historical vehicle that makes the direct *apprehensio Christi in corde* possible in factual faith, he

---

[241] Barth, "Der christliche Glaube und die Geschichte," p. 344.

[242] In "Der christliche Glaube und die Geschichte," Barth begins by saying that he wants to critique not only theological method, but the "method of the actual origin and state of Christian experience and history" p. 160. In "Moderne Theologie und Reichsgottesarbeit," he says, "Wissenschaft ... is method, not matter," p. 346, which is obviously different from what he said in Rom II: "Wissenschaftlichkeit means Sachlichkeit," Rom II, p. 515.

[243] Barth, "Moderne Theologie und Reichsgottesarbeit," p. 355.

claims, is biblical authors such as Paul, as well as "an entire ancestral line of *mediating* individuals," who, by the "transparency" of their thoughts, words, and deeds, bear witness to their faith, to their *Anschauung* of Christ. "It is believing individuals, those who have become alive, who are the rocks upon which and with whom, again and again, the church is being built." And the specific means by which we may encounter "the light that was lit in them" is *Einfühlung*. "Through the psychological process of *Einfühlung* we are put *beyond* all the things which initially separate us, yet *through* them, into the *soul* of the inspired, i.e., the Christ-inspired, biblical author. We see what he has seen, we experience what he has experienced, we henceforth believe not because of His words, but because we ourselves have heard and recognized that he is truly the Christ, the world's Saviour." "Christ's righteousness becomes my righteousness, Christ's piety becomes my piety. He becomes I."[244] This is what Luther experienced when he established by means of *Einfühlung* "an inner relationship with Paul," and this can be our experience as well.

Whatever it was that ultimately caused Barth to change his mind, this is a very different approach than the one he pursued after 1915.

E. A Hermeneutics of Love and Trust

Karl Barth's break with liberalism brought about many changes in his theology, but nowhere is this more apparent than in his approach to biblical exegesis. Barth's break with liberalism entailed a fundamental break with the empathetic tradition of interpretation and a "conversion from all romanticism to *Sachlichkeit*."[245] In retrospect, Barth said in 1927 with reference to his 1910/12 essay, "I thought I could easily unite idealistic-romantic and Reformed theology. Along these lines I allowed to be printed a large treatise on faith and history which would have been better left unprinted."[246] Barth may have been trying to unite idealistic-romantic and Reformed theology in other ways in this essay, but it is clear that one of the ways he was trying to do so was by uniting Calvin's doctrine of inspiration (with its intimations regarding "the inspiredness of the believer") with the idealistic-romantic concept of *Einfühlung*. That Barth recognized in his early *Römerbrief* period that such an attempt could only fail, we now know from his preface drafts to Rom I. Twice in these preface drafts he states: "No art of empathy [*Einfühlungskunst*] can offer the slightest substitute for this participation."[247] The specific form of participation he was inter-

---

[244] Barth, "Der christliche Glaube und die Geschichte," p. 200.
[245] Rom II, p. 471.
[246] Karl Barth, "Autobiographische Skizze Karl Barths aus dem Fakultätsalbum der Ev.-Theol. Fakultät in Münster," Karl Barth-Rudolf Bultmann, *B-B Br.*, p. 295; ET pp. 153-154.
[247] Appendix 2, Preface Drafts IA, p. 281 (p. 587) and II, p. 284 (p. 591).

ested in, he eventually realized, was better accounted for by Calvin's doctrine of inspiration and not by any art or psychological process of empathy. As we shall see, the difference between these two approaches for Barth was the difference between a more attentive and loving approach to exegesis on the one hand, which Barth claimed he wished to promote, and a more inattentive and loveless approach on the other, which he felt was prevalent among his contemporaries. In the following pages I shall outline: 1) Barth's specific problems with the concept of *Einfühlung* as it relates to the task of exegesis, 2) his alternative to it, viz., a hermeneutics of love and trust, and finally, 3) a distinction between these two approaches that should help to clarify the specifically "critical" aspect of Barth's approach to exegesis.

1. No Art of Empathy Can Offer the Slightest Substitute

Barth's basic problem with the hermeneutical concept of empathy was that it was intrinsically speculative and tended toward a presumption of familiarity with authors not warranted by the text itself. Nowhere was such presumption more apparent to Barth than in the way the dominant science of exegesis treated the apostle Paul. Paul Wernle, to recall, had described approaching Paul empathetically as "a psychological task," one that required identifying with Paul's spirit, "living in [him] in such a way that only and entirely *his* time, *his* environment, *his* addressees, *his* circumstances are before one's eyes." To understand Paul it was necessary to understand Paul's "character," "disposition," "temperament," and above all, his "sharply distinguished individuality," etc.[248] But what this typically amounted to, in Barth's view, was psychologism. Empathy was simply a means of ascribing all sorts of motives and intentions to Paul, and it was depictions based on such insights that led Barth eventually to say, "The modern portraits of Paul are for me no longer believable at all even historically."[249]

Interestingly enough, it was precisely these sorts of insights that Barth himself had cultivated before his break with liberalism. Around 1913, for example, Barth led a Bible study in his congregation at Safenwil, for which he prepared the following observations *about* Paul:

> ... narrow, strict spirit in parent's household, many commands and prohibitions. Saul accepts the necessity of it, he wants to be good, but he reaches the contrary. A tendency toward the forbidden because it is forbidden. By his own choice and by parental will, he is destined to take up the profession of a rabbi ... a man of will, [yet] a man of contrast: a) weakly, sick, often uncertain, yet able to accomplish, tough; b) depressive, yet self-confident, absolute, authoritarian; c) emotional softness (compassion, sympathy, love, en-

---

[248] See pp.130f. above.
[249] Rom II, p. xiv.

thusiasm), yet hard (judgmental, consistent, stiff). No saint, a man of contradiction, but also mighty in his failures. All his life he had to fight with himself and does so.[250]

Drawing a psychological profile of this sort had been important to Barth because this was part of the process of feeling one's way into an author. On the basis of these kinds of insights one could begin to establish an inner relationship with Paul, to immerse oneself in his thought-world and piety, and thereby to begin to see what Paul saw and experience what he experienced. It must be emphasized, however, that discussing Paul in these terms was not uncommon at the turn of the century, particularly among leaders of the dominant science of biblical exegesis.[251]

Given Barth's earlier interest in these matters, it is remarkable to see such a thoroughgoing absence of these sorts of observations in Barth's writings *after* his break with liberalism. Indeed, given all that he had said about the importance of empathy, about identifying with Paul, immersing oneself in his thought-world and piety, establishing an inner relationship with him, etc., Barth's comments about Paul after 1915 are striking. In his preface to Rom I, he states: "The powerful voice of Paul was new to me."[252] In his preface drafts he describes the voice of Paul as "strange."[253] Far from having achieved a depth of familiarity with Paul, Barth describes Paul as anything but familiar throughout the *Römerbrief* period.[254] At one point in his correspondence with Thurneysen, he states:

> How many there may have been before me who after a heated struggle with all these puzzling words have thought the task was 'finished,' until they (the words) look at the next exegete just as mysteriously. During the work it was often as though something was blowing on me from afar, from Asia Minor or Corinth, something very ancient, early oriental, indefinably bright, wild, original, that somehow is hidden beneath these sentences and is so ready to let itself be drawn forth by ever new generations. *Paul* – what a man he must have been, and what men also those for whom he could so sketch and hint at these pithy things in

---

[250] Karl Barth, "Paulus," *Vorträge und kleinere Arbeiten*, 1909-1914, pp. 555-557.

[251] Paul Wernle discusses the apostle Paul in similar fashion in several books: *Der Christ und die Sünde bei Paulus* (Freiburg: J.C.B. Mohr [Paul Siebeck], 1897); *Paulus als Heidenmissionar* (Freiburg: J. C.B. Mohr [Paul Siebeck], 1899); *Die Anfänge unserer Religion* (Freiburg: J.C.B. Mohr [Paul Siebeck], 1901); *Was haben wir heute an Paulus?* (Basel: Helbing & Lichtenhahn, 1904) the first of which Barth knew well and alludes to several times in his early work as well as in Rom I. And there are many other prominent figures in the dominant science of biblical exegesis who do the same: A. Deissmann, A. Jülicher, J. Weiss, et al.

[252] Rom I, p. 4.

[253] Appendix 2, Preface Draft III, p. 287 (p. 595), Preface Draft IV, p. 291 (p. 599), Preface Draft V, p. 292 (p. 601).

[254] "I peered with astonishment into a world of new, original, important, and fertile thoughts as if created for the purpose of being understood today; but I also saw, notwithstanding all Pauline-literature, how little these thoughts actually had become known in today's Christendom, let alone acknowledged by it and effective in it." Appendix 2, Preface III, p. 287 (pp. 594-595).

a few muddled fragments! I often shudder in such company. The Reformers, even Luther, are *far* from the stature of *Paul*; only now has that become convincingly clear to me. And *behind Paul*: what realities those must have been that could set this man in motion in *such* a way! What a lot of farfetched stuff we compile then in commentary on his words, of which perhaps 99 percent of their real content eludes us![255]

As I mentioned earlier, Barth described his encounter with Paul as the great turning-point of his life. Of course, it was the *subject matter* to which Paul's words bore witness that he claims was ultimately decisive. Still, Paul the man, Paul the individual, Paul the religious personality, had also deeply disturbed him. Barth's description of this experience is discussed in more detail in Appendix I. But the point here is that *after* 1915 and throughout his *Römerbrief* period, Barth says nothing whatsoever about attaining or having attained "personal" intimacy with Paul. Rather, he stresses how utterly "distant" and "removed" we are from Paul the man, Paul the religious personality.[256] To the extent that we know anything about Paul's personality at all – and Barth was convinced we did not know much[257] – he says one gets the impression that Paul, among other figures in the Bible, may *personally* have been an "insufferable eccentric" or "odd-ball."[258] In any case, "we must really marvel what harmless and inoffensive books most commentaries on *Romans* and other books about Paul are. And why not? It is probably because in them the 'disagreeable points' are handled according to Wernle's formula."[259]

This raises a second problem Barth had with the hermeneutical concept of empathy. The empathetic tradition of interpretation presupposed a general anthropology, a common, universally intuitable core of humanity. For Schleiermacher as for everyone in the emphathetic tradition of interpretation, the act of transforming oneself into the author and gaining an immediate comprehension of the author as an individual was based on "the assumption that each person contains a minimum of everyone else."[260] It was based, in other words, on a "comparison with oneself." Barth's problem with this, as I have suggested, was that it imposed unnecessary limits upon individuality. To the extent an author's individuality could be "subsumed under a general type" and "corroborated by comparisons," how much does this really tell us about the author as an individual? Does it necessarily capture the essence of his or her individuality?

---

[255] Karl Barth to Eduard Thurneysen, 27 Sept., 1917, *B-Th. Br.* I, p. 236.

[256] Appendix 2, Preface Draft III, p. 287 (p. 595).

[257] Barth states in preface drafts to Rom I: "Whoever, for instance, wants to be informed about the little one knows and the great amount one does not know about Paul's 'personality,' about the members and the character of the Roman Christian church, about Pauline formulas in the context of the history of religions ... will be disappointed here." Appendix 2, Preface Draft IA, p. 278 (p. 583); Preface Draft II, pp. 282-283 (p. 589).

[258] Barth, "Biblische Fragen, Einsichten und Ausblicke," p. 87.

[259] Rom II, p. xv.

[260] See p. 154 above.

And even if it were possible on the basis of their writings alone to classify the apostle Paul or the prophet Jeremiah under the rubric of a personality type, how important would such information be for interpreting their writings? Such information was certainly of great importance to the history of religions school. As Wernle said: "In the end, the strange must again be understood according to human nature and by all available means of psychological empathy."[261] For the history of religions school and a great many biblical exegetes of the day, comparing one religion, one religious personality with another, was ultimately *all* that scholars could do. Anything more would be to engage in metaphysics. Barth, of course, refused to accept this. He challenged the so-called "omnipotence of analogy" (Troeltsch).[262] Whereas the history of religions school claimed there was only *variation* based on comparisons according to the analogical method, Barth claimed on the basis of revelation there was *otherness* ("wholly otherness") and as a result tried to adopt an exegetical method which honored, or at least refused to set limits on, the quality of otherness.[263]

A third problem Barth had with the hermeneutical application of empathy was not merely its presupposition, but its aim. As a means of "getting into the mind" of an author, the empathetic tradition of interpretation focused attention as never before upon the author as an individual personality. Wernle and his contemporaries are prime examplars of this tendency. Barth, however, suggests that this trend began much earlier. Focus on an author's personality, and especially his religious personality, had its roots in Schleiermacher, which is why in sorting out his own theological heritage in 1916 Barth said (to repeat):

> Our grandfathers were right after all when they so passionately defended the fact that revelation is in the Bible and not only religion, and when they would not allow the subject matter to be turned upside down for them by so pious and clever a man as Schleiermacher. And our fathers were right when they guarded warily against being drawn out upon the shaky ground of the religious personality cult.[264]

Barth himself had been drawn to religion and drawn out, at least part way, upon that same shaky ground of the religious personality cult. What had been important to him then about the Bible was that it had been "written down by men who experienced themselves the glory of Christian certainty to the liveli-

---

[261] See p. 131 above.

[262] Troeltsch, "Über historische und dogmatische Methode in der Theologie," p. 732; ET p.14.

[263] This appears to be why Barth states in his preface to Rom II, "It is consistent with my principle of exposition that I cannot see how the contemporary parallels which in other commentaries are about all there is, should be more instructive for understanding and explicating *Romans* than the events of which we ourselves are witnesses" Rom II, p. xv. Barth's point is that infinite comparisons between the biblical witness and other religions are of relatively little value if one denies that "God speaks," which is the very thing Barth himself claimed to be witness of.

[264] Barth, "Die neue Welt in der Bibel," p. 28.

est degree."[265] It was primarily about religion, piety, about "people who *experienced* God and who now communicate these experiences."[266] But this conviction which he shared with a vast number of his contemporaries dramatically changed when he discovered the Bible's true subject matter, content, and theme.

This discovery, as I discussed in chapter three, changed the entire course of Barth's life and led him to adopt a *sachlicher, inhaltlicher, wesentlicher* approach to the Bible. His discovery, in a nutshell, was:

> The Bible has only *one* theological interest and it is not speculative: interest in God himself. ... *God* is the new, incomparable, unattainable, who has drawn the regard of the men of the Bible to himself. ... He cannot be grasped, brought under management, and put to use; he cannot serve. He must rule. He must himself grasp, seize, manage, use. ... He is not a thing among other things, but the Wholly Other, the infinite aggregate of all merely relative others. ... But whereas elsewhere consideration of him is left to the last, an imposing background, an esoteric secret ..., in the Bible he is the first consideration, the foreground, the revelation, the one all-dominating theme.[267]

In comparison to this one all-dominating theme, Barth realized what he had not realized before, namely, "the surprisingly meager interest the Bible has in *biography*, in the development of its heroes."[268] He realized that the Bible was not primarily a "document of piety" or about "the *personal relationship of men to God*" as the empathetic tradition of interpretation had insisted it was.[269] He realized how approaching the Bible as a document of piety had actually directed his attention *away* from the Bible's real subject matter, content, and theme, which is why he responded to critics in his preface to Rom II, "I shall accept criticism only from those who have shown that they have seen the real riddle (and truly not only the biographical, psychological one!)."[270] Approaching the Bible with the chief aim of establishing an "inner relationship" with the

---

[265] Barth, *Konfirmandenunterricht 1909-1921*, p. 67.

[266] Barth, *Konfirmandenunterricht 1909-1921*, p. 69.

[267] Barth, "Biblische Fragen, Einsichten und Ausblicke," pp. 84-85.

[268] "There is no gripping history of the youth and conversion of Jeremiah, no report of the edifying death of Paul. To the grief of our theological contemporaries there is above all no 'Life of Jesus.' What we hear of these men they never tell themselves; we do not read it in their 'life and letters.' The man of the Bible stands and falls with his task, his work." Barth, "Biblische Fragen, Einsichten und Ausblicke," p. 83; "The prophets and apostles do not *wish* to be what they are; they *have* to be. And therefore they *are*" (p. 82).

"... they are all such distraught, humanly unsatisfactory figures, uncertain of their souls and of their practical success, the direct opposite of heroes, their life stories unconcluded, their life work unfinished. So far from founding any *institutions*, the criteria of the *historical* worth of things, they do not even attempt it! Whether we think of Jacob or David or Jeremiah, or of Peter or Paul, there is a living witness not to humanity but to the *end* of humanity" (p. 87).

[269] Appendix 2, Preface Draft I, p. 277 (p. 582); Barth, "Biblische Fragen, Einsichten und Ausblicke," p. 82.

[270] Rom II, p. vii.

author on the basis of the "psychological process of empathy," Barth realized, had been a mistake because the true subject matter, content, and theme of the Bible is *"Totaliter aliter*! 'That which is born of the flesh is flesh; and that which is born of the spirit is spirit.' There are no transitions, intermixings, or intermediate stages. There is only crisis, finality, new insight."[271] Barth's discovery that "*God is God*" meant that God could not be identified with any medium of revelation, even that made available by direct contact with the pious self-consciousness of mediating individuals such as Paul (or any others having immediate experience of the affecting appearance of Christ). Thus his problem with the empathetic tradition's focus on Paul's piety, inner life, personality, etc., in short, was that it "ignores what is important and develops with *loving interest* that which is paltry."[272]

Yet, finally, beyond directing attention away from the Bible's true subject matter, content, and theme, and beyond its presupposition of a general anthropology which led to a leveling down or flattening out of individuality, and beyond the fact that it was intrinsically speculative and tended toward a presumption of familiarity not warranted by the text itself, empathetic interpretation was problematic to Barth for another reason. Empathetic identification with an author implied a kind of aesthetic submissiveness or surrender to the spirit of an author or age, but the presupposition which governed it was that of a free, autonomous, self-positioning subject who could stand in other ways *above* the spirit of that same author or age, which is what Barth was referring to when he spoke of those who with respect to the prophets and apostles would stand on the one hand "smiling sympathetically beside them" and yet take up "a cool and indifferent distance from them" on the other.[273] What was so disturbing to Barth about the dominant science of exegesis of his day – and this goes to the heart of why he referred to its approach as basically "inattentive and loveless" – was that it assumed that having read Paul empathetically, having examined him historically and psychologically, it had understood or at least had made a serious effort to understand him. It assumed that if only we could understand Paul or any author in his specific historical and psychological context or set of relations, we would then truly understand him or at least understand him *better*.

Barth rejected this assumption. Throughout his *Römerbrief* period he insisted that to understand Paul apart from the subject matter to which his words bear witness is not to understand him *at all*. Yet for Barth it was not simply

---

[271] Barth, "Biblische Fragen, Einsichten und Ausblicke," pp. 95, 91.

[272] Appendix 2, Preface Draft II, pp. 284-285 (pp. 591-592). See also Preface Draft III, p. 288 (p. 596).

[273] Appendix 2, Preface Draft II, p. 284 (p. 591). In Preface Draft IA, it is similarly stated: "... it does not take the prophets and apostles in earnest, but while it stands smiling sympathetically albeit condescendingly beside them, it conceitedly distances itself from them and outwardly examines them historically and psychologically" (p. 281 [p. 587]).

that those who refused to do so missed the point. It was in claiming to have understood an author on the basis of empathy that they ineluctably reduced the author to his historical and psychological context, to the reconstructible influences of his immediate or distant horizon, while ignoring the substance of what he has to say or attributing it to the power of these contingent forces. This is what Barth was accusing the dominant science of biblical science (and specifically Jülicher) of in his Rom II preface:

> ... How quickly ready, by means of a few rather banal categories of [Jülicher's] own religious thought (feeling, experience, conscience, conviction), to have *already* understood and explained [Paul] then and there; but how quickly he is ready, if all this cannot be done in the twinkling of an eye, to save himself from the Pauline ship with a clever leap, and to ascribe responsibility for the meaning of the text to the 'personality' of Paul, to the 'Damascus experience' (which evidently can explain the most incredible things), to Late Judaism, to Hellenism, to the ancient world in general, and to some other demigods.[274]

The art of empathy in Barth's view served only to mask this sort of historical and psychological reductionism. While smiling sympathetically at the prophets and apostles, it reduced them to the sum of their psychological parts or to the aggregate total of their historical relations, not taking their words in earnest but merely examining the historical-psychological surface. Although empathizing with an author gave every appearance of love (and Herder, Schleiermacher, Dilthey, Troeltsch, and Wernle each clearly equate such an approach with love),[275] to the extent it tried to do so apart from the subject matter about which the author writes, it is an approach Barth viewed as actually inattentive and loveless. To try to interpret an author "*in abstracto*," that is, apart from that which he by the very act of writing or speaking has obviously sought to make himself understood, Barth later described as an act of "shameless violence" against the author, something fundamentally dehumanizing.[276] The great irony, of course, is that what was of utmost importance to the empathetic tradition of interpretation was, ostensibly, the humanity, the individuality of authors! Yet Barth claims it is just such an approach which forms the basis for all manner of "isolation and impoverishment forced upon individuals."[277] This is why Barth described the dominant science of exegesis of his day as basically "inattentive and loveless" and this is why, despite all that appeared to suggest "loving interest" in Paul, for example, interest in his historical and psychological context,

---

[274] Rom II, p. xi.
[275] With reference to Herder, see pp. 148-149 above. Dilthey states: "Concerning morality Schleiermacher has observed that if sympathy is the basis of all understanding, then the highest understanding requires love." *Hermeneutics and the Study of History*, p. 230. As for Wernle, see pp. 130-132 above, and Troeltsch, *Glaubenslehre*, pp. 37-38; ET pp. 38-39.
[276] KD I/2:515; CD I/2:465. More shall be said about this in a moment.
[277] KD I/2:515; CD I/2:465.

his personality, inner life, etc., he said in his preface drafts to Rom I: "How cold-bloodedly we today, for the most part, ignore Paul."[278]

Barth's problem with the art of empathy, in sum, was that although it resembled participation with the author (for what kind of participation could aim higher than one in which the interpreter seeks, as Schleiermacher described it, to "transform himself into the author"?), it really did not participate with the author at all because it failed to regard the subject matter about which the author actually writes or speaks as the decisive matter. Rather than standing *with* the author by standing on his side and following the direction in which his words actually point, it is content merely to write *about* the author, and "to speak *about* someone," Barth said, "seems to me to be hopelessly condemned to speak *past* him, and to seal his grave even tighter."[279]

This does not mean, however, that the manner in which an interpreter seeks to relate to an author was for Barth simply arbitrary. There is a way of relating to authors which Barth discusses throughout his *Römerbrief* prefaces, and it is to this that we now turn.

2. A Relationship of Faithfulness

At the end of the last chapter I asked whether there was any connection between the hermeneutical tradition of Schleiermacher and Dilthey and Barth's provocative claim, "As one who would understand, I must press forward to the point where insofar as possible I confront the riddle of the *subject matter* and no longer merely the riddle of the *document* as such, until I can almost forget that I am not the author, until I have almost understood him so well that I let him speak in my name, and can myself speak in his name." (As I indicated, Georg Eichholz and others have posed this question as well). Given what has been subsequently said about the art of empathy, there certainly *appears* to be a connection. And given Wernle's remark in his review of Rom I that Barth had interpreted Paul with such a depth of "*Kongenialität*" (a favorite term of the empathetic tradition of interpretation),[280] it may well be that Barth was trying

---

[278] "It became to me one of the greatest riddles how cold-bloodedly we today, for the most part, ignore Paul. We have examined him 'historically,' we have appropriated a few slogans from his workshop, we have with quiet sympathy shrugged our shoulders precisely at *his* decisive thoughts and are going precisely the ways of *our* decisive thoughts, against which he most strongly warned." Appendix 2, Preface Draft III, p. 287 (p. 595).

[279] It is worth pointing out, however, that the decision made by many exegetes at the turn of the century to write *about* Paul rather than *with* him did not necessarily have to do with any loveless predisposition *against* Paul. On the contrary, many interested in writing *about* Paul obviously held him in high regard. Yet even among those holding Paul in high regard, many did so only in terms of his identity as a religious personality, in terms of his identity as someone who could relate meaningful and perhaps even interesting psycho-religious experiences, or in terms of his historical significance as a religious founder, etc. Rom II, third edition, p. xxi.

[280] The term 'Kongenialität' has a long history in the empathetic tradition of interpretation. See Gadamer, *Wahrheit und Methode*, pp. 193-195; 237, 244-245; ET pp. 189-191, 233, 240.

to identify with the empathetic approach to interpretation, yet – in a fashion he would become famous for – only to outbid it in the manner of an *Aufhebung*.[281] Whether this was Barth's aim, closer analysis in light of his comments about the art of empathy in his preface drafts to Rom I indicates that although there is certainly a similarity between the approach of the empathetic tradition of interpretation and Barth's statement above, there is also a very significant difference.

First, the *basis* of participation that Barth discusses is different. As I have already suggested, the basis of participation Barth describes has primarily to do with allegiance to the author's words, with standing *with* the author while looking in the same direction his words point until one sees and can participate in the *subject matter* which the author claims is there (whether one can actually see and participate in the subject matter which the author claims is there, of course, comes with no guarantee), whereas the empathetic tradition's basis of participation does not have primarily to do with the author's words or the subject matter to which they point but with knowledge of the author himself, in knowing various historical and psychological circumstances *about* the author and having an empathetic capacity (*Einfühlungsvermögen*) to identify with them. Secondly, Barth qualifies the *manner* in which he claims to participate with the author. He does not, for example, necessarily claim to identify with the author in any interior sense, i.e., in terms of a relationship which might involve a state of complete, undifferentiated consciousness (which implies the essential difference between a sympathetic [*mitfühlen*] and empathetic [*einfühlen*] relationship). Nor does Barth necessarily even claim interior identification as his goal. (He does this by using the qualifier "almost": "until I can *almost* forget that I am not the author, until I have *almost* understood him so well that I let him speak in my name.") Thus, unlike Schleiermacher who claimed it was necessary that the interpreter "transform himself, so to speak, into the author in order to gain an immediate comprehension of the author as an individual," or Wernle who insisted the interpreter "must seek to live in an author in such a way that only and entirely *his* time, *his* environment, *his* addressees, *his* circumstances are before one's eyes," Barth's goal is simply to stand as close to the author as possible, not in order to look *at him*, much less to get inside him psychologically, but to look in the direction his words point, from exactly the same angle or vantage point, as it were, in a definite direction, as definite a direction as John the Baptist's finger points in Grünewald's painting. Barth describes taking a stand beside an author in such a way as a relationship of faithfulness (*ein Treueverhältnis*).

---

[281] Barth's often tried to outbid other views (typically his opponents' views) in the manner of a kind of *Aufhebung*. An example of this is found in Barth's preface to Rom II, where he says he wishes the so-called "critical" exegetes would be "*more critical*" Rom II, p. xii.

Maintaining a relationship of trust or faithfulness with the author is one of Barth's most important hermeneutical principles. Though the words trust and faithfulness do not appear in his prefaces to Rom I or II, the word trust does appear in his preface drafts to Rom I. As mentioned earlier, Barth states: "Here I am forced to indicate with a few sentences the chasm which separates me from the method of today's dominant science of biblical exegesis. To understand an author means for me mainly to *stand with him*, to take each of his words in earnest, so long as it is not proven otherwise that he does not deserve this trust, to participate with him in the subject matter in order to interpret him from the inside out." As I discussed in the last chapter, Barth goes on to describe how the dominant science of exegesis (in the name of scientific objectivity) does quite the opposite. Rather than approaching the author's words with trust, it approaches them with "mistrust." But it is in the preface to the third edition of his *Römerbrief*, where the word is mentioned four times, that Barth most clearly elaborates what he means by a *Treueverhältnis*. Bultmann, to recall, had praised Barth's statement, "until I can almost forget that I am not the author," etc., as "the high point of exegetical understanding," to the extent, that one does so from the standpoint of the subject matter. He criticized Barth, however, for not taking into account the fact that Paul himself did not always speak "from the subject matter itself" and that "in him there are other spirits speaking besides the *pneuma Christou*."[282] Barth responded to Bultmann's criticism by agreeing that there are certainly other spirits speaking in Paul. In fact, he says, "I must still really go a little further than he does and say that what speaks in the *Epistle to the Romans* is nothing but the 'others,' the various 'spirits' which he adduces, such as the Jewish, the popular Christian, the Hellenistic, and others." Calling Bultmann's assumption into question – as if at one place "one could point one's finger with the observation that *there* assuredly the *pneuma Christou* speaks? Or to turn the matter around, is the Spirit of Christ perhaps a spirit which can be presented *along with* other spirits?" – Barth then asserts: "My conclusion therefore is that in no case can it be a question of playing off the Spirit of Christ, the 'subject matter,' in such a way against the 'other spirits,' that in the name of the former certain passages are praised, but certain others, where Paul is not speaking 'from the subject matter' are belittled. Rather, it is a question of seeing and making clear how the 'Spirit of Christ' is the crisis in which the whole finds itself." It is at this point that Barth introduces the notion of a relationship of faithfulness:

> The exegete is faced with the either-or, whether or not he, knowing himself what is at stake and entering into a relationship of faithfulness to the author, intends to read him with the hypothesis that the author also knew with more or less clarity down to the last word (for where should the limit be set – surely not through the discovery of relationships of historical dependence?) what is at stake. He will then not write his commentary *about* Paul, but,

---

[282] See pp. 92-93 above.

certainly not without frequent sighs and shaking of the head, as well as he can, down to the last word, write it *with* Paul. The measure of the 'Spirit of Christ' which he thereby discovers in Paul and can make perceptible in his rendering will certainly not be equally great everywhere, but will be a 'more or less.' He feels, however, that he is responsible in this matter. He never lets himself be entirely befuddled by the voice of the 'other' spirits who often make the dominant notes of the 'Spirit of Christ' almost inaudible. He always looks first for the lack of understanding in himself and not in Paul. He spares no pains to see and to show to what degree what is scattered is still paradoxically part of the context of the subject matter, and how all the 'other' spirits really are somehow subject to the *pneuma Christou*.[283]

Three points about this passage are noteworthy: First, Barth returns to themes of his Rom I preface drafts, namely, writing "*with*" rather than "*about*" Paul" and the importance of maintaining a relationship of trust or faithfulness. Second, the general application of this hermeneutical principle is implied; that is, it applies to "any author." Third, Barth's remark, "down to the last word" suggests he obviously holds a different view of the significance of biblical language than he did before 1915.[284] The significance of maintaining a relationship of faithfulness with Paul and the general application of this principle in any case becomes more explicit as Barth continues:

> Naturally the exegete can also approach Paul without that hypothesis, and refuse to trust him. Perhaps he himself does not know, or does not know clearly enough, what might be at stake in such a writing as the *Epistle to the Romans*. Or perhaps he has despaired of the task of discerning, from the chorus of the 'other' spirits which rings out from all lines of his text, the voice of that knowledge. He will then write his commentary *about* Paul, and at most occasionally *with* Paul, when Paul chances to say something that is clear to him as well. The measure of the Spirit of Christ in Paul, if he decides to define those things at all which are clear as such, will appear to him under the formula "in part-in part." He stands as an irresponsible observer *beside* the conglomeration of Spirit and spirits, which is what the text means for him. He does not know this restlessness with respect to the meaning of the text because he does not know a relationship of faithfulness to it, because, even when under certain conditions he travels a little way beside it, he is still by no means determined to stand and to fall with it. I hold that it is impossible for anyone to do justice to any author, to be able really to bring any author to speak again, if he does not dare to assume that hypothesis, does not enter into that relationship of faithfulness to him. I understand that we must in despair travel this road from time to time. There are truly enough phenomena that seem to permit us only to talk *about* them, although in this there is always the question

---

[283] Rom II, third edition, p. xx.

[284] More shall be said about this in the next chapter. Prior to 1915, as I have shown, Barth held a basically Lutheran view of Scripture ("*Was Christus treibt*"). This changed at some point in his *Römerbrief* period. The either-or position Barth articulates above in opposition to Bultmann foreshadows what he would later say in 1925: "With God there is no more or less, only an either-or. The Reformed Church has always put special emphasis on this determination. It basically never approved of Luther's self-satisfied way of setting up a kind of selective Bible due to an individually qualified Dogmatic. And we think the Church did right to do so." Karl Barth, "Das Schriftprinzip der reformierten Kirche" (1925), *Vorträge und kleinere Arbeiten 1922-1925*, ed. Holger Finze (Zürich: Theologischer Verlag Zürich, 1990), pp. 512-513.

whether what is enigmatic and puzzling is to be sought for more on their side, or more on the side of us who observe them. But what I cannot understand is the invitation which Bultmann issues to me to mix fire and water, to think and to write *with* Paul, that is, first of all in the entirely foreign language of his Jewish-popular-Christian-Hellenistic thought-world, and then suddenly, when this may get to be too much for me – as if something struck me as especially strange where everything is strange! – to speak 'critically' *about* and *against* Paul. Does Bultmann not perceive that, even considered only from the point of view of purity of style, this will not do; that, as I see it, this would be a matter of bad taste, a falling back into the method of the "temporarily conditioned remnants" and "disagreeable points"?[285]

Barth goes on to address Bultmann's charge that behind his work is a "modern dogma of inspiration," but to sum up what Barth means by a relationship of faithfulness with an author, it means writing *with* the author rather than *about* the author. Rather than becoming preoccupied with the reconstructible circumstances that may or may not on the basis of historical probability lie behind the text, it means focusing primarily on the text itself in light of its central subject matter, content, and theme. It means making a sincere effort to understand the author on his own terms and in his own stated and not merely speculatively reconstructed context. It means trying to understand the author's text with an openness at least to the possibility that he might tell us something we did not already know but perhaps could know if we would only take his "thoughts at least as seriously as one takes one's own." It means rather than assuming the author did not really know what he was talking about, approaching his text with the hypothesis "that the author knew with more or less clarity down to the last word what is at stake." It means instead of assuming the author was writing for effect or to make some sort of impression, accepting the possibility that the author was writing to describe what was or is in fact the case. It means rather than trying as an interpreter to "play the schoolmaster," "always looking first for the lack of understanding in oneself and not in [the author]." It means rather than presuming familiarity with the author or the author's situation, rather than trying to understand him ultimately according to various general types or categories, respecting the author's individuality and otherness and extending such respect, of course, to the subject matter about which he writes. Above all, it means exercising patience and trust. It means accepting the challenge of "stubbornly occupying" oneself with the author's words until they render a specific theme or subject matter. It means making an earnest commitment to travel with the author's text, not just "a little way ... under certain conditions," but with a willingness to "to stand and fall with it." It means wrestling with the author's text – as in the case of Calvin's wrestling with Paul – "until the wall between the first and sixteenth centuries becomes transparent, until Paul speaks there and the man of the sixteenth century hears here, until the conversation between document and reader is concentrated entirely on the

---

[285] Rom II, third edition, pp. xx-xxi.

subject matter."²⁸⁶ Characterized hardly by dogmatic self-assurance but by "frequent sighs and shaking of the head" and a profound sense of "restlessness with respect to the meaning of the text," this determination to struggle with the author's text is what Barth means by maintaining a relationship of faithfulness and a more attentive and loving approach to the task of interpretation.²⁸⁷

3. An Emergency Clause

Karl Barth's answer to the hermeneutics of suspicion, in short, was a hermeneutic of trust. Though a hermeneutic of suspicion was already pervasive among biblical scholars at the turn of the century, Barth saw a hermeneutic of trust as basic and primary. Indeed, he saw the decision to maintain a relationship of faithfulness with an author as the most important decision an interpreter could make. It would be a serious mistake, however, to confuse this attitude of trust with simple-minded naiveté, for even though he insisted that we try to enter into a relationship of faithfulness with every author, he did not insist that we maintain every such relationship. Barth did not make this clear in his *Römerbrief* prefaces and was severely criticized as a result. But in his preface drafts to Rom I, he repeatedly stipulates that an author's words are to be taken "in earnest, so long as it is not proven otherwise that he does not deserve this

---

²⁸⁶ Rom II, p. xi.
²⁸⁷ In recent years, some have suggested that Barth was ambivalent regarding such concepts as authorial intention. Mark I. Wallace, for example, claims: "Barth stands alongside both New Critical and current deconstructive critics of the Bible in maintaining that all literary creations, the Bible included, are primarily works of art, not by-products of history – as such, they possess a life of their own, a life relatively independent from the cultural and authorial milieus that produced them. Possessing semantic autonomy, the 'literary work exists, in a sense, outside of history, in a kind of aesthetic preserve' where the text's surplus of meaning escapes the finite conditions that gave rise to it in the first place." Wallace, "Karl Barth's Hermeneutic: A Way Beyond The Impasse," *Journal of Religion*, 68 (1988), p. 403. This is typical of many 'post-modern' readings of Barth. The problem is that nowhere does Barth suggest that we read the Bible or any text as if they possessed "a life relatively independent from the cultural and authorial milieus that produced them." While never guilty of the so-called 'intentional fallacy,' Barth was not, particularly in light of what maintaining a relationship of faithfulness to an author entailed for him, ambivalent, in any sense, to the fully human, historical determination of texts. This is clear from the beginning of the *Römerbrief* period. Yet discussing an author's intentions for Barth, unlike many of his contemporaries influenced by the empathetic tradition of interpretation, as he later claimed, was based upon the fact that "we cannot make any essential distinction between the thinking and speaking of the prophets and apostles and their writing, either in the sense in which many attempts have been made recently to limit inspiration to their thinking and speaking or even to the prophetic experience which precedes and underlies their thinking. ... As men, who lived then and there and not here and now, the prophets and apostles do, of course, exist for us only in what they have written" (KD I/2:560-1; CD I/2:505). Interestingly, Schleiermacher says we must draw no distinction between what the apostles *said* and wrote, not between what they *thought* and wrote. See Schleiermacher, *Hermeneutik*, p. 85; ET p. 107.

trust."[288] He refers to this as an "emergency clause" (*eine Notklausel*), and given interpreters like Wernle and Jülicher who in face of so many "disagreeable points" in Paul tended all too hastily, in Barth's view, "to save [themselves] from the Pauline ship with a clever leap," it is easy to see why Barth stresses his reluctance to invoke it. His reason: "The Bible has been approached much too carelessly with the application of this emergency clause."[289] For the dominant science of biblical exegesis, this so-called emergency clause had simply become an all too convenient escape clause for not maintaining a relationship of faithfulness. Nevertheless, the fact that Barth raises the issue of an emergency clause which would allow him *not* to trust an author indicates something very important about Barth's understanding of what it means to interpret texts critically.

Exegesis which is truly critical, in Barth's view, involves a willingness to question one's own questions, to try again and again to strip oneself of unjustified assumptions by foregrounding one's most basic presuppositions about the text. To be critical means, fundamentally, to be *self*-critical.[290] It is this kind of criticism that Barth was talking about when he said: "The historical critics must be *more critical* to suit me!"[291] This is why the decision not to trust an author's words should never be made in haste and only in the last resort. Still, Barth acknowledges that there are occasions when an author's words do not deserve our trust, and the question this raises is: What is the basis, according to Barth, for deciding whether an author's words do not deserve our trust? From an epistemological standpoint it would appear that what lies behind Barth's assertion is some sort of correspondence theory of truth, that is, a given statement should be trusted so long as it does not fail to correspond to the subject matter about which it purports to bear witness. This is essentially what "measuring everything in light of the subject matter" is about. Bultmann, as I indicated earlier, applauded this approach. However, the fact that Barth did not seem to recognize or wish to acknowledge that Paul did not always speak in his *Epistle to the Romans* from the subject matter suggested to Bultmann that

---

[288] Appendix 2, Preface Draft IA, p. 281 (p. 587); Preface Draft II, p. 284 (p. 591); Preface Draft III, p. 288 (p. 596).

[289] Appendix 2, Preface Draft III, p. 288 (p. 596).

[290] "We can say that the use of a human scheme of thought in the service of scriptural exegesis is legitimate and fruitful when it is a critical use, implying that the object of the criticism is not Scripture, but our own scheme of thought, and that Scripture is necessarily the subject of this criticism." KD I/2:823; CD I/2:734.

[291] Rom II, p. xx. The first time Barth expressed this concern for a "more critical" approach *vis à vis* his contemporaries appears to have been in his letter to Paul Wernle of Oct.24, 1919: "We are not accusing you of criticism but of lack of criticism with respect to the gestaltless rubble heap of individual relative truths which you presented to us as the result of scientific work at the New Testament" (See p. 19n.41 above). What seems to have triggered this concern was Wernle's failure to interpret the parts in light of the whole.

Barth was not "radical enough." But it suggested to Barth that Bultmann had a very different basis for deciding which words of Paul were worthy of trust.

Though Bultmann had praised Barth's statement, "until I can almost forget that I am not the author, until I have almost understood him so well that I let him speak in my name," as "the high point of exegetical understanding," what this fundamentally implied for Bultmann was *understanding Paul better than he understood himself.* He expresses this view in his 1926 review of Barth's commentary on I Corinthians 15 and attributes it to Barth himself.[292] Barth, however, notwithstanding his statement about almost forgetting that he was not the author, never accepted that this was what he had achieved with respect to Paul, nor that this was something he even aspired to. On the contrary, throughout his career, Barth explicitly rejected the goal of understanding Paul or any other apostle better than he understood himself, and it appears that this was already the case in the *Römerbrief* period.[293] Gadamer, as I previously mentioned, claims it is through the various ways interpreters have sought to understand an author better than he understood himself that "the whole history of modern hermeneutics can be read."[294] Given the implicit differences between Barth and Bultmann on this issue, it is important to reflect upon Gadamer's claim, because I think it provides a key insight into why he referred to Barth's *Römerbrief* as "a hermeneutical manifesto."

---

[292] Characterizing Barth's approach, Bultmann states: "It means interpreting Paul really critically; it means understanding him better than he understood himself! And I can only repeat that the *hazard* of this kind of exegesis must always be explicitly recognized, and the exegesis must be developed on a basis of the most exact knowledge of the contemporary background and by means of careful and penetrating analysis of the content." R. Bultmann's "K. Barth's 'Die Auferstehung der Toten," pp. 12f.; ET pp. 92-93.

[293] Given the popularity of this exegetical goal, it would appear that the reason Barth qualifies his provocative statement with "almost" – "until I can *almost* forget that I am not the author, until I have *almost* understood him so well that I let him speak in my name" (italics mine) – is that he did not want to claim that he had understood Paul better than Paul had understood himself. Barth's problem with understanding an author better than he understood himself is indicated in his Jan.28, 1924 lectures on Schleiermacher's hermeneutic, *Die Theologie Schleiermachers*, pp. 324f.; ET p. 180f. His rejection of this exegetical goal with respect to Paul and other apostles appears throughout the *Church Dogmatics*, even the lecture drafts for IV.4: "If we ask how is it possible that the coming of Jesus Christ and in and with it that of God's kingdom could present itself to the first disciples and the apostolic communities as one which was already perfectly past but still perfectly future, then, *abandoning any attempt to understand the New Testament better than it understood itself*, our simple answer must be that this apparent impossibility became an actuality in the Easter history which expounds, illustrates, and crowns the history of Jesus Christ." Karl Barth, *Das christliche Leben, 1959-1961*, ed. Eberhard Jüngel (Zürich: Theologischer Verlag Zürich, 1976), p. 440; ET *The Christian Life* (Grand Rapids: William B. Eerdmans, 1981), pp. 254-255. (Italics mine).

[294] See pp.150f. above.

Much has been written about what it means to "understand an author better than he understood himself" and about the origins of this formula.[295] I mentioned earlier its role in Herder, Schleiermacher, and Dilthey and said that in seeking to understand an author better than he understood himself much has always hinged on what has been meant by *better*. Better in relationship to what? Better awareness of the author's *Sitz im Leben*? Better awareness of grammatical rules the author presupposed?, etc. Gadamer, as I said earlier, says, "What it means for Schleiermacher is clear. He sees the act of understanding as the reconstruction of the production. This inevitably renders many things conscious of which the writer may be unconscious."[296] In other words, to understand an author *better* than he understood himself is to become *more conscious* of things of which the writer may have been totally unconscious or simply less conscious. It is this notion of understanding an author better than he understood himself, the notion championed by Schleiermacher and the empathetic tradition of interpretation, that has been dominant since the beginning of the nineteenth century, and according to Gadamer, this represents a fundamental departure from the way previous interpreters conceived their task.

Throughout *Truth and Method*, Gadamer distinguishes between two different notions of understanding. Georgia Warnke has described them as follows:

> The first form of understanding refers to the kind of substantive knowledge one has when one is justified in claiming that one understands Euclidean geometry or an ethical principle, for example. Here understanding means seeing the 'truth' of something, grasping that the sum of the squares of the two sides of a right triangle is equal to the square of the hypotenuse, that the validity of Euclidean geometry is relativized by the discovery of other forms of geometry or that murder is wrong. Understanding in this sense involves insight into a subject-matter or, as Gadamer puts it, an understanding of *die Sache*. The second sense of understanding, in contrast, involves a knowledge of conditions: the reasons why a particular person says that murder is wrong or the intentions behind someone's claiming that a geo-

---

[295] There is considerable debate about who came up with this formula first. Herman Patsch says it was Friedrich Schlegel, "Friedrich Schlegel's 'Philosophie der Philologie' und Schleiermachers frühe Entwürfe zur Hermeneutik: Zur Frühgeschichte der romantischen Hermeneutik," *Zeitschrift für Theologie und Kirche* 63 (1966), pp. 437-72. Kurt Mueller-Vollmer states in his essay, "To Understand An Author Better Than The Author Himself: On The Hermeneutics Of The Unspoken," *Language and Style* 5 (1971), pp. 43-52, that "The classical philologist Boeckh was responsible for having introduced it for the first time into a systematic theory of interpretation," p. 43. Dilthey's student, O.F. Bullnow, "Was heißt, einen Schriftsteller besser verstehen, als er sich selber verstanden hat?" *Das Verstehen: Drei Aufsätze zur Theorie der Geisteswissenschaften* (Mainz: Kirchheim, 1949), pp. 7-33, claims that it appears even earlier in Kant (*Critique of Pure Reason*, B 370) and Fichte (*Werke* 6, p. 337). Gadamer points out, however, as we shall see, that it has a very different connotation in Kant and Fichte than in the Romantic tradition, *Wahrheit und Methode*, p. 197f.; ET pp. 194f. Barth, in any case, appears to have found a reference to it even earlier in Herder. See pp. 150-151 above. See also Ernst-Wilhelm Kohls, "Einen Autor besser verstehen, als er sich selbst verstanden hat" in *Theologische Zeitschrift* 26 (1970) pp. 321-337.

[296] See pp. 150f. above.

metrical proposition is true. This kind of understanding thus involves an understanding of the psychological, biographical or historical conditions behind a claim or action itself. What is understood is not the truth-content of a claim or the point of an action but the motives behind a certain person's making a certain claim or performing a given action.[297]

According to the latter notion of understanding, the one embraced by Schleiermacher and the empathetic tradition of interpretation, understanding an author better than he understood himself has to do with retracing the author's path of creative production, becoming more conscious of that which he may have been unconscious or only partially conscious of, such as, for example, his own psychological motives, historical or biographical circumstances, etc. The former notion, on the other hand, the one Gadamer defends and claims is more classical, is obviously quite different. It does not aim at understanding an author better than he understood himself, rather it defines understanding basically in terms of agreement (*Einverständnis*), i.e. agreement with another regarding a specific subject matter. Gadamer asserts in an important passage: "Understanding is first of all agreement. So human beings usually understand one another immediately or they communicate until they reach an agreement. Reaching an understanding is thus always: reaching an understanding about something. Understanding each other is always understanding each other with respect to something."[298]

These two notions of understanding are clearly juxtaposed in Barth's *Römerbrief* prefaces and preface drafts, which is why he stresses throughout that understanding is always understanding *about something*, about the *truth* regarding a given *subject matter*, apart from which there is no understanding, whereas for so many of his contemporaries, particularly in the dominant science of exegesis, understanding has to do with knowledge about all sorts of conditions and circumstances relative to a given subject matter yet not necessarily about the subject matter itself. This is also why Barth stresses: "As one who would understand, I must press forward to the point where insofar as possible I confront the riddle of the *subject matter*" etc., and then immediately asks: "What else do we call 'understanding' and 'explanation' – has Lietzmann, for example, ever seriously asked himself this question?"[299] As early as

---

[297] Georgia Warnke, *Gadamer: Hermeneutics, Tradition, and Reason* (Standford: University Press, 1987), pp. 7-8.

[298] Gadamer, *Wahrheit und Methode*, pp. 183-184; ET p. 180. "Verstehen heißt zunächst, sich miteinander verstehen. Verständnis ist zunächst Einverständnis. So verstehen die Menschen einander zumeist unmittelbar, bzw. sie verständigen sich bis zur Erzielung des Einverständnisses. Verständigung ist also immer Verständigung über etwas. Sich verstehen ist sich verstehen in etwas." Gadamer goes on to say "From language we learn that the subject matter is not merely an arbitrary object of discussion, independent of the process of mutual understanding, but rather is the path and goal of mutual understanding itself." Barth would agree, but for him it is not ultimately "from language" *itself* that we learn this.

[299] Rom II, p. xii.

his *Römerbrief* period, Barth realized that his notion of understanding was very different from that of many of his contemporaries, which explains why he makes so many comments about understanding (more than a dozen) throughout the *Römerbrief* prefaces and preface drafts: "One can only *understand* that for which one *stands*"[300]; "To understand an author means for me mainly *to stand with him*, to take each of his words in earnest"[301]; "The words 'history' and 'understanding' make no sense for me at all without this living context between the past and the present which cannot be achieved through some empathetic art, but is *given* in the subject matter and in which one must *be*."[302]

Here we return to the main thesis of this study. The theological movement that Barth's *Römerbrief* launched, he later explained, represented an attempt "to reverse the current understanding of the New (and Old) Testament, and understanding in general."[303] Understanding in general had become confused because ever since Schleiermacher, theologians had turned their attention more and more to the subject of understanding (viz., themselves) rather than to the object they claimed they wished to understand (viz., God). Instead of recognizing that "man's knowledge depended on his being known by the object of his knowledge,"[304] they convinced themselves that man's knowledge depended on the way taken in knowing. Of course, Schleiermacher, "the father of modern hermeneutics," had much to do with this shift in focus. No theologian had talked more about the problem of human understanding than he. The task he set up for himself, as Gadamer says, was "precisely that of isolating the procedure of understanding. He endeavored to make it an independent method of its own."[305] Yet it is precisely at this point that Barth sought to overcome Schleiermacher. He attempted to do so by championing a *sachlicher* approach to theology and exegesis. Schleiermacher's influence, however, was still so great when Barth's *Römerbrief* appeared that even many who admired its *sachlicher* approach still did not recognize the depth of its implications. Bultmann, for example, praised Barth's *sachlicher* approach but still demonstrated by seeking to understand Paul better than he understood himself on the "basis of the most exact knowledge of the contemporary background *and* by means of careful and penetrating analysis of the content" that he had not overcome the notion of understanding that the hermeneutical tradition of Schleiermacher had pioneered. Rather he demonstrated that he was still caught up in the same bi-

---

[300] Appendix 2, Preface Draft III, p. 288 (p. 596).
[301] Appendix 2, Preface Draft IA, p. 281 (p. 587) and Preface Draft II, p. 284 (p. 591).
[302] Appendix 2, Preface Draft IA, p. 302 (p. 587).
[303] Barth, *Ein Versuch, ihn zu verstehen*, p. 60; ET p. 127.
[304] Barth, *Ein Versuch, ihn zu verstehen*, p. 60; ET p. 127.
[305] Gadamer, *Wahrheit und Methode*, p. 174; ET p. 185. The implications of this, of course, were profound. Gadamer adds: "Hence it is likely that not until Schleiermacher – with whom hermeneutics became an independent method, detached from all content – could the interpreter claim superiority over his object" (p. 182; ET pp. 194-195).

furcated, "double-entry book-keeping" approach of his contemporaries. That Bultmann, in Barth's view, "had gone back to the old idea of understanding" in light of his essay of 1950, "The Problem of Understanding," in which he aligned his own project in the trajectory of the hermeneutical tradition of Schleiermacher and Dilthey, therefore, could hardly have been a great surprise to Barth. Bultmann had actually never been far from it.

Barth's attempt to overcome this "old idea of understanding" with a more *sachliche* notion of understanding, a notion of understanding that focused primarily on the truth-content of a given text, is what Gadamer seeks to describe from a strictly hermeneutical, non-theological, perspective in *Truth and Method*. Again, Georgia Warnke provides a nice summary of Gadamer:

> In his own reconstruction of the development of hermeneutics from Schleiermacher through Dilthey, Gadamer tries to show that what Dilthey described as a liberation from dogma is instead a move from one sense of understanding, an understanding of truth-content, to the other, an understanding of conditions of genesis. Despite their differences both Tridentine Catholicism and the Protestantism of the Reformation are concerned with the truth-content of the Bible. ... As hermeneutics develops, however, attention is redirected away from the understanding of the truth content of a text and toward the understanding of intentions. The aim of understanding is no longer seen as a knowledge of *die Sache* – a substantive knowledge of claims to truth or normative authority. It is seen rather as insight into the historical or biographical circumstances behind their expression. The question of understanding thus becomes the genetic one: what were the conditions under which agents acted, spoke or wrote as they did? The question of the validity of their words or actions is no longer considered part of the theory of understanding.[306]

This is why Gadamer refers to the first edition of Barth's *Römerbrief* as "a virtual hermeneutical manifesto." It was "the first revolutionary eruption" against the hegemony of the hermeneutical tradition of Schleiermacher and Dilthey.[307] It aimed at understanding the truth-content of Paul's *Epistle to the Romans*, rather than merely the historical or biographical circumstances behind it. Instead of trying to understand Paul better than he understood himself, it focused above all on understanding the subject matter about which Paul wrote.

It is very important to point out, however, that even though Barth did not *aim* at understanding *Paul* better than he understood himself, nowhere does he

---

[306] Warnke, *Gadamer: Hermeneutics, Tradition, and Reason*, pp. 9-10.

[307] Major differences between Barth and Gadamer must not be overlooked, however. Gadamer's hermeneutics are strictly philosophical, thus his discussion of 'truth' is, compared to Barth's, highly abstract and, from a dogmatic perspective, speculative. Moreover, Gadamer's comment in the passage above, viz., "Bultmann's combination of historical-critical research with theological exegesis and his reliance on philosophy (Heidegger) for methodological self-awareness prevents Barth from recognizing himself in Bultmann's method," demonstrates that he, like Bultmann, does not understand the basis of Barth's *sachlicher* approach (viz. "the sovereign freedom of the subject matter" at issue) or the depths of its implications. Nevertheless, it is to Gadamer's credit that he acknowledged, however belatedly, the hermeneutical significance of Rom I.

exclude the *possibility* that *any* author, including Paul, might be understood better than he understood himself. In fact, there are many cases when an author *must* be understood better than he understood himself, which is why Barth mentions the necessity of an "emergency clause." For Barth, *it is possible* to understand an author better than he understood himself *if* one has a better understanding of the subject matter about which the author writes or speaks. However, the problem with trying to understand the apostle Paul better than he understood himself, or any other apostle for that matter, is that in Barth's view we have no immediate or independent access to the subject matter about which Paul and the other apostles wrote, apart from Paul and the other apostles themselves. This, of course, is not necessarily the case with respect to other subject matter. There are cases in which we *do* have knowledge of a given subject matter apart from the words of others and can demonstrate that their words do not sufficiently correspond to the subject matter they purport to bear witness to. In such cases, it is possible to understand an author better than he understood himself. Nevertheless, Barth insists, this is an emergency measure! It is not a *goal*. It is certainly not something we set out to do upon first encountering an author. Rather, understanding an author better than he understood himself is something that occurs only after the most painstaking effort to understand an author has been made, and then only after an interpreter has come to a firm understanding of what the author is talking about, or at least trying to talk about, and can demonstrate that the author's words do not sufficiently correspond to it. Only then is it possible to understand an author better than he understood himself. Until then, however, we are obliged according to Barth to maintain a relationship of trust with the author and to take each of his words "in earnest, so long as it is not proven otherwise that he does not deserve this trust."

Interestingly, Gadamer points out that the formula "understanding an author better than he understood himself" appears in two places before Schleiermacher, viz., in Fichte and Kant,[308] in a way very similar to this and in contrast to Schleiermacher. According to Gadamer, for Fichte and Kant and almost everyone before Schleiermacher, understanding an author better than he understood himself had to do with

> achieving greater conceptual clarity ... it claims, solely through thought, through elaborating the implications of an author's ideas, to achieve insights into the real intention of an author's ideas – intentions he would have shared if his thinking had been clear enough. ... Thus the disputed formula makes no claim beyond that of philosophic critique of the subject matter. Someone who is better able to think his way through what an author is talking about will be able to see what the author says in the light of a truth hidden from the author. In this sense the principle that one must understand an author better than he understands

---

[308] Gadamer, *Wahrheit und Methode*, p. 197; ET p. 194.

himself is a very old one, as old as scientific critique itself. ... As such it has a sense completely different from Schleiermacher's philological rule.[309]

Whether it was Barth's studies in Kant or his discovery of the supremacy of the Bible's subject matter over all things (or both) that alerted him to these two very different notions of understanding, the point is that Barth appears to have realized from very early on in his *Römerbrief* period that the only basis for understanding an author better than he understood himself is on the basis of a knowledge of the *subject matter* about which the author writes and not on the basis of a knowledge of any genetic process behind the author's words, such as the historical circumstances or psychological motives which may have given rise to them. This is not to suggest that questions regarding the author's historical or biographical circumstances or psychological disposition are simply irrelevant or inconsequential. On the contrary, Barth repeatedly claims that such knowledge may be very interesting and illuminating. Nevertheless, his point is that until we have understood the author on the basis of the subject matter about which he writes, we have still not understood him at all.

But why did the hermeneutical tradition of Schleiermacher on the basis of this genetic notion of understanding seek to understand authors better than they understood themselves? Here, finally, we come to the fundamental difference between Barth and the hermeneutical tradition of Schleiermacher. For the latter, the focus of understanding is not on the subject matter or truth-content of what the author says, but on the conditions and circumstances which gave rise to the author's words as an individual personality in a particular place and time. Given this focus, Schleiermacher was convinced that there were two ways to go about "the art of understanding" which he elaborates in his hermeneutics. First, "There is a less rigorous practice of this art which is based on the assumption that understanding occurs as a matter of course. The aim of this practice may be expressed in negative form as: 'misunderstanding should be avoided.'" Second, "There is a more rigorous practice of the art of interpretation that is based on the assumption that misunderstanding occurs as a matter of course, and so understanding must be willed and sought at every point."[310] It is this second, more rigorous approach that Schleiermacher pursued and that was the basis for his hermeneutical reflections. He later said: "We can formulate the task of hermeneutics in negative terms: to avoid misunderstanding at every point."[311] Gadamer claims, "This is something fundamentally new. For from now on we no longer consider the difficulties and failures of understanding as occasional but as integral elements that have to be prevented in advance."[312] And here, Gadamer makes a crucial observation:

---

[309] Gadamer, *Wahrheit und Methode*, pp. 198-199; ET p. 195.
[310] Schleiermacher, *Hermeneutik*, p. 86; ET pp. 109-110.
[311] Schleiermacher, *Hermeneutik*, p. 160; ET p. 218.
[312] Gadamer, *Wahrheit und Methode*, p. 188; ET p. 185.

> Schleiermacher's idea of a universal hermeneutics starts from this: that the experience of the alien and the possibility of misunderstanding is universal. It is true that that this alienation is greater, and misunderstanding easier, in artistic than in non-artistic utterance. ... But precisely Schleiermacher's extending the hermeneutical task to 'meaningful dialogue,' which is especially characteristic of him, shows how fundamentally the meaning of alienation, which hermeneutics is supposed to overcome, has changed in comparison to the task of hermeneutics as hitherto conceived. In a new and universal sense, alienation is inextricably given with the individuality of the Thou.[313]

The point has been made that the basis for understanding an author's text for the hermeneutical tradition of Schleiermacher and Dilthey is a common anthropology. Here we discover something decisive about that anthropology. It is an anthropology based on alienation. This is why the main task of interpretation for Schleiermacher is "to avoid misunderstanding at every point." The reason is because misunderstanding is the norm. And the reason misunderstanding is the norm is because the experience of alienation is the norm. Gadamer was not the first to recognize this, however. Barth recognized it much earlier, which is why he said in the 1930s, "general hermeneutics has been so mortally sick for so long ..."[314] In fact it appears that Barth already recognized this early in his *Römerbrief* period, for in his preface drafts to Rom I (in perhaps his most direct challenge to the hermeneutical tradition of Schleiermacher) he says: "But, of course, I wanted to *understand*, not *misunderstand* Paul."[315] The entire hermeneutical enterprise ever since Schleiermacher had been dedicated not to understanding but to the avoidance of misunderstanding because of the profound sense of alienation allegedly experienced by most individuals. For Schleiermacher and most of his progeny throughout the nineteenth and twentieth centuries, it is this sense of "alienation," as Gadamer says above, "which hermeneutics is supposed to overcome." Barth never denied this sense of alienation experienced by individuals, but neither did he make it the basis of his hermeneutics.[316] Nor did he see

---

[313] Gadamer, *Wahrheit und Methode*, pp. 182-183; ET p. 179.

[314] Barth, KD I/2:523; CD I/2:472.

[315] Appendix 2, Preface Draft IA, p. 281 (p. 587); Preface Draft II, p. 284 (p. 591). That Barth recognized in his *Römerbrief* period that the presupposition of *misunderstanding* played a decisive role in Schleiermacher's hermeneutic is evident from Barth, *Die Theologie Schleiermachers*, pp. 326-327; ET p. 183. See pp. 255f. below.

[316] Barth was once asked, "What objection do you have to so-called 'existential exegesis'?" Barth's answer applies to "existential exegesis" as it does to the hermeneutical tradition of Schleiermacher and Dilthey: "The existential exegete presupposes not only his own dialogue with the text, but a specific anthropology, that is, a pattern of thought. In my case mistakes are possible; in the existentialist's case mistakes are necessary." *Karl Barth's Table Talk*, p. 28. Barth says something similar to this earlier on in his *Church Dogmatics* when, after elaborating several hermeneutical propositions, he asks: "At this point the question arises: What is the source of the hermeneutic teaching which we have just sketched? Well, the fact that in spite of its inherent clarity it still does not enjoy recognition is in itself an indication that it does not

hermeneutics as a means of overcoming such alienation, but rather chose what he believed was a more excellent way.

4. Caritas: An Excursus

Barth speaks of love and attentiveness elsewhere in his preface drafts to Rom I,[317] but beyond what has been said thus far Barth does not say much more in his *Römerbrief* period about the differences between a more attentive and loving approach to the Bible on the one hand and the inattentive and loveless approach of his contemporaries on the other. In light of Gadamer's comments about hermeneutics becoming a means of overcoming individual alienation after Schleiermacher, however, it is interesting to note one of Barth's later comments about "the problem of hermeneutics." Describing the distracted, insecure, extroverted church of his day, Barth says in the last volume of his *Church Dogmatics*:

> It is the church which for the sake of security wants to construct an ontology before beginning theology; which instead of expounding the Bible gives itself with deadly seriousness to the problem of hermeneutics (to love of love instead of love itself!); which instead of speaking of the Word entrusted to it speaks constantly of the speech event; which constantly analyzes humanity instead of speaking simply and directly to it (because it knows what it wants and has to say). Supposedly to reach people where they are, this church is forever paying regard to them, adjusting to them, trying to win their attention and sympathy, attempting to be – or to appear to be – as pleasant as possible to them. It is the distracted and therefore the chattering church, the squinting and therefore the stuttering church.[318]

In characterizing his contemporaries' preoccupation with the problem of hermeneutics as a "love of love instead of love itself!," Barth was stating something that had been apparent to him, at least to some degree, from the beginning of his *Römerbrief* period, viz., the real problem of hermeneutics is love.[319] And where love's relationship to hermeneutics is most apparent in Barth's thought is in the *Church Dogmatics* I/2 §18. Because of its relevance to many of the concerns earlier discussed in this chapter, a brief excursus on this material seems in order.

Immediately preceding his treatment of the doctrine of Holy Scripture in §19-21, Barth discusses "The Life of the Children of God" in §18. The main

---

arise out of any general considerations on the nature of human language, etc., and therefore out of a general anthropology. Why is it that, as a rule, general considerations on the nature of human language do not lead to the propositions indicated? My reply would be: because the hermeneutic principles are not dictated by Holy Scripture, as they are in our case." KD I/2:515; CD I/2:465-466.

[317] Appendix 2, Preface Draft IA, p. 280 (pp. 585-586) and Preface Draft II, p. 286 (p. 593).

[318] Barth, *Das christliche Leben*, p. 230; ET p. 139.

[319] Here again, though wishing to avoid a backwards historical argument, as I mentioned at the outset (See p. 8 n.20 above), I merely want to highlight this theme in the trajectory of Barth's thought.

topic here is love, which is discussed on the basis of an extended exegesis (more than fifty pages) of the Great Commandment: "You shall love the Lord your God with all your heart, and with all your soul, and with all your strength, and with all your mind; and your neighbor as yourself" (Lk.10:27, also in Matt.22:37f., Mk.12:29). Discussing love before taking up the doctrine of Holy Scripture is necessary, we discover, because we cannot truly understand the Holy Scripture apart from love. This is one of Barth's most important hermeneutical presuppositions, though he, of course, is not the first to espouse it. Augustine did so long ago in *De doctrina Christiana*.[320] And there are others, such as each of the representatives of the empathetic tradition of interpretation I mentioned earlier, who in various ways have also advocated a hermeneutic of love. But Barth's understanding of love, as we shall see, differs from these more recent advocates of love in at least three ways, and these differences yield important insights into Barth's hermeneutic and theirs.

a. Love is a Gift, a Miracle

Christian life, Barth claims, begins and ends with love. "Love is the essence of Christian living."[321] "As Christians, we are continually being asked about love, and in all that we can ever do or not do, it is the decisive question." Barth says many things about love in §18, but the most important thing he says is that we cannot love of ourselves. Love is not something innately within us. "We cannot offer a love which is the work of our own hands or heart."[322] We cannot love without God first loving us. "To know what love is, we have first to ask concerning the unique love of God for us."[323] That unique love of God is known to us *in concreto* in Jesus Christ. Our love can only be understood as an answer to this love of God for us.[324] In other words, love is a gift, it is a miracle. "It is the miracle of all miracles."[325] It is a miracle that God loves us and a miracle that we can love God. And "If it is a real miracle that we can love God, it is necessarily a real miracle that we can love our neighbor."[326] "Love to God," Barth says, "is the real cause and expository principle of love to the neighbor."[327] It is "the real cardinal and interpretative principle" of our love of one another,[328] but it is always, first and last, a gift, a miracle (which is a point

---

[320] Augustine, *On Christian Doctrine*, trans. D.W. Robertson (Indianapolis: Bobbs-Merrill, 1958); See also *The Confessions of St. Augustine*, bk.xii, chs.18 and 25, trans. Rex Warner (New York: Penguin, 1963).
[321] KD I/2:409; CD I/2:372.
[322] KD I/2:422; CD I/2.384.
[323] KD I/2:413; CD I/2:376.
[324] KD I/2:418; CD I/2:380.
[325] KD I/2:431; CD I/2:392.
[326] KD I/2:458; CD I/2:416.
[327] KD I/2:452; CD I/2:410.
[328] KD I/2:444; CD I/2:403.

Barth realized as early as his *Römerbrief* period that not all his theological contemporaries necessarily shared).[329]

But if Christian love (*caritas*) is truly a gift, a miracle, then it is not the same thing as empathy. It is not the same thing because it has a different basis. In fact, Christian love does not necessarily have anything to do with empathy.[330] Barth claims even "the concept of sympathy is inadequate" to describe what the Bible tells us love is.[331] If the condition for the possibility of love of God and love of our neighbor is the love of God for us in Jesus Christ and is therefore truly a gift, a miracle, then love can hardly be described as a "natural capacity"[332] such as an *Einfühlungsvermögen* or even a "supernatural capacity" such as a "habitus."[333] Nor can it be described as a "talent" or a "special art"[334] such as an *Einfühlungskunst*. Yet this, as I have shown, is how love is described by members of the empathetic tradition of interpretation. Barth, on the other hand, believed that such a view turns love into a work, a method, a technique, a law,[335] which is why he emphasizes that love is fundamentally an act,

---

[329] In his famous correspondence-debate of 1923 with Barth, Adolf von Harnack posed this question (the fifth of fifteen), "If God and world (life in God and worldly life) are absolute contrasts, how are we to understand the close connection, even equating, of love for God and love for one's neighbor which constitutes the heart of the gospel? How is this equation possible without a high regard for morality?" Harnack-Barth, *Anfänge*, pp. 323-324; ET p. 165. Barth responded: "It is precisely the bringing together in the gospel of love for God and love for our neighbor that is the clearest indication that the relationship between our 'life in the world' and our 'life in God' is that of an 'absolute contrast' which can be overcome only by the miracle of the eternal God himself. Or is there anything more strange, more incomprehensible, any fact in the world more in need of the revelation of God, than that of 'neighbor'? 'High regard for morality,' yes, but do we *love* our neighbor, or can we love him? And if we do *not* love him, what is the state of our love of *God*? Does anything show more clearly than this 'heart' (not of the gospel, but of the Law), that God does not make alive unless he first slays?" Barth-Harnack, *Anfänge*, p. 326-327; ET p. 168.

[330] "The afflicted fellow-man offers himself to us as such. And as such he is actually the representative of Jesus Christ. As such he is actually the bearer and representative of the divine compassion. As such he actually directs us to the right praise of God. For him to be and do this, we do not need to know anything about his mission, about the sacramental character of his existence. At first we will simply not be able to know anything about it. We need to take him simply as what he actually is: as the neighbor who is near us *propinquissimus* in his misery." KD I/2:474; CD I/2:429-430.

[331] KD I/2:492; CD I/2:445.

[332] "The biblical passages do not know anything of a natural love to God which is proper to us apart from divine revelation, or of a natural capacity for love which is prior to revelation." KD I/2:410; CD I/2:373.

[333] KD I/2:440; CD I/2:400.

[334] KD I/2:431; CD I/2:391. It is not "a special art or striving on the part of those who have already proposed and undertaken the task, or a wonderful flower of piety which has grown in the garden of those who are already particularly suited for it." KD I/2:431; CD I/2:392.

[335] KD I/2:486f.; CD I/2:439f.

an act of God's free grace,[336] not a disposition, an attitude, or mood (though it certainly has to do with these).[337] Thus to love is to rely on God's free grace, and to rely on God's free grace means we must pray: "In the last resort we can only love the neighbor by praying for ourselves and for him: for ourselves, that we may love him rightly, and for him, that he may let himself be loved; which means that either way prayer can have only one content and purpose: that according to His promise Jesus Christ may let His work be done for and to ourselves and to our neighbor."[338] In short, for Barth, neither empathetic, existential, nor any other form of participation with our neighbor can substitute for that participation which is born of love and prayer.

b. Love is Always for Another

The second most important thing Barth says about love in §18 is that love is always love for *another*. "God has no need to love us, and we have no claim upon his love. God is love, before He loves us and apart from it. Like everything else that He is, He is love as the triune God in Himself. Even without us and without the world and without the reconciliation of the world, He would not experience any lack of love in Himself."[339] "He is love in Himself without and before loving us, and without being forced to love us."[340] But God *has* chosen to love us and as such He loves us as another, that is, as *other* than Himself, and this has significant implications.

> God alone – because He is God and man's Creator – can confront man as another. But His confrontation means that He gives Himself to be man's own. And therefore in this confrontation, which is not the removing but the form of His presence in the heart, He can and will be loved by man. The decisive element which is revealed in this fact is that love is love for another. Of course, this element is real only in love to God, and in the love to the neighbor which it includes and posits. All other loving is compromised as such by the uncertainty of the objectivity or otherness of the one who is loved, by the possibility that the one who supposedly loves is perhaps really alone. Where there is no otherness of the one who is loved, where the one who loves is alone, he does not really love.[341]

---

[336] "We have to rely on the miracle, the free grace of God, to make good what we with our own foresight can only bungle. We have to trust in the fact that Jesus Christ will be present in this meeting with my neighbor. It will be his business, not mine, however badly I play my part, He will conduct His business successfully and well. ... We have to rely on the fact that Jesus Christ is the Lord, in whose hand the other is the neighbor; that He became man and died for him; that my lack of love cannot and will not prevent Him calling the other to Him by me." KD I/2:502-503; CD I/2:453.

[337] KD I/2:496; CD I/2:447f.

[338] KD I/2:503-504f.; CD I/2:453f. That we must pray here means that we *will* pray on the basis of His promise.

[339] KD I/2:417; CD I/2:379.

[340] KD I/2:415; CD I/2:377.

[341] KD I/2:425-426; CD I/2:386-7.

This is exactly Barth's problem with the empathetic tradition of interpretation. Its conception of love is based on "the Romantic, concept of the mutual losing of oneself in another."[342] Barth quotes Hegel, who he claims typifies this Romantic conception of love:

> "Love is a differentiating of two, who are not at all divided for one another. The consciousness, the feeling of this identity, this being outside myself and in the other is love: I have my self-consciousness, not in myself, but in the other. But this other in whom alone I am satisfied and am at peace with myself – and I only am as I am at peace with myself; without it, I am the contradiction which falls apart – this other, by being outside himself, has his self-consciousness only in me, and both are just the consciousness of apartness from self and identity, the perception and feeling, and awareness of unity. That is love, and all talk about love is empty talk if we do not see that it is the differentiating and the removal of the differentiation. God is love, i.e., the differentiating and unreality of the differentiation is a game of differentiating, which cannot be taken seriously, the differentiation is posited as at once removed, i.e., the simple eternal idea."[343]

Barth repudiates this definition of love. Christian love, he insists, is not "'a game of differentiating which cannot be taken seriously.'" On the contrary, it must be taken seriously. "God in His love for us acts in serious distinction from us, without either having his self-consciousness in us or losing it to us. 'Not that we loved God, but that he loved us.' (I John 4:10) – that is how it is. And if we return God's love, that does not mean that we have our self-consciousness in God or lose it to God. Our differentiation before God is a serious thing, and it is only in this differentiation that we can and will love Him."[344] And this applies to our neighbor as well. If we are to love our neighbor, then our differentiation from him and his differentiation from us must be acknowledged. Yet this is precisely what the empathetic tradition of interpretation refuses to do. For all its talk about the mystery of individuality, it is not really prepared to accept the otherness of others. Instead it seeks "the removal of differentiation" and sets limits upon individuality on the basis of a general anthropology, that is, by positing – as we saw with each of its previously mentioned representatives – a commonly, universally intuitable core of humanity which presupposes that "each person contains a minimum of everyone else." In other words, it posits that ultimately (or at least at a decisive point, viz., at the point of "divination") interpretation is based on a "comparison with oneself."[345] Just as Herder said: "For it is and must ever be true that we love our neighbor only as we love ourselves. How can we be true to others if we are not true to ourselves? The degree of our sense of self is at the same

---

[342] KD I/2:414; CD I/2:377.
[343] KD I/2:413-414; CD I/2:376.
[344] KD I/2:376; CD I/2:414.
[345] Schleiermacher, *Hermeneutik*, p. 109; ET p. 150.

time the measure of our feeling for others: for it is only our self that we can as it were project [*hineinfühlen*] into the feelings of others."[346]

Barth rejects this view not only because nowhere are we commanded to love ourselves, but also because it compromises the objectivity or otherness of the one who is loved, that is, because it is not really love for another. Contrary to Augustine[347] and many others throughout the history of the Church (including Tertullian, Chrysostom, Aquinas, and modern figures such as Polanus and Kierkegaard), Barth claims to side with Luther and Calvin on this issue of "self-love":

> Our self-love can never be anything right or holy and acceptable to God. It is an affection which is the very opposite of love. God will never think of blowing on this fire, which is bright enough already. His demand is that the impulse should be "reversed" [Calvin]. ... We have to admit that the Reformers were right. Of course, there is the man who loves himself: this is assumed in our text and in Matt.7:12. But there is no commandment to do this. Self-love is not on the same level as the commanded love to God and our neighbor. Where the latter begins, the former ceases and *vice versa*. Loving himself, man does not love or no longer loves in the sense of the children of God: and to the extent that this love is the only true love, we must add that loving himself he does not love or no longer loves at all. Loving himself, he is alone. That is the predicament of most of what passes for "love." Man is supposed to love, but the truth is that man is concerned only with himself and therefore does not love at all. Love must always have an opposite, an object. It is only an illusion that we can be an object of love to ourselves.[348]

In short, the reason we are not commanded to love ourselves is because we do this pretty well already and because true love is always love of *another*, which "self-love" is not.[349]

---

[346] See p. 149 above.

[347] Augustine, *On Christian Doctrine*, bk. I, ch. 22f., pp. 18f.

[348] KD I/2:427; CD I/2:388. "What we love – if we love at all – is always something else or someone else. Of much apparent loving another we have to ask whether the other really is another, whether it has in fact a basic object, and therefore whether it is real love at all. And, in spite of Augustine, the invention of a commandment to love oneself was a cardinal error. As the wrath of Calvin rightly felt, it meant the elevation of something negative in itself into a principle." Barth later adds: "Self-love means, and must mean, to be alone with ourselves, to seek ourselves, to serve ourselves, to think of ourselves. Now it is true that we do this. It is true that we do it even when we love our neighbor. ... But the commandment: Thou shalt love thy neighbor, is not a legitimation but a limitation of this reality. If I love my neighbor, that is the judgment on my self-love and not its indirect justification. When I love my neighbor I do not apply to him the same good thing as I do to myself when I love myself. Far from it. When I love my neighbor I confess that my self-love is not a good thing, that it is not love at all." KD I/2:499; CD I/2:450.

[349] Barth develops this theme in terms of "other regard" under the rubric "The Basic Form of Humanity" in KD III/2:264f.; CD III/2:222f.

c. To Love is to Receive and to Be a Witness

Finally, Barth says in §18 that love has to do with receiving and being a witness. If love is truly a gift, a miracle, and we cannot really love of ourselves, if we cannot offer a love which is the work of our own hands or heart but can love only because He has first loved us, then love is a matter of receiving and being a witness to the love of God in Jesus Christ. If we have known this love, Barth says, we cannot help but testify to it, we cannot help in our very existence to become a sign and testimony of His love.[350] Of course, "it is unequivocally clear that the reality, the work and effectiveness of our witness – if we do bear witness, if we are witnesses – are not of our own power and disposing."[351] Nevertheless, the gift, the miracle, the promise remains true: "Ye shall be my witnesses" (Acts 1:8), and specifically, witnesses of the love of God in Jesus Christ. But this is where Barth's argument takes a decisive turn: before we can *be* a sign, a witness of the love of God to our neighbor, we must *receive* the witness of our neighbor, and this raises a very important question, "Who is my neighbor?"

On the basis of an exegesis of Lk. 10:25-27, "the parable of the Good Samaritan" (where Jesus responds to this question put to him by a lawyer who can faithfully recite the twofold commandment regarding love of God and love of neighbor), Barth argues against "current exegesis" and with the more "primitive exegesis" of this parable that our neighbor is not simply our fellow-man or he or she whom we find in need, but actually he or she who is our "benefactor."[352] "My neighbor is the man who emerges from amongst all my fellow-men as this one thing in particular, my benefactor."[353] What is the par-

---

[350] KD I/2:456f.; CD I/2:413f.

[351] KD I/2:501; CD I/2:452. Barth states earlier: "love to the neighbor can only have the significance of a free sign" KD I/2:447-448; CD I/2:406.

[352] Without citing examples, Barth claims that "current exegesis" tends to interpret the parable along these lines: "that Jesus would have said to the teacher of the Law: This Samaritan did not ask questions like you ["Who is my neighbor?"]. He found his neighbor in the man that had fallen among thieves. He treated him accordingly. Go and do likewise." In other words, it tends to interpret the parable moralistically, whereas "primitive exegesis" suggests that Jesus Christ Himself is the Good Samaritan! How is it possible that the lawyer who asks this question can be summoned to go and do likewise when he lacks all the necessary presuppositions and does not even know who his neighbor is, much less see him as a benefactor? "Well, it is Jesus Christ who gives the summons, and we cannot abstract Jesus Himself from the summons which He gives. On His lips the 'Go and do thou likewise' is only Law because it is first Gospel. The good Samaritan, the neighbor who is a helper and will make him a helper is not far from the lawyer. The primitive exegesis of the text was fundamentally right. He stands before him incarnate, although hidden under the form of one whom the lawyer believed he should hate, as the Jews hated the Samaritans." See KD I/2:461f.; CD I/2:418f..

[353] KD I/2:463; CD I/2:420. "In the biblical sense of the concept my neighbor is not each of my fellow-men as such. It is not, therefore, a matter of telling myself and realizing that humanity as such consists of mere individuals, who are all my neighbors. ... It is not therefore the

ticular benefit which comes to me through my neighbor? Barth answers: "that through my neighbor I am referred to the order in which I can and should offer to God, whom I love because He first loved me, the absolutely necessary praise which is meet and acceptable to Him."[354] My neighbor is my benefactor, in other words, because he is "a living sign of the grace of God."[355] "To what extent my benefactor?," Barth asks.

> To the extent that, in virtue of a special commission and authority here and now, he proclaims and shows forth Jesus Christ within this world, thus giving to my praise of God direction and character ... enabling me even as I offer it really to live in this world really by faith. That is the Samaritan aid which my neighbor gives to me. That is the meaning and content of the event in which he is to me a neighbor and not merely a fellow-man.[356]

It is not because "he has this role and significance because of some inherent value in himself as such," but because God has summoned him to be so that "simply as he is, as a man, he can be a neighbor to me here and now at any moment, as the Samaritan was to the man half-dead by the roadside."[357] By his sheer corporeality, he can become my benefactor because even as such he can bear witness to Jesus Christ, namely, that He became incarnate and took on human flesh, misery, and weakness. "Our fellow-man in his oppression, shame and torment confronts us with the poverty, the homelessness, the scars, the corpse, at the grave of Jesus Christ."[358] This is how my fellow-man becomes my benefactor and proves himself to be my neighbor: "Our fellow-man becomes to us the compassionate neighbor because he is seen in the reflection of the sign which gives to the great sign of the Church, in all its meaning for humanity generally, its origin, basis and stability, in the reflection of the human nature of Jesus Christ."[359] Barth immediately adds: "Of course, I have my own part. I have to go and do likewise. I myself have to be a neighbor and therefore a bearer and representative of that divine mercy in the world. I have to be a child of God. It is only then that this will come to me through the neighbor. But again that does not alter the fact that this thing has to come to me through my neighbor."[360]

---

case that the question: Who is my neighbor? really means: Is this or that individual one of my neighbors? On the contrary, my neighbor is an event which takes place in the existence of a definite man definitely marked off from all other men. My neighbor is my fellow-man acting towards me as a benefactor." KD I/2:462-463; CD I/2:419-420.

[354] KD I/2:462-463; CD I/2:419-420.
[355] KD I/2:484; CD I/2:437.
[356] KD I/2:464; CD I/2:421.
[357] KD I/2:457, 466; 414, 423.
[358] KD I/2:473; CD I/2:428. Barth emphasizes however that outward misery is not the only veil. Our neighbor's actual misery "may just as well be hidden behind an aspect of soundness, strength and victory."
[359] KD I/2:467-468; CD I/2:424.
[360] KD I/2:464-465; CD I/2:421.

"To love the neighbor, therefore, is plainly and simply to be to him a witness of Jesus Christ. That the duty of love is the duty of witness results from the fact that I am summoned by my encounter with the neighbor to expect to find in him a brother of Jesus Christ and therefore my own brother."[361] The fact is: "The primary and true form of the neighbor is that he faces us as the bearer and representative of divine compassion."[362] How can we not, therefore, receive his witness?

But Barth presses further: "To what extent has a fellow-man commission and authority to emerge in this way, and therefore to be in a position to act towards me as the bearer and representative of the mercy of God?"[363] "How can we ever trust that man will be my neighbor like that?"[364] Here we begin to see what this discussion has to do with hermeneutics in general and biblical exegesis in particular. Barth's "first general and decisive answer" is the Church. "It is the Church which introduces the Good Samaritan. To understand this, we must first remember that the Church as such and in itself is simply the work of the service which men render one another by mutually proclaiming and showing forth Jesus Christ."[365] "Who and what a neighbor is, we can best realize from those who founded the Church, the biblical prophets and apostles. What they do is the purest form of that work of divine mercy which is assumed by the children of God. They bear witness to Jesus Christ. In that way they order the praise of the children of God; they make it possible as a real praise of the real God."[366] It is through them, the prophets and apostles, that we learn "this original order, this new destiny of man"; it is through them that we see for the first time that "Man himself now becomes a sign"; it is through them that we see fulfillment of God's promise: "Ye shall be my witnesses."[367]

We cannot stop here, however, because "service of the compassionate neighbor is certainly not restricted to the life of the Church in itself and as such. ... Humanity as a whole can take part in this service."[368] "If we know the incarnation of the eternal Word and the glorification of humanity in Him, we cannot pass by any man, without being asked whether in his humanity he does

---

[361] KD I/2:487; CD I/2:440.
[362] KD I/2:459; CD I/2:416.
[363] KD I/2:465; CD I/2:421.
[364] KD I/2:467; CD I/2:424.
[365] KD I/2:465; CD I/2:421-422. See also: "The commandment to love is not directed to humanity, or to men in general in their natural or historical groupings. Humanity or men in general are not even considered as the recipients of this commandment and as those who will fulfill it. The commandment is given to Israel. Indeed, it is given only in the sense of the synoptic Jesus. It is given to the community declared in the twelve apostles as representing the new twelve tribes." KD I/2:419; CD I/2:381.
[366] KD I/2:465; CD I/2:422.
[367] KD I/2:468; CD I/2:424.
[368] KD I/2:465-466; CD I/2:422.

not have this mission to us, he does not become to us this compassionate neighbor."[369] Barth claims: "Jesus Christ is always concealed in the neighbor," yet he adds: "The neighbor is not a second revelation of Jesus Christ side by side with the first. When he meets me, the neighbor is not in any sense a second Christ. He is only my neighbor. And it is only as such and in his difference from Christ, only as a sign instituted by Christ, that we can speak of his solidarity and identity with Christ."[370] The fact that Jesus Christ is originally and properly our brother "does not exclude, but includes the fact that in every man we have to expect a brother," a "hidden neighbor."[371] "What man is there who might not one day meet us as a messenger of the Word of God, a witness to the resurrection?"[372] But, again, *that* a man or woman can actually become my neighbor, that is, a sign or witness to Jesus Christ, should not be taken for granted as something "self-evident."[373] It is a gift, a miracle, and one we can know only by means of the prophets and apostles:

> For if in the prophets and apostles we see men to whom Jesus Christ has become a neighbor, and they themselves have become helpful and compassionate neighbors by bearing witness to Him, if it has become a general possibility in the Church that men can have this function, then we must obviously be prepared and ready for the fact that man, our fellow-man generally, can become our neighbor.[374]

Here, finally, we come to Barth's basic problem with the leading hermeneutical tradition of his day, the problem he had from the beginning of his *Römerbrief* period with the dominant science of biblical exegesis, the problem that has been at issue throughout the entire preceding chapter. The prophets and apostles bear witness to Jesus Christ and in so doing show us who and what a neighbor is. It is through them that we see fulfillment of God's promise: "Ye shall be my witnesses," that we learn "this original order, this new destiny of man," that we see for the first time that "Man himself now becomes a sign." Yet the dominant science of biblical exegesis does not receive the prophets' and apostles' witness. It does not even grant them – at least in any fundamental or primary sense – the role or status of witnesses. Instead they are regarded primarily and fundamentally as sources. This is what is at issue in Barth's early lament, "Today's theology does not stand by the prophets and the apostles ... it does not take the prophets and apostles in earnest, but while it stands smiling sympathetically albeit condescendingly beside them, it conceitedly distances itself from them and outwardly examines them historically and psycho-

---

[369] KD I/2:470; CD I/2:426.
[370] KD I/2:480; CD I/2:435.
[371] KD I/2:469; CD I/2:425.
[372] KD I/2:471; CD I/2:427.
[373] KD I/2:463; CD I/2:420.
[374] KD I/2:468-469; CD I/2:425.

logically."[375] This failure to take the prophets' and apostles' role and status as witnesses is *the* hermeneutical problem Barth addresses in §19 of the *Church Dogmatics*; and as we see from the following, it is a problem that threatens not only our relationship to the prophets and apostles, but every human relationship:

> My exposition cannot possibly consist in an interpretation of the speaker. Did he say something to me only to display himself? I should be guilty of a shameless violence against him, if the only result of my encounter with him were that I now knew him or knew him better than before. What lovelessness! Did he not say anything to me at all? Did he not therefore desire that I should see him not *in abstracto* but in his specific and concrete relationship to the thing described or intended in his word, that I should see him from the standpoint and in the light of this thing? How much wrong is being continually perpetrated, how much intolerable obstruction of human relationships, how much isolation and impoverishment forced upon individuals has its only basis in the fact that we do not take seriously a claim which in itself is as clear as the day, the claim which arises whenever one person addresses a word to another.[376]

The "lovelessness" that Barth describes here is the same lovelessness he describes in the preface drafts to Rom I. Barth's problem with the dominant science of biblical exegesis was that despite all its empathy and all its efforts to smile sympathetically at the prophets and apostles, it did not take their words in earnest. It sought merely to interpret Paul, as if he were writing merely to "display himself," rather than what Paul wrote about. Following the hermeneutical tradition of Schleiermacher and Dilthey, the dominant science of exegesis approached its task as if the goal of one's encounter with Paul "were that I now knew him or knew him better." Instead of trying to understand Paul in terms of "his specific and concrete relationship to the thing described or intended in his word," it tried to interpret him "*in abstracto*," that is, apart from the subject matter about which he wrote. But at the heart of all this Barth realized – and to some extent early in his *Römerbrief* period – was love. Barth claimed, as mentioned above, that "the duty of love is the duty of witness." Thus for him, accepting our neighbor's role and significance as a witness is the primary way in which we love our neighbor, while refusing to accept our neighbor's role and significance as a witness is a primary way in which we fail to love our neighbor.

But accepting our neighbor's role and significance as a witness does not mean for Barth that we must believe "in" our neighbor. On the contrary, the Great Commandment forbids this:

> We cannot believe in our neighbor, nor are we required to do so in this second commandment. To confuse or confound the two demands, to be related to our fellow-man in such a way that we believe in him, that we give to him what we owe to God, is to make us incapable of fulfilling what we do owe to him. Yet we cannot seek the One in whom we believe

---

[375] Appendix 2, Preface Draft IA, p. 281 (p. 587).
[376] KD I/2:515; CD I/2:465.

and without whom we cannot live, we cannot love God, without this loving, as it were, manifesting itself, not as a second, repeated light of revelation, but as the light of our human and earthly witness to revelation, in the praise of God commensurate with us in our humanity within this world and time.[377]

Yet though we do not believe in our neighbor this does not mean that we do not expect to find him to be a witness. Everyone, even those we think we already know, even those who stand "outside and over against" the Church and are "indifferent or hostile to it," may become witnesses to us of God's love and mercy.[378] "The Samaritan in the parable shows us incontestably that even those who do not know that they are doing so, or what they are doing, can assume and exercise the function of a compassionate neighbor."[379] Thus even Goethe or Lao-tzu can have this function. But for Goethe and Lao-tzu to have this function, to bear witness to God's love and mercy, it may well be that we must understand them better than they understood themselves.

I discussed earlier the reason why Barth refused any attempt to understand the apostle Paul better than he understood himself, and his reason for refusing to set this as the goal for interpreting any author. But I also mentioned that there are many cases in Barth's view in which understanding others better than they understand themselves is necessary.[380] This is a concern he explicitly expresses in the *Römerbrief* period.[381] But where we find Barth actually trying to do this is in his *Protestant Theology in the Nineteenth Century*. Here, in a manner even many of his critics described as remarkably sympathetic,[382] Barth tells us that what Kant may have really wanted to say "from the point of view

---

[377] KD I/2:455; CD I/2:413.
[378] KD I/2:466; CD I/2:422.
[379] KD I/2:466; CD I/2:422.
[380] See pp. 198-199 above.
[381] "There is no wisdom in stopping at the next to the last or the next to the next to the last want of the people; and they will not thank us for doing so. They expect us to understand them better than they understand themselves, and to take them more seriously than they take themselves. We are unfeeling, not when we probe deeply into the wound, which they carry when they come to us for healing, but rather when we pass over it as if we did not know why they had come" in Karl Barth, "Not und Verheißung der christlichen Verkündigung" (1922) *Vorträge und kleinere Arbeiten 1922-1925*, ed. Hinrich Stoevesandt (Zürich: Theologischer Verlag Zürich, 1990), p. 76f. See also in the same volume, "Das Wort Gottes als Aufgabe der Theologie" (1922), p. 151f.
[382] In his introduction to the English edition, Jaroslav Pelikan praises Barth's "sympathy and perception" and suggests that "Perhaps the most striking feature of the chapters presented here is their willingness to treat theologians of the past on their own terms. Anyone who expects Karl Barth the dogmatician to become the judge of the quick and the dead when he functions as a historian of theology will find, to his surprise, that Barth has made a genuine effort to comprehend the theologians of the nineteenth century from within their own frame of reference." *Protestant Theology in the Nineteenth Century*, p. 8. Even Paul Tillich described it as "beautiful" in *Perspectives on 19th and 20th Century Protestant Theology* (New York: Harper & Row, 1967), p. 92.

of a philosophy attentive to the concerns of 'mere reason'" – and did say even if tinged with ridicule – was that *"The biblical theologian proves that God exists by means of the fact that he has spoken in the Bible!"*[383] What Herder was really trying to describe was "the autonomy and independence in faith which belief derives from its object, and only from its object ... an insight which truly and finally explodes the Enlightenment conception of religion."[384] What Schleiermacher really was after was a theology of the third article even if the result of his theology was that man "alone is the subject, and Christ has become his predicate ... which could not be what Schleiermacher intended."[385] One figure after another is interpreted in light of what he might have said or might have been trying to say, had he been thinking more clearly. Even Feuerbach and Strauss, we are told, are to be "loved," for they bear witness to "difficulties just at the point where proper theology begins."[386] Thus, even here understanding an author better than he understood himself does not necessarily mean abandoning trust or a refusal to maintain a relationship of faithfulness or loyalty to the author. Loyalty to an author can still be maintained even if it is a loyalty of opposition.

Again, however, understanding an author better than he understood himself is not the goal of interpretation. It is always an "emergency clause," something to be invoked only when the *Sachlichkeit* of an author's words has been compromised or confused. This of course is not always easy to discern. It is often difficult, even "interpreting everything and everyone in *optimam partem*," to understand what an author is really saying or trying to say. Sometimes we can only speak of our "attempt to understand" (e.g. *"Rudolf Bultmann – ein Versuch, ihn zu verstehen"*). But because "Love is patient" (I Cor. 13:4), our claims to understand or not to understand can never be made hastily or with any sense of final determination. Rather our understanding is always provisional, reformable, open-ended. Barth expresses this again and again throughout his *Römerbrief* prefaces with respect to Paul. And this is also reflected in many of the figures he treats throughout his *Protestant Theology in the Nineteenth Century*, which is why he typically asks so many questions throughout his exposition as to what a given philosopher or theologian may or may not have been really trying to say. Certainly one of the best examples of this is seen in Barth's famous "Nachwort" and especially the five questions he poses at its conclusion. His openness here, his refusal to pronounce a final verdict over Schleiermacher (to "latch the door" as it were) his effort to ask again and again, at every decisive point, "Have I indeed understood him correctly?" or

---

[383] Barth, *Die protestantische Theologie im 19. Jahrhundert*, p. 278; ET p. 196.
[384] Barth, *Die protestantische Theologie im 19. Jahrhundert*, p. 300; ET p. 222.
[385] Barth, *Die protestantische Theologie im 19. Jahrhundert*, p. 424; ET p. 354.
[386] Barth, *Die protestantische Theologie im 19. Jahrhundert*, p. 515; ET p. 389.

"Could he not be understood differently?" goes to the very heart of what a more loving approach to interpretation was about for Barth.[387]

In sum, Barth's hermeneutic may be best characterized in terms of faith, hope, and love: *faith* in the promise that "Ye shall be my witnesses"; *hope* that we shall actually find our fellow-man to be a witness; and, finally, *love* that we too might actually be witnesses to others of the love and mercy of God. In a day dominated perhaps as much as our own by a hermeneutic of suspicion, when it could be said that the "greatest" biographies of Jesus had been written by men filled with hate, and that "hate sharpened their historical insight,"[388] Barth obviously tried to set a different course. At the outset of his study of Schleiermacher in the 1930s, he said: "Anyone who has never loved here and is not in a position to love again and again may not hate here either."[389] And in his opening lecture in his first course on Schleiermacher on Nov.1, 1923, he told his Göttingen students: "Love, when one can love, is *a priori*, in history too, a relatively surer way to knowledge than alienation or aversion."[390] Whether Barth was always as loving or charitable as he could have been in his interpretation of others is certainly a question which should continue to be debated. Nevertheless, as far as he was concerned, this was *the* question. But as I have suggested, love meant something different to Barth than it did to his contemporaries, and such differences had profound hermeneutical implications, which I suspect, given all the talk about "the ethics of interpretation" in our day, we have hardly begun to understand or appreciate.[391]

---

[387] Barth, "Nachwort," pp. 307f.; ET pp. 274f.

[388] Albert Schweitzer, *The Quest of the Historical Jesus* (1906), pp. 4-5.

[389] Barth, *Die protestantische Theologie im 19. Jahrhundert*, pp. 380-381; ET p. 308.

[390] Barth, *Die Theologie Schleiermachers*, p. 9; ET p. xvii.

[391] For a bibliography on the growing discussion surrounding "the ethics of interpretation" see A.K.M. Adam, "Twisting to Destruction: A Memorandum on the Ethics of Interpretation" in *Perspectives in Religious Studies*, 23:2 (1996), p. 215 n.2. I find it rather ironic that many so-called 'post-modern' biblical scholars who have argued for some time against having hermeneutical principles are some of the same ones who are now concerned with the ethics of interpretation.

Chapter 6

The Meaning of the Bible Itself

Finally, in addition to a reading that is more in accordance with the Bible's "subject matter, content, and substance," and beyond his insistence upon an approach which "enters into the meaning of the Bible with more attention and love," Barth insists in his first preface draft to Rom I and throughout his *Römerbrief* period upon a reading of the Bible that is more in accordance with "the meaning of the Bible itself." What did Barth mean by a reading that is more in accordance with the meaning of the Bible itself? How is such a reading achieved? And what role does historical understanding play in the process? Though anticipated to some extent already, these are some of the questions I shall attempt to answer in this chapter. But first, in order to understand one of the basic presuppositions behind Barth's principle of reading the Bible more in accordance with the meaning of the Bible itself, it is necessary to compare one of Barth's most firmly held convictions before his break with liberalism with one of his most firmly held convictions afterwards.

A. The Language and the Content Are One

Before his break with liberalism, Karl Barth expressed no interest in reading the Bible according to the meaning of the Bible itself. One wonders if it ever even occurred to him as a possibility. To read the Bible according to the meaning of the Bible itself presupposes that there is a meaning or sense of the Bible itself to be understood, and there is no indication that Barth ever held such a presupposition prior to 1915. On the contrary, in contrast to the consistent theme sung by "the chorus of prophets and apostles" which he later referred to in his "*Die neue Welt in der Bibel*" essay of 1917, the Bible seems to have represented for him little more than a cacophony of disparate voices, something impossible to read or understand on its own terms or according to its own meaning.[1] As I discussed at length in the previous chapter, before 1915 it was primarily for Barth about religion, about piety, about individuals "who *experienced* God and who now communicate these experiences."[2] What was important about it was not so much its words or its letters or even its thoughts, but

---

[1] Barth, "Die neue Welt in der Bibel," p. 20.
[2] Barth, *Konfirmandenunterricht, 1909-1921*, p. 69.

the pious feelings, affections, or more precisely, "the justifying and reconciling *Anschauung* of Christ" *behind* its thoughts, words, and letters. The reason Barth and his contemporaries emphasized the necessity of getting behind the thoughts, words, and letters of the Bible was because, as Schleiermacher had said, "stepping forth in thought and word is everywhere the vacillating; the innermost which lies back of thought and word is that which is in agreement with itself, the identical, but that can never be communicated externally as such."[3] Of course, it was more than a romantic conception of language that determined this particular approach for Barth; it was an approach which also conformed to his understanding of revelation. Even before his break with liberalism, Barth's understanding of revelation was *actualistic* in the sense that revelation always had the character of an event and was not bound to the Bible, to church doctrine, or to any other normative conceptualization.[4] The Spirit "blows where it wills" (John 3:8), Barth was fond of quoting prior to 1915, and what this implied for him was that "faith in revelation on the one hand and the authority of the scriptural letter on the other are completely heterogeneous categories. One might as well speak about wooden iron."[5]

Barth's disdain (one might even say antipathy) for the letter and his specific concern that the scriptural letter might be confused or in any way identified, even indirectly, with revelation itself, were noted in the previous chapter and represent one of his most firmly held convictions before his break with liberalism. It is a conviction he clearly inherited from Schleiermacher and one he consistently highlighted in his essays on Schleiermacher throughout the mid-

---

[3] See pp. 175-176 above. Similarly, what was really significant about the Bible's portrait of Jesus was "not his outer life, not his words, not his deeds," but His "inner life." See Barth, "*Moderne Theologie und Reichgottesarbeit,*" p. 194.

[4] Whether Barth's understanding of revelation before his break with liberalism can be described as properly "actualistic" is an interesting question. Can there be an actualistic understanding of revelation apart from a normative conceptualization of faith's object? Moreover, Barth does not say much if anything about God's 'acting' prior to 1915, but he does refer to revelation as an 'event.' It is in this sense and only in this sense that I would relate the concept of actualism to his understanding of revelation before his break with liberalism. For the best discussion of the theme of actualism in Barth's theology, see George Hunsinger's *How To Read Karl Barth: The Shape of His Theology*, passim. Hunsinger states: "Actualism emphasizes the sovereign activity of God in patterns of love and freedom. ... The church, the inspiration of scripture, faith, and all other creaturely realities in their relationship to God are always understood as events. They are not self-initiating and self-sustaining. They are not grounded in a neutral, ahistorical, or ontological relationship to God independent of the event of grace. Nor are they actualizations of certain ontologically given creaturely capacities. Rather, they have not only their being but also their possibility only as they are continually established anew according to the divine good pleasure. They have their being only in act – in the act of God which elicits from the creature the otherwise impossible act of free response. God is thus the Lord – not only of the mysterious event which constitutes the divine being, but also of the mysterious event which constitutes our being in relation to God" (pp. 30-31).

[5] Barth, "*Moderne Theologie und Reichgottesarbeit,*" p. 203.

1920s.⁶ Yet it is precisely here that we see one of the most dramatic changes in Barth's thought after his break with liberalism. Prior to 1915 his comments about the scriptural letter had been consistently disparaging. He could not stress its inadequacy enough. But soon after his break he expressed a newfound appreciation for the scriptural letter. The words of the Bible, the specific language of Holy Scripture, he regards as indispensable, even irreplaceable and unsubstitutable. In his preface drafts to Rom I, he even goes so far as to say that "the language and the content are one."⁷ This is by no means to suggest that Barth no longer recognized a distinction between the language of the Bible and its content. On the contrary, the Bible's *signa* and its *res*, what is written and what is written about, remained two very different things. His understanding of revelation and its relationship to the Bible, as I said above, remained actualistic in the sense that he still did not believe that revelation was intrinsically bound by or contained in the Bible. The difference now however was that Barth believed that he had heard God speak through the words of the Bible, that he himself had witnessed the words of the Bible bearing witness to revelation, and as a result he had come to recognize that even though there was no *direct* identification between its words and the actual content of revelation, there was by means of revelation, as he later referred to it, an *indirect* identification between them. In other words, there was an indirect identification be-

---

⁶ In his essay, "Schleiermacher," which was first delivered as a lecture in his course on the history of modern theology at Münster in 1926, Barth states: "We come directly to a most important characteristic of Schleiermacher's theology, if we select, from the plenitude of questions which have been raised, those which bear on the general relation between the factor finally presented as 'speech' and the reality, that is to say the Christian religious attitude out of which the speech and thought have arisen, and which they 'express'[*ausdrücken*]. ... He is convinced, as few men have been, of the inexpressibility of the divine. He foresees a future time when speaking on religion will be replaced by the 'palid silence' of the 'holy virgins.' How rigid this conviction was he has made plain in his *Celebration of Christmas*. ... Words 'are only the shadows of our insights and feelings.' ... Obviously, for Schleiermacher, even the most religiously adequate expression and presentation of reality in words is an emptying, a kenosis, if not a profanation, of that reality. ... [His] vehemence appeared most often when he was speaking against the 'dead letter.' ... His pulpit polemic was never more vigorous than when he was bringing up this charge." Karl Barth, "Schleiermacher" (1926), *Die Theologie und die Kirche* (Munich: Evangelischer Verlag, 1928), pp. 138-145; ET "Schleiermacher," *Theology and Church*, trans. Louise Pettibone Smith (New York: Harper & Row, 1962), pp. 161-165. Barth makes similar sorts of statements in: "Schleiermachers 'Weihnachtsfeier'" (1924), *Vorträge und kleinere Arbeiten 1922-1925*, ed. Holger Finze (Zürich: Theologischer Verlag Zürich, 1990), pp. 458-489; ET "Schleiermacher's Celebration of Christmas," *Theology and Church*, pp. 136-158; "Das Wort in der Theologie von Schleiermacher bis Ritschl" (1927), *Vorträge und kleinere Arbeiten 1925-1930*, ed. Hermann Schmidt (Zürich: Theologischer Verlag Zürich, 1994), pp. 183-214; ET "The Word in Theology from Schleiermacher to Ritschl" (1927), *Theology and Church*, pp. 200-216; and *Die Theologie Schleiermachers*; ET *The Theology of Schleiermacher*, passim.

⁷ Appendix 2, Preface Draft IA, p. 279 (p. 584) and Preface II, p. 283 (p. 590).

tween the Word and the words of the Bible, but it was an indirect identification made possible and real only by the former, not by the latter, that is, by way of the Holy Spirit and not by any inherent characteristic or intrinsic quality having to do with the language of the Bible itself. Thus, although Barth recognized a distinction (even if he did not yet describe it as an infinitely qualitative distinction) between the words of the Bible and its actual content before his break with liberalism, it was only after his break with liberalism that he insisted that this distinction (which was by then for him an infinitely qualitative distinction) could only be made rightly if one refused to separate the words of the Bible from its actual content.[8] This is why he claimed "the language and the content are one," and this is why from 1917 on he speaks so often about "the Bible itself" and our need to interpret the Bible according to "the meaning of the Bible itself."[9]

The key phrase above is "bear witness." As I described it in chapter three, Barth's great discovery was that God, that revelation, is the actual content, subject matter, and theme of the Bible. But the immediate consequence of this discovery was his discovery that God had used and continues to use *the words of the Bible* – not simply the faith or piety behind the words, but the words themselves – *to bear witness* to this specific content, subject matter, and theme.[10] This was something new. Before his break with liberalism Barth had understood the Bible primarily as a *source*. After his break with liberalism, after he understood himself to have become a witness to the fact that *Deus dixit*, that God spoke and continued to speak through the words of the Bible, he began to understand the Bible primarily as a *witness*. This is not to say that the Bible – the testimony of the prophets and apostles – did not bear witness in any sense in Barth's view prior to 1915. In 1910/12, he said: "What they [the apostles] left behind for us in reports and thoughts about him is the *witness* of their faith, of their intuition of Christ, which they passed on in the transparency of their words."[11] Clearly the Bible in some way bore witness to something. Yet what it bore witness to was not God or the content of revelation itself, but merely the faith, the piety, the *Anschauung*, which had given rise to it. In other words, that Barth characterized the witness of the apostles' faith as being "passed on in the transparency of their words" suggests that their words still did not really bear witness at all, at least in any sense he later regarded as con-

---

[8] One is reminded here of Augustine's statement: "God should not be said to be ineffable, for when this is said something is said," *On Christian Doctrine*, I, vi, p. 11. The question is: how do we know that God is ineffable apart from His saying so?

[9] Barth, "Die neue Welt in der Bibel," pp. 22, 24; Preface Draft I, p. 277 (p. 582), etc.

[10] This is obviously why Barth spoke thereafter not simply of the Bible's inspiration but of 'verbal inspiration.'

[11] Barth, "Der christliche Glaube und die Geschichte," p. 204.

stitutive,[12] since they did not really point in any particular direction beyond themselves as *signs*, but instead were merely *expressions*,[13] the outward overflow or residue of the inner life, faith, or piety of the author.[14]

Still, however, even as a liberal, Barth saw himself as in some sense bound to the words of the Bible. As I mentioned earlier, Barth told his 1909 confirmation class that the Bible was important "because it is there that we find the

---

[12] As Barth later defined it: "Witnessing means pointing in a specific direction beyond the self and on to another. Witnessing is thus service to this other in which the witness vouches for the truth of the other, the service which consists in referring to the other. This service is constitutive for the concept of the prophet and also for that of the apostle. ... Standing in this service, the biblical witnesses point beyond themselves. If we understand them as witnesses, and only as such do we authentically understand them, i.e., as they understand themselves, then their self, which in its inner and outer determination and movement constitutes as it were the matter of their service, must be decisively understood by us from the standpoint of its form as a reference away from themselves. They do not speak and write for their own sakes, nor for the sake of their deepest inner possession or need; they speak and write, as ordered, about that other. They do not try to push themselves, not even as champions or advocates of the cause they represent; beyond all immanent teleology they are forced to speak and write about that other. They do not want to offer and commend themselves to the Church, and especially not their own particular experience of God and relationship to God, but through themselves that other. And not even 'through themselves' in the sense that man himself must be a more or less perfect organ for the revelation of objective facts and values or subjective stimulations (as is true enough in the achievements of science, politics, and art), but through themselves in such a way that what makes man a witness is solely and exclusively that other, the thing attested, which constrains and limits the perfect or imperfect human organ from without. ... At this point we cannot reflect assiduously enough 'on the difference between an apostle and a genius,' (Kierkegaard, 1847)" KD I/1:114-115; CD I/1:111-112.

[13] Even in his liberal period, however, Barth was never an 'expressivist,' at least as this term has been defined in recent years, since he never affirmed the basic "underlying unity of religious experience" in general. See George Lindbeck, *The Nature of Doctrine: Religion and Theology in a Postliberal Age*, pp. 31f. Barth's talk about religious experience was, by contrast, even in his liberal period, specifically and consistently christocentric. Like Schleiermacher (at least, of the *Glaubenslehre*), Barth believed the content of revelation had to do not with just any religious experience or *Anschauung*, but the religious experience or *Anschauung* of Jesus Christ. Thus, contrary to what expressivists assume, religious people are not all talking about *the same thing* merely using different words. And for Barth not only did revelation have to do with a specific content, but the *form* of revelation was specific as well and not simply vague or arbitrary. Though he certainly did not limit the form of revelation to language, his criterion, to recall from his confirmation instruction, was: "Everything that is *Jesus-like* in people can be revelation, a message from God" (See p. 67 above).

[14] Here again: "To understand an author means for me mainly to *stand with him*, to take each of his words in earnest, so long as it is not proven otherwise that he does not deserve this trust, to participate with him in the subject matter, in order to interpret him from the inside out." The phrase "in order to interpret him from the inside out" is an interesting one and has not yet been commented on. It is clear from the context of this statement that interpreting an author "from the inside out" is being juxtaposed with the empathetic tradition of interpretation's approach of interpreting authors from the *outside in*.

earliest reports and thoughts about Jesus, written down by men who experienced themselves the glory of Christian certainty to the liveliest degree."[15] In other words, the words of the Bible were still important because they were a means of coming into contact with the faith and piety of those who experienced Christ in an especially lively way. They were important not only because they put us in closest historical proximity to the extraordinary people and events surrounding Jesus Christ but because they served to awaken some sort of divine impulse, inclination, or longing deep within our souls.

Yet Barth described his relationship to the words of the Bible in a very different way after his break with liberalism. Whereas before he saw himself bound to the words of the Bible because they were primarily a means of coming into contact with the faith and piety of those who experienced themselves the glory of Christian certainty to the liveliest degree, after his break with liberalism he no longer considered the words of the Bible primarily a "means" in this or any other sense. Instead of using the words of the Bible to awaken some divine impulse already in us (and thereby relegating the inspiration and authority of the Bible to a result rather than a presupposition of exegesis), Barth discovered he could no longer 'use' the Bible at all, as a means or tool for coming into contact with revelation or even devotionally as a means of finding comfort or inspiration.[16] Barth's encounter with the Bible taught him that there was a "Word in the words," that is, an external word (*externum verbum*) and an internal word (*internum verbum*) in the Bible. Contrary to what he formerly believed, what he discovered to be lying behind the words of the Bible were not merely pious feelings, attitudes, and perceptions, but a Word, *the* Word, a divine word, an alien word (*verbum alienum*) which stands over and against all human words, yet is a word no less in its own right. What he discovered was really behind the words of the Bible was a *concretissimum* – though not at the expense of an *alienissimum* – a specific object, rather than something merely vague, non-cognitive, or unthematizable.[17] What he discovered was an *intellectum*, something that is really a matter of knowledge and not something merely a matter of feeling or intuition. Because this "Word in the words" was an alien word with a specific intellectual, even rational – as opposed to non-rational or irrational – content, Barth realized it was not something he at some level already knew or could have somehow said to himself. Nor was it something he could have anticipated or presupposed. This is why

---

[15] Barth, *Konfirmandenunterricht, 1909-1021*, p. 67.

[16] Barth refers to the problem of coming to the Bible for comfort or inspiration ("*Trost*" or "*Anregung*") in "Die neue Welt in der Bibel," p. 25.

[17] KD I/1:141; CD I/1:137.

he felt bound in a way he had never felt before to the words of the Bible. It was there and there alone that he had heard this Word, this divine, alien word.[18]

This changed everything. Whereas before his break with liberalism Barth tried consistently to deverbalize (*Entwörtlichung*)[19] the content of revelation, to play the spiritual content of revelation off against its verbal form, one of the most striking features of Barth's approach after his break with liberalism was his refusal to separate the two and his consistent effort to interpret the one in light of the other. Whereas before he refused to acknowledge that revelation had any intrinsic linguistic character at all, after he refused to acknowledge revelation apart from language, even if it were never exhausted by language.

Whereas before it had been a matter of using the words of the Bible to get at something that he, like Schleiermacher, in some sense and at some level, already knew and could say to himself, after his break he learned he could never again be so presumptuous. Interpreting the Bible became not a matter of being a 'master' or "virtuoso of the Word" (as he later often referred to Schleiermacher),[20] but a servant of the Word, clinging steadfastly to the weak, broken, vacillating human words of the Bible like a beggar. Whereas before it had been a matter of trying to decide which of the Bible's words might contain the voice of the Spirit, after it became no longer a matter of traveling "under certain conditions a little way beside" the language of the Bible, but a matter of "standing or falling with it ... without regard for the consequences."[21] It became a matter of standing *under the Word* rather than over it. Like the Reformers, Barth discovered there was no way to understand the Spirit apart from the letter, just as there was no way to understand the letter apart from the Spirit; and while it is the letter that bears witness to the Spirit, it is the Spirit who brings us back constantly to the letter, which is the basic point at issue in the preface to the third edition of his *Römerbrief*:

> My conclusion therefore is that in no case can it be a question of playing off the Spirit of Christ, the 'subject matter,' in such a way against the 'other spirits,' that in the name of the former certain passages are praised, but certain others, where Paul is not speaking 'from the subject matter' are belittled. Rather it is a question of seeing and making clear how the 'Spirit of Christ' is the crisis in which the whole finds itself. Everything is litera, the voice of 'other' spirits, and whether and in how far everything can be understood also in the context of the 'subject matter' as the voice of the spiritus (of Christ) is the question by which the litera must be studied.[22]

Of course, Barth considered none of this self-evident. "God's Word, heard by *human* ears, proclaimed by *human* lips, is only *God's* Word when the miracle

---

[18] As Barth later put it: "This is why the letter of Scripture is the very reverse of a *pudendum* or *negligendum*." KD I/1:138; CD I/1:134.
[19] KD I/1:143f.; CD I/1:138f.
[20] Barth, *Die protestantische Theologie im 19.Jahrhundert*, pp. 399f.; ET pp. 327f.
[21] Rom II, p. xxi.
[22] Rom II, p. xx.

occurs. Otherwise it is a human word like any other."[23] There was nothing about the words of the Bible themselves that indicated that there was, had been, or could ever be, a Word in the words. In this respect it appears that nothing about his view of human language changed at all after his break with liberalism. He continued to see human language, the language of the Bible, as weak, corrupt, broken, vacillating, etc. But even here there was a change. It was not that he became more confident or hopeful about the potential or capacity of the language of the Bible or human language in general. From many of his comments after his break, it would appear that if anything he became less confident, less hopeful about the capacity or potential of human language. But this was not really the case either. The actual change that occurred in Barth's thought really had nothing to do with becoming more or less confident, more or less hopeful, more or less optimistic or pessimistic about anything. It had to do with a *crisis*, a crisis not from below, but from above, not of human language as such (which seems to have been one of the primary crises for Barth prior to 1915), but of revelation. It was not *human language's* relationship to revelation that changed but *revelation's* relationship to human language; not human language's capacity to bear witness to revelation that changed but revelation's capacity to bear witness to itself through human language. Barth could still say after his break with liberalism what he said before: "Faith in revelation on the one hand and the authority of the scriptural letter on the other are completely heterogeneous categories. One might as well speak about wooden iron." He could also still say, given the opportunity to qualify his terms, "the innermost which lies back of thought and word is that which is in agreement with itself, the identical." But what he could not say after his break with liberalism was: "the innermost which lies back of thought and word is that which is in agreement with itself, the identical, *but that can never be communicated externally as such*" (italics mine). Whereas before, Barth held a view of language that said that language could not be "commissioned," "conscripted," or "commandeered" by God to bear witness to Himself, after 1915, after he claimed to hear God speak through the Bible, he found he could no longer be so legalistic; he could no longer hold such an "iron law" regarding what God could or could not do with human language.[24] God had used the weak, fragile, stammering words

---

[23] Rom II, pp. 350-1.

[24] Barth certainly discovered an "iron law," but it was a different law than the one he had learned from Kant, et al, i.e., one not established 'from below' on the basis of an abstractly absolutized view of 'human powerlessness.' The iron law he discovered said that it is impossible for man to speak of God, but it was based on a revelation that had really occurred: "This iron law itself cannot be understood without the prior assumption that the proclamation of the Church is the Word of God. It is not understandable as something in itself, nor as a general truth. The mystic and agnostic philosophers apparently use the same phrases. They speak of God and they say the same things about Him in what seems to be very much the same language: that it is not possible for us to speak of Him. ... What they mean is the unutterableness

of the Bible to bear witness to Himself, and this event and this alone is the truly decisive event that changed the course of Barth's life.

This also goes a long way toward explaining why Matthias Grünewald's painting of the crucifixion with John the Baptist's finger "pointing in an almost impossible way" made such a deep impression on Barth. This painting, which he seems to have discovered sometime around or shortly after 1915,[25] represented a brand new possibility: not a brand new human possibility as such or a possibility latent within humanity or human language itself, but an "impossible possibility." Before his break with liberalism it was simply impossible, even as a divine possibility, that one could bear witness so decisively, so unambiguously, as John the Baptist is depicted as doing in this painting.[26] In Barth's view, prior to 1915, the most that the prophets and apostles could do, even under grace, was *express* their own experience and thereby 'witness' to their own faith. Human language was simply too corrupt, too vacillating. After 1915, however, Barth discovered that human language's corrupt, vacillating character was not an insuperable obstacle for God. God *could* and indeed *had* used the corrupt, vacillating human language of the Bible to bear witness to Himself. Human language could, therefore, be used to point, to signify, to bear witness. What is written could actually be used to refer to what is written about. And if God had used the weak, corrupt, vacillating language of the Bible to bear witness to Himself, what about human language in general? Even if it is only with the language of the Bible that we are given a special promise in this regard, is it not possible, is it not right to expect, given the promise of John 16:13, that God could, according to His own good pleasure, use language found elsewhere to bear witness to Himself? And what about human language's relationship to other genuine objects of knowledge? It would take Barth another two or three decades to elaborate his answer to this question,[27] but it was, as I have indi-

---

of the ultimate depth of the mystery of the world and the human soul. ... But what is there common between this depth which man himself discovers and controls, and the depth of God? Nothing but the name." KD I/2:839; CD I/2:750-1.

[25] It would be difficult to overestimate the significance of this painting for Barth. A reproduction of it (the one from the Isenheim altar, Colmar) hung over his writing desk, facing him, throughout his career. He mentions it in: Karl Barth to Eduard Thurneysen, 3 June, 1919, *B-Th. Br. I*, p. 332; "*Biblische Fragen, Einsichten, und Ausblicke*," p. 79 (See p. 143 above); Rom II, p. 118; KD I/1:115, 277; CD I/1:112, 262. His most detailed discussion of it occurs in *Unterricht*, p. 186; ET pp. 151-152. But his first reference to it is in Rom I, in his exegesis of Rom.4:9-12, wherein he states: "This art is from God" p. 164.

[26] Interestingly, Barth said of Schleiermacher: "That is why he has little liking for the figure of John the Baptist in the New Testament," *Die protestantische Theologie im 19. Jahrhundert*, p. 404: ET p. 333. Rather than serving as a witness, "for Schleiermacher proclaiming God means proclaiming one's own piety ... for him preaching consists of a self-imparting by the preacher" (p. 406; ET p. 335).

[27] It is on the basis of this impossible possibility that Barth claims human language can again serve its original purpose and fulfill its function, namely, to bear witness, to serve as a

cated, a question he was already concerned with in his *Römerbrief* period. In his preface to the third edition of his *Römerbrief* he said, "I cannot understand how there could be any other way to the spirit of a writing (whatever it is!) than the hypothetical expectation that its spirit would speak to our spirit precisely through the letter," a point very difficult to imagine him emphasizing before his break with liberalism.[28]

The point, in any case, is that one of the great crises of Barth's day as he described it in Rom II was that "the signpost has become meaningless."[29] This was one of the great crises Barth himself had wrestled with up until 1915. But sometime thereafter Barth found himself faced with a far deeper crisis, a crisis which yielded insight into all others, which made the words of the Bible, the biblical signposts, far from meaningless but, in the strictest sense of the word, *significant* in a way they had never been before. This, in sum, is the basic presupposition at issue in Barth's attempt to read the Bible in accordance with the meaning of the Bible itself.

B. The Service of Historical Criticism

Barth's attempt to read the Bible more in accordance with the meaning of the Bible itself, however, has not yet been described but already raises an important question: If reading the Bible more in accordance with the meaning of the Bible itself means focusing on the words of the Bible rather than all that might lie behind them, what about all that does lie behind the biblical text? What about the *Sitz im Leben* out of which it arose? Does this not have some bearing on what actually stands in the text? In short, what role does historical criticism play for Barth if his main focus is on interpreting the biblical text itself? Barth's relationship to historical criticism has already been discussed and can be summarized as follows: historical criticism as generally practiced was not critical enough of its own presuppositions. It did not recognize the relativity of its judgments or of historical understanding in general. In the name of scientific objectivity it presumed to take up a position of unprejudiced, nonparticipatory observation outside or above history even though its judgments were often highly prejudiced and speculative.[30] And because of its preoccupa-

---

sign. This theme appears in various places throughout the *Church Dogmatics* and is one I hope to unravel in a subsequent volume. See pp. 237-238n.47 below, e.g., particularly with respect to Barth's phrase "the future of every human word."

[28] Rom II, p. xxii. "Understanding," as Barth later said, has always to do with "a return to the word, an inquiry into the word itself." KD I/2:514; CD I/2:465.

[29] Rom II, p. 49.

[30] As Barth said in 1920: "Why can't we come to the obvious conclusion that our sense of being outside, our naturalism, our historicism, and our aestheticism will not do?" Barth, "Biblische Fragen, Einsichten und Ausblicke," p. 73.

tion with the individual parts of the Bible rather than its whole – its focus on the historical-psychological circumstances behind the biblical text rather than its actual content, subject matter, and theme – its judgments were often reductionistic.

Yet this reflects only one aspect of Barth's relationship to historical criticism. As I have tried to make clear, Barth did not see his approach to exegesis as in any way a repudiation of or as an alternative to historical critical exegesis. On the contrary, he insisted in his Rom II preface, "I am no 'declared enemy of historical criticism.'" Moreover, even before he was labeled as such he said in his preface to Rom I: "The historical-critical method of biblical research has its place; it points to a preparation for understanding that is never superfluous."[31] So given his criticisms, the question that must now be raised is: what *constructive* role did historical critical research actually play for Barth? How did it serve as "a preparation for understanding"? To answer this question, it is necessary to go back again to statements made in the *Römerbrief* prefaces, such as the following:

> I do not reproach them for their historical criticism, the justification and necessity for which I to the contrary do specifically recognize, but for their contentment with an explanation of the text which I cannot regard as any explanation at all, but only as the first primitive attempt at one: the establishing of 'what is there' by means of translation and paraphrasing the Greek words and phrases in the corresponding modern language by means of philological, archaeological exposition of the results so achieved, and by means of a more or less plausible ordering of the individual elements according to historical and psychological pragmatism. *How* uncertain, *how* very dependent the historians are on the often questionable assumptions even in this establishment of 'what is there,' Jülicher and Lietzmann know better than I. This primitive attempt at an exposition is also not exact science. An exact science of the Letter to the Romans would have to limit itself to the deciphering of the manuscripts and the compilation of a concordance. But the historians rightly do not want to limit themselves to that. Rather [they] press beyond this primitive attempt and try to *understand* Paul, that is, to discover not only how what is there can somehow be repeated in Greek or German, but how it can be *re-thought*, and what it may perhaps *mean*. And it is here, and not with the obvious use of historical criticism in reference to the work which must be done before, that the dissension begins. While I follow the historians attentively and thankfully as long as they are occupied with that primitive attempt at explanation ..., I am always astonished at the modesty of their claims when I consider their attempts to press forward to a real understanding and explanation.[32]

Properly applied historical criticism provides a primitive attempt at understanding what is there. Of course, 'what is there' is precisely the question, as I pointed out in chapter three.[33] Historical critical research can certainly contribute to our understanding of what is there, but a "philological, archaeological exposition ... by means of a more or less plausible ordering of the individual

---

[31] Rom I, p. v. See also Appendix 2, Preface Draft V, p. 291 (p. 600).
[32] Rom II, p. x.
[33] See pp. 84-85 above.

elements according to historical and psychological pragmatism" is not enough. Historians "rightly do not want to limit themselves to that," and it is here that Barth says "dissension begins." The problem, he claims, arises "when I consider their attempts to press forward to a real understanding and explanation." It is not that historians seek to go beyond what they can know as historians that astonishes Barth, it is "the modesty of their claims" when they do.[34] He cites the "banal categories" of Jülicher's "religious thought" as an example. Jülicher tries "to ascribe responsibility for the meaning of [*Romans*] to the 'personality' of Paul, to the 'Damascus experience' (which evidently can explain the most incredible things), to Late Judaism, to Hellenism, to the ancient world in general, and to some other demigods." But what makes this so astonishing to Barth is not merely the result itself, i.e., historical and psychological reductionism, but *how* readily it is established, the relative *ease* with which historical critics such as Jülicher attempt to move from text to referent, from *signa* to *res*, from what is written to what is written about. For Barth, by contrast, as for Luther and Calvin, there is a 'wall' which prevents this move from being such an easy one. Comparing Jülicher's attempt to move from text to referent with Calvin's, Barth says: "How energetically the latter goes to work after he has conscientiously established 'what is there' to think the thoughts of the text after it, that is, to come to terms with it until the wall between the first and sixteenth centuries becomes transparent, until Paul speaks there and the man of the sixteenth century hears here, until the conversation between document and reader is concentrated entirely on the *matter* (which *cannot* be different here and there!)." I discussed this passage earlier in terms of the differences it reflects in Jülicher's and Calvin's approach, namely, the diligence, patience, and focus shown by the latter in contrast to the former.[35] Now it is necessary to say a bit more about what this 'wall' (*Mauer*) represents.

Barth does not say much about what this wall represents in his *Römerbrief* period, but in his Göttingen lectures he talks about a "barrier" (*eine Schranke*) that confronts us when we approach the Bible as God's Word. This barrier has to do with the fact that when we read the Bible as God's Word we are reading human words. "His own Word comes to me only in this broken form. ... This is the barrier that confronts us. We believe we find it in the fact that *the* Word comes to us only in *words*, in human words. We must halt at this barrier and acknowledge it."[36] Barth's problem with historical critics was that they did not halt. They recognized the words of the Bible as weak, corrupt, vacillating, etc., and that as ancient, distant, and foreign, the biblical witness represented a kind of wall which must be broken through. Still, they tended to see it as something

---

[34] What astonishes Barth is how content historians can be with such "meager results," Rom II, p. xii.

[35] See p. 118 above.

[36] Barth, *Unterricht*, pp. 280-281; ET pp. 230-231.

more or less transparent, something that could be more or less penetrated with the proper historical tools and psychological skills, because what it obviously referred to was certain historical events or expressions of religious self-consciousness. Barth, by contrast, found the Bible's words more opaque. Because the Bible was primarily a witness to revelation rather than a source-book of historical facts, its words were not so obviously transparent. And this is why Luther's and Calvin's focus on the words of the Bible themselves made so much more sense. As he explained in his essay of 1925, "*Das Schriftprinzip der reformierten Kirche*":

> The prophetic-apostolic witness is the form in which the Bible mediates revelation and in this respect it is the Word of God itself. One cannot separate the revelation from this witness as something that in itself stands behind it, something in itself to be observed. The historian cannot be denied in his attempt to reach beyond the sources to the *facts* which are beyond the sources; he will for example run up there against the inner life of the biblical author, a religious-historical development, and at an especially important place he will run up against dark hues which are usually called, somewhat optimistically, the 'life of Jesus.' He will run up against the beginning of the tragedy called church history. There is no doubt that all this somehow, more or less, recognizably exists. But all this has nothing to do with revelation. Revelation is or rather *happens* for us in the *Scriptures*; it happens, there is no way to avoid this, in the biblical *texts*, in the words and the sentences, in that which the prophets and apostles *wanted* to say and *have* said as their witnesses. That is the relative right of the doctrine of verbal inspiration against which so much injustice has been done as we shall discuss shortly. Its *right* lies in the following: the texts do not concern us as sources but as a *witness*. And the witness is not to be looked for in some fact behind the sources but within the texts.[37]

The reason Luther's and Calvin's focus on the words of the Bible themselves made so much sense to Barth is because revelation, the real subject matter, content, and theme of the Bible, occurs not *behind* the words of the Bible but *in* them. Why not behind the words of the biblical witness? Because one "cannot separate the revelation from this witness as something that in itself stands behind it, something in itself to be observed." This is not to deny historical critical analysis of the Bible nor to identify it directly with revelation itself as if it were some kind of oracle. On the contrary, there is a wall that separates us from having any immediate access to revelation which must be broken through. And "the wall [*die Wand*] to be broken through," Barth says, "is the fully to be acknowledged historical limitedness of the biblical witness. Whoever ignores or denies this wall and makes the Bible into an oracle denies the revelation because he denies the decision."[38] Of course, "the decision" Barth is referring to here is not *our* decision, e.g., our decision to try to penetrate through the biblical witness, it is *God's* decision to reveal Himself in the human words of the

---

[37] Barth, "Das Schriftprinzip der reformierten Kirche," pp. 516-517.
[38] Barth, "Das Schriftprinzip der reformierten Kirche," p. 517.

Bible,[39] and this decision is just as easily denied by making the Bible into a source as it is by making it into an oracle, which brings us back to the fundamental question of this section.

If the actual subject matter, content, and theme of the Bible is not a historical fact which can be grasped by historical critical investigation, if it is not something a historian *qua* historian can find *behind* the biblical witness, what role does historical criticism play for Barth? Despite his various, scattered remarks it appears that Barth did not provide a very clear answer to this question in his *Römerbrief* period. But shortly thereafter in his Göttingen lectures he offers this description:

> The witness of the prophets and apostles is a collection of records of concrete historical situations. As I study these, I unavoidably try to reconstruct these situations. On the basis of what is in the text I try to establish how things were then, what the authors had in mind when they said this or that, and apart from the authors and the texts how the events took place which they record. I combine these findings with other things that the same authors might have said about the same subjects or others. When the text is silent, I try to supplement its thoughts with cautious conjectures so as to form them into a whole. I try to understand them on the basis of what earlier or contemporary authors say on whom they might be dependent or with whom they might share a common legacy. I will especially use this procedure in relation to historical reports, and with the aid of further sources I will try to construct a picture of the events that the authors record. As I have either earlier or at the same time, by a similar procedure, formed some picture of the whole period, its events, relationships, and movements, its external and internal makeup, I fit the pictures that I have taken from the texts into this larger picture, and when I adduce similarly achieved pictures of the times that precede and follow, set these pictures in the framework of historical development, and look at them in this way, then I have carried through what might be called the act of historical investigation.[40]

Here we have Barth's first truly substantive description of the constructive role of historical criticism. Here all the procedures, "all the crowbars and wrecking tools," of historical critical investigation which he alluded to in his preface to Rom II are plainly described. Source criticism, form criticism, redaction criticism, and all other means of understanding the text and reconstructing the concrete historical situation out of which it arose may be employed. None are rejected. Yet the fundamental purpose of historical criticism brought out here is that it serves to construct "a picture," (*ein Bild*). This is its essential contribution and the significance of this task must not be underestimated. But there are two things which must be said about this picture which historical criticism

---

[39] This is not to suggest that we do not have decisions to make as readers of the Bible. Immediately after the sentence above, Barth writes: "The statement that the Bible is the Word of God, describes a decision that takes place on the razor's edge between unbelief and faith." Barth, "Das Schriftprinzip der reformierten Kirche," p. 517. Later he adds: "The decision *has been* made in and through him ... Jesus Christ; and it is continually *being made* on the battlefield between faith and unbelief" (p. 543).

[40] Barth, *Unterricht*, p. 313: ET pp. 255-256.

helps to form. First, it is a picture which is formed solely in the mind of the interpreter. It is not to be confused with the events themselves or with the real subject matter, content, and theme the prophets and apostles' words bear witness to. "We must be aware that this act is subjectively conditioned. We may respect its findings, but there is no reason to make an idol of them, as though the speaking of God's Word in scripture took place in the mere contemplation of such a historical picture (e.g. to mention the most important, the historical Jesus). Perhaps it does, but if so something else has to happen."[41] This "something else" that has to happen I will discuss in a moment, but Barth's problem with modern historical critics clearly was not only that they tended not to be cautious about their conjectures and tended not to acknowledge the subjective conditioning involved in their depictions. His problem was that they tended to make idols of them. They tended to identify or confuse their portraits with the actual subject matter of the Bible itself or act as if there were a second subject matter, a second *res*, namely, the historical fact or situation their picture depicts.

The second thing to be said about such pictures is that not only are they necessary, they are inevitable. The witness of the prophets and apostles has to do with historical situations. Barth says, "I unavoidably try to reconstruct these situations." With or without historical criticism, in other words, pictures are always formed in the minds of readers. The only question is the quality or appropriateness of the pictures formed. Barth claims, "The degree of skill and method and competence will vary, as will also the apparatus used. ... There is a wide gap between the refined research of a Harnack or Holl and the simple investigation of an old peasant sitting down with a Luther Bible."[42] Some pictures are obviously better than others. Some are more appropriate, more fitting, more historically plausible than others. This is why historical criticism remained such an important tool for Barth. Historical criticism could serve to shatter the false images, the inappropriate and unwarranted conjectures and constructions we often bring to the Bible, which is why rejecting historical criticism was never a question for Barth. Even after his break with liberalism when he expressed concern in a letter to Thurneysen on Jan.1, 1916, that he had become "frightfully indifferent" to historical questions, he said: "Of course that is nothing new for me. Already under the influence of Herrmann, I always thought of historical criticism as merely a means of attaining freedom over

---

[41] Barth, *Unterricht*, pp. 313-314; ET p. 257. "We can speak of the objectivity of this picture only with the reservation that we must make in relation to all scholarly depictions. We certainly cannot speak of an authority. Its objectivity is disputable to the degree that I depart from the sources and from the lexicographical findings and resort to combinations and conjectures and constructions. The canon has authority, and so does the text that the church has received, but not a construct that is defended, perhaps very plausibly, even though it goes beyond the text and canon" (p. 313; ET pp. 256-257).

[42] Barth, *Unterricht*, p. 313; ET p. 256.

against tradition, not, however, as a constitutive factor in a new liberal tradition as apparently Wernle and his like want to have it."[43] In other words, even as a liberal Barth recognized that although its contribution was not enough, historical criticism still had a role to play, a service to render. It could liberate readers from layers of false presuppositions and conceptions laid upon the text by the history of interpretation.

But what Barth realized after his break with liberalism that he had not realized before was that the Reformers had approached the task of interpretation in a very similar fashion. They too had recognized that there were layers of traditional interpretation that tended to obscure the literal sense of the Bible, and in their effort to get beyond these layers to the meaning of the text itself they too had tried to take the humanity of the Bible seriously. They too had recognized that the words of the Bible were human words written in specific times, in specific places, by specific individuals, under specific circumstances. "This is why the Reformers demanded the grammatical investigation of scripture."[44] And to this extent even though their tools were not as sophisticated as those of modern historical critics, they too were interested in a real historical understanding of the Bible.[45] Yet what the Reformers realized that modern historical critics did not was that there was a wall separating what is written from what is written about, and it could not be penetrated merely on the basis of their own efforts or skill. Certainly there is always "a kind of crust" which must be broken through, a crust of unfamiliarity, with regard to any text, not least the Bi-

---

[43] Karl Barth to Eduard Thurneysen, 1 Jan., 1916, *B-Th Br.* I, p. 121.

[44] Barth, *Unterricht*, p. 313; ET p. 257.

[45] As Barth later said: "The demand that the Bible should be read and understood and expounded historically is, therefore, obviously justified and can never be taken too seriously. The Bible itself posits this demand: even where it appeals expressly to divine commissionings and promptings, in its actual composition it is everywhere a human word, and this human word is obviously intended to be taken seriously and read and understood as such. To do anything else would be to miss the reality of the Bible and therefore the Bible itself as the witness of revelation. The demand for a 'historical' understanding of the Bible necessarily means, in content, that we have to take it for what it undoubtedly is and is meant to be: the human speech uttered by specific men at specific times in a specific situation, in a specific language and with a specific intention. It means that the understanding of it has honestly and unreservedly been one which is guided by all these considerations. If the word 'historical' is a modern word, the thing itself was not really invented in modern times. And if the more exact definition of what is 'historical' in this sense is liable to change and has actually changed at times, it is still quite clear that when and wherever the Bible has been really read and expounded, in this sense it has been read 'historically' and not unhistorically, i.e., its concrete humanity has not been ignored. To the extent that it has been ignored, it has not been read at all." KD I/2:513; CD I/2: 464. Barth adds: "All the care and love which we may apply to the biblical text within the framework of that other understanding cannot alter the fact that the understanding as such is inadequate. Luther and Calvin, on the other hand, have at this very point shown a real historical understanding for the Bible" (KD I/2:517; CD I/2:468).

ble, which neither Barth nor the Reformers denied.[46] But as far as any real breaking through the biblical text is concerned, this is something that they realized happens primarily from the other side, i.e., it is not so much that we penetrate the text and establish what its subject matter is, it is the subject matter that breaks forth through the text and establishes itself as such. And Barth was prepared on this specific basis to approach other texts with a similar expectation, e.g., the works of Goethe and Lao-tzu, even if the subject matter of their works did not establish itself nearly so powerfully and unequivocally as the subject matter of the Bible establishes itself.[47]

---

[46] Barth, "Die neue Welt in der Bibel," p. 27.

[47] This is the basis of Barth's move from special to general hermeneutics, which has been discussed already and is perhaps best elaborated in the following passage: "... there is no question of a peculiarity of the biblical word or its subject-matter, beside which we have normally to ascribe to other human words and their subject matter a different peculiarity. It is rather that the peculiarity of the Bible has the force of an example, i.e., that we learn from it what is to be learned concerning the peculiarity of the human word in general. Everything that is said in a human word is as such always wrapped in a mystery, in this mystery, even when it is not divine revelation. But it is because what is said in the biblical word of man is divine revelation, and as such the *analogia fidei*, that everything which is said by human word is drawn into the darkness and light of its mystery. Is it not the case that whatever is said to us by men obviously wants – and it is with this claim that it confronts us with something said to us – to make itself said and heard? It wants in this way to become to us a subject matter. It wants us for our part to bring it a true objectivity, i.e., interest for its own sake. ... [It] wants to be heard openly and not with the mixture of our hearing and our own speaking and interrupting. In order to be understood by us, it wants not to be mastered by us, but to lay hold of us. It wants to be evaluated in its relation to what is said in it. ... In short, whatever is said to us by men always demands of us what God's revelation in the human word of Holy Scripture – but that alone – can actually achieve in relation to us. God's revelation in the human word of Holy Scripture not only wants but can make itself said and heard. It can become for us real subject matter, and it can force us to treat it objectively. ... God's revelation in the human word of Holy Scripture is distinguished from everything else that is said to us by men by the fact that a majesty belongs to the one which obviously is radically lacking in the other, a majesty without which the latter would be meaningless if the former were only an exception and not the law and the promise and the sign of redemption which has been set up in the sphere of all other human words, and of all that is said by them. How can we deny or ignore the distinction between what merely wants to be the thing said by other men, and what can be God's revelation in the human word of Holy Scripture? We have to accept this distinction. But knowing this distinction, how can we regard the false hearing and understanding and expounding of the human word, and therefore the meaninglessness with which it is delivered, as the norm and law of our words, just because it is the rule under which they labor, and the power of the revelation of God in the human word of Holy Scripture only as an outside exception? Even though as an exception it may confirm the rule, it necessarily breaks through it and reveals itself to be the norm and law in the light of which all human words now actually stand. Their aim and intention cannot possibly be concealed if we start with the hearing and understanding and expounding of the human word of the Bible. They cannot themselves become witnesses of revelation. Good care is seen to that. But when we start with the witnesses of revelation, we have to approach all other human words with at least the question what it is that however feebly and ineffectively they want to say, and

The point is that while the Reformers sought to take the humanity of the Bible's words seriously and were open to using practically any tool in order to do so, they also approached the words of the Bible with a certain respect and reserve. They did so because they recognized the elusive, enigmatic character of human language and because they recognized the sovereign freedom of the Bible's subject matter. Unlike so many modern historical critics, they knew that the Bible's subject matter could not be grasped, mastered, or subdued by any exegetical method. This is what finally impressed Barth so much about Calvin's approach. Instead of trying to get *behind* the text in order to seize or capture its subject matter, Calvin tried after taking pains to establish what is there "to think the thoughts of the text after it, that is, to come to terms with it until the wall between the first and sixteenth centuries becomes transparent, until Paul speaks and the man of the sixteenth century hears here, until the conversation between document and reader is concentrated entirely on the *matter*." Unlike so many of Barth's contemporaries, Calvin remained "wholesomely restrained" *before* the text because he did not assume that he already knew what it had to say or that his exposition could provide anything more than hints as to its real content.[48] He focused patiently *on* the text because he knew that if he was to understand it truly, "something else" had to happen, something which was beyond his control.

This is what happened to Barth when he heard 'God speak' through the words of the Bible. "Holy Scripture," he announced in 1917, "interprets itself despite all our human limitations."[49] But the reason is not because of any intrinsic quality having to do with the words of Holy Scripture themselves, but as he makes clear throughout his "Die neue Welt in der Bibel" essay, because the subject matter, content, and theme of Holy Scripture establishes itself as such. This was a brand new possibility for Barth and a brand new way of thinking about the doctrine of verbal inspiration.[50] The immediate consequence of it,

---

what would make itself said and heard in them. There will then be no question of the assurance of an hermeneutics which is based on the necessity of irrelevance, nor of the meaninglessness to which human words generally would in fact be condemned, were it not that they had with them with all its promise the human word of Holy Scripture, and their own future was revealed by this human word. In view of the future of every human word which is already present in Holy Scripture, we will, of course, read Homer and Goethe and even the newspaper rather differently than if we did not know the future." KD I/2: 521-522; CD I/2:471-472.

[48] KD I/2:521; CD I/2:470.

[49] Barth, "Die neue Welt in der Bibel," p. 22.

[50] Though it is difficult to pinpoint what it was exactly that changed Barth's mind regarding the doctrine of verbal inspiration, and specifically *Calvin's* doctrine of verbal inspiration, the point that he subsequently emphasized in discussing Calvin's teaching on this topic, viz., II Tim.3:16 (e.g. *"Das Schriftprinzip der reformierten Kirche,"* p. 542 and KD I/2:516-517; CD I/2:467-468) is that *God and God alone* is the main subject, the prime acting agent, at issue in this doctrine. To this extent, therefore, Barth's discovery that the subject matter, content, and theme of the Bible establishes itself as such was already implicit in Calvin.

however, was not that he felt he understood the Bible more but that he understood it less. To really understand the Bible, he discovered, required much more than he ever realized. It required not only that he understand the words in light of the *subject matter* but that he understand the subject matter in light of the *words*. This is what the dominant science of biblical exegesis of the day in Barth's view had failed to do. Scholars had become preoccupied with understanding the historical and psychological antecedents behind the text rather than understanding the text itself in light of its actual subject matter, content, and theme. Barth, as I have emphasized, had no objections to historical critical analysis. On the contrary, he saw it as an indispensable tool for shattering the false images and unwarranted pictures we often bring to the task of interpretation and as a real help in reconstructing better ones. Still, reconstructing better pictures of what might have happened behind the text Barth could not "regard as any explanation at all, but only as the first primitive attempt at one." It could serve only as a "preparation." Real hearing, understanding, and explaining, he insisted, occur only when the words of the text are understood in light of its actual subject matter, which includes the possibility that even the best pictures we reconstruct in our minds with the help of historical criticism may be revised, reshaped, and if necessary, even shattered, in light of the subject matter.[51]

Historical criticism thus provides an indispensable preparatory service in Barth's view. Yet relative to the larger task of *theological* exegesis, this is its *only* service. Interestingly enough, Schleiermacher, as well as some of his more astute followers such as Paul Wernle, had a similar view of historical criticism's role, as I discussed at length in the last chapter. For Schleiermacher, historical interpretation was a basically "comparative" task, one that "should be done even before interpretation begins, since it is the means for re-creating the relationship between speaker and the original audience, and interpretation cannot begin until that relationship has been established."[52] For

---

[51] It may be that all will be "newly defined and broadened and eventually shattered and remoulded" in light of the subject matter, KD I/2:812; CD I/2:724. Is there any value thus to understanding the humanity of authors? Barth states: "We certainly cannot despise such knowledge as worthless. When their word is heard, and in the hearing attention is paid to what is signified and intended in this word, and there is an understanding of the full meaning and scope of their humanity in the light of this object of their word, then a proper exposition of their word can take account of their humanity in all its scope and meaning – not, however, *in abstracto* but in its connexion with the object revealed in their word as it is heard and understood. An exposition of their humanity *in abstracto* may be very full historically. It may be informed and penetrated by a very great understanding of their religion. It may be carried out with the greatest possible zeal. But we still have to reject it as an interpretation of the Bible – and on the very ground that it does not take the human word of the Bible as seriously as according to the Bible itself it ought to be taken" (KD I/2:516; CD I/2:467).

[52] Schleiermacher, *Hermeneutik*, p. 84; ET p. 104.

Wernle, using the same language as Barth, the purpose of historical criticism was to create "a general picture" of the facts which lie behind the text even if such a picture bears only "hypothetical character."[53]

The reason historical interpretation must occur before the larger task of interpretation begins for Schleiermacher is that something else has to happen. The reason the general picture that historical criticism creates bears only hypothetical character for Wernle is that the very act of creating such a picture requires that something else happen. That "something else" according to Schleiermacher and Wernle, as I have shown, has decisively to do with the psychological or divinatory process of *Einfühlung*. The "something else" that has to happen, according to Barth, however, has decisively to do with the subject matter establishing itself as such. And implicit in this difference is another. So decisive is it for Barth that the subject matter of a text establish itself as such, that unlike Schleiermacher or Wernle, he allows no restrictions, no preconceived notions as to what may be possible, to be set up in advance by historical criticism, since such restrictions would limit the subject matter of the text from freely determining itself as such.[54] Barth's problem with those who accused him of not taking historical criticism seriously enough, in short, was that they had not yet taken the freedom of the Bible's subject matter seriously enough. This was his basic conflict with historical critics from the very beginning of his *Römerbrief* period, and it remained so throughout his career.

C. The Art of Paraphrasing

Barth insisted from the beginning of his *Römerbrief* period and throughout his career that he *had* interpreted Paul's *Epistle to the Romans* historically. In his preface drafts to Rom I he said: "Fundamentally, as much as this might be held against me, I must say that, in my opinion, I have offered a historical presentation of Pauline thoughts and not an outpouring of my own or other modern ones."[55] In his preface to Rom II, he challenged readers "to read the book very carefully, not too quickly, not without checking my progress against the Greek text and other commentaries, and, please, preferably not 'enthusiastically.'"[56]

---

[53] Wernle, *Einführung*, pp. 35-36.

[54] KD I/2:814-815; CD I/2:726.

[55] Appendix 2, Preface Draft II, p. 284 (p. 591).

[56] Rom II, xvi. Three paragraphs later Barth adds: "Concerning textual notes, which Jülicher in his zeal to turn me out into the quiet pastures of practical theology wished I had omitted entirely, it may be said that I introduced them in those places where I felt I had to deviate from the text of Nestle, which I assumed to be in the hands of most of my theological readers. I do not intend to intervene in matters in which I am notoriously incompetent. Yet I could not simply for that reason entirely decline to give a brief explanation of why I prefer other

Even after the smoke of his bombshell-commentary and the wide-ranging pneumatic exegesis discussion of the mid- and late-1920s had begun to clear, Barth said in his preface to the English edition of his *Römerbrief* of 1932:

> It may not be irrelevant if I now make it quite clear both to my future friends and to my future opponents in England that in writing this book I set out neither to compose a free fantasia upon the theme of religion nor to evolve a philosophy of it. My sole aim was to interpret Scripture. I ask readers not to say to me too quickly (as a few in Germany have said to me all too quickly), that I am not an exegete or rather: that I am a 'pneumatic' exegete. This reproach which is implied in the word 'pneumatic' may well fall back heavily on those who so easily raise this reproach. The publication of this book in English may perhaps lead to a fresh formulation of the problem, "What is exegesis?" [57]

Here, while affirming that his "sole aim" in writing his *Römerbrief* was to interpret Scripture, Barth expresses what he had hoped from the beginning it would accomplish, namely, "a fresh formulation of the problem, 'What is exegesis?'" Of course, given his contemporaries' definition, many simply could not believe that exegesis could have been his true aim, which is why it was so important to Barth to reiterate what his original intentions had been:

> No one can, of course, read anything out of a text without at the same time reading something into it. Moreover, no interpreter is rid of the danger of reading in more than he reads out. I neither was nor am free from this danger. And yet I should be altogether misunderstood if my readers refused to credit me with the honesty of, at any rate, *intending* to explain the text. I must assure them that, in writing this book, I felt myself bound to the actual words of the text, and did not in any way propose to engage myself in free theologizing. It goes without saying that my interpretation is open to criticism; and I hope to hear as soon as possible of important and proper criticism of it at the hands of my English-speaking theological colleagues. But I do not want to hear criticisms which proceed from some religious or philosophical or ethical 'point of view.' Proper criticism of my book can be concerned only with the interpretation of the text of the Epistle. In other words, criticism or approval should move strictly within the realm of Theology. I shall not be impressed in the least by general propositions concerning the value or lack of value of my 'spiritual outlook,' or of my 'religious position,' or of my 'general view of life.' My book deals with one issue, and with one issue only. Did Paul think and speak in general and in detail in the manner in which I have interpreted him as thinking and speaking? Or did he think and speak altogether differently? The fourth and last request I have to make of my English readers is therefore quite direct. Of my friendly readers I ask that they should take nothing and believe nothing from me which they are not of themselves persuaded stands within the meaning of what Paul wrote. Of my unfriendly readers I ask that they should not reject as an unreasonable opinion of my own what, in fact, Paul himself propounded. The purpose of this book neither was nor is to delight or annoy its readers by setting out a New Theology. The purpose was and is to direct them to Holy Scripture, to the Epistle of Paul to the Romans, in order that, whether they be delighted or annoyed, whether they are 'accepted'

---

readings in passages, not all of which are unimportant, though I am always ready to be corrected" (Rom II, xvii-xviii).

[57] Barth, "Vorwort zur englischen Ausgabe," pp. 480-481; ET ix-x [translation revised].

or "rejected," they may at least be brought face to face with the subject matter of the Scriptures.[58]

After more than a decade of criticism, Barth remained adamant that his sole intention in writing his commentary had been to interpret Paul's *Epistle to the Romans*. Indeed he insisted to his dying day that this had been his intention.[59] Of course this is exactly what his contemporaries had trouble believing. From the beginning, even those sympathetic to Barth, as I pointed out in chapter two, could not understand how he could call his *Römerbrief* a "commentary."[60] To repeat Schlatter: "*The Epistle to the Romans* for Barth is a timeless, entirely modern, entirely contemporary word. All that is human, all that is historical, sinks away. . . . *The Epistle to the Romans* ceases to be an epistle to the Romans."[61] Or, as Krister Stendahl, representing a younger generation of biblical scholars, later charged: "[Barth] is admittedly incapable of enough patience and enthusiasm for keeping alive the tension between what the text meant and what it means. There are no criteria by which they can be kept apart; what is intended as a commentary turns out to be a theological tractate, expanding in contemporary terms what Paul should have said about the subject matter as understood by the commentator."[62]

While it is certainly true that Barth had "no criteria" – *a priori* or *a posteriori* – for keeping what the text meant and what it means apart, Stendahl is wrong in alleging "that Barth speaks as if it were a very simple thing to establish what Paul actually meant in his own terms" or that he became "primarily concerned with the present meaning" and lost "his enthusiasm or his ultimate respect for the descriptive task," i.e., for establishing "what it meant."[63] On the contrary, Barth repeatedly acknowledged that Paul's *Epistle to the Romans* was addressed to a specific people, in a specific place, at a specific time and that there *was* a difference between what it meant and what it means. But what was

---

[58] Barth, "Vorwort zur englischen Ausgabe", pp. 480-481; ET ix-x [translation revised].

[59] "So at that time (and indeed later) I read the text of the Bible with very many different kinds of spectacles and naively displayed the fact. But by using all those different kinds of spectacles, what I honestly wanted to express (and was convinced that I was expressing) was the word of Paul" Barth, "Nachwort," p. 295; ET p. 265 [slightly revised]. "In both cases it was my intention – and it will remain my intention in the future, if I again have to say something about the Epistle to the Romans – to let Paul speak for himself. No interpreter could escape from the qualification: 'as I understand him,' and that naturally applies to me too. But I did and do hope that Paul is strong enough to make himself heard even through the medium of interpretations which are still and ever remain inadequate." Karl Barth, *Kurze Erklärung des Römerbriefes* (Munich: Christian Kaiser Verlag, 1956), p. 8; ET *A Shorter Commentary on Romans* (Richmond: John Knox Press, 1959), p. 8.

[60] See p. 15n.3 above.

[61] Schlatter, *Anfänge*, pp. 143, 145; ET pp. 121, 123.

[62] Krister Stendahl, "Biblical Theology: A Program," *Interpreter's Dictionary of the Bible*, 1 (Nashville: Abingdon Press, 1962), p. 420. Hereafter, "Biblical Theology: A Program."

[63] Stendahl, "Biblical Theology: A Program," p. 420.

so deeply disturbing to his critics was his refusal to draw a fundamental distinction between what it meant and what it means at any particular point. As Barth put it, from what standpoint could one possibly do so?[64] Given "the living context" found within the subject matter of the Bible, there was no place he felt he could point to and say with any certainty "Here, *this* is a 'dead relic' whereas *there* is a 'living link.'" Moreover, exegesis which was truly scientific, he insisted, demanded a perpetual openness to the possibility that what was once thought a "dead relic" of the past could become at any moment a "living link." Nor was he willing to separate the question of what it means from what it meant in any *safe*, two-stage, bifurcated process which might hermetically seal the former off from the latter. This sort of "double-entry bookkeeping," which I discussed earlier in chapter three, is what is at issue in Barth's comment in his preface to Rom II: "Do the historians then really think that by doing so they have fulfilled their duty to human society, that with a *re bene gesta* they have imparted the Word by adding a supplementary commentary by Niebergall?"[65]

The fact that biblical exegetes could be so preoccupied with what Paul's text meant then and there yet never seem to get around to talking about what it means here and now, or that they could miss the significance of its meaning both then and there as well as here and now, indicated to Barth that they still did not understand what it was really about, that they were not willing to wait "until Paul speaks there and the man of the sixteenth [or twentieth] century hears here, until the conversation between document and reader is concentrated entirely on the *matter* (which *cannot* be different here and there!)." Thus, from Barth's perspective, it was not that he did not have "enough patience and enthusiasm for keeping alive the tension between what the text meant and what it means" (as if such a tension were *ours* to keep alive), it was that his contemporaries did not have enough patience and enthusiasm "to wait" for the Bible's subject matter to establish itself as such.

Barth's attempt to bring about "a fresh formulation of the problem, 'What is exegesis?,'" as I have said, arose out of his conviction that modern historical-critics had largely neglected genuine theological interest in the Bible. He did

---

[64] Of course we always interpret from a particular standpoint, but as Barth said in his preface to the third edition of his *Römerbrief*, "The *pneuma Christou* is not a position on which one can take a stand," Rom II, xxii.

[65] Rom II, xiii. Friedrich Niebergall (1866-1932), professor of Practical Theology at Heidelberg from 1908 to 1922 and thereafter at Marburg, was a member of the history of religions school. The volume Barth is referring to, *Praktische Auslegung des Neuen Testaments: Für Prediger und Religionslehrer* (Tübingen: J.C.B. Mohr [Paul Siebeck], 1909), was the last in a multi-volume series entitled, *Handbuch zum Neuen Testament*, edited by Hans Lietzmann. In its preface, Niebergall states that he "seeks to build a connection between historical-critical exegesis and the content of the New Testament thought as should occur in worship, teaching, and counseling."

not, however, seek a theological understanding of the Bible at the expense of a genuine historical understanding, as many of his critics claimed. Rather, for the sake of a better theological understanding of the Bible he sought a more thorough integration of historical understanding into the larger task of theological exegesis, even if his own commentary fell far short in reflecting it (which he freely admitted was the case). But in addition, Barth's effort to reformulate the task of exegesis, as I have already alluded to, was based on his conviction that the text of the Bible *itself* had been neglected. He expressed this concern many times in his *Römerbrief* prefaces, but in one of his preface drafts to Rom I he adds the following which sheds light on what interpreting the text itself actually meant to him:

> Because this book is not my dogmatic but an exegetical work, I was not able to say everything about each of the topics touched upon, but only about that which lies directly in the path of Paul's words. One is not allowed, therefore, to read its statements as a treatise but should rather be interested, first of all, in the understanding of the text itself. My statements have no importance of their own, nor do the quotations of other writings. Everything is meant only as movement of the text. I do not want to be right anywhere, even where I speak very definitely in the name of Paul. I only want to point out doors that are now closed which could perhaps open if this text were to speak again.[66]

The phrase that stands out above is "I do not want to be right anywhere," and it implies a very different approach than the one pursued by most of Barth's contemporaries. For most of his contemporaries, certainly for most members of the dominant science of biblical exegesis, the goal of interpreting a book such as *Romans* was a matter of getting Paul 'right' in the sense of accurately depicting the content that lies behind his text. But getting Paul 'right' was not the goal of interpretation for Barth because of what it implied about that content. It implied there was something fixed, static, inert about it; that interpreting Paul's words was more or less a matter of deducing the correct "result" of some mathematical equation, as if what were at issue was merely data or information. It implied that the "object" or "thing" Paul had written about was something one could capture, or an especially skilled interpreter could master or a particularly determined one could put under the hot lights of historical criticism and interrogate. In short, it implied that there was something dead or frozen in time about what Paul had written about. Of course, in Barth's view there was nothing dead or frozen about what Paul had written about. What Paul had written about was alive, and alive not as a caged bird but as "a bird in flight."[67] Thus any attempt to paint or photograph this bird in flight or get it "right," as it were, was as such always a distortion, indeed, a betrayal of its reality.

---

[66] Appendix 2, Preface Draft III, pp. 289-290 (p. 598).
[67] Barth, "Der Christ in der Gesellschaft," pp.40f. See also Rom I, pp.384, 391.

In other words, it was not that Barth believed there was no such thing as a right or wrong interpretation of *Romans*, as many deconstructionists and postmodernists claim. (One could hardly give as much attention to the Greek text as he did without believing that some interpretations were more right, i.e., more faithful to what Paul actually said, than others.) Rather, Barth did not want to be right anywhere, even where he spoke definitely in the name of Paul, because what Paul wrote about was not, in the strictest sense, something one could be 'right' about.[68] It was never something simply 'given' or something one could merely 'observe' as such. Moreover, as I discussed earlier, what Paul wrote about was not subject to independent corroboration or verification, which is why with respect to his own interpretation Barth said, "verification can only be a relative, more or less certain verification."[69] But the main problem with seeking to get Paul 'right' as I have suggested was that it implied a certain ossification of the subject matter of Paul's text. This is why Barth emphasized throughout his career that his *Römerbrief* was, at most, merely a "preliminary work" and his interpretation strictly "provisional."[70] Given the nature of its subject matter, "How could such a lively and responsible enterprise as the explanation of the *Epistle to the Romans* remain fixed for any length of time?"[71]

This leads us to consider one of the most important concepts in the *Römerbrief* prefaces. Given his objective of interpreting the text itself, the only alternative to getting Paul right, as Barth saw it, was to attempt "to paraphrase" what Paul said. The "presumption" involved even in trying to paraphrase Paul, he claimed, was "embarrassing enough for me . . . as if I were really permitted to say what Paul said." Nevertheless, it "could not be avoided."[72] If the goal was to say what the text said, the most anyone could do, given the nature of the subject matter, was to point readers in the direction the text itself pointed by means of a paraphrase.[73] This required pointing not just in any direction but in a particular direction, to a particular space which as such – that is, apart from the event of God speaking – was always empty. To Barth, this was the great

---

[68] Deconstructionists typically deny 'right' or 'wrong' interpretations of texts because they believe language is inherently corrupt, ambiguous, arbitrary, or meaningless; and they write many books to prove it. Barth, on the other hand, objected to getting Paul 'right' not because of the inadequacy of language (*signa*), but because of the sovereign freedom, that is, the transcendent alterity of the subject matter (*res*) of Paul's text. Barth believed Paul was right. Whether he as an interpreter was right was another question. "Our questions, if we understand ourselves aright, are the questions of Paul, and Paul's answers, if their light illumines us, must be our answers," Appendix 2, Preface Draft IV, p. 290 (p. 599). The point for Barth is that it is ultimately only the Holy Spirit who establishes the rightness of a given interpretation.

[69] Rom II, p. xiv.

[70] Barth uses the word "provisional" [*vorläufig*] four times in his Rom II preface, pp. xiii-xiv.

[71] Rom II, preface to third edition, p. xix.

[72] Appendix 2, Preface Draft III, p. 289 (p. 597)

[73] Barth, "Der Christ in der Gesellschaft," pp. 40f.

challenge of paraphrasing *Romans*. The word paraphrase, however, has a variety of connotations. To gain a better understanding of what Barth meant by it, it is necessary to consider how he uses it in his *Römerbrief* prefaces.

A paraphrase (*Umschreibung*) is typically defined as a freer form of translation, freer in the sense that it does not stick as closely to the actual wording of the text or speech in question. All attempts at translation, of course, run the risk of saying something *other* than what the author or speaker actually said, but the risk involved in paraphrasing is obviously even greater, precisely because one does not stick as closely to the actual wording of the text or speech in question. Barth was very much aware of this risk with respect to paraphrasing the apostle Paul. He knew that he could not substitute "easier language" and still communicate the same thoughts as Paul, which is why, referring to his commentary as a whole, he said:

> It only wants to interpret by *paraphrasing* the thoughts of Paul, not by translating them into our easier thoughts. For the language and the content are one. The 'easier' Christian way of thinking ... does *not*, unfortunately, by any means indicate that we, after all, have arrived upon the same subject matter as Paul and the Bible. If ears will be once again open to the *subject matter* with which Paul was concerned, then will his language be once again understood as well, as was obviously the case in the first century.[74]

Barth's claim that "the language and the content are one" and his concern that priority be given to understanding the subject matter of the Bible have already been discussed. The point to be emphasized here is that, contrary to those who suggest that paraphrasing gave him greater liberty in his attempt to interpret Paul's words, Barth recognized that in trying to paraphrase Paul's words he was still bound to them. And implied in this concern was his recognition of a problem which he later regarded as one of the most serious problems of Neo-Protestantism, viz., its preoccupation with 'translating' the gospel or, more precisely, illustrating it, rather than first 'hearing' it.[75] As he said in the early 1930s, "Interpretation means saying *the same thing* in other words. Illustration means saying the same thing *in other words*."[76] This is precisely the prob-

---

[74] Appendix 2, Preface Draft IA, p. 279 (p. 584). Barth correlates "easier language" with "easier thoughts" in Preface Draft II, pp. 283-284 (p. 590).

[75] For Barth translation is always secondary to hearing (See Barth, *Ein Versuch ihn zu verstehen*, pp. 13-15; ET pp. 88-89). This is why Barth said the fundamental problem of Neo-Protestantism is that it seeks to be an *ecclesia docens* (a "teaching church") before being an *ecclesia audiens* (a "hearing church"). It already knows *what* needs to be translated. Translation, it should come as no surprise, was the main concern of "the new hermeneutic." See James M. Robinson, *The New Hermeneutic*, p. 58f.

[76] KD I/1:364; CD I/1:345. It is interesting to compare the following quotations from Luther's *Tischreden, D. Martin Luther's Werke: kritische Gesamtausgabe* (Weimar: Hermann Böhlaus, 1912-1921): "Languages themselves do not make a theologian but they are of assistance, for it is necessary to know the subject matter before it can be expressed through languages" (2, 2758a, b, of 28 September to 23 November 1532, pp.639-640); "It is not enough to

lem with using "easier language" to paraphrase Paul. One could end up with a *metabasis eis allo genos*. The first thing to be said about Barth's notion of paraphrasing, therefore, is that it did not give him license to say something other than what Paul said. On the contrary, it obliged him to say *the same thing*.

Still, to paraphrase means to use other words. More than simply a repetition or wooden recapitulation, the purpose of a paraphrase is to express what the text says in relevant, contemporary language. Barth placed special emphasis on this in his Rom II preface: "I intend now for this first primitive attempt at paraphrase and what belongs with it to constitute only the starting point for a dialectic movement as inexorable as it is elastic, using all the crowbars and wrecking tools needed to achieve *relevant* treatment of the text."[77] But unlike other modern paraphrasers, the primary purpose in using relevant, contemporary language for Barth was not to communicate the content of Paul's message to those unfamiliar with it, nor to make it 'fresh' to those to whom it was more or less familiar, rather it was to communicate the same thoughts, ideas, and concepts in *all* their contemporary relevance to the modern situation. And here again it must be emphasized, for Barth it was not a matter of 'making' such thoughts, ideas, and concepts contemporary or relevant. They already were. Nor was it a matter of simplifying or making such thoughts, ideas, and concepts "easier" or more accessible to the modern mind. It was a matter of reproducing them in a way which reflected – in all their rich, manifold complexity – their immediate implications for the thought world of the present. This is how Barth could discuss "The Law and Romanticism" in light of Rom. 7:7-13 or "The Law and Pietism" in light of Rom.7:14-25, and many other topics such as liberalism, bolshevism, bourgeois socialism, etc. Convinced that Paul's thoughts impinged immediately upon the present, Barth felt he had no choice but to discuss such topics. This is what a commentary was for. To do anything less would be to fail to write a commentary. To do anything less would only prove that one had failed to understand what Paul actually said. This is why Barth was so adamant: "I was not able to say everything about each of the topics touched upon, but only about that which lies directly in the path of Paul's words. ... Everything is meant only as movement of the text." And it is noteworthy that at the time even severe critics acknowledged that Barth had restated many of Paul's thoughts in a remarkably penetrating way. Even Jülicher said of Rom I:

> Without losing itself in the details of scholarly exegesis, [it] reproduces the basic thoughts of that letter in the language of our time, indeed recast in the conceptual world of today, and shows its own value in steady confrontation with the religious and moral problems of the

---

know grammar but one must pay attention to the sense: for the knowledge of the subject matter brings out the meaning of the words" (4, 5002, of 21 May and 11 June 1540, p. 608).

[77] Rom II, p. xi-xii.

present day. The author has at his disposal superb gifts for attaining his goal. With passionate commitment he stands in the middle of the struggle with the problems. He did not inherit his position in the battle, but won it for himself, earnestly sought it by various solutions. He knows how to speak penetratingly, at times charmingly, and always with colorful vividness.[78]

The problem is that even though Jülicher and others could not deny the power of Barth's exegesis and many of the connections he drew between Paul's ideas and modern ones, they basically felt he had failed to reckon with the contingency of Paul's thought. To repeat Schlatter, to Barth "the word should encounter us free from all restrictions of time, and loosed from all historical conditions, 'vertically from above.'" Instead of talking about "the conviction and concerns of that Christian community to which Paul is speaking," he talks about "the religious chaos of the present."[79] Jülicher perhaps summed it up best when he said: "The great gifts of the author make it possible for him to evoke a strong impression with his transferal of the Pauline world of ideas into the present. Because he knows so precisely how it concerns him, and what the whole of truth means for him, and because he has learned to control the spirits, he forces all of Paul into his own course."[80] Jülicher's problem with Barth, in short, was that he took such "liberties" with Paul's words that his so-called "paraphrase" too often betrayed "the hand of a scribe making insertions."[81]

Barth claimed he did not wish to make insertions of his own. He said in one preface draft: "I have no message of my own, I have only statements about the message of Paul to make."[82] Yet he also recognized there was no such thing as reading out without reading in. He recognized that interpreting Paul was a matter of reckoning with various tensions. It was not only a matter of reading in and reading out or interpreting the parts in light of the whole or the whole in light of its parts, it was also a matter of saying the same thing on the one hand yet saying it in terms of its contemporary relevance on the other. It was not only a matter of entering into the meaning of the Bible but doing so according to the meaning of the Bible itself, or, as he said in his Rom II preface, it was a matter of measuring "all that *can* be said" in light of "all that *is* said" with as little as possible "left over."[83] Reckoning with these sorts of tensions did not mean that interpretation was necessarily a matter of striking a balance, however. Throughout his *Römerbrief* period Barth never expressed interest in achieving 'balance' with respect to anything. On the contrary, unlike Schleier-

---

[78] Jülicher, *Anfänge*, p. 88; ET p. 72.

[79] Schlatter, *Anfänge*, p. 145; ET p. 123.

[80] Jülicher, *Anfänge*, p. 97; ET p. 80.

[81] Jülicher, *Anfänge*, p. 89, 93; ET pp. 73, 76-77.

[82] Appendix 2, Preface Draft III, p. 287 (p. 595). "My intention was not to say this or that about a passage, but to understand and explain the Letter to the Romans." Rom II, xiv-xv.

[83] Rom II, xii.

macher for whom truth was always in the middle (as he saw it),[84] Barth believed – and nowhere is this better illustrated than in his exegesis of *Romans* – there were times when thoroughgoing onesidedness was needed. The balanced remarks of a scholar would not suffice. The bold strokes of a preacher, the hammer blows of a prophet, were necessary in order to say what Paul said. Barth did not want to say *more* than Paul said, but in order not to say *less* he believed there were points at which he had no choice but to say more.

The point is that faithfulness to the text for Barth did not mean devotion to the letter at the expense of the spirit. On the contrary, it meant that a "critique of the letter by the spirit" was "unavoidable." As he said in his preface to the third edition of his *Römerbrief*: "Faithfulness to the text necessarily demands that the ideas in the individual words of the text be expanded or contracted (either tacitly or explicitly), while formal, verbal consistency results in an obvious suppression of what should, and indeed must, be expressed."[85] This appears to be a gloss on his rather cryptic reference in his preface to Rom II to "a dialectic movement as inexorable as it is elastic," but the thrust of it is that interpretation is a matter of allowing the subject matter of the text to be the criterion by which "the ideas in the individual words of the text be expanded or contracted." All ideas, all words, are subject to expansion or contraction. The art of interpretation is the art of deciding the degree to which each needs to be expanded or contracted in light of the subject matter. Barth denied that this had to do with a *Sachkritik*, at least in Bultmann's sense. Bultmann's notion of *Sachkritik* implied playing off the spirit against the letter, concluding that "Paul himself did not always speak 'from the subject matter itself,'" in short, "playing the schoolmaster" to Paul. Rather than allowing the ideas in the individual words of the text to be *expanded* or *contracted* in light of the subject matter, it required that some be *suppressed* or even *silenced* in light of the subject matter. The presuppositions behind this kind of criticism were discussed at length in the last chapter. The point here is that Barth's notion of criticism was very different. It was not that he believed any less firmly than Bultmann that everything must be understood in light of the subject matter. It was that he believed that the primary purpose of trying to understand everything in light of the subject matter was to arrive at an understanding of the text itself. "Calvin practiced *this* type of criticism in a masterful manner," Barth said, "without neglecting the discipline which must certainly be exercised in this connection. I have not avoided the necessity of this type of criticism, as the perceptive reader will notice at once, hopefully without succumbing unrestrainedly to the accompanying danger that is bound up with it."[86] The "discipline" Barth is referring to "which must certainly be exercised in this connection" has to do with

---

[84] Barth, *Die Theologie Schleiermachers*, p. 324; ET p. 182.
[85] Rom II, preface to third edition, p. xxii.
[86] Rom II, preface to third edition, pp. xxi-xxii.

the focus Calvin kept on the text itself. The "accompanying danger that is bound up with it," to which Barth hoped he had not unrestrainedly succumbed, has to do with eisegesis.

D. Calvin as Exemplar

Calvin's name, as we have seen, appears throughout Barth's *Römerbrief* period. In his preface drafts to Rom I, Barth said that he wished "to advance the assertion that the 'uncritical' works of a Calvin or J.T. Beck are *more concerned with the subject matter* than, for example, those of Jülicher or Lietzmann," and he hoped that his own work would be seen in their trajectory.[87] In his preface to Rom II, Barth argues the superiority of Calvin's exegetical approach over Jülicher's. And as we saw above in his preface to the third edition of his *Römerbrief*, Calvin – notwithstanding his doctrine of verbal inspiration – is a model to Barth *not* because he is "uncritical" but precisely because of the "type of criticism" he employs. Barth was obviously significantly indebted to Calvin. But beyond the *Römerbrief* prefaces, where this is most apparent is in the lectures he gave on Calvin during the summer semester of 1922. Near the end of these lectures, while discussing Calvin's commentary on *Romans,* Barth describes three distinctive features of Calvin's exegetical approach which provide considerable insight into his own.

The first distinctive feature of Calvin's exegesis, according to Barth, is its "extraordinary *Sachlichkeit*":

> We can learn from Calvin what it means to stay close to the text, to focus with tense attention on what is actually there. Everything else *derives* from this. But it has to derive from *this.* If it does not, then expounding is not real questioning and readiness to listen. Calvin once wrote of Luther's exegesis that he was not too much concerned about the literal wording or the historical circumstances of the text but was content to derive fruitful doctrine from it (*Briefe*, 217). We see gentle criticism here. Calvin wanted to derive fruitful doctrine *from* the actual wording and historical circumstances, not by ignoring them. ... Thus he engaged in textual criticism insofar as he was able with the tools available. ... Nor did he shrink from higher criticism, seriously questioning the authenticity of 2 Peter and Jude, and definitely contesting Paul's authorship of Hebrews.
>
> The actual exposition follows the text word for word. Only rarely does Calvin allow himself brief digressions. Naturally he does engage in what we call eisegesis, and rightly so, for if we read nothing into the Bible we will also read nothing out of it. But whichever he is doing he keeps his eye firmly on the actual text. He proceeds methodically and steadfastly, seeking diligently to follow the text in all its twists and turns. His aim is to do justice to everything in it. ... He stays close to what is there because what is there is enough for him, because the *one* biblical truth is dear and important to him precisely in the form and

---

[87] Appendix 2, Preface Draft III, p. 288 (p. 596). "As related to its *intention*, I desire this book to stand beside the commentaries of Calvin, the forgotten Carl Heinrich Rieger (1828) and the honorable teacher of my father, J.T. Beck." Preface Draft IA, p. 278 (p. 596).

passage in which it is communicated and not in some other. ... Each passage has its own truth. Each is self-grounded. Each must be expounded in its own context. The harmony of the whole will emerge of itself without having to be more or less questionably documented in detail. What he still *reads into* the Bible at every point, in contrast to more recent historical study with which his approach must not, of course, be confused, is the unity of truth, the assumption that though there are *many* voices, in the last resort they are all seeking to say the same thing. This did not prevent him, however, from seeing what was *distinctive* as such, from finding the reason for it, and from emphasizing it and establishing its validity in its own place.[88]

The second distinctive feature of Calvin's exegetical method Barth points out is its *"uniformity"* [*Einheitlichkeit*]:

> We see this even outwardly in his commentaries in the equal way in which each word and chapter is taken up and exploited. He does not give special prominence to Romans 1-8 because these chapters are the biblical basis of Reformation soteriology. He expounds the whole epistle with the same care and attention. Nor does he stop at Romans and some other leading and central writings. Romans is for him, as he says, an entrance that has been opened up to an understanding of all scripture. In gentle criticism he complained that Melanchthon expounded only a few particularly essential chapters and because he was occupied with these he neglected many others that ought not to be neglected. If in principle it is seen to be right to listen to the Bible, then we should listen to the whole Bible.
>
> Calvin, too, of course, did allow himself some tacit exceptions. I have already mentioned Revelation. In the OT he omitted especially the works attributed to Solomon. The feeling of being engaged in battle on a long and extended front enabled him to deal with detailed passages in a relaxed and sober manner. He had his eye on the whole, and therefore did not need to break out and win victories at every point which could be in his view only sham victories. The whole of a single book and the whole of all the books speaks for itself.[89]

Finally, the third distinctive feature of Calvin's exegesis Barth singles out is its *"relevance"* [*Aktualität*] .

> This is the more striking in Calvin because his objectivity often borders on what we call historicism. At this point we see one of the tensions in which his theology is so rich. Like no other Reformation exegete, he gives free play to what is unique in each passage. He really emerges above all the others as a true biblical investigator and scholar. But then he can handle the material in such a way that we do not have the impression with him any

---

[88] Karl Barth, *Die Theologie Calvins*, ed. Hans Scholl (Zürich: Theologischer Verlag Zürich, 1992), pp. 526-528; ET *The Theology of John Calvin*, trans. Geoffrey Bromiley (Grand Rapids: William B. Eerdmans, 1995), pp. 389-391. Hereafter cited as *Die Theologie Calvins*.

[89] Barth, *Die Theologie Calvins*, pp. 528-529; ET p. 391. Barth adds, "I do not think that we should view the doctrine of verbal inspiration, which is obviously in the background here, in the rigid and mythological way in which people usually see it. What does it amount to in practice but the hypothesis that in some sense the text is trustworthy, the premise that there has to be a meaning in it, a meaning, indeed, in its wording? This premise did not prevent Calvin in fact from closely examining that trustworthiness any more than his doctrine of predestination prevented him from taking our human responsibility in bitter earnest. But it gave him also a consistent zeal to track down the content of the whole Bible, a zeal that incidentally would also stand historical investigation of the Bible in good stead."

more than with others that all we have here is mere history. History is indeed being studied, but it is also being made. It did not simply need such common expressions as "Hence we say" and "Hence we recall," or the occasional attacks on papists, monks, and schoolmen, to make clear to us that the commentary has a purpose, that something is happening in it, that a fruitful dialogue and living dialogue is in fact taking place here across the cleft of the centuries. We are in the 1st century but we are equally in the 16th. We hear Paul, and we also hear Calvin. The voices merge into one another so that we can hardly distinguish them, and we get some sense of the truth of the saying that the Spirit who spoke by the prophets must penetrate into our hearts. This relevance of Calvin's exposition, quite apart from specific applications, means that it still speaks and teaches and persuades today. We believe Calvin the more readily because he is not deliberately trying to make us believe but simply setting out what he finds in Paul, yet not, of course, without being able or even trying to hide the fact that he himself believes it. This quiet kinship between the apostle and the exegete speaks for itself.[90]

Barth concludes his discussion of Calvin's exegesis with the following comments which show the extent of Calvin's influence upon him:

We have to read Calvin attentively, of course, if we are to profit from him. At a glance most of us might find him rather tedious. Initially his thoroughness, restraint, and uniformity seem overdone. But finally, especially when we compare him enough with others, we are grateful for these qualities and rejoice to see how here and there between the lines of the commentaries there can be just as powerful lightning flashes as in Luther, but with the advantage that we never lose sight of the primary goal of exposition as we often do in Luther. Whenever I have myself consulted Calvin's commentaries for my own use,[91] I have found pleasure in his distinctive combination of historical and pneumatic exegesis even when I have permitted myself to go my own way. His work not only provided an external model for my own special study of Romans but also laid a firm foundation for its content.[92]

These three features of Calvin's exegesis to which Barth calls attention go a long way in summarizing much that has been discussed throughout this study. Each of these features is clearly manifest in Barth's own exegetical approach. But given all that has been said about Barth's relationship to Calvin, particularly in light of Barth's explicit rejection of Calvin's doctrine of *verbal* inspiration prior to 1915 and the enthusiasm he expressed at the same time for Luther's exegetical approach as discussed in the previous chapter, it appears that the most important thing Calvin taught Barth was to focus on the text itself. Granted Barth remained interested in the "powerful lightning flashes" that Luther's exegesis so often yields even if it does sometimes stray from the literal sense of the text (which Barth refers to as "Luther's merry chasing after

---

[90] Barth, *Die Theologie Calvins*, p. 530; ET p. 392.

[91] Hans Scholl adds: "The form of this statement rests on a pencil correction, Barth made in the MS. He originally wrote: 'As one who for years has never preached without consulting Calvin's commentaries I can finally do no more than bear witness that I have always found pleasure in this distinctive combination of historical and pneumatic exegesis even when ...'" Barth, *Die Theologie Calvins*, p. 531 n. 24; ET pp. 392-393 n. 23.

[92] Barth, *Die Theologie Calvins*, pp. 530-531; ET pp. 392-393.

deer").[93] But what clearly distinguishes Barth's exegetical approach after 1915 which is so characteristic of Calvin's is that it aims never to "lose sight of the primary goal of exposition," which is to understand "the meaning of the text itself."

---

[93] Barth, *Die Theologie Calvins*, pp. 531, 528; ET pp. 392, 390.

Chapter 7
Conclusion

Karl Barth's attempt to overcome the hermeneutical tradition of Schleiermacher did not end at the conclusion of his *Römerbrief* period. As I mentioned in the Introduction, in his 1923/24 course on Schleiermacher, Barth lectured on his hermeneutics "because here we shall have the chance to get to know Schleiermacher at his best and most brilliant, in his natural strength, on his home ground, for, to use his own expression, he was a virtuoso in the field whose method hermeneutics describes."[1] His analysis of Schleiermacher's hermeneutics here, as I said, is as sharply nuanced and erudite as one can find in the early 1920s. But the main problem, according to Barth, is that for all its sophistication and breadth, for all its insight into the manifold problems of understanding and the mystery of individuality, it fails to do justice to the freedom of the Word of God or man as a hearer of it. "Apart from this fourfold expository method" of balancing the grammatical and the psychological, the comparative and the divinatory sides of interpretation, Schleiermacher makes the "momentous declaration" that "there is no other."[2] In other words, "Schleiermacher's hermeneutics not only has not enough idea but no idea at all what to make of the concept of inspiration."[3] Barth concludes:

> How very simply and triumphantly Schleiermacher deals with the ancient doctrine of inspiration. He seems not to have known, considered, or at any rate understood it except in the crude form that the biblical authors were recording instruments of the Holy Spirit. It is eliminated along with poor allegorizing and the spirit-theory of Ast, and Schleiermacher's system prevails. How remarkable that he does not seem to have considered the possibility that the thought which I understand in what is said by someone else, whether with or without his system or any other hermeneutics, might be contingently, without any qualitative or quantitative possibilities of misunderstanding, the truth or Word of God, and that I should then have good reason to treat this address more specifically and more seriously than any other as the bearer of this content, a reference to this subject. What if special New Testament hermeneutics, whether gratefully employing Schleiermacher's method or any other general method, were to consist quite simply of taking these texts more seriously in this specific sense? Why should not God have spoken to man in a way that is necessarily and

---

[1] Barth, *Die Theologie Schleiermachers*, p. 318; ET p. 178.
[2] Barth, *Die Theologie Schleiermachers*, p. 325; ET p. 182.
[3] Barth, *Die Theologie Schleiermachers*, p. 314; ET p. 175.

compellingly understandable as God makes it so? If God is God? But here we come up against the frontier which we do not pass in Schleiermacher or in his tracks.[4]

The reason "Schleiermacher's system proves a match for the Holy Spirit,"[5] or at least purports to be, in Barth's view, is because it tries to substitute something else for the inspiration of the Holy Spirit. I have tried to give an account of what that *something else* is in tracing the empathetic tradition of interpretation. I have also tried to suggest that Schleiermacher's aversion to the doctrine of inspiration is, at least in part, understandable. As a child of Romanticism, Schleiermacher had a deep appreciation not only for the great mystery of human individuality and personality but for the enormous power of the human imagination and of human creativity. He simply could not embrace a doctrine which, as he saw it, docetically demeaned human thought and action, annulled human freedom and creativity, and made human authors "merely passive tools of the Holy Spirit."[6] Moreover, he was also enough of a child of the Enlightenment to be suspicious of any concept that deferred to the Holy Spirit while at the same time suspending all philological and historical rules (which Gadamer claims is one of the main reasons he tried to construct a general hermeneutic).[7] In short, Schleiermacher saw the doctrine of inspiration as dehumanizing, and like Herder before him, strove to achieve a more fully human reading of the Bible.[8] Yet on a different front, he also strove, according to Barth, to prevent the wholesale collapse of theology into history which he saw as perhaps an even greater threat.[9] He knew that what was really at issue in theology was beyond history and psychology, and he firmly refused to reduce it to either. Nevertheless, despite his reputation as a theologian of the third article, Schleiermacher could not ultimately, in Barth's view, keep the work of the Holy Spirit "from being confused with a mode of human cognition."[10] I have

---

[4] Barth, *Die Theologie Schleiermachers*, pp. 326-327; ET p. 183.

[5] Barth, *Die Theologie Schleiermachers*, p. 326; ET p. 182.

[6] Schleiermacher, *Hermeneutik*, p. 85; ET p. 107.

[7] Gadamer, "The Problem of Language in Schleiermacher's Hermeneutic," pp. 83-84.

[8] Rather than as inspired, "every element must be treated as purely human." Schleiermacher, *Hermeneutik*, p. 84; ET p. 106. As to Herder, see Barth, *Die protestantische Theologie im 19.Jahrhundert*, p. 298; ET p. 218.

[9] Barth, *Die protestantische Theologie im 19. Jahrhundert*, p. 384; ET p. 311.

[10] Barth, *Die protestantische Theologie im 19. Jahrhundert*, pp. 414f; ET pp. 343f. In fairness to Schleiermacher, Barth's deeper, systematic concern was: "A pure teaching of the Word will take into account the Holy Spirit as the divine reality in which the Word is heard. ... It was with this thought in mind that the Reformers propagated the teaching of the Word of God in its correlation with faith as the work of the Holy Spirit in man. ... Schleiermacher reversed the order of this thought. What interests him is the question of man's action in regard to God. We must not condemn him for this out of hand. If we call to mind the entire situation of theology in the modern world then we shall find it understandable that it fastened upon the point which had come to the center of the entire thought of modern man" (pp.410-411; ET p.340). Nevertheless, "*The Word is not so assured here in its independence in respect to faith as should be*

discussed that mode of human cognition in the course of this study in terms of divination, genius, *Kongenialität*, and *Einfühlung* and it was just such a mode of human cognition Barth himself had in mind when he spoke in 1910/12 of a "psychological-historical vehicle that makes the direct *apprehensio Christi in corde* possible."

Barth's break with liberalism, I have argued, involved a break with the empathetic tradition of interpretation. Although his famous statement in his preface to Rom II – "As one who would understand, I must press forward to the point where insofar as possible I confront the riddle of the *subject matter* and no longer merely the riddle of the *document* as such, until I can almost forget that I am not the author, until I have almost understood him so well that I let him speak in my name, and can myself speak in his name" – might appear to betray this claim, closer examination of it, particularly in light of the preface drafts to Rom I, actually confirms that what is really at issue here is something beyond divination, *Einfühlung*, or *Kongenialität*. And further confirmation that this is really what is at issue in this statement comes after the *Römerbrief* period in his Göttingen lectures on dogmatics. In his last major subsection on his chapter on "The Word of God as Holy Scripture," Barth discusses the concept of freedom, individual believers' freedom which is historical, relative, and formal freedom, and the direct, absolute, and material freedom which can be ascribed only to Scripture as God's Word. He claims that Christian freedom, in contrast to secular notions of freedom, is always related to authority, and that in contrast to modern Protestants who tend to identify Roman Catholicism with authority and Protestantism with freedom, "the original Reformation had an idea of authority and freedom according to which the two do not confront one another partially, quantitatively, and competitively but are conjoined in a dialectical unity as the objective and subjective possibility of the same thing."[11] To put it concretely, when it comes to understanding Scripture as the Word of God, there are historical authorities and historical freedoms that individual believers ought to recognize. On the one hand, there are the concrete historical events and circumstances recorded and collected through the witness of the prophets and apostles. On the other hand, there are the pictures I reconstruct of

---

the case if this theology of faith were a true theology of the Holy Spirit. In a proper theology of the Holy Spirit there could be no question of dissolving the Word. Here, quite seriously, there is a question of such a dissolution. The only thing which prevents it is Schleiermacher's good will in not allowing things to develop so far. This good will must once again be formally acknowledged, but that in no way alters the fact that we feel ourselves here in all seriousness threatened by this dissolution. Thus it seems necessary for us after all to begin to consider whether what has happened here is that it is not the Holy Spirit, but, as Schleiermacher claims, merely man's religious consciousness which has after all become the theme of theology. In some depth of his mind Schleiermacher must have intended otherwise" (pp. 422-423; ET pp. 352-353).

[11] Barth, *Unterricht*, p. 307; ET p. 252.

these historical events and circumstances (the relativity and necessity of which I discussed in the last chapter). On the one hand, there are the creeds and confessions of the church which should indeed serve as historical authorities for me. On the other hand, there are "the ineluctabilities of my thinking," the fact that no matter how sophisticated or primitive, no matter how much a free and independent thinker I may think myself to be and may actually be, I always bring, for better or for worse, a philosophy to every text I read.[12] Finally, there is on the one hand, "the church's teaching office," e.g., the lights of Calvin and Luther, *et al.*, and "over against this authority, on the side of freedom," Barth says, there is "the concept of prophecy." He describes it as such:

> I mean by this what secularists might call congeniality [Kongenialität] with the witnesses of revelation and what yesterday I described as thinking the thoughts of Scripture for oneself. In the second edition of my Romans I caused some offense by saying that in exposition a point is reached when I almost forget that I am not the author, since I almost understand him so well that I can have him speak in my name or can even speak in his. This is what I have in mind here. The sharpest historical observation and the most intensive thinking after and thinking with do not help me at all if first and last there does not enter in something of this identification between me and the author, the author and me. I number this among the relative conditions of hearing. Over against this congeniality the absolute freedom with which the Spirit gives witness that the Spirit speaks the truth is something different. But in the relative sphere this congeniality should not be overlooked as the last and concluding definition of the concept of freedom. With it the whole process of hearing finally moves out of the empirical sphere and the reflective sphere into the existential sphere. I do not merely investigate or think. No, the witness to revelation now appears to me in this very special light. Historical distance and conceptual abstraction are overcome. The witness becomes for me a Word, a Word for the hour. Even as I do this, Romans, which I observe and reflect on, becomes a letter to me and a letter which I must now write to the people of Göttingen and to anyone who will listen.[13]

Here Barth not only returns to one of the most controversial statements of his *Römerbrief* period but to the place where everything turns, where his theological revolution was born. Historical investigation of the Bible is not enough! Schleiermacher knew that. Something more is needed. But what? Identification with the biblical author. Yes, but what kind of identification? *Empathetic* identification or that achieved by some sort of psychological or aesthetic *Kongenialität*? "Secularists," Barth says, might call it that. But prophetic identification with the author is a very different matter, even if there is a kind of secular analogy to it. But beyond this, Barth's point – the point around which his entire discussion of freedom and Scripture as the Word of God turns – is that even a sanctified sort of congeniality or empathy born of prayer and learned in

---

[12] Barth adds: "True hearing of the Word in Scripture depends upon my thinking something in relation to what I hear. I cannot maintain that what I think is Christian philosophy. It bears too plainly the marks of human and profane philosophy. But I can and should *hope* that it is." *Unterricht*, p. 317; ET p. 260.

[13] Barth, *Unterricht*, pp. 318; ET pp. 260-261 [translation slightly revised].

the school of the Holy Spirit is not enough. Why? Because: "Over against this congeniality the absolute freedom with which the Spirit gives witness that the Spirit speaks the truth is something different." No amount of empathy or congeniality can substitute for the inward illumination of the Holy Spirit. No exegetical method, no matter how learned, loving, or spiritual, can substitute for that moment "in which the Spirit speaks to spirit."[14] The Word of God is free and we cannot force Holy Scripture to speak to us as such.

Still, Barth insists that this 'congeniality,' which cannot be understood as such but only as a concept of prophecy, "should not be overlooked as the last concluding definition of the concept of freedom." To be sure, identifying with an author in such a way "is not at all a personal aspiration which someone might have, nor is it, of course, something for which one has to be specifically a theologian. We have here a category that applies wherever there is real hearing of the Word."[15] Nor does it mean that we become prophets or confuse ourselves with the apostle Paul or put our witness on a level with his. "The only thing is that the Word is certainly not heard if hearing does not reach a climax in this *moment* in relation to which all observation and reflection can be no more than *preparation*." But even here Barth states, "It is essential that over against this last and supreme freedom there should stand directly as a corrective the last and supreme authority of the church in its office as present-day watchman and teacher."

> If we are clear about this, about the relativity of this last and supreme freedom, not erasing the boundary but realizing and considering that I am saying this, not the Lord [cf. I Cor.7:12], even at the moment when I seem to stand on the same level as Scripture in my understanding and reception and further witness; if I keep in mind the distance which unconditionally separates even this moment of congenial freedom – Christian freedom, we hope – from the absolute freedom of the Word itself, then there can be no talk of enthusiasm or the like without doing harm to the living character of the Word. Instead, we may then see that even in this final matter we do not merely have a permission but an unconditional demand.[16]

The point, in short, is this: if congenial or empathetic identification with an author is no substitute for the prophetic, "congenial," Christian freedom learned in the school of the Holy Spirit, then it is certainly no substitute for the absolute freedom of the Word of God itself. But there is a freedom for which we as hearers of the Word of God have been set free, and that freedom, "The freedom of the children of God," as Barth later said, "begins only where the freedom, which we think we experience in our humanity, ends."[17]

---

[14] Barth, *Unterricht*, p. 308; ET p. 253.
[15] Barth, *Unterricht*, pp. 318-319; ET p. 261.
[16] Barth, *Unterricht*, p. 319; ET pp. 261-262.
[17] KD I/2:447; CD I/2:405.

Barth continued to emphasize this theme of freedom and contemporaneity with the prophets and apostles throughout his career. In his *Christian Dogmatics*, again with reference to his famous statement in his preface to Rom II about almost forgetting that he is not the author, he repeats almost word for word what he said above in his Göttingen lectures.[18] In his *Church Dogmatics* he elaborates it even further, though in greater contrast to the secular concept of *Kongenialität*.[19] In the *Church Dogmatics*, however, Barth claims that achieving contemporaneity with the prophets and apostles and interpreting them as contemporaries has been one of the chief preoccupations of modern theologians. It is the reason "they think they have discovered the revelation of God in history afresh for the first time properly in emancipation from the rigid antithesis of the old Church and theology."[20] "Lessing," he claims, "is the epoch-making name in this regard" because, for all his talk about an "'ugly, wide ditch'" (between the Bible and us), of which he said in a well-known passage "... that he could not jump across," the fact is: "Lessing could make this jump. So could Herder and *Schleiermacher* after him, and others up to A. Ritschl, and Harnack, Lagarde and *Troeltsch*, always with increased excellence and skill." Although Lessing rightly saw that the "problem was the lack of contemporaneity between Christ, the apostles, and us. ... He abandoned it for an immanent lack of contemporaneity that could be overcome by way of immanence. From now on all the more lively thinkers, in contrast to the Enlightenment and Kant, found no further difficulty or stumbling block in interpreting revelation as history and history as revelation."[21] This "way of immanence" that overcomes the "ugly, wide ditch" between the Bible and us is, of course, something richly complex and multifaceted. But concretely, with respect to achieving contemporaneity with Christ and the prophets and apostles, it has to do with a hermeneutical skill which presupposes a common anthropology and is based on our ability to identify with other personalities, especially, other *religious* personalities. This is what I tried to describe earlier in tracing the empathetic tradition of interpretation. But the point Barth makes in this passage is that beyond these efforts to achieve contemporaneity with Christ and the prophets and apostles by "way of immanence," there is another way.

Barth claims that the Word of God creates its own hearer and overcomes the "ugly, wide ditch" between Christ, the prophets and apostles, and us, from an entirely different direction. It is a way which does not deny the value of hermeneutical skill, but neither is it dependent on it, for, as he says, "When God's Word is heard and proclaimed, something takes place that for all our herme-

---

[18] Barth, *Die christliche Dogmatik*, pp. 527-529. This appears under the rubric of "3. Die Momente der konkreten Freiheit" in §22 "Die Freiheit des Gewissens."

[19] KD I/1:150f.; CD I/1:145f.; KD I/2:784; CD I/2:700f.

[20] KD I/1:151; CD I/1:146 [translation slightly revised].

[21] KD I/1:152; CD I/1:147.

neutical skill cannot be brought about by hermeneutical skill."[22] Nor is it a way which denies genuine historical understanding or any of the tools that can be properly employed to achieve it. "Here again," Barth insists, "there is and has to be a specific relation of historical understanding with all the relevant components from philological analysis to the so-called art of empathy [*zur Kunst der sogenannten Einfühlung*]. Proclamation is possible only in this relation of understanding, just as there could be prophecy and the apostolate only in a specific relation of understanding."

> But in this relation proclamation of the Word of God does not come about through the individual or corporate components of the relation, e.g., through philological perspicacity or the most ingenius or refined empathy [*die genialste oder raffinierteste Einfühlung*]. It comes about solely and simply through the power of the biblical Word itself, which now makes a place for itself in a very different time, and becomes the content of this place, as Paul steps forth in proclamation, not as a religious personality, but as an apostle of Jesus Christ, so that Jesus Himself is present in him. As the Word of God is this act, then in this step from revelation to Scripture and then to the proclamation of the Church, in a full and strict differentiation of the times, it is one, it is contemporaneous.[23]

At the beginning of this study, I suggested that before pronouncing any final verdict on Barth's contribution as an exegete, we might find it worthwhile to consider once again what he "was really trying to do, what he was up against and trying to overcome, and see if there are specific exegetical principles he employed which might still be worthy of our attention." I am convinced that the exegetical principles of Barth's *Römerbrief* period are as important and relevant today as ever, and this is why. In his widely celebrated 1962 essay on "Contemporary Biblical Theology" in which he sharply criticized Barth for failing to keep "alive the tension between what the text meant and what it means," Krister Stendahl asserts: "What emerged [out of the "history of religions school" at the end of the nineteenth and beginning of the twentieth century] was a descriptive study of biblical thought – empathetic in the sense that it was beyond sympathy or antipathy. This was actually a new phenomenon in biblical studies, and yet it came as a mature outgrowth of the historical and critical study of the Scriptures."[24] Stendahl, I believe, is right. This was a relatively new phenomenon in biblical studies, at least in terms of the extent to which it was applied. But the empathetic approach to interpretation which Stendahl praised in 1962, in my estimation, is as pervasive today among rank and file scholars in biblical and religious studies departments throughout this country and Europe as ever, and with it the same historicizing and psychologizing assumptions.

---

[22] KD I/1:153; CD I/1:148.
[23] KD I/1:154; CD I/1:149.
[24] Krister Stendahl, "Biblical Theology: A Program," p. 418f..

Of course, recently, in the wake of 'post-modern' approaches to interpretation, there has been, despite its predominance, somewhat of a trend away from the empathetic approach and its tendency toward historical and psychological reductionism. In particular, *deconstruction*, which can be seen in part as a reaction to if not a rather drastic *over*reaction against the empathetic tradition of interpretation, has served to remind (or should remind) Christian readers – not in spite of but because of its tendency to deny or "bracket" such notions as meaning or truth – that what is written and what is written about are two different things, and that *our* attempt to move "from text to truth or from language to reality," as Hans Frei once said, "is almost always premature."[25] Yet here too, and perhaps especially here, Karl Barth's hermeneutical principles are worthy of our attention.

In Chapter 2, I mentioned a series of lectures Barth delivered on the Apostles' Creed in Utrecht, Holland in February and March of 1935.[26] At the end of these lectures, Barth responded to ten questions put to him by those in attendance. Two of the ten questions, as I said earlier, had to do with his exegetical method and the second specifically with his understanding of the relationship of "theological exegesis" to the "science of history." Barth's response to an especially concrete form of this latter question I believe is instructive:

> And now in this connection one of you has put to me concretely the specifically Dutch question, whether the serpent in Paradise 'really' spoke? – I would oppose characterizing this incident as 'myth.' No more can I, on the other hand, characterize it, in the sense of historical science, as 'historical' ['*historische*'], for I am as little able to imagine a speaking serpent (apart from everything else!) as anyone. But I should like to ask the dear friends of the speaking serpent whether it would not be better to hold fast to the fact that "it is written" and to go on and interest themselves in *what* the serpent said? To me they appear to be very important and momentous words that I should not like under any circumstances to miss from the Bible. The serpent's speech is indeed the invitation to man to face God with the question so significant for the very problem of theological exegesis: "Hath God said?" Where this question is heard, there a man *must* have the idea of being as God, there the fruit *must* be eaten. There he stands reflecting over the Word of God, and to that Word he will then most certainly not be obedient. The attitude of standing over it apologetically, should

---

[25] "At the very least," Frei adds, "the Christian reader has to stop soberly in front of a barrier that in its own way is as impenetrable as the 'death strips' that separate two countries at cold war with one another." Hans W. Frei, "Conflicts in Interpretation: Resolution, Armistice, or Co-existence" in *Theology & Narrative: Selected Essays*, editors George Hunsinger and William C. Placher (Oxford: University Press, 1993), p.163. I might add that for Frei, Barth, and others committed to biblical realism, the reason our attempt to move "from text to truth or from language to reality is almost always premature" is not because God has not spoken clearly but because "all men are liars" (Psalm 116:11. See also Romans 3:4 and *The Confessions of St. Augustine*, bk. xiii, ch. 25).

[26] See pp. 30-31 above.

be given up. The fact that we do not give it up proves very palpably that the serpent has really spoken, yes, indeed![27]

Many conservatives both in this country and abroad have interpreted Barth's response to this question as "pure subjectivism" and as proof that Barth did not take history seriously.[28] The problem, of course, is that such critics have often not understood that the modern "science of history" works only on the basis of analogy with the present and that there is thus a distinction to be made between *Historie* and *Geschichte*.[29] But it must be said that conservative critics are not the only ones who have been dissatisfied with Barth's response here. Emil Brunner, a "neo-orthodox" theologian if there ever was one, referred to Barth's response above as "a clever evasion of the problem."[30] And it is easy to see why he would. Brunner, who understands the distinction between *Historie* and *Geschichte* very well, opposes Barth's juxtaposition of a theology of the Word of God versus a so-called "natural theology" which is implied in Barth's statement above, i.e., a theology which begins with the Word of God written versus a theology which begins with "the idea of being as God"; a theology which holds "fast to the fact that 'it is written'" versus a theology which, at least in Barth's view, begins with preconceived notions as to what constitutes reality and then – taken as real, incontrovertible knowledge – proceeds to interrogate with the question, "Hath God said?"; a theology which begins with *trust* in God's Word rather than *mistrust*, a theology which stands *under* the Word rather than *over* the Word.

Barth's point – at least his immediate point with respect to whether the serpent in Paradise "really" spoke – is that rather than *speculating* on *how* a serpent might speak or *what* a speaking serpent might look like (which a number of contemporary Dutch theologians were quite willing to do,[31] which is why he refers to it as a "specifically Dutch question") – it is "better to hold fast to the fact that 'it is written'..." In other words, it is better to allow a bit of "breath-

---

[27] Barth, *Credo*, pp. 163-164; ET pp. 190-191 [translation slightly revised].

[28] Klaas Runia, *Karl Barth's Doctrine of Holy Scripture* (Grand Rapids: William B. Eerdmans, 1962) pp. 100f.; Heinrich Jochums, *Die grosse Enttäuschung: Karl Barth und die Theologien, Philosophien, Anthropologien und Ideologien der Gegenwart, sonderlich im deutschen Sprachraum* (Wuppertal: Verlag und Schriftenmission der Evangelischen Gesellschaft für Deutschland, 1986), p.65; Lothar Gassmann, *Karl Barth: Das Verhängnis der Dialektik*, (Berneck: Schwengeler-Verlag, 1995), pp. 40-41, et al.

[29] Barth refers to this bone of contention between himself and conservative American critics in the "Foreword to the American Edition" of his *Evangelical Theology: An Introduction*, p.xi. As to the significance of this distinction for Barth, see above pp. 103-104.

[30] Emil Brunner, *Man in Revolt*, trans. Olive Wyon (Philadelphia: Westminster Press, 1947), p. 88.

[31] According to Klaas Runia, there was a controversy in the Reformed Church in Holland in 1926 over this matter which was sparked by "Dr. J.G. Geelkerken, who assumed the possibility that Gen.3 had not to be taken literally." He was subsequently 'condemned.' *Karl Barth's Doctrine of Holy Scripture*, p. 101 n. 53.

ing space" (as Hans Frei calls it) between what is written and what is written about and, without succumbing at all to the temptation to mythologize the account, to permit the Holy Spirit to disclose what the real referent of the text is – to reveal the connection between text and truth – and to accept it as such, which means focusing on the *sachlicher, inhaltlicher, wesentlicher* issue of "*what* the serpent said."

The larger point, however, and the reason I think Barth's hermeneutical principles are so important today, is because – amid all our continuing preoccupation with all that lies behind the text (e.g., the author's context) and now all our preoccupation with all that lies in front of the text (e.g., the reader's context) – Barth calls us, once again, to pay attention to *the text itself*. He calls us, once again, to take the words of the Bible seriously. And because there is *by grace* – which means always beyond our control – a possibility (indeed, the promise) of a fit or correspondence between what is written in the Bible and what is written about, he has reminded us that we have good reason for trying to take the words of others seriously as well, even if our attempt to proceed on the basis of a hermeneutics of trust sometimes forces us to invoke an "emergency clause."

I am convinced that we are still a long way from understanding all that Barth has to teach us about theological exegesis and absolutely certain that the principles of exegesis I have attempted to elucidate in this study do not begin to exhaust the richness of Barth's approach to the task of interpretation. There is a great deal more to be said about Barth's hermeneutics, particularly in light of his development after his *Römerbrief* period and his more formal elaboration of his move from special to general hermeneutics in the *Church Dogmatics*. But if there was ever a time when the Church needed to rediscover *theological* exegesis as Barth understood it (even in his *Römerbrief* period), and if there was ever a time when the Church and the academy needed to approach the Bible "more in accordance with its subject matter, content, and substance, entering with more attention and love into the meaning of the Bible itself," it seems to me that that time is now.

Appendix 1

The Historical Background of the Preface to the First Edition of Barth's *Römerbrief*

Karl Barth's struggle to write a preface for his commentary began in the spring and lasted throughout the summer of 1918, and the preface was not completed until the last week of August, only days before his publisher's deadline of September 1. Four years earlier, in October of 1914, he had experienced the greatest cataclysm of his life, which was brought to a head by his discovery that ninety-three German intellectuals had signed a manifesto supporting the war policy of the Kaiser and among the signatories were several of his teachers under whom he had studied in Germany. It was in the aftermath of this discovery, as Barth later described it, that "an entire world of theological exegesis, ethics, dogmatics, and preaching, which up to that point I had accepted as basically credible, was thereby shaken to the foundations, and with it everything which flowed at that time from the pens of the German theologians." Barth said of himself and Eduard Thurneysen, "We made a fresh attempt to learn our theological ABCs all over again. More reflectively than ever before, we began reading and expounding the writings of the Old and New Testaments. And behold, they began to speak to us – very differently than we had supposed we were obliged to hear them speak in the school of what was then called 'modern' theology."[1] Shortly thereafter, in the summer of 1916,[2] with the sound of bombshells exploding on the distant horizon, Barth said, "I sat down under an apple tree and began, with all the tools at my disposal, to apply myself to the Epistle to the Romans." Two years later, he produced a "bombshell" of his own, as his commentary was later famously described.[3]

Writing the *Römerbrief* had not been easy for Barth. Though he said in his final preface that he had written his commentary with a certain "joy of discovery," this phrase – the one most often repeated by early reviewers of the first edition – he later admitted, had been stated "somewhat romantically."[4] This is

---

[1] Barth, "Nachwort," pp. 293-294; ET pp. 263-264.
[2] In a letter from Barth to Thurneysen, Thurneysen inserts an editorial note: "We decided on a walk to set a course for some revolutionary theological studies. Soon thereafter Barth began with the exegesis of *Romans*." Karl Barth to Eduard Thurneysen, 26 June, 1916, *B-Th. Br. I*, p. 145 n. 1.
[3] See p. 42n.127 above.
[4] See pp. 18-19 above.

corroborated by his correspondence with Thurneysen. Between July 19, 1916 and December 12, 1918, Barth's work on his *Römerbrief* is mentioned in these letters no less than sixty-two times, and they provide an interesting perspective on the circumstances surrounding its genesis. A few of his remarks in these letters, as he claimed, reflect moments which do seem characterized by a certain "joy of discovery," particularly when, for example, he makes discoveries which he regards as having been ignored by modern commentators,[5] or when he is surprised by what he discovers in older commentators.[6] Yet at least as often do his letters reflect moments of deep perplexity and frustration. For example, on September 1, 1916, Barth writes, "I am presently at my wits end over the *Römerbrief* at the granite boulders in 3:20ff. What all is behind it, I will hardly be able to discover and lift out with this first attempt."[7] On March 8, 1917, "In Romans 4 still a few mighty blocks are surfacing."[8] On November 1, he writes, "I am in a fix with my preparations for Romans 6-8."[9] On December 17, "With respect to the *Römerbrief*, I am [now] in a terrible fix."[10] On February 6, 1918, he reports "I am deep into the commentary at [chs.] 9-11, but I see no land at all in sight; very strange things are stated there."[11] Sometimes his letters reflect little more than the groanings of slow, plodding labor: "I am right now working through the most boring studies of Weiß, Godet, Lipsius ... in order to acquire the right and possibility of exegeting Rom. 5."[12] Other times he expresses astonishment at how much more there still is to be discovered in *Romans*.[13] But beyond perplexity and frustration, clearly the most common sentiment Barth expresses in writing his commentary is a sense of

---

[5] E.g., "I am working day in and day out at Rom.6-8 and still have a lot of work ahead until I can go to the interpretation. ... I am reading in the evenings modern theologians on Paul and I am more and more amazed about a world that allows all this to happen and also about the patience and forbearance of God who could have long ago declared an end to all this through an earthquake." Karl Barth to Thurneysen, 26 Oct., 1917, *B-Th. Br.* I, p. 238 or "The work on Rom.3 will soon come to an end. I am surprised about all the exegetes who actually overlooked the context of this chapter. Or is it finicky if I see the *pistis theou* in v.3 as key to the whole?" Karl Barth to Thurneysen, 23 Oct, 1916, *B-Th. Br.* I, pp. 159-160.

[6] E.g. "Discovered a gold mine: J.T. Beck!! As a Bible-interpreter he is simply towering over the rest of the guild, also above Schlatter and he is also for us implicitly in his systematic ways partly accessible again and exemplary. I discovered him through the Römerbrief and want to follow him there in the context with the others from Calvin to Tholuck ... a whole cloud of witnesses." 27 July 1916, *B-Th. Br.* I, p. 148 or "And now I have taken up again my journey through [chs.] 9-11. What shall become of this? I am just now working at Calvin who is here at his best." Karl Barth to Eduard Thurneysen, 23 Jan. 1918, *B-Th. Br.* I, p. 260.

[7] Karl Barth to Eduard Thurneysen, 1 Sept., 1916, *B-Th. Br.* I, p. 152.
[8] Karl Barth to Eduard Thurneysen, 8 March, 1917, *B-Th. Br.* I, p. 180.
[9] Karl Barth to Eduard Thurneysen, 1 Nov., 1917, *B-Th. Br.* I, p. 241.
[10] Karl Barth to Eduard Thurneysen, 17 Dec., 1917, *B-Th. Br.* I, p. 252.
[11] Karl Barth to Eduard Thurneysen, 3 Feb., 1918, *B-Th. Br.* I, p. 264.
[12] Karl Barth to Eduard Thurneysen, 27 July, 1917, *B-Th. Br.* I, p. 220.
[13] Karl Barth to Eduard Thurneysen, 27 Sept., 1917, *B-Th. Br.* I, p. 236.

awe and bewilderment. Throughout his letters, he uses terms such as: "strange" (*fremd*),[14] "curious" (*merkwürdig*),[15] "mysterious" (*geheimnisvoll*),[16] "peculiar" (*seltsam*),[17] "astonishing" (*erstaunlich*)[18], even "dangerous" (*gefährlich*)[19] to describe what he finds while exegeting *Romans*.[20] I have already discussed at length what it was he discovered as so strange, so mysterious, etc.[21] But what he says in his early preface drafts to Rom I stands in sharp contrast to the "joy of discovery" he spoke of in his final preface:

> The certain horror of modern readers before the monotone rhythm of Pauline thoughts is thoroughly understandable to me ... The task of understanding Paul verse by verse has been ... an assault upon me and the whole of today's thought and sensibilities. ... I had to write entire chapters and sections entirely against myself. ... [It] is embarrassing enough for me yet it could not be avoided [that] I had to set my speech next to Paul's as if I were really permitted to say what Paul said. ... It has been afflicting and humiliating for me to venture so close as I have to the fire ... in face of the gravity of Paul's pronouncements I would have gladly hidden in some kind of anonymity if that would have fundamentally changed the situation.[22]

Overwhelmed by the magnitude of the project he had undertaken, by the "rich treasures" of *Romans* yet untapped, and by the sheer "gravity of Paul's pronouncements," he wrote to Thurneysen as his work drew near completion on February 11, 1918, "My *Römerbrief* often seems to me a virtual tower of Babel. Perhaps it would be better to ceremoniously burn it in the end rather than let it be printed. Does the dear God really want this scribble. It is merely another new theology."[23] Thurneysen replied the next day, February 12, consolingly, "Under no circumstances may you burn the *Römerbrief*, perhaps in the preface you can provide a hearty little oration which would prevent it from being understood only 'theologically.' But the *Römerbrief* itself will already

---

[14] Karl Barth to Eduard Thurneysen, 12 June, 1918, *B-Th. Br.* I, p. 281.
[15] Karl Barth to Eduard Thurneysen, 24 April, 1918, *B-Th. Br:* I, p. 274
[16] Karl Barth to Eduard Thurneysen, 12 June, 1918, *B-Th. Br.* I, p. 281.
[17] Karl Barth to Eduard Thurneysen, 3 Feb.,1918, *B-Th. Br.* I, p. 264.
[18] Karl Barth to Eduard Thurneysen, 25 March, 1918, *B-Th. Br.* I, p. 271.
[19] Karl Barth to Eduard Thurneysen, 1 Sept., 1916, *B-Th. Br.* I, p. 152.
[20] It is worth noting that Paul's other letters evoked a similar response: With reference to *First Corinthians* 15, Barth states: "I am in haste for the time being to close the New Testament at this point and to busy myself with passages in which the fire does not burn so disturbingly." Karl Barth to Eduard Thurneysen, 11 Nov., 1919, *B-Th. Br.* I, p. 350; "*Second Corinthians* sweeps over me like a torrent. Only the smallest part can flow on in the form of sermons," 31 May, 1920, *B-Th. Br.* I, p. 392; "I am doing my preparatory work on II Corinthians 5. That is indeed a chapter! If only one could succeed even a little in letting such passages speak once more. It is all packed full of 'insights and vistas,' but how hard it is to grasp them!" 16 June 1920, *B-Th. Br.* I, p. 399.
[21] See pp. 186-187 above.
[22] Appendix 2, Preface Draft IA - Preface III, pp. 290, 289 (pp. 587, 591, 597-598), passim, italics mine.
[23] Karl Barth to Eduard Thurneysen, 11 Feb., 1918, *B-Th Br.* I, p. 265.

take care of that."[24] This brief exchange is interesting not only for the insight it provides into the depths of Barth's frustration while writing the *Römerbrief*, but also because of what it says about the specific challenge both he and Thurneysen recognized they were facing. Both were aware of how provocative their particular *method* of exegesis would likely appear to their contemporaries, and it is precisely this that Barth recognized he needed to address in his preface. From Thurneysen's response above, it appears that a major source of Barth's concern, even months before writing his first preface draft, was over how his commentary *as a commentary* would be received. His concern was that his commentary would be summarily dismissed as merely an abstract or eccentric 'theological' reading of Paul's *Romans*, that it might be regarded as a highly original and creative theological treatise written in the name of a 'commentary' but was not *really* a commentary at all. As I pointed out in Chapter 2, Barth's concerns in this regard were not unfounded.[25]

Barth's critics, as he suspected, did, for the most part, regard his 'theological' reading of *Romans*, apart from being historically and critically *naive*, as the product of eisegesis. This is what he was responding to when in his preface to Rom II he said, "This book does not intend to be anything else but a part of the conversation of a theologian with theologians. Jülicher's and Eberhard Vischer's triumphant discovery that I am also a theologian is quite superfluous. I have never intended to do anything else but *theology*."[26] But Thurneysen's advice that Barth give a "hearty little oration which would prevent it from being understood only 'theologically'" implies that he and Barth were not only conscious of the narrowness of their contemporaries' understanding of theological exegesis but already anticipated their criticisms. In placing the word in quotation marks, it appears that Thurneysen was juxtaposing, ironically, the narrowness of their contemporaries' understanding with his and Barth's more comprehensive understanding of *theological* exegesis. But it is Thurneysen's further comment that "the *Römerbrief* itself will already take care of that," that is perhaps even more significant. As I suggested in Chapter 2 with reference to Barth's preface to Rom II, Thurneysen was consistently inclined to advise Barth *not* to elaborate his views on exegetical method.[27]

For Barth, of course, finishing his commentary and writing a preface for it was one problem, finding a publisher was another. His proposed commentary was rejected by at least three Swiss publishers. On September 6, 1917, through the generous ministrations of his friend Rudolf Pestalozzi, a wealthy businessman, Barth secured a publisher, G.A. Bäschlin of Bern.[28] On September 10,

---

[24] Eduard Thurneysen to Karl Barth, 12 Feb., 1918, *B-Th Br.* I, p. 266.
[25] See pp. 14-16 above.
[26] Rom II, p. viii.
[27] See pp. 20-21 above.
[28] Karl Barth to Eduard Thurneysen, 6 Sept., 1917, *B-Th Br.* I, p. 227. Pestalozzi offered a subsidy to cover losses if the first printing could not be sold.

Barth visited Bern to meet his publisher and discuss his commentary and a book of sermons he and Thurneysen hoped to publish.[29] Immediately upon his return Barth wrote to Thurneysen on September 11, "The *Römerbrief* must be finished by September 1, 1918, because the publisher wants the book out before the Christmas season in order to catch business," adding, "Without some weeks' or months' leave of absence it will hardly come off even if things should go well. And even so it will be a crowded year for me."[30] To make a long story short, after more than two years of intensive labor, while attempting to fulfill his responsibilities as pastor of a Reformed church in the small, industrial village of Safenwil (which he admitted had taken a toll not only on his congregation, but on his family and even his own physical health), Barth finally produced a full manuscript sometime near the end of May or the beginning of June, 1918. On June 4th, Barth announced to Thurneysen,

> I have two good reports to make to you today. First, that yesterday a first proof-reading of the Römerbrief was completed, including a preface with it, so that I would now be ready for the mug you, Eduard, once promised me in Uerkheim for this occasion. Secondly, I have already begun with the second proof-reading so that the beginning might be brought to greater fullness by means of the conclusion. If I were a chicken, I would allow myself now to cluck pompously around the house. Rejoice with me![31]

This is the first time Barth himself mentions a preface to the *Römerbrief* and, as Hermann Schmidt suggests, it refers to Preface Draft I, which is less than one page in length.[32] It is clear that Barth is not yet finished with his manuscript, but the end is clearly in sight. Thurneysen responds two days later on June 6, "I search for short and simple words to tell you how very glad I am and how I take a sigh of relief with you ... that the accomplishment is now secure." His letter concludes with the following appraisal:

> It is not just a book, a treatise or study, rather it is about a matter which you have been called to carry out, and in which we all are deeply participating. It will be tremendously helpful to those who follow along, who know themselves to be moved and grasped [by it]. I myself have richly experienced this. And even if the book should only slowly succeed, it is now here and can wait until it finds eyes which can read and understand.[33]

Whether Thurneysen's appraisal is partially responsible for prompting Barth to draft another preface, it is clear that it made an impression on Barth, for he repeats several words and phrases from it in Preface Drafts IA-V, the most famous of which is the one suggesting that the *Römerbrief* "can wait. ..."[34] At

---

[29] Karl Barth and Eduard Thurneysen, *Suchet Gott, so werdet ihr leben!* (Bern: Bäschlin, 1917).
[30] Karl Barth to Eduard Thurneysen, 11 Sept., 1917, *B-Th Br.* I, pp. 229-230.
[31] Karl Barth to Eduard Thurneysen, 4 June, 1918, *B-Th Br.* I, pp. 279-280.
[32] Rom I, editor's preface, xv.
[33] Eduard Thurneysen to Karl Barth, 6 June, 1918, *B-Th Br.* I, p. 280.
[34] Hermann Schmidt suggests that Barth may owe the phrase, "it is now here and can wait until it finds eyes which can read and understand," to Thurneysen (see Schmidt's footnote,

any rate, between June 6 and June 12, Barth had written another preface. On June 12, he wrote back to Thurneysen: "I am sending you here the preface before it is sent to Bäschlin so that you might examine this important piece with your tested tact and taste regarding arrogant, careless places, etc., which should definitely be removed as well as its gaps."[35] This, in all probability, refers to Preface Draft II which contains fewer emendations and is only a slightly modified version of Preface Draft IA. It is nearly seven times longer than Preface Draft I and, given its specific content, causes Barth concern. He shares his reservation about it in the same letter: "Actually the tone of this preface is much too confident for the uncertainty in which I find myself with regard to [*Romans*] and the subject matter."[36] By this stage Barth appears to have become much more conscious of the fact, as he says above, that the preface is an "important piece." Thurneysen responded two days later on June 14, "I find your preface excellent. That you in one passage became clear against the theologians is simply necessary. It must remain in order to keep distance from them."[37] Yet, notwithstanding his friend's approval, Barth was still obviously not satisfied with his preface.

With the original deadline of September 1 drawing near,[38] Barth spent the rest of June, July, and August editing his manuscript. On July 11, he reports to Thurneysen, "Once I am finished I will look spiritually like a decimated division brought back from the front."[39]

On July 23, in the final stages of revising his manuscript (which he described as useless "chewing of the cud"), he again shares the same doubt with Thurneysen as he expressed in February six months earlier: "... working on it, I often have doubts whether the dear God now really wants this or whether it would have been better to let the whole thing disappear into a drawer as a successful writing exercise. In any case, I am through with it as soon as it is finished. ... Please send me some directions regarding the preface. I have too little of an overview."[40] Again the same anxiety manifests itself as earlier in Febru-

---

Rom I, p. 600 n. 7). If so, one might also want to note other important phrases such as being "moved and grasped," "deeply participating," etc. I use the word "famous" to describe the "can wait" phrase, but Barth, in his preface to Rom II, described it as "notorious" (*berüchtigt*) obviously because of the way critics responded to it, e.g., Jülicher, "Ein moderner Paulusausleger" p. 453f.

[35] Karl Barth to Eduard Thurneysen, 12 June, 1918, *B-Th Br.* I, pp. 280-281.
[36] Karl Barth to Eduard Thurneysen, 12 June, 1918, *B-Th Br.* I, pp. 280-281.
[37] Eduard Thurneysen to Karl Barth, 14 June, 1918, *B-Th Br.* I , p. 282.
[38] Eduard Thurneysen to Karl Barth, 14 June, 1918, *B-Th Br.* I , p. 282. Barth writes: "And now a lot of sour work lies ahead. So far everything had to be worked out entirely new and who knows how the end of the [Römerbrief] will then look at me again. I could probably rewrite for years but now I have to be done by October 15 at the very latest."
[39] Karl Barth to Eduard Thurneysen, 11 July, 1918, *B-Th Br.* I , p. 285.
[40] Karl Barth to Eduard Thurneysen, 23 July, 1918, *B-Th Br.* I, pp. 287-288.

ary: Does "the dear God really want this ...?"; the same temptation to simply forget it all, and the same struggle to draft a fitting preface.

We have no evidence that Thurneysen ever sent Barth any further directions regarding the preface. In fact, after July 23 there is no evidence of any communication between them until Barth's letter of August 19. Still struggling over his preface, Barth writes:

> The *Römerbrief* is now completed, but I have no true joy over it. The whole of it stands there like a sheep but without a victory flag[41] and things of that sort. And now the necessity of a preface becomes greatly important. Nelly[42] rejects all my new drafts as clumsy, overly humble, and Ragaz-like.[43] Presently I simply cannot think of anything at all to say. ... So now, in order to be punished for all that I have written, I find myself in a special little Hell.[44]

The "new drafts" Frau Barth rejected as "clumsy, overly humble, and Ragaz-like" probably refer to Preface Draft III and perhaps II.[45] Preface Draft III is only a little shorter than II. Though there is some overlapping material, it represents a new train of thought and adds many new details. Recognizing as never before the significance of finding an appropriate preface, but deeply frustrated at this point as to what to say, Barth again receives encouragement from Thurneysen the next day, August 20:

> In spite of all the special demons from some psychic sphere which want to spoil the *Römerbrief* for you, in spite of the preface idols {götzleins}, that you cannot manage to prop up (which is actually a good sign since all these prefaces or afterwords and self-interpretations have something awkward about them), we rejoice![46]

Thurneysen's gentle admonishment, it would appear, is that Barth has perhaps made too much out of the preface and risks making an idol of it. For whatever reason, neither Barth nor Thurneysen ever again mention the preface to the first edition of his *Römerbrief* in their correspondence. As a result, we have no fur-

---

[41] This is a reference to the *Agnus Dei* of christological art.

[42] Frau Barth.

[43] The term "ragazisch" refers to Leonhard Ragaz (1868-1945), pastor of the Münster cathedral in Basel (also Professor in Zürich 1908 to 1921) and leader of the religious socialist movement in Switzerland. What this term denotes in its adjectival sense is difficult to define precisely. However, given the content of Prefaces Drafts II and III and Barth's characterization of Ragaz elsewhere in his correspondence, "ragazisch" probably refers to a certain melodramatic, overtly tragical, or sensational quality associated with Ragaz's habit, as Barth characterizes it, of "shouting at every moment, see, here or there is the kingdom of God!" (5 Feb., 1915, *B-Th Br*: I, 29). This also seems to be the sense in which Barth uses the phrases: "*ragazisch-tragisch*" (14 July, 1915, *B-Th Br*: I, p. 64) and "*Ragazis Tragik*" (23 Jan., 1918, *B-Th Br*: I, p. 260).

[44] Karl Barth to Eduard Thurneysen, 19 Aug., 1918, *B-Th Br.* I, p. 288.

[45] Hermann Schmidt states, "The 'new drafts,' which Frau Barth rejected, are probably identical to Preface Draft III." However, since Frau Barth rejected more than one draft, it seems likely, that this refers to Preface Drafts III *and* II (and perhaps IA).

[46] Karl Barth to Eduard Thurneysen, 30 Aug., 1918, *B-Th Br.* I, p. 289.

ther information why Barth ultimately decided on a very different and much shorter version.

Whether it was because he had weighed Nelly's criticisms so heavily or because he maintained reservations of his own, Barth was still obviously not satisfied with what he had written. Between August 19 and August 31, he composed three more preface drafts: IV, V, and his final draft which was eventually published in 1919.[47] Preface Drafts IV and V are only slightly different from the final version. They represent a brief synthesis of the content of the earlier preface drafts. Each begins, "Paul spoke to his contemporaries as a child of his age. But much more important than this truth is the other, that he speaks as a prophet and apostle of the kingdom of God to all men in all ages." Each asserts that "the differences between then and now, there and here, have to be considered, but are not of serious import" and that "what was once serious is still serious today. ..." Each announces that "Paul's questions" are really "our questions" and "Paul's answers" should be "our answers." Each states that "historical understanding is a continuous, more and more honest and penetrating conversation between the wisdom of yesterday and the wisdom of today, which is one and the same" and illustrates this point with the same lines from Goethe (instead of the more provocative lines of Nietzsche in Preface Drafts IA and II). Each insists upon "substantive participation alongside Paul instead of facing him with the cool detachment of an observer." Each claims that "this book was written with a certain joy of discovery." But next to this latter claim, probably the single comment among these drafts most remembered by his critics was Barth's statement that although "the historical-critical method of biblical research has its place ... , if I had to choose between it and the old doctrine of inspiration, I would definitely choose the latter."

What is most striking about Preface Drafts IV, V, and the final version, however, is how irenic they are compared to the earlier Preface Drafts (I, IA, II, III). In fact, the only remark that could possibly be construed as polemical is the one above regarding the importance of "substantive participation alongside Paul instead of facing him with the cool detachment of an observer" and perhaps, indirectly, his remark about if given the choice between the historical-critical method and the old doctrine of inspiration he would choose the latter. Yet in Preface Draft V and the final version, even this remark is softened by the comment, "I am glad that I do not have to choose between the two." Preface Draft IV is shorter and contains no material beyond what is found in Preface Draft V, but the differences, though small, between it and Preface Draft V and the final published version are interesting, for they demonstrate further attempts to soften edges. In Preface Draft V, for example, Barth states, "The differences between then and now, there and here, have to be considered, *but no longer and no more endearingly than is absolutely necessary* for a knowledge

---

[47] Karl Barth to Eduard Thurneysen, 30 Aug., 1918, *B-Th Br.* I, p. 290.

of their *essential insignificance.*" In the final draft this reads, "The differences between then and now, there and here, must be considered. But the purpose of this consideration can only be the recognition that these differences have *no* significance for what really matters." Certainly compared with the earlier drafts, the final preface represents a significant modification in tone. Concluding with the self-deprecating plea that other "better qualified" individuals should join in digging even more wells in *Romans*, the final preface constitutes a far more irenic distillation of the concerns he sought to address in his earlier preface drafts.

Why was writing a preface for his *Römerbrief* so difficult for Barth, and why did he ultimately choose a more irenic approach? As to why it was so difficult, there are several plausible reasons. First of all, writing the preface required him to look back on where he had been and what he had accomplished. This was not easy. Barth's turn to the Bible had begun as early as the summer of 1915. Much had changed since then. When he began work on his preface the fate of the war was still much in doubt.[48] But by late August, at the time when Barth was composing his final preface drafts, the fate of the war, to practically all observers, had become unmistakably clear.[49] Now, in the latter half of what he would later describe as an "apocalyptic year," with over twenty million lives lost and many more wounded, with dozens of national economies ruined, and the signs of war, devastation, and carnage all around, Barth had to write a preface which would put his work into some kind of perspective. In Preface Draft III, written earlier in August, Barth had mentioned writing his commentary "under the cosmic pressure of this time of war. ..." He later struck this phrase.[50] In the preface drafts of late August no reference whatsoever is made to the war. The real 'crisis' at issue, of course, to Barth, was still the same. But the question of relevance was now acute. "What does the world of the Bible and the world of the newspaper have to do with one another?" Such

---

[48] Karl Barth to Eduard Thurneysen, 25 March, 1918, *B-Th Br.* I, p. 271. "Yes, the German offensive! If it succeeds now, things may go well. We shall then experience something. At any rate the later continuation of the war would be provided for. If it succeeds?" The "German offensive" is a reference to "the great 'Michael offensive'" of March 21, 1918, which Gordon A. Craig describes in his chapter, "The Great War" in *Germany 1866-1945* (Oxford: University Press, 1978), pp. 393f.

[49] According to Craig, "On 8 August Rawlingson's Fourth British Army, supported by French units, struck with dramatic suddenness east of Amiens, and masses of Allied tanks tore the German lines to shreds. This was 'the black day of the German army,' and it recoiled, never to seize the initiative again. By the beginning of September the Allied armies were sweeping forward in every sector: the British were through the Somme and hammering at the Hindenburg line; the French were pushing forward in the Champagne; and the Americans, whom the German navy had vowed to keep out of Europe, had won their first fight at St. Mihiel and were advancing in the Meuse-Argonne." Craig, *Germany 1866-1945*, pp. 394-395.

[50] Appendix 2, Preface Draft III, p. 287 (p. 594).

concerns were weighing heavily on Barth at this time.[51] Another reason why drafting a preface may have been difficult is because *he* had changed. Writing his commentary had been a life-changing experience.[52] He referred to the whole experience as a 'conversion' and by the time it was necessary to write his preface remarked: "How different everything looks at me now than it did the first time, actually much more strange and mysterious. Oh my! ..."[53]

But beyond the changes that had taken place in the times and in himself what was clearly most difficult was the fact that *the task* had changed. Barth recognized that his preface would require him to take a step back from the task of exegesis itself. Not only would he have to reflect on what he had done but on *how* he had done it. He knew that in his preface some sort of explanation of his method would be required. What made it difficult was, as he says in his first preface draft, "Here I am forced to indicate with a few sentences the chasm which separates me from the method of today's dominant science of biblical exegesis."[54] Barth had written a commentary which constituted, as Gadamer aptly described it, a "hermeneutical manifesto." He needed an appropriate preface to introduce it. Given the provocative content of his *Römerbrief*, the stakes were already high. Putting his hermeneutical principles on the table would only raise them. This is why writing the preface was such a struggle and why, apparently, in the end, he chose a much briefer, far less polemical preface draft from among those he had written. Whether, as a tactical maneuver, this achieved the purpose of focusing readers' attention on the content of the *Römerbrief* rather than on its exegetical method, questions regarding the

---

[51] Karl Barth to Eduard Thurneysen, 14 Nov., 1918, *B-Th Br*. I, pp. 301-302. "What goes on around us? What is there to say? One stands astonished, does he not, and can only state how the face of the world changes visibly: on *this* side of things. But the *other* side: the meaning and content, the actual trend of it all, the movements in the spiritual realm that now take place, the doors of God that now open or close, the progress or standstill in the *eleutheria tes doxes ton teknon tou theou*? Who is there now with a comprehensive view who is able to see to the very roots of world events in order to speak and act from that standpoint? ... It seems to me that we come just too late with our bit of insight into the world of the New Testament. How needful it is now that one should be able with full hands to draw out, to interpret, to clarify, to point the way and lay open paths – how thinly flows the little stream of knowledge. ... If only we had been converted to the Bible *earlier* so that we would now have solid ground under our feet! One broods alternately over the newspaper and the New Testament and actually sees fearfully little of the organic connection between the two worlds concerning which one should now be able to give a clear and powerful witness. Or is it different for you? You stand there with a clearer conscience since you do not have to be reading the proofs of a book almost every day as I do."

[52] See pp. 140-141 above.

[53] Karl Barth to Eduard Thurneysen, 12 June, 1918, *B-Th Br*. I, pp. 280-1. Given all that has been said thus far about how strange and bewildering Barth discovered the contents of the *Römerbrief* to be, it is interesting to note that Barth makes the same kind of remarks (and almost as frequently!) in preparing his second edition.

[54] Appendix 2, Preface Draft IA, p. 281 (pp. 581-582).

latter would not go away and, as the preface to the second edition of the *Römerbrief* demonstrates, neither would the necessity to respond to them.

Appendix 2

The Preface Drafts to the First Edition of Barth's *Römerbrief* [1]

Preface Draft I

The following book is an attempt to read the Bible differently than we were generally taught at universities under the dominance of the theology of the 1890's. Question: in what way different? I wish to answer: more in accordance with its subject matter, content, and substance, focusing with more attention and love upon the meaning of the Bible itself. I speak not only in my name. For even if I have communicated only to a few in this regard, I know nevertheless from many indications that a whole generation of young pastors and students is emerging who are supported by enough non-theologians who have questions on their hearts regarding the positive meaning of the Bible, who in the present, scientific trade of theology, are hardly given a voice.

We were introduced to the Bible as the "classical document of piety." What can be said in this regard about the Bible has been brilliantly and impressively stated in today's theology. We are sincerely thankful for it. It had to be said and had to be heard. We *have* heard it, but we cannot stop with it now. For with all due respect to the faithful and successful work which has been accomplished in its field, it is precisely this notion which we perceive today as, in the end, inattentive and loveless with regard to the meaning of the Bible.

Preface Draft I A [2]

This book must itself say what it contains and what it intends. If, after having written it, I should write something else *about it*, it would be necessary to dispute the treatment which has befallen and continues to befall the *Römerbrief*, Paul himself, and the entire Bible at the hands of theology. I do not wish to do this to please certain curious readers and reviewers, but neither do I wish my

---

[1] The Preface Drafts to the First Edition of Karl Barth's Römerbrief are printed in the Gesamtausgabe edition of Rom I, pp. 581-602. The publication of this translation has been granted by the Karl Barth Nachlaßkommission and follows the transcription and footnotes supplied by Herbert Anzinger which includes the corrections, additions, and deletions Barth made in pencil after drafting them.

[2] Preface Draft IA is obviously hurriedly written and contains no less than 25 additions at the margin.

thoroughly positive and edifyingly intended work to suffer. All naysaying is so ambiguous and unclear. I must really, therefore, request the reader's trust that I would have been capable of distinguishing the difference as well, but was not willing to do so at this time.[3] The book contains enough inherent criticism. The informed reader will find it on almost every page, but it would be of no value to point it out to the uninformed. Whoever understands how it is meant, has sufficiently grasped how it is *not* meant.

It remains for me then only to add a few instructions regarding my work. First of all, one should not wonder too much about the book's style which simultaneously treats various literary genres. It will seem to historians, too modern; to moderns, too historical; to philosophers, too edifying; and to those seeking to be edified, too philosophical; to theologians, too unscientific; and to non-theologians, too learned. It will not fit in anywhere. I only want to reply to all sides that the *Römerbrief* itself does not really fit in anywhere either and that all such complaints, first of all, do not strike against me, but against Paul. The approach I have taken seemed to me the most appropriate one in order to let Paul speak for himself. Even if he now *speaks* only a little, my not entirely common approach is therefore justified.

The second request is that one should not seek in this book what is not intentionally stated there – especially all that which I would characterize as "*antiquarian.*" Whoever, for instance, wants to be informed about the little one knows and the great amount one does not know about the personality of Paul, about the composition[4] of the Roman, Christian church, about Pauline "formulas" in the context of the history of religions, or about the questions of authenticity which become particularly acute at the end of the letter, will be disappointed here. I have dared confidently to be quiet about these matters, for as interesting in my opinion as they are, they are not really important questions for understanding the text itself, questions which can be and should be considered, but their discussion should by no means, as has occurred, replace explication itself. Whoever insists upon knowing *about* Paul and his letter, will find – according to need, direction, and taste – better things than I could ever write in B. Weiß, Godet, Lipsius,[5] Jülicher, Lietzmann and Zahn. I think I have offered instead a few things *from* Paul which are not found in the books of these scholars. As related to its *intention*, I desire this book to stand beside the commentaries of Calvin, the forgotten Carl Heinrich Rieger (1828) and the honorable teacher of my father, J.T. Beck. Just as little did I want at every moment to interrupt the flow of interpretation by *substantiating* my interpretation. The reasons which are given from verse to verse for one or the other view

---

[3] Correction: " desire to" instead of "want to."

[4] Correction: "the members and the character" instead of "the composition."

[5] Barth mentions only here the Römerbrief commentary by R.A.Lipsius (in: *Handbuch zum Neuen Testament, II/2*, Tübingen, 1891).

have been abundantly provided in other literature. The informed reader will not fail to recognize in this matter, that I have considered these as well; they have been expounded for the umpteenth time and there is no cause for doing it again. If the whole which I intended to present is substantiated in itself, then it also substantiates the particular, despite all differences of opinion, whereas more than one stunning book about Paul serves to warn us that a thousand correct particulars certainly do not always make an intelligible and well-founded whole. An exception to this rule I have made regarding essentially textual-critical questions by briefly mentioning and substantiating in footnotes a number of variations from Nestle's edition. Quotations from other writings have in this book the same function as Old Testament quotations in Paul. I found them necessary when I thought I had discovered in them a particularly striking, strong and, as it were, prophetic formulation of the content of the text. Also, this book does *not* consciously use *easier language* than the *Römerbrief* itself. It only wants to interpret by *paraphrasing* the thoughts of Paul, not by translating them into our "easier" thoughts. For the language and the content are one. The "easier" Christian way of thinking, which perhaps leaves the reader soon longing for more of the same, does *not*, unfortunately, by any means indicate that we, after all, have arrived upon the same subject matter as Paul and the Bible. If ears will be once again open to the *subject matter* with which Paul was concerned, then will his language be once again understood as well, as was obviously the case in the first century.

Fourth, an answer to the question: What kind of reader did I have in mind as I wrote? I say, the same as Paul himself had in mind, namely, everyone who is in any way moved by the same matter which the *Römerbrief* is all about. For everyone who is able to have the need and the joy to allow the truth that it declares to be called to their "memory" (Rom.15:15), for it is also in them. In particular, I have often naturally had my colleagues in the ministry and the more reasonable ones among students of theology in mind. For I know how confused and perplexed we, particularly as 'experts,' often are with respect to the content of the Bible. And if, as we all wish, it should once again speak to the inwardly and outwardly torn race of man of our day, it must first of all speak again powerfully, decisively, and clearly in an entirely different way to those of us who should be its mouthpiece. Frankly, dear colleagues, we surely notice that at present the "explication" *à la* Niebergall[6] and the easy churchly

---

[6] In the preface to Rom II, p. xi (later editions: p. xiii) the corresponding sentence says: "For do the historians really think that they would have fulfilled their duty with respect to human society by allowing Niebergall *re bene gesta* to speak in Volume V?" *Das Handbuch zum Neuen Testament*, published by H. Lietzmann, et al, was in its first revised edition designed in the following way: Vol.I Linguistic and Historical Matters, Vol.II-IV Commentaries on the New Testament writings, Vol. V, Fr. Niebergall, *Praktische Auslegung des Neuen Testaments für Prediger und Religionslehrer*, Tübingen 1909. Niebergall's book though came out

counterfeiting of the Bible is really inadequate, and that the flight from the misunderstood Bible to the philosophers, to the aesthetes, or to the socialists is only a flight from our real task. In the midst of all this, we do not have a good conscience. For "He who tills his land will have plenty of bread, but he who follows worthless pursuits is a fool," (Prov.12:11). This longing for more subject matter, content, and substance in our understanding of the Bible, in our knowledge of God and in our preaching has been in us all for a long time. If we would only once again[7] take our place, standing in attention before the rich treasures of *the* one and only *Römerbrief* (the real one, not the theologically worked-over one) as our predecessors at the time of the Reformation![8] How much more would we *know* and know what to *say*! And how much more there still is besides the *Römerbrief* in this so highly praised yet so little known Bible! If through my attempt at this *one* point I were only able to encourage one or another to dare to dig for the sources here or elsewhere with love and attentiveness *deeper* than has been given to me now. But I hope that a few non-theologians will not fail to take the trouble to investigate alongside as well. It is just as much their concern as it is ours. The 'laity' have the theologians they deserve, and if they rightly demand that the theologians offer them something more and better, they ought even less deny them, as it is almost always still the case, their inner participation precisely with the main task which they must perform today with respect to the question of the Word of God. Yet I really do not like to think of all readers as leafing nibblers, who are quickly satisfied or judge after merely sampling, but as readers who actually read. The worth or worthlessness of a book will depend upon whether it sooner or later finds such readers. For the same relationship stands between book and reader as between a work of art and its observer: the book is not only what the author is able and wants to make it, but just as much so what the reader is able and wants to take from it. I am conscious of the great responsibility I have taken upon myself by writing this book. But I desire to lay the same responsibility also upon those who read it – and those who will not read it.

Safenwil, ...[9]

The Author

---

in 1914 in a second edition not as part of the *Handbuch*. It was later replaced in the *Handbuch* by editions of New Testament texts in pericope form by L. Fendt (1931 and 1941).

[7] Addition: "with open hands."

[8] Addition: "instead of today placing ourselves beside it with our terrible historical-psychological 'objectivity' (which is not)!"

[9] Under "Safenwil, ...", written with ink at the margin: "Schwierigkeiten Lektüre des Textes."

[There are six free lines following this original ending. Barth then changed the beginning of his last paragraph (originally): "Thirdly ..." into "Fourthly. ..." He then added on the next two pages following his third point:]

A third request is that one should not be too amazed at all the exposition in this book which lies seemingly so far from the 'historical' Paul. The superficial reader will hardly be able to avoid this, but it should not cause one to hastily reproach what is written here as 'too much' eisegesis of the text. I am gladly willing to have my errors pointed out to me in all their detail if I find precisely this occurring in my text. But, fundamentally, as much as this might be held against me, I must say that I have offered a historical presentation of Paul's views and not my own or the views of other moderns' regarding the issues here at hand. The task of understanding Paul verse by verse has been enough of an assault upon my and the whole of today's thought and sensibilities. But, of course, I wanted to *understand*, *not* misunderstand Paul. Here I am forced to indicate with a few sentences something of the chasm which separates my method from that of today's dominant science of biblical exegesis. To understand an author means for me mainly *to stand with him*, to take each of his words in earnest so long as he does not prove that he does not deserve this trust, in order to interpret him from the inside out. But today's theology does not stand by the prophets and the apostles, does not participate in the same subject matter with them, but rather stands with the modern reader and his prejudices; it does not take the prophets and apostles in earnest, but while it stands smiling sympathetically albeit condescendingly beside them, it conceitedly distances itself from them and outwardly examines them historically and psychologically. That is what I have against it. What I call "to stand with him" means to begin with the presupposition that what was once true will always be true and that, conversely, the problems with which we are concerned today, if they are really serious problems, are the same as those with which serious people of all times have wrestled. Without this presupposition history is chaos. The words 'history' and 'understanding' make no sense for me at all without this living context between the past and the present which cannot be achieved through some empathetic art [*Einfühlungskunst*], but is *given* in the subject matter and in which one must *be*. Understanding history in this context can be nothing other than a continuous dialogue between the truth which was and which comes. The art of historical description must then consist precisely in suspending from this dialogue unimportant differences of former and present ways of thought and sensibilities, instead of continually emphasizing them as the decisive matter. Whoever in this sense does not 'read in,' i.e., participate in the subject matter, cannot read out. I speak therefore of Paul's questions as if they were *our own* questions in the belief that they really *are*. And I let Paul speak about *our* questions in the belief that he really *has*. If it were otherwise, what would we have to do with him? "You may only interpret the past out of the highest power of the present: only in the strongest efforts or your noblest qualities will you divinize what in the past is great, worth knowing and preserving. Like through like! Or else you will pull the past down to yourself!" (Nietzsche, 1874).[10] Whoever has ears to hear, let him hear! I, on the contrary, will readily accept the reproach that I have "read in" *too little*.

Preface Draft II[11]

This book must say itself what it contains and what it intends. [...][12] to be said must almost inevitably turn into an argument with other interpreters of Paul and his *Römerbrief*. But I do not wish my positive and edifyingly intended work to suffer. Such comparisons always have something ambiguous and unclear about them. Perhaps the reader may grant trust that I do not refrain from them for lack of ability, but for not wanting to. The book contains enough inherent criticism. The informed reader will find it on almost every page, but it would be of no value to point it out to the uninformed. Whoever understands how it is meant, has sufficiently grasped how it is *not* meant. I would therefore only like to give a few instructions for my work as it makes its way to the readers.

First of all, one should not be too upset about the book's formal style which simultaneously treats various literary genres. It will speak too modernly for the historians, too historically for the modern, too edifyingly for the philosophers and too philosophically for those seeking to be edified, too unscientifically for the theologians and too learnedly for the non-theologians. It will not fit in anywhere. I only want to remind all sides that the *Römerbrief* itself with its manner of speaking does not fit in anywhere either and that all such complaints, first of all, do not strike against me, but against Paul. As must be the purpose of such a commentary, I have taken the course which seemed to me the simplest and most appropriate one in order to let the words of Paul speak. Should it be that he speaks even a little in this book, then my not entirely common approach is therefore justified.

The second request is that one should not seek in this book what is not intentionally stated there – especially all that which I would summarize as "*antiquarian.*" Whoever, for instance, wants to be informed about the little one

---

[10] Fr. Nietzsche, *Unzeitgemäße Betrachtungen, II. Vom Nutzen und Nachteil der Historie*, in: *Werke*, I, Munich 1954, p. 250.

[11] Preface Draft II is preserved on eight arabically paginated, unruled pages. It is written as a finished Latin copy and contains very few corrections. In contrast to the rest of the manuscript, Barth did not allow any free space on the margins of these pages. But there are some later additions made in pencil, of which the longer ones – for lack of room at the margins – are written on an extra half page in handwriting clearly not intended for the printer.

[12] Two or three words are erased, probably, "What is ..."

knows and the great amount one does not know about Paul's "personality," about the members and the character of the Roman, Christian church, about Pauline formulas in the context of the history of religions, or about the questions of authenticity which become particularly acute at the end of the letter, will be disappointed here. I have dared confidently to be quiet about these matters, for as interesting as they are, they are not really important questions for understanding the text itself, questions which can be and should be considered, but their discussion should by no means, as has occurred, replace explication itself. I would not know, for instance, what I would have to change about my book if – according to the assumption of the most extreme critics – the entire letter were 'inauthentic.' It is a wonderful wellspring and would hence flow enigmatically in the old Catholic church of the second century, but it would indeed flow. Whoever insists upon knowing *about* Paul and his letter, will find according to need, direction and taste better things than I could ever write in B. Weiß, Godet, Lipsius, Jülicher, Lietzmann and Th. Zahn.[13] I think I have offered instead a few things *from* Paul which are *not* found in them. Just as little did I not want constantly to interrupt the flow of interpretation by *substantiating* my conception of the text. The reasons which are given from verse to verse for one or the other interpretation have likewise been abundantly provided in other literature. The informed reader will not fail to recognize in this matter, that I have considered these as well. They have been expounded for the umpteenth time and there was no cause for doing it again. If the whole which I wanted to present is substantiated in itself, then it also substantiates the particular, despite all differences of opinion, whereas more than one stunning book about Paul serves to warn us that a thousand correct particulars do not always make an intelligible and well-founded whole.

An exception to this rule I have made by briefly mentioning and substantiating in footnotes a number of variations in Nestle's edition. Quotations from other writings have in this book the same function as Old Testament quotations in Paul: I found them necessary when I thought I had discovered in them a particularly striking, strong and, as it were, prophetic formulation of the content of the text. – Also this book does not consciously use *easier language* than was thought appropriate to the dignity of the object. It was necessary to interpret by paraphrasing Paul's thoughts and not by translating them into our 'easier' thoughts. For the language and the content are one. The 'ease' of our usual

---

[13] Addition: "All of them, as well as the older commentaries of Bengel, Tholuck, and Meyer and the Catholic exegesis of Loch and Reischl, have been faithful and indispensable counselors for me throughout. I have always been especially grateful for Lietzmann's excellent translation. But my book is not a continuation of the theological work along *this* line, but follows along another line in the company of the commentaries of Luther, Calvin (crossed out: "I find myself in the company of Luther's *Scholien* of 1516, Calvin's commentary of 1538 of"), Spener, C.H. Rieger, J.T. Beck and Schlatter. It will therefore not enrich the professional (zünft{ige}?) literature on Paul."

Christian way of thinking by no means indicates that we, after all, have arrived upon the same subject matter as Paul and the Bible. If ears will be once again open to the subject matter with which Paul was concerned, then will his language be once again understood as well. This was obviously the case in the first century.

A third request is that one should not be too amazed at all that is in this book which lies seemingly so far from the 'historical' Paul. The superficial reader will hardly be able to avoid this, but it should not cause one to hastily reproach what is written here as "too much eisegesis of the text." I am gladly willing to have my errors pointed out to me in all their detail if I find that this or that thought occurs in my text. But, fundamentally, as much as this might be held against me, I must say that, in my opinion, I have offered a historical presentation of Pauline thoughts and not an outpouring of my own or other modern ones. The task of understanding Paul verse by verse has been enough of an assault upon my and the whole of today's thought and sensibilities. But, of course, I wanted to *understand*, not *misunderstand* Paul. Here I am forced to indicate with a few sentences the chasm which separates me from the method of today's dominant science of the biblical exegesis. To understand an author means for me mainly to *stand with him*, to take each of his words in earnest, so long as it is not proven that he does not deserve this trust, to participate with him in the subject matter, in order to interpret him from the inside out. But today's theology does not stand with the prophets and the apostles; it does not side with them but rather with the modern reader and his prejudices; it does not take the prophets and apostles in earnest, instead, while it stands smiling sympathetically beside them or above them, it takes up a cool and indifferent distance from them; it critically or merrily examines the historical-psychological surface and misses its meaning. That is what I have against it. When I speak about "standing by an author" I mean beginning with the presupposition that what once was a serious problem, is still one today and that, conversely, the problems with which we are concerned today, if they are really serious problems and not merely fads, must be the same as those with which the notable people of all times have wrestled. The decisive prerequisite for the interpretation of a text for me therefore is participation in its *subject matter*. No historical meticulousness and no art of empathy and no trip to the Orient can offer even the slightest substitute for this participation. Without this living context of past and present which is given within the *subject matter*, the words "history" and "understanding" have no meaning at all: history then remains a chaos and the willingness to understand, a fiddling about with empty forms. Mixed into this lively context of the subject matter, the understanding of history is a continuous, ever more honest dialogue between the truth which *was*, which *comes*, and which is *one* and *the same*. And the art of history will have to consist precisely in suspending from this dialogue the insignificant differences of former and present ways of thought and sensibilities, rather than ignoring what is important and developing with loving interest that which is paltry. Whoever does not continually 'read in' because he participates in the subject matter, cannot 'read out' either. Thus I speak in the following of Paul's questions as our own questions in the belief that they really *are*, and let Paul speak about our questions in the belief that he really *has*. If it were not so, then one should actually not bother us with these old stories! "You may only interpret the past out of the highest power of the present: only in the strongest efforts of your noblest qualities will you divinize what in the past is great, worth knowing and preserving. Like through like! Or else you will pull the past down to yourself!" (Nietzsche 1874).[14] I, on the contrary, will readily accept the reproach of approaching the *Römerbrief* much too presuppositionlessly and therefore having 'read in' too little.

Finally, an answer to the question: What kind of reader did I have in mind as I wrote? I say, none other than those that Paul himself had in mind, namely, everyone who is in any way moved by the same matter which the *Römerbrief* is all about, for everyone who is able to have the need and the joy to allow the truth that it declares to be called to their "memory" (Rom.15:15), for it is also in them. In particular, I have often naturally had the more open ones among my colleagues[15] in the ministry and the more reasonable ones among students of theology in mind. For I know from my own experience how confused and perplexed especially we 'experts' often are are with respect to the great content of the Bible; and if, as we all wish, it should once again speak to the inwardly and outwardly torn race of man of our day, it must first of all speak again clearly, decisively, and powerfully in an entirely different way to those of us who should be its mouthpiece. What are we moaning about, as long as we ourselves do not even know what we want or if we want anything at all? The *Römerbrief* might tell us unmistakably. Frankly, dear colleagues, we surely notice that at present the 'explications' *à la* Niebergall are really inadequate.[16] Only with displeasure and embarrassment and with the constant, quiet question: Keeper, is the night soon over?, do we endure the miserableness of our modern church proclamation, which is no longer even worthy of the name.[17] We begin to notice that the flight from the misunderstood Bible to the philosophers, to the pedagogues, to the aesthetes, or to the socialists is only a flight from our real task.[18] In the midst of all this we do not have a good conscience; we cannot

---

[14] Compare above to Preface Draft IA, pp. 281-282n.10.
[15] Correction: "my colleagues."
[16] Addition: "I Corinthians 15:34."
[17] Correction: "which no longer has an object."
[18] Addition: "But we are even more indignant about the spirit of the modern church which constantly wishes to capture us to do its aimlessly 'positive work' in all kinds of small things ('which need to be done as well'), if we are still foolish enough to let them capture us. This, too, is flight and nothing but flight from our *Verbi Divini Ministerium*."

have it; for "He who tills his land will have plenty of bread, but he who follows worthless[19] pursuits is a fool," (Prov.12:11). This longing for more subject matter, content, and substance in our understanding of the Bible in our knowledge of God and in our preaching has been in us all for a long time. If we would only again take our place, standing in attention with open hands before the rich treasures of the *one and only Römerbrief* as our predecessors at the time of the highly praised Reformation! How much more would we *know* and know what to *say*! For the *Römerbrief* is only one *part* of the Bible and I know better than anyone else that the following is only an attempt to let it speak once again more clearly, more originally, more simply than we are accustomed to hearing it. I would be delighted if through my attempt at this point, I were able to encourage others to dare to dig with love and attentiveness for sources here or elsewhere deeper than it has turned out for me thus far. But I am hoping for non-theologians who will not fail to take the trouble to investigate alongside as well. It is just as much their concern as it is ours. They are not helping us theologians with their shrugging shoulders and sneering aphorisms; nonetheless, they are not free of their joint responsibility for the situation. For the "laity" have the theologians they deserve. And if they today rightly demand that we theologians should achieve something more and better, as it is almost always still the case, they must even less deny us their inner participation precisely with the main task which we have to do today with respect to the question of the word of God. A purer, fresher, more genuine atmosphere for which they long together with us for our poor church will then not fail to emerge. – Yet I really do not like to think of all readers, not for my own sake but for the sake of the object itself, as curiously superficial, leafing nibblers, who are quickly satisfied or judge after merely sampling, but as readers who actually read. The worth or worthlessness of this book will depend on them as well. For the same relationship stands between reader and book as between an observer and a work of art: it is not only what the author is able and wants to make it, but just as much so what the reader is able and wants to take from it. I am conscious of the great responsibility I have taken upon myself by writing this book. But I desire to share this responsibility with those who read it – and those who will not read it.[20]

---

[19] Correction: "unnecessary."
[20] Addition: "Since long ago the True was found/ A group of noble men it bound/ *Hold fast then* – that ancient Truth! (Goethe) 15, 18 Tertius, Apology, Statement, not personal message.

Preface Draft III[21]

The bold venture of a Romans commentary and the manner by which it came about requires a few clarifying remarks. The *Römerbrief* has actually engaged me in a remarkable way ever since I have tried to read the Bible. As I began to make a sketch of the following work, I thought I would only produce a private summary of exegetical studies. But precisely under the cosmic[22] pressure of this time of war, the subject matter led me further. I peered with astonishment into a world of new, original, important, and fertile thoughts, as if created for the purpose of being understood today; but I also saw, notwithstanding all Pauline-literature,[23] how little these thoughts actually had become known in today's Christendom, let alone acknowledged by it and effective in it. It became to me one of the greatest riddles how cold-bloodedly we today [?], for the most part, ignore Paul. We have examined him 'historically,' we have appropriated a few slogans from his workshop, we have with quiet sympathy shrugged our shoulders precisely at *his* decisive thoughts and are going precisely the ways of *our* decisive thoughts, against which he most strongly warned. What has become today of the "power of God" of his gospel (Rom.1:16)? We are again at least as removed from Paul as the late [?] Jewish-Christians of the first century or the Catholic Church before the Reformation. I mean no particular confession or direction, I mean the whole of Protestant Christendom, when I say: What is today preached and believed as 'gospel,' stands in [...][24] contrast to the knowledge of God of the *Römerbrief*. It was out of this insight, which I did not seek, yet could also not avoid, that I came to the conclusion that I would allow my work to become a book. Its intention is to bring to hearing the strange voice of Paul and thus at least point to the existence of this riddle. As long as not many are shocked by it,[25] there is no prospect for getting rid of it. I really do not presume to offer anything more than the material for this[26] to occur. I have no message of my own, I have only statements about the message of Paul to make. But this undertaking is already enough of a burden for me.

From what has been said it will be perhaps understandable why I have consciously raised again the method, which has long since been repudiated in theology, of 'reading in' our own problems into the thought world of the Bible. In fact, I know that this book is already scientifically done for, even before it ap-

---

[21] Preface Draft III is written on squared paper in a smaller format and includes eight pages without numbers. Barth did not leave room for a margin, hence, it is difficult to read his numerous corrections. The footnotes record only the later corrections done in pencil.

[22] Deleted: "cosmic."

[23] Deleted: "notwithstanding all Pauline literature."

[24] illegible.

[25] Correction: "*many* are amazed about it."

[26] Correction: "this amazing experience."

pears. But it could not be otherwise. It was not only because, from the beginning, I felt I was participating in it much too strongly, because I had heard Paul speaking directly *to us* so clearly, that I could not continue with the *preliminary* work of the historical method any longer than was absolutely necessary. Rather, it was because I had to directly advance the assertion that the "uncritical" works of a Calvin or J.T. Beck are more *concerned with the subject matter* [*sachgemäßer*] than, for example, those[27] of Jülicher or Lietzmann. It is not about "reading something into" the Bible, it is about understanding it. One can only *understand* that for which one *stands*. An author can never ever be interpreted through the historical-psychological surface, but only by joining with him in the subject matter, by working with him, by taking each word of his in earnest, so long as it is not proven that he does not deserve such trust. The Bible has been approached much too carelessly with the application of this emergency clause. The mistrust one has, the Unwillingness-To-Understand, the non-participatory, distancing of oneself has simply been made into a scientific principle. I consider, on the other hand, the doctrine of verbal inspiration more fruitful. It at least contains the wise challenge of stubbornly occupying readers with a biblical text until it is brought forth to significant speech, until it stands before us not as a dead relic of Jewish or near-eastern nonsense, but as a living link in a movement which should move us as well. What was once serious, is still also today and what is serious today and not merely chance or a fad, stands also in the immediate relation to that which has always been serious. Only through this living context of the past and present will historical understanding be at all possible. I take historical understanding to be a continuous, ever more honest and penetrating dialogue between the truth which *was*, which *comes*, and which is one and the same. And the art of history must consist precisely in suspending from this dialogue the insignificant differences of former and present ways of thought and sensibilities, rather than ignoring what is important and developing with loving interest that which is paltry. Whoever does not continually 'read in' because he participates in the subject matter cannot 'read out' either. Thus I speak in the following of Paul's questions as our own questions in the belief that they really *are*, and let Paul speak about our questions in the belief that he really *has*. The fact that beyond historical labor, the reigning theology of today does not know to offer anything better than psychological and pastoral banalities *à la* Niebergall, I take as a serious symptom of the spiritual decay of our time. I do not think that I have yet offered anything better or have disclosed the relation of then and now in such a way that Paul *must* once again be heard, as the Reformers succeeded to accomplish for their time. I think also in this regard I have shown only possibilities which shall still require much work to be realized and for which the collaboration of a serious philosophy shall be indispensable. And I do not take lightly that today's theo-

---

[27] Addition: "solely critical [nur kritischen]."

logy will reject this attempt from the start. I would have really rather written something else that it would not *have* to reject.

From this basic attitude a further circumstance resulted which is embarrassing enough for me, yet could not be avoided: I am talking about the naivetè with which I had to set my speech next to Paul's as if I were really permitted to say what Paul said. I would gladly bear the blame for this presumption personally, but I regret, for the sake of the subject matter, having to think about the fact,[28] with all the dire focus our educated world places upon the personal, that many will not get *beyond* this outrage. It has been afflicting and humiliating enough for me to venture as close as I have to the fire. In this regard, I can only repeat that I really do not think I present my own message but that of Paul by serving in the role of "I[29] Tertius, the writer of this letter," (Rom.16:22). I did this, in spite of its continuous relation to the present, not because I sought it out, but because, as it stands, it lies in the content. I had no need to speak out about idealism, pietism, the church, the state, etc. Had it been up to me I would have done so in an entirely different way. Instead, I had to write entire chapters and sections directly against myself. Perhaps this apology will be accepted, perhaps it will be interpreted deliberately as arrogance. Accusers should only believe that in view of the gravity of Paul's pronouncements I would have gladly hidden in some kind of anonymity if that would have fundamentally changed the situation.

In closing, here are a few instructions for the friendly reader.

1. One must not seek historical and philological information here. The little one knows historically about Paul and his letter and the state of exegetical questions is better presented than I could ever do in the works of B. Weiß, Godet, Lipsius, Jülicher, Lietzmann, Th. Zahn. I have gratefully and attentively used them. However, in the book itself, I have presented only results without further comments.[30] One understandable exception is a few variations from Nestle's edition in the footnotes. Conscientiously inquiring readers will, of course, not avoid taking the trouble to compare these with the remaining literature.[31]

2. Because this book is not my dogmatic but an exegetical work, I was not able to say everything about each of the topics touched upon, but only about that which lies directly in the path of Paul's words. One is not allowed, therefore, to read its statements as a treatise but should rather be interested, first of all, in the understanding of the text itself. My statements have no importance of their own, nor do the quotations of other writings. Everything is meant only

---

[28] Deleted: "about the fact."
[29] Deleted: "I."
[30] Deleted: "without further comments."
[31] Correction: "with other translations and commentaries" instead of "with the remaining literature."

as movement of the text. I do not want to be right anywhere, even where I speak very definitely in the name of Paul. I only want to point out doors that are now closed which could perhaps open if this text were to speak again.

3. One cannot simply leaf through and sample this book. The *Römerbrief* itself has been leafed through and sampled enough and the result was that one did not understand it. So it goes for this exegesis. The certain horror of modern readers before the monotone rhythm of Pauline thoughts is thoroughly understandable to me. Whoever is not capable of overcoming this should keep his hands off them. But whoever has ears to hear should try to think along with them in their context.

Preface Draft IV[32]

Paul spoke to his contemporaries as a child of his age. But *much* more important than this truth is the other, that he speaks as a prophet and apostle of the kingdom of God to all men in all ages. The differences between then and now, there and here, have to be considered, but are not of serious import[33] at the central point where Paul stands. What was once serious is still also serious today, and what today is serious, and not merely chance or a fad, stands also in immediate relation to that which was formerly serious. Our questions are at their deepest level the questions of Paul and Paul's answers should be our answers. I take historical understanding to be a continuous and ever more honest and penetrating conversation between the wisdom of yesterday and the wisdom of today,[34] which is one and the same.

> Das Wahre war schon längst gefunden
> Hat edle Geisterschaft verbunden
> Das alte Wahre – faß es an![35]
> Since long ago the True was found
> A group of noble men it bound
> Hold fast then – that ancient Truth!

The historical-critical method of reading the Bible has its rightful place. But if I had to choose between it and the doctrine of inspiration, I would definitely seize hold of the latter; for it maintains a greater, deeper, more important place. It is certain that it has been more natural for all ages hungering and thirsting for righteousness to take a position of substantive participation alongside Paul instead of facing him in the cool detachment of an observer. Perhaps we are

---

[32] Preface Draft IV is found on two pages of the same paper which Barth used for Preface Draft III.

[33] Correction: "are not crucial."

[34] Correction: "tomorrow" instead of "today."

[35] J.W. von Goethe, "legacy," beginning of the second stanza.

presently entering such a time. If I am not mistaken, there will be no lack of those who will gladly let the *Römerbrief* "remind" (Rom.15:15) them of that which really *is*. One will note that this book was written with a certain joy of discovery. Paul's strange voice was really[36] new to me and it seems to me that it should be new to many others as well. But it is quite clear to me at the end of this work that there still remain far away lands[37] to be discovered. It is intended to be nothing more than a preliminary work. If only many would come in order to dig for more wells here (Ps. 84:7)! But should I be mistaken in the joyful expectation of an age of new questions and inquiries for the biblical message, then this book together with the *Römerbrief* itself has time – to wait.[38]

Preface Draft V[39]

Paul spoke to his contemporaries as a child of his age. But *much* more important than this truth is the other, that he speaks as a prophet and apostle of the kingdom of God to all men in all ages. The differences between then and now, there and here, have to be considered, but no longer and no more endearingly than is absolutely necessary for attaining a knowledge of their essential insignificance. The historical-critical method of reading the Bible has its rightful place: it compels one to preliminary work which cannot be ignored at any point.[40] But if I had to choose between it and the old doctrine of inspiration, I would definitely seize hold of the latter; for it has a greater, deeper, more *important* place because it forces one to the work itself, without which all preparation is worthless.[41] I am in the fortunate position not to have to choose between the two;[42] but my whole attention and effort was[43] focused upon looking

---

[36] Deleted: "really."

[37] Addition: "and rich treasures."

[38] On June 6, 1918, Eduard Thurneysen writes to Barth upon the news of the conclusion of its first reading: "and even if the book will only slowly be a success, it now is complete and can wait until it finds eyes which can read and understand" Eduard Thurneysen to Karl Barth, 6 June, 1918, B-Th. Br. I, p.280. Since the preface was certainly written later, Barth could possibly owe to his friend this closing remark which was added to the final text – as well as several others. See Rom II, p. xvii (later reprints: p. xviii).

[39] Preface Draft V is like Preface II written in Latin fair copy on two unruled pages which carry the page numbers I and II. The work of correction began by Barth's underlining with a thick blue pen – the same one he probably used for numbering his drafts I-V – those words and parts of sentences he was not yet satisfied with. The corrections are then written with pencil in between the lines. Several other changes have been added in the printed preface and can be compared there.

[40] Correction: "it points to a preparation for understanding which is never superfluous."

[41] Correction: "because it points to the task of understanding."

[42] Correction: "I am glad that I do not have to choose between the two."

through the historical into the spirit of the Bible which is an eternal spirit. What was once serious is still also serious today, and what today is serious, and not merely chance or a fad, stands also in immediate relation to that which was formerly serious. Our questions are at their deepest level[44] the questions of Paul and Paul's answers – if correctly understood[45] – should be our answers.

> Das Wahre war schon längst gefunden
> Hat edle Geisterschaft verbunden
> Das alte Wahre – faß es an!
> Since long ago the True was found
> A group of noble men it bound
> Hold fast then – that ancient Truth!

I take historical understanding to be a continuous and ever more honest conversation between the wisdom of yesterday and the wisdom of tomorrow, which is one and the same. Here I remember my father, Professor *Fritz Barth*, with respect and gratitude whose entire lifework has been an application of this insight.

It is certain that it has been more natural for all ages hungering and thirsting for righteousness to take a position of substantive participation alongside Paul instead of facing him in the cool detachment of an observer. Perhaps we are presently entering such a time. If I am not mistaken, there might soon be those[46] who will gladly let the *Römerbrief*[47] "remind" (Rom.15:15) them of that which really *is*. The reader will notice that this book was written with a certain joy of discovery.[48] Paul's strange[49] voice was new to me and it seems to me that it should be new to many others as well. But it is quite clear to me at the end of this work that there still remain far away lands and rich treasures to be discovered.[50] It is intended to be nothing more than a preliminary work.[51] If only many would come in order to dig for more wells here (Ps. 84:7). But should I be mistaken in the joyful expectation of an age of new questions and investigations[52] for the biblical message, then this book (together with the *Römerbrief*) itself has time – to wait.

---

[43] Correction: "is."
[44] Correction: "Our questions are, if we understand ourselves correctly."
[45] Correction: "if their light again shines on us."
[46] Correction: "there are already those here, even now."
[47] Correction: "of Paul."
[48] Correction: "with the joy of discovery."
[49] Correction: "strong."
[50] Correction: "that there is still much unheard of and undiscovered."
[51] Correction: "which asks for participation."
[52] Correction: "in the joyful hope of a common quest and investigation."

Bibliography

I. Primary Literature

A. Works by Karl Barth

A.1. Books and Book-length Lecture Series

———. *Die Auferstehung der Toten. Eine akademische Vorlesung über I. Kor. 15*. Munich: Chr. Kaiser Verlag, 1924. Trans. H. J. Stenning under the title *The Resurrection of the Dead* (New York: Hodder & F. H. Revell Company, 1933).

———. *Die christliche Dogmatik im Entwurf I. Die Lehre vom Worte Gottes: Prolegomena zur christlichen Dogmatik 1927*. Ed. Gerhard Sauter. Zürich: Theologischer Verlag Zürich, 1982.

———. "Der christliche Glaube und die Geschichte" (1910). In *Vorträge und kleinere Arbeiten, 1909-1914*. Eds. Hans-Anton Drewes and Hinrich Stoevesandt. Zürich: Theologischer Verlag Zürich, 1993, 155-212. This essay was first published in *Schweizerische theologische Zeitschrift* 29 (1912), 1-18, 49-72.

———. *Das christliche Leben, 1959-1961*. Ed. Eberhard Jüngel. Zürich: Theologischer Verlag, 1976. Trans. Geoffrey Bromiley under the title *The Christian Life* (Grand Rapids: Eerdmans, 1981).

———. *Credo: Die Hauptprobleme der Dogmatik dargestellt im Anschluß an das apostolische Glaubensbekenntnis*. Munich: Chr. Kaiser Verlag, 1935. Trans. J. Strathearn McNab under the title *Credo: A Presentation of the Chief Problems of Dogmatics with Reference to The Apostles' Creed* (New York: Charles Scribner's Sons, 1936).

———. *Einführung in die evangelische Theologie*. Zürich: Evangelischer Verlag Zürich, 1962. Trans. Grover Foley under the title *Evangelical Theology: An Introduction* (New York: Holt, Rinehart, and Winston, 1963).

———. *Erklärung des Johannes Evangeliums 1-8: Vorlesung, Münster, Wintersemester 1925/26*. Ed. Walther Fürst. Zürich: Theologischer Verlag Zürich, 1976.

———. *Erklärung des Philipperbriefes*. Munich: Chr. Kaiser Verlag, 1927. Trans. James W. Leitch under the title *The Epistle to the Philippians* (Richmond: John Knox Press, 1962).

———. "Das Evangelium in der Gegenwart." *Theologische Existenz heute* 25 (1935).

———. *Fides quaerens intellectum: Anselms Beweis der Existenz Gottes im Zusammenhang seines theologischen Programms*. Eds. Eberhard Jüngel and Ingolf U. Dalferth. Zürich: Theologischer Verlag Zürich, 1981. Trans. Ian W. Robertson under the title *Anselm: Fides Quaerens Intellectum* (Richmond: John Knox Press, 1960).

———. "Gespräch in Princeton I." *Gespräche, 1959-1962*. Ed. Eberhard Busch. Zürich: Theologischer Verlag Zürich, 1995.

———. *Die Kirchliche Dogmatik*, I/1, I/2, Die Lehre vom Wort Gottes. Zürich: Theologischer Verlag Zürich, 1932/1939.

———. *Konfirmandenunterricht, 1909-1921*. Ed. Jürgen Fangmeier. Zürich: Theologischer Verlag Zürich, 1987, 60-61.

———. *Kurze Erklärung des Römerbriefes*. Munich: Chr. Kaiser Verlag, 1956. Trans. under the title *A Shorter Commentary on Romans* (Richmond: John Knox Press, 1959).

———. *Die protestantische Theologie im 19. Jahrhundert. Ihre Geschichte und Vorgeschichte.* Zürich: Evangelischer Verlag Zürich, 1947. Trans. Brian Cozens and John Bowden under the title *Protestant Theology in the Nineteenth Century* (London: SCM, 1972).

———. *Der Römerbrief (Erste Fassung) 1919.* Ed. Hermann Schmidt. Zürich: Theologischer Verlag Zürich, 1985.

———. *Der Römerbrief, 1922.* Zürich: Evangelischer Verlag Zürich, 1954.

———. *Suchet Gott, so werdet ihr leben!* Bern: G.A. Bäschlin, 1917.

———. *Die Theologie Calvins, 1922.* Ed. Hans Scholl. Zürich: Theologischer Verlag Zürich, 1993. Trans. Geoffrey Bromiley under the title *The Theology of John Calvin* (Grand Rapids: Eerdmans, 1995).

———. *Die Theologie Schleiermachers 1923/24.* Ed. Dietrich Ritschl. Zürich: Theologischer Verlag Zürich, 1978. Trans. Geoffrey Bromiley under the title *The Theology of Schleiermacher* (Grand Rapids: Eerdmans, 1982).

———. *Die Theologie und die Kirche.* Munich: Chr. Kaiser Verlag, 1928.

———. *Theologische Fragen und Antworten.* 2nd ed. Zürich: Theologischer Verlag. Zürich, 1986.

———. "Unterricht in der christlichen Religion" 1924, I. Ed. Hannelotte Reiffen. Zürich: Theologischer Verlag Zürich, 1985. Trans. Geoffrey Bromiley under the title *The Göttingen Dogmatics: Instruction in the Christian Religion I* (Grand Rapids: Eerdmans, 1991).

———. "Unterricht in der christlichen Religion" 1924/1925, II. Ed. Hinrich Stoevesandt. Zürich: Theologischer Verlag Zürich, 1990.

———. "Vorwort zur englischen Ausgabe der Römerbriefauslegung." *Zwischen den Zeiten* (1932), 477-481. Trans. Edwyn C. Hoskyns under the title *The Epistle to the Romans* (Oxford: University Press, 1933, v-x).

———. *Das Wort Gottes und die Theologie.* Munich: Chr. Kaiser Verlag, 1924.

———. *Rudolf Bultmann – ein Versuch, ihn zu verstehen.* Zürich: Evangelischer Verlag Zürich, 1952. Trans. Reginald H. Fuller under the title "Rudolf Bultmann: An Attempt to Understand Him," *Kerygma and Myth*, Vol. II (London: SPCK, 1962, 83-132).

A.2. Shorter Articles, Essays and Addresses

———. "Antwort auf Herrn Professor von Harnacks offenen Brief." *Die Christliche Welt* 37 (1923), 244-252. Also: "Ein Briefwechsel mit Adolf von Harnack." In Karl Barth, *Theologische Fragen und Antworten*, 7-31; *Anfänge der dialektischen Theologie* I. Munich: Chr. Kaiser Verlag, 1962, 323-347. Trans. Keith R. Crim under the title "Correspondence Between Adolf von Harnack and Karl Barth," *The Beginnings of Dialectic Theology*, ed. James M. Robinson (Richmond: John Knox Press, 1968, 165-187).

———. "Autobiographische Skizzen Karl Barths aus dem Fakultätsalbum der Ev.-Theol. Fakultät in Münster." In *Karl Barth-Rudolf Bultmann Briefwechsel, 1922-1966.* Ed. Bernd Jaspert. Zürich: Theologischer Verlag Zürich, 1971, 290-300. Trans. Geoffrey Bromiley under the title *Karl Barth-Rudolf Bultmann Letters 1922-1966* (Grand Rapids: Eerdmans, 1981, 150-157).

———. "Biblische Fragen, Einsichten und Ausblicke." In Karl Barth, *Das Wort Gottes und die Theologie*, 70-98.

———. "Brunners Schleiermacherbuch." *Zwischen den Zeiten* 2 (1924), 49-64.

———. "Der Christ in der Gesellschaft." In Karl Barth, *Das Wort Gottes und die Theologie*, 33-69.

———. "Die dogmatische Prinzipienlehre bei Wilhelm Herrmann." In Karl Barth, *Die Theologie und die Kirche*, 240-284. Trans. Louise Pettibone Smith under the title "The Principles of Dogmatics According to Wilhelm Herrmann" in Karl Barth, *Theology and Church*, 238-271.

———. "Die Gerechtigkeit Gottes." In Karl Barth, *Das Wort Gottes und die Theologie*, 5-17.

———. "Die Missionstätigkeit des Paulus nach der Darstellung der Apostelgeschichte." In *Vorträge und kleinere Arbeiten 1905-1909*. Eds. Hans-Anton Drewes and Hinrich Stoevesandt. Zürich: Theologischer Verlag Zürich, 1992, 148-243.

———. "Moderne Theologie und Reichgottesarbeit." *Zeitschrift für Theologie und Kirche* 19 (1909), 317-321. Also in *Vorträge und kleinere Arbeiten 1905-1909*. Eds. Hans-Anton Drewes and Hinrich Stoevesandt. Zürich: Theologischer Verlag Zürich, 1992, 341-347.

———. "Nachwort." In F. D. E. Schleiermacher, *Schleiermacher-Auswahl*. Ed. Heinz Bolli. Munich: Siebenstern-Taschenbuch-Verlag, 1968, 290-312. Trans. George Hunsinger under the title "Concluding Unscientific Postscript on Schleiermacher" in *The Theology of Schleiermacher* (Grand Rapids: Eerdmans, 1982, 261-279).

———. "Die neue Welt in der Bibel." In Karl Barth, *Das Wort Gottes und die Theologie*, 18-32.

———. "Nocheinmal: Jesus und die Psychiatrie" (1913). Karl Barth, *Vorträge und kleinere Arbeiten 1909-1914*. Ed. Hans-Anton Drewes and Hinrich Stoevesandt. Zürich: Theologischer Verlag Zürich, 1993, 563-571.

———. "Not und Verheißung der christlichen Verkündigung" (1922). In Karl Barth, *Vorträge und kleinere Arbeiten 1922-1925*. Ed. Hinrich Stoevesandt. Zürich: Theologischer Verlag Zürich, 1990, 65-97.

———. "Paulus" (1913?). In Karl Barth, *Vorträge und kleinere Arbeiten 1909-1914*, 555-557.

———. "Von der Paradoxie des 'positiven Paradoxes': Antworten und Fragen an Paul Tillich." *Theologische Blätter* 2 (1923), 287-296. Trans. Keith R. Crim under the title "The Paradoxical Nature of the 'Positive Paradox': Answers and Questions to Paul Tillich" in *The Beginning of Dialectical Theology*, 142-154.

———. "Reformierte Lehre, ihr Wesen und ihre Aufgabe." In Karl Barth, *Das Wort Gottes und die Theologie*, 179-212.

———. "Schleiermacher." In Karl Barth, *Die Theologie und die Kirche*, 136-189. Trans. Louise Pettibone Smith under the title "Schleiermacher" in *Theology and Church* (London: SCM, 1962, 159-199).

———. "Schleiermachers 'Weihnachtsfeier.'" *Zwischen den Zeiten* 3 (1925), 38-61. Also in *Vorträge und kleinere Arbeiten 1922-1925*. Ed. Holger Finze. Zürich: Theologischer Verlag, 1990, 458-489. Trans. Louise Pettibone Smith under the title "Schleiermacher's Celebration of Christmas," *Theology and Church*, 136-158.

———. "Unerledigte Anfragen an die heutige Theologie." In Karl Barth, *Die Theologie und die Kirche*, 1-25. Trans. Louise Pettibone Smith under the title "Unsettled Questions for Theology Today" in *Theology and Church*, 55-73.

———. Das Wort Gottes als Aufgabe der Theologie." In Karl Barth, *Das Wort Gottes und die Theologie*, 156-178.

———. "Das Schriftprinzip der reformierten Kirche." *Zwischen den Zeiten,* 3 (1925), 215-245. Also in *Vorträge und kleinere Arbeiten 1922-1925*. Ed. Holger Finze. Zürich: Theologischer Verlag Zürich, 1990, 512-513.

———. "Das Wort in der Theologie von Schleiermacher bis Ritschl" (1927). In Karl Barth, *Vorträge und kleinere Arbeiten 1925-1930*. Ed. Hermann Schmidt. Zürich: Theologischer Verlag, 1994, 183-214. Trans. Louise Pettibone Smith under the title "The Word in Theology from Schleiermacher to Ritschl" (1927) in *Theology and Church*, 200-216.

———. "Zwinglis '67 Schlussreden' auf das erste Religionsgespräch zu Zürich 1523" (1906). In *Vorträge und kleinere Arbeiten, 1905-1909*. Eds. Hans-Anton Drewes and Hinrich Stoevesandt. Zürich: Theologischer Verlag Zürich, 1992, 104-119.

A.3. Collections of Letters

───. "Adolf Schlatter/Karl Barth: Ein Briefwechsel [1924-1936]." *Theologische Beiträge* 17 (1986) 96-100.

───. *Karl Barth-Rudolf Bultmann: Briefwechsel 1911-1966*. 2nd ed. Ed. Bernd Jaspert. Zürich: Theologischer Verlag Zürich, 1994.

───. *Karl Barth-Eduard Thurneysen: Briefwechsel: I, 1913-1921*. Ed. Eduard Thurneysen. Zürich: Theologischer Verlag Zürich, 1973.

───. *Karl Barth-Eduard Thurneysen: Briefwechsel: II, 1921-1930*. Ed. Eduard Thurneysen. Zürich: Theologischer Verlag Zürich, 1974.

II. Secondary Literature

Adam, Karl. "Die Theologie der Krisis." *Hochland: Monatsschrift für alle Gebiete des Wissens, der Literatur und Kunst,* 23 (1926/27), 271-286. Also in *Gesammelte Aufsätze zur Dogmengeschichte und Theologie der Gegenwart*. Augsburg: Literar. Institut P. Haas & CIE., K-G., 1936, 319-337.

Althaus, Paul. "Paulus und sein neuster Ausleger." *Christentum und Wissenschaft* 1 (1925), 20-30, 97-102.

Avis, Paul. "Karl Barth: The Reluctant Virtuoso." *Theology* 86 (May 1983), 164-171.

Bachmann, Philipp. "Der Römerbrief verdeutscht und vergegenwärtigt" [Review of Rom I]. *Neue Kirchliche Zeitschrift* 32 (1921), 517-547.

───. "Der Römerbrief und Barths Auslegung desselben." *Allgemeine evangelisch-lutherische Kirchenzeitung: Organ der Allgemeinen evangelisch-lutherischen Konferenz* 59 (1926), 434-440, 458-463, 484-492.

Bakker, Nico T. *In der Krisis der Offenbarung: Karl Barths Hermeneutik, dargestellt an seiner Römerbrief-Auslegung*. Neukirchen: Neukirchener Verlag, 1974.

Barbour, R. S. "Karl Barth: The Epistle to the Romans." *The Expository Times* 88 (1979), 264-268.

Baur, Hans. "Selbstkritik oder Selbstzerfleischung?" [Review of Rom I]. *Schweizerisches Protestantenblatt* 43 (1920), 275-277.

Baxter, Christina. "Barth a Truly Biblical Theologian?" *Tyndale Bulletin* 38 (1987), 3-27.

───. "The Movement from Exegesis to Dogmatics in the Theology of Karl Barth." Ph.D. diss., University of Durham, England, 1981.

Behler, Ernst. "What it Means to Understand an Author Better than He Understands Himself: Idealistic Philosophy and Romantic Hermeneutics." In *Literary Theory and Criticism. Festschrift presented to Rene Wellek in Honor of his Eightieth Birthday*. Ed. Joseph P. Strelka. I. Bern/Frankfurt am Main/New York: Lang, 1984, 69-92.

Behm, Johannes. *Pneumatische Exegese? Ein Wort zur Methode der Schriftauslegung*. Schwerin: Fr. Bahn, 1926.

Beintker, Michael. *Die Gottesfrage in der Theologie Wilhelm Herrmanns*. Berlin: Evangelische Verlagsanstalt, 1976.

───. "Der Römerbrief von 1919." *Verkündigung und Forschung* 30:2 (1985), 22-28.

Biggar, Nigel. *The Hastening that Waits: Karl Barth's Ethics*. Oxford: Clarendon Press, 1993.

Boehmer, Julius. [Review of Rom II]. *Die Studierstube: kirchlich-theologische Monatsschrift* 20 (1922), 146-149.

Breitenstein, Jules. [Review of Rom I]. *La Semaine religieuse de Genève: journal evangelique protestant* 10:5 (1919), 19.

Bromiley, Geoffrey W. "The Authority of Scripture in Karl Barth." In *Hermeneutics, Authority, and Canon*. Ed. Geoffrey W. Bromiley. Leicester: Inter-Varsity Press, 1986, 275-294.

Brunner, Emil. "'Der Römerbrief' von Karl Barth: eine zeitgemäß-unmoderne Paraphrase" [Review of Rom I]. *Kirchenblatt für die reformierte Schweiz* 34 (1919), 29-32.

———. *Man in Revolt*. Trans. Olive Wyon. Philadelphia: Westminster, 1947.

Bullnow, F. O. "Was heißt, einen Schriftsteller besser verstehen, als er sich selber verstanden hat?" In *Das Verstehen: Drei Aufsätze zur Theorie der Geisteswissenschaften*. Mainz: Kirchheim, 1949, 7-33.

Bultmann, Rudolf. "Ethische und mystische Religion im Urchristentum [II]." *Die christliche Welt* 34 (1920), 738-743.

———. "Ist voraussetzungslose Exegese möglich?" *Theologische Zeitschrift* 13 (1957), 409-417. Trans. Schubert Ogden under the title "Is Exegesis Without Presuppositions Possible?" in Rudolf Bultmann, *Existence and Faith* (New York: Meridian Books, 1960, 289-296).

———. "Karl Barth, Die Auferstehung der Toten." *Theologische Blätter* 5 (1926), 1-14. Trans. Louise Pettibone Smith "Karl Barth, *The Resurrection of the Dead*" in Rudolf Bultmann, *Faith and Understanding*, ed. Robert Funk (Philadelphia: Fortress Press, 1987, 66-94).

———. "Karl Barths 'Römerbrief' in zweiter Auflage." *Die christliche Welt*, 36.Jg. 1922, 320-323; 330-334; 358-361; 369-373. Also in *Anfänge der dialektischen Theologie* I. Munich: Chr. Kaiser Verlag, 1962, 119-142; Trans. Keith R. Crim under the title "Karl Barth's Epistle to the Romans in its Second Edition" in *The Beginnings of Dialectic Theology*, 100-120.

———. "Neues Testament und Mythologie. Das Problem der Entmythologisierung der neutestamentlichen Verkündigung." *Kerygma und Mythos*. Ed. Hans Werner Bartch. Hamburg: Herbert Reich-Evangelischer Verlag, 1951, 15-48. Trans. Schubert M. Ogden under the title "New Testament and Mythology: The Problem of Demythologizing The New Testament Proclamation," *New Testament and Mythology and Other Basic Writings* (Philadelphia: Fortress Press, 1984, 1-44).

———. "Das Problem einer theologischen Exegese des Neuen Testaments." *Zwischen den Zeiten* 3 (1925), 334-357. Trans. Keith R. Crim under the title "The Problem of a Theological Exegesis of the New Testament," in *The Beginnings of Dialectical Theology*, 257-74.

———. "Das Problem der Hermeneutik." *Zeitschrift für Theologie und Kirche* 47 (1950), 47-69. Also in *Glauben und Verstehen II*. Tübingen: J. C. B. Mohr (Paul Siebeck), 1952, 211-35; Trans. Schubert M. Ogden under the title "The Problem of Hermeneutics," in *New Testament and Mythology and Other Basic Writings* (Philadelphia: Fortress Press, 1984).

Busch, Eberhard. *Karl Barths Lebenslauf*. Munich: Chr. Kaiser Verlag, 1975. Trans. John Bowden under the title *Karl Barth: His Life From Letters and Autobiographical Texts* (Philadelphia: Fortress Press, 1976).

Buschbeck, Karl. "Der Römerbrief" [Review of Rom II]. *Evangelisches Kirchenblatt für Schlesien* 25:45 (1922), 335-337.

Childs, Brevard S. *Biblical Theology of the Old and New Testaments: Theological Reflection on the Christian Bible*. Philadelphia: Fortress, 1993.

———. "Karl Barth as Interpreter of Scripture." In *Karl Barth and The Future of Theology*. Ed. David L. Dickerman. New Haven: Yale Divinity School Association, 1969, 30-35.

———. "Toward Recovering Theological Exegesis." *Pro Ecclesia* 6 (1997), 16-26.

Craig, Gordon A. *Germany: 1866-1945*. New York: Oxford University Press, 1978.

Cullmann, Oscar. "Les problèmes poses par la methode exegetique de l'ecole de Karl Barth." *Revue d'histoire et de philosophie religieuses* 8 (1928), 70-83.

Cunningham, Mary Kathleen. *What Is Theological Exegesis? Interpretation And Use of Scripture in Karl Barth's Doctrine of Election*. Valley Forge, Pennsylvania: Trinity Press International, 1995.
Curran, T. H., "Schleiermacher: True Interpreter." In *The Interpretation of Belief. Coleridge, Schleiermacher, and Romanticism*. Ed. David Jasper. London: MacMillan, 1986, 97-103.
Dalferth, Ingolf U. "Karl Barth's Eschatological Realism." In *Karl Barth: Centenary Essays*. Ed. Stephen W. Sykes. Cambridge: University Press, 14-45.
Davison, James E., "Can God Speak a Word to Man? Barth's Critique of Schleiermacher's Theology." In *Scottish Journal of Theology* 37 (1984), 189-211.
Deißner, Kurt. [Review of Rom II]. *Die Theologie der Gegenwart* 16 (1922), 270.
Demson, David E. *Hans Frei & Karl Barth: Different Ways of Reading Scripture*. Grand Rapids, Michigan: Eerdmans, 1997.
Dilthey, Wilhelm. "Die Entstehung der Hermeneutik." In *Gesammelte Schriften*, V. Leipzig and Berlin, 1914-1936, 317-331. Trans. Fredric Jameson under the title "The Rise of Hermeneutics," *New Literary History* 3 (1972), 229-244.
―――. *Gesammelte Schriften, I, Einleitung in die Geisteswissenschaften*. Berlin: B. G. Teubner, 1922.
―――. *Gesammelte Schriften, V. Über vergleichende Psychologie: Beiträge zum Studium der Individualität*. Berlin: B. G. Teubner, 1924.
―――. *Gesammelte Schriften, VII. Der Aufbau der geschichtlichen Welt in den Geisteswissenschaften*. Berlin: B. G. Teubner, 1927. Trans. under the title *The Hermeneutics Reader*, ed. Kurt Mueller-Vollmer (New York: Continuum, 1992, 152-164).
―――. *Gesammelte Schriften, VIII. Die Typen der Weltanschauung und ihre Ausbildung in dem metaphysischen System*. Berlin: B. G. Teubner, 1931.
―――. "Das hermeneutische System Schleiermachers in der Auseinandersetzung mit der älteren protestantischen Hermeneutik." *In Gesammelten Schriften, II.1. Leben Schleiermachers*. Berlin: Walter de Gruyter, 1966, 595-785. Trans. Theodore Nordenhaug and Rudolf Makkreel under the title *Hermeneutics and the Study of History, Selected Works, Vol. IV*, ed. Rudolf Makkreel (Princeton: University Press, 1996, 33-234).
―――. *Leben Schleiermachers*. 2nd ed. Berlin: Walter de Gruyter, 1922.
Dobschütz, Ernst von. "Die Pneumatische Exegese, Wissenschaft und Praxis." In *Vom Auslegen des Neuen Testamentes*. Göttingen: Vandenhoeck & Ruprecht, 1927, 49-64.
Ebeling, Gerhard. "Wort Gottes und Hermeneutik," *Wort und Glaube*. Tübingen: J. C. B. Mohr (Paul Siebeck), 1960, 319-348. Trans. James W. Leitch under the title "Word of God and Hermeneutic" in *Word and Faith* (Philadelphia: Fortress Press, 1963, 305-332).
Eichholz, G. "Der Ansatz Karl Barths in der Hermeneutik." *Antwort: Karl Barth zum siebzigsten Geburtstag*. Ed. Rudolf Frey, et al. Zürich: Theologischer Verlag Zürich, 1956, 52-68.
Epprecht, Robert. "Der Römerbrief von Karl Barth" [Review of Rom I]. *Religiöses Volksblatt: Organ für kirchlichen Fortschritt* 51 (1920), 182-184.
Fascher, Erich. *Vom Verstehen des Neuen Testamentes: Ein Beitrag zur Grundlegung einer zeitgemäßen Hermeneutik*. Gießen: Alfred Töpelmann, 1930.
Ford, David F., *Barth and God's Story: Biblical Narrative and the Theological Method of Karl Barth in the Church Dogmatics*. Frankfurt am Main: Verlag Peter Lang, 1981.
―――. "Barth's Interpretation of the Bible." In *Karl Barth, Studies of His Theological Method*. Ed. S. W. Sykes. Oxford: Clarendon Press, 1979, 55-87.
Forstman, H. Jackson. "The Understanding of Language by Friedrich Schlegel and Schleiermacher." *Soundings* 51 (1968), 146-165.
―――. "Barth, Schleiermacher and The Christian Faith." *Union Seminary Quarterly Review* 21:3 (1966), 305-319.

———. *Word and Spirit: Calvin's Doctrine of Biblical Authority*. Stanford: University Press, 1962.
Frei, Hans W. "The Doctrine of Revelation in the Thought of Karl Barth, 1909 to 1922." Ph.D. diss., Yale University, 1956.
———. "Karl Barth – Theologian." In *Karl Barth and The Future of Theology*. New Haven: Yale Divinity School Association, 1969, 5-12.
———. *The Eclipse of Biblical Narrative: A Study of Eighteenth and Nineteenth Century Hermeneutics*. New Haven: Yale University Press, 1974.
———. "Barth and Schleiermacher: Divergence and Convergence." In *Barth and Schleiermacher: Beyond the Impasse?* Eds. James O. Duke and Robert F. Streetman. Philadelphia: Fortress Press, 1988, 65-87.
———. "Conflicts in Interpretation: Resolution, Armistice, or Co-Existence?" In *Theology & Narrative: Selected Essays*. Eds. George Hunsinger and William C. Placher. Oxford: University Press, 1993, 153-166.
———. *The Identity of Jesus Christ: The Hermeneutical Bases of Dogmatic Theology*. Philadelphia: Fortress Press, 1975.
———. "The 'Literal Reading' of Biblical Narrative in the Christian Tradition: Does It Stretch or Will It Break?" In *The Bible and Narrative Tradition*. Ed. Frank McConnell. New York: Oxford, 1986, 36-77.
———. *Types of Christian Theology*. New Haven: Yale University Press, 1992.
Freundenberg, Matthias. *Karl Barth und die reformierte Theologie. Die Auseinandersetzungen mit Calvin, Zwingli und den reformierten Bekenntnisschriften während seiner Göttinger Lehrtätigkeit*. Neukirchen-Vluyn: Neukirchener Verlag, 1996.
Frick, Heinrich. *Wissenschaftliches und Pneumatisches Verständnis der Bibel*. Tübingen: J. C. B. Mohr (Paul Siebeck), 1927.
Fuchs, Ernst. *Marburger Hermeneutik*. Tübingen: J. C. B. Mohr (Paul Siebeck), 1968.
———. "Das Neue Testament und das hermeneutische Problem." *Zeitschrift für Theologie und Kirche* 58 (1961). Trans. and ed. James M. Robinson under the title "The New Testament and the Hermeneutical Problem" in *The New Hermeneutic* (New York: Harper & Row, 1964).
Fueter, Karl. "Allerlei Theologisches" [Review of Rom I]. *Neue Züricher Zeitung und schweizerisches Handelsblatt* 140:2008 (21 Dec. 1919).
Gadamer, Hans-Georg. *Wahrheit und Methode*. 2nd edition (revised). Tübingen: J. C. B. Mohr (Paul Siebeck), 1965. Trans. Joel Weinsheimer and Donald Marshall under the title *Truth and Method* (New York: Crossroad, 1989).
———. "The Problem of Language in Schleiermacher's Hermeneutic." In *Schleiermacher as Contemporary*. Ed. Robert W. Funk. New York: Herder & Herder, 1970, 68-84.
Gerber, Ernst. "Ein neues Buch über den Römerbrief" [Review of Rom I]. *Brosamen: Evangelisches Volksblatt* 32/17 (27 April 1919), 2-3.
Girgensohn, Karl. *Die Inspiration der heiligen Schrift*. Dresden: C. L. Ungelenk,1925.
Godsey, John D. *Karl Barth's Table Talk*. Richmond: John Knox Press, 1962.
Gogarten, Friedrich. "Vom heiligen Egoismus des Christen: eine Antwort auf Jülichers Aufsatz in Nr.29 'Ein moderner Paulusausleger.'" *Die Christliche Welt* 34 (1920), 546-550. Trans. Keith R. Crim under the title "The Holy Egoism of The Christian: An Answer to Jülicher's Essay: 'A Modern Interpreter of Paul'" in *The Beginnings of Dialectical Theology*, 82-87.
Greene-McCreight, Kathryn. *Ad Litteram: Understandings of The Plain Sense of Scripture in the Exegesis of Augustine, Calvin and Barth of Genesis 1-3*. Ann Arbor, Michigan: UMI, 1994.
Hadorn, Friedrich Wilhelm. [Review of Rom I]. *Berner Tagblatt* 32:33 (1920), 2.
Hamilton, Kenneth. "Under Schleiermacher's Banner." In *Religion in Life*, 1963, 564-573.

Harrisville, Roy A. "Karl Barth and the Römerbrief." *Dialog: A Journal of Theology* 28:4 (1989), 276-281.
Harvey, Van A. "A Word in Defense of Schleiermacher's Theological Method." *The Journal of Religion* 42 (1962), 151-170.
Herder, Johann Gottfried. "Briefe an Theophron." In *Sämtliche Werke*, xi. Ed. Bernhard Suphan. Hildesheim: Georg Olms Verlagsbuchhandlung, 1967, 163.
Herzog, Frederick. "The Possibility of Theological Understanding: An Inquiry in the Presuppositions of Hermeneutics in Theology." Th.D. diss., Princteon Theological Seminary, 1953.
Hoffmann, Konrad. "Karl Barths Römerbrief in zweiter Auflage" [Review of Rom II]. *Kirchlicher Anzeiger für Württemberg: Organ des Evangelischen Pfarrvereins* 31 (1922), 129-130.
Hunsinger, George. *How to Read Karl Barth: The Shape of His Theology*. New York: Oxford, 1991.
———. "Beyond Literalism and Expressivism: Karl Barth's Hermeneutical Realism." *Modern Theology* 3:3 (1987), 209-223.
Jeanrond, Werner G. "The Impact of Schleiermacher's Hermeneutics on Contemporary Interpretation Theory." In *The Interpretation of Belief. Coleridge, Schleiermacher, and Romanticism*. Ed. David Jasper. London: MacMillan, 1986, 81-96.
———. "Karl Barth's Hermeneutics." In *Reckoning with Barth*. Ed. Nigel Biggar. Oxford: Mowbray, 1988, 94.
Jelke, Robert. "Historisch-kritische und theologisch-dogmatische Schriftauslegung." In *Das Erbe Martin Luthers: Festschrift für Ihmels*. Leipzig: Dörffling and Franke, 1928, 215-235.
Johnson, Robert C. "The Legacy of Karl Barth." In *Karl Barth and The Future of Theology*. Ed. David L. Dickerman. New Haven: Yale Divinity School Association, 1969, 1-4.
Jülicher, Adolf. "Ein moderner Paulusausleger" [Review of Rom I]. *Die christliche Welt* 34 (1920), 453-457. Also in Moltmann, *Anfänge der dialektischen Theologie* I. Munich: Chr. Kaiser, Verlag, 1962, 87-98. Trans. Keith R. Crim under the title "A Modern Interpreter of Paul" in *The Beginnings of Dialectical Theology*, 72-81.
———. "Der Römerbrief" [Review of Rom II]. *Theologische Literaturzeitung* 47:25 (1922), 539-540.
Jüngel, Eberhard. *Gottes Sein Ist Im Werden*. Tübingen: J. C. B. Mohr (Paul Siebeck), 1965. Trans. Horton Harris under the title *The Doctrine of the Trinity: The Being of God is in Becoming* (Grand Rapids: Eerdmans, 1976).
———. "Einführung in Leben und Werk Karl Barths." In *Barth-Studien*. Zürich: Benziger Verlag, 1982, 22-60. Trans. Garrett E. Paul under the title "Barth's Life and Work" in *Karl Barth: A Theological Legacy* (Philadelphia: Westminster, 1986, 22-52).
———. "Theologie als Metakritik. Zur Hermeneutik theologischer Exegese." In *Barth-Studien*. Zürich: Benziger Verlag, 1982, 83-97. Trans. Garrett E. Paul under the title "Theology as Metacriticism: Toward a Hermeneutic of Theological Exegesis" in *Karl Barth: A Theological Legacy*, 70-82.
Kelsey, David H. *The Uses of Scripture in Recent Theology*. London: SCM, 1975.
Kimmerle, Heinz. "Hermeneutical Theory or Ontological Hermeneutics." Trans. Friedrich Seifert. *Journal for Theology and the Church* 6 (1967), 107-121.
Kirschstein, Helmut. *Der souveräne Gott und die heilige Schrift: Einführung in die biblische Hermeneutik Karl Barths*. Aachen: Shaker Verlag, 1998.
Koepp, Wilhelm. *Die gegenwärtige Geisteslage und die 'dialektische' Theologie: eine Einführung*. Tübingen: J. C. B. Mohr (Paul Siebeck), 1930.

Kohls, Ernst-Wilhelm. "Einen Autor besser verstehen, als er sich selbst verstanden hat. Zur Problematik der neueren Hermeneutik und Methodik am Beispiel von Wilhelm Dilthey, Adolf von Harnack und Ernst Troeltsch." *Theologische Zeitschrift* 26 (1970), 321-337.

Kraus, Hans-Joachim. "Das Problem der Heilsgeschichte in der 'Kirchlichen Dogmatik." In *Antwort: Karl Barth zum siebzigsten Geburtstag*. Eds. Rudolf Frey, et al. Zürich: Evangelischer Verlag Zürich, 1956, 69-83.

Krüger, Gerhard. "Dialektische Methode und theologische Exegese. Logische Bemerkungen zu Barths 'Römerbrief.'" *Zwischen den Zeiten* 5:2 (1927), 116-157.

Lafargue, Michael. "Are Texts Determinate?: Derrida, Barth, and the Role of the Biblical Scholar." *The Harvard Theological Review* 81 (1988), 341-357.

Lindbeck, George. "Barth and Textuality." *Theology Today* 43 (October 1986), 361-76.

———. *The Nature of Doctrine: Religion and Theology in a Postliberal Age*. Philadelphia: Westminster, 1984.

Lindemann, Walter. *Karl Barth und die kritische Schriftauslegung*. Hamburg-Bergstedt: Evangelischer Verlag, 1973.

Loew, Wilhelm. "Noch einmal Barths Römerbrief" [Review of Rom I]. *Die Christliche Welt* 34 (1920), 585-587.

Lütz, Dietmar. *Homo Viator: Karl Barths Ringen mit Schleiermacher*. Zürich: Theologischer Verlag Zürich, 1988.

Macholz, Woldmar. "Pneumatische Exegese – eine berechtigte theologische Forderung." *Pastoralblätter* 69, 70ff.

Maddox, Randy I. "Hermeneutic Circle: Vicious or Victorious." *Philosophy Today* (Spring 1983), 66-75.

Margolis, Joseph. "Schleiermacher Among the Theorists of Language and Interpretation." *The Journal of Aesthetics and Art Criticism* 45 (1986/1987), 361-368.

Marquardt, F.-W. "Exegese und Dogmatik in Karl Barths Theologie." In *Registerband to Kirchlichen Dogmatik of Karl Barth*. Zürich: Evangelischer Verlag Zürich, 1970, 651-76.

Marshall, Bruce D. "Hermeneutics and Dogmatics in Schleiermacher's Theology." *The Journal of Religion* 67 (Jan. 1987), 14-32.

McCormack, Bruce L. *Karl Barth's Critically Realistic Dialectical Theology: Its Genesis and Development 1909-1936*. Oxford: Clarendon, 1995.

———. "Historical-Criticism and Dogmatic Interest in Karl Barth's Theological Exegesis of the New Testament." In *Biblical Hermeneutic in Historical Perspective: Studies in Honor of Karlfried Froehlich on his Sixtieth Birthday*. Eds. Mark S. Burrows and Paul Rorem. Grand Rapids: Eerdmans, 1991, 322-338.

McGlasson, Paul. *Jesus and Judas: Biblical Exegesis in Barth*. Atlanta, Georgia: Scholars Press, 1991.

Meinecke, Friedrich. "Zur Entstehungsgeschichte des Historismus und des Schleiermacherschen Individualitätsgedankens" [1939]. In *Zur Theorie und Philosophie der Geschichte*. Werke, 4. Ed. Eberhard Kessel. Stuttgart: Köhler, 341-357.

Mennicke, Carl. "Auseinandersetzung mit Karl Barth" [Review of Rom I]. *Blätter für religiösen Sozialismus* 2 (1920), 5-8.

Merz, George. [Review of Rom I]. *Christentum und Gegenwart: evangelisches Monatsblatt* 11:3 (1920), 48.

Miescher, Ernst. [Review of Rom I]. *Christlicher Volksfreund: Blätter zur Förderung christlichen Glaubens und Lebens* 45:6 (8 Feb. 1919), 71.

Minear, Paul Sevier. "Barth's Commentary on the Romans, 1922-1972; or Karl Barth vs. The Exegetes." In *Footnotes to a Theology: The Karl Barth Colloquium of 1972*. Ed. Martin Rumscheidt. Waterloo, Ontario: The Corporation for the Publication of Academic Studies in Religion in Canada, 1974, 8-29.

Miskotte, Kornelis H. *Als De Goden Zwijgen*. Amsterdam: Uitgeversmaatschappij, 1956. . Trans. John W. Doberstein under the title *When the Gods are Silent* (New York: Harper & Row, 1967).

———. "Die Erlaubnis zur schriftgemäßen Denkform." In *Antwort: Karl Barth zum siebzigsten Geburtstag*. Eds. Rudolf Frey, et al. Zürich: Evangelischer Verlag, 1956.

———. "Das Problem der Theologischen Exegese." In *Theologische Aufsätze*. München: Chr. Kaiser Verlag, 1936.

Moltmann, Jürgen. *Anfänge der dialektischen Theologie*, 2 vols. Munich: Chr. Kaiser Verlag, 1962-1963.

Mueller-Vollmer, Kurt. "To Understand an Author Better than the Author Himself: On the Hermeneutics of the Unspoken." *Language and Style* 5 (1971), 43-52.

Müller, Emil. "Der Römerbrief" [Review of Rom I]. *Monatsblatt für das reformierte Volk des Aargaus* 29:7 (1919), 51-54.

Müller, Karl. "Karl Barths' Römerbrief" [Review of Rom I]. *Reformierte Kirchenzeitung* 71 (1921), 103-105.

Münch, Alexander. [Review of Rom I]. *Das neue Werk: Der Christ im Volksstaat* 1 (1919), 487-488.

Neuberg, Artur. [Review of Rom II]. *Pastoralblätter für Predigt, Seelsorge und kirchliche Unterweisung* 64 (1921), 497-504.

Neven, G.W. "Dialektik als Sprachform der Theologie Karl Barths." *Zeitschrift für dialektische Theologie* 11:2 (1995), 211-228.

Niebergall, Friedrich. *Praktische Auslegung des Neuen Testaments: Für Prediger und Religionslehrer*. Tübingen: J. C. B. Mohr (Paul Siebeck), 1909.

Niebuhr, Richard R. "Schleiermacher On Language and Feeling." *Theology Today*, July, 1960, 150-167.

Nietzsche, Friedrich. "Unzeitgemäße Betrachtungen, II. Vom Nutzen und Nachteil der Historie." In *Werke*, 1. München: Carl Hanser Verlag, 1954.

Otto, Rudolf. "How Schleiermacher Rediscovered the Sensus Numinis." In *Religious Essays: A Supplement to 'The Idea of the Holy.'* Trans. B. Lunn. Oxford: University Press, 1931.

Palmer, Richard E. *Hermeneutics: Interpretation Theory in Schleiermacher, Dilthey, Heidegger, and Gadamer*. Evanston: Northwestern University Press, 1969.

Pfau, Thomas. "Immediacy and the Text: Friedrich Schleiermacher's Theory of Style and Interpretation." *Journal of the History of Ideas* 51 (1990), 51-73.

Plantinga, Theodore. *Historical Understanding in the Thought of Wilhelm Dilthey*. Toronto: University of Toronto Press, 1980.

Procksch, O. "Über pneumatische Exegese." *Christentum und Wissenschaft* 1 (1925), 145-158.

Provence, Thomas. *The Hermeneutics of Karl Barth*. Ann Arbor: Michigan: UMI, 1980.

Radler, Aleksander. "Die Theologie Schleiermachers" [Rezension von Barths Die Theologie Schleiermachers, 1923/24]. *Verkündigung und Forschung*, 30:2 (1985), 28-44.

Redeker, Martin. *Friedrich Schleiermacher. Leben und Werk (1768 bis 1834)*. Berlin: de Gruyter, 1968.

Ricoeur, Paul. *Essays on Biblical Interpretation*. Ed. Lewis S. Mudge. Philadelphia: Fortress, 1980.

———. "Schleiermacher's Hermeneutics." *The Monist* 60 (1977) 181-197.

———. "The Hermeneutical Function of Distanciation." *Philosophy Today* 17 (1973), 129-141.

Robinson, James M. "Hermeneutics After Barth." In *The New Hermeneutic*. Ed. James M. Robinson. New York: Harper & Row, 1964, 1-77.

Schaeder, Erich. "Die Geistesfrage in der neueren Theologie der Gegenwart." *Zeitschrift für systematische Theologie* 3 (1925), 424-460.

Schlatter, Adolf. "Karl Barths 'Römerbrief'" [Review of Rom II]. *Die Furche* 12 (1922), 228-232. Also in *Anfänge der dialektischen Theologie* I. Ed. Jürgen Moltmann. Munich: Chr. Kaiser, Verlag, 1962, 142-147. Trans. Keith R. Crim under the title "Karl Barth's Epistle to the Romans" in *The Beginnings of Dialectical Theology*, 121-125.

Schleiermacher, Friedrich. *Der christliche Glaube*. 2 vols. Berlin: de Gruyter, 1960. Trans. H. R. Mackintosh under the title *The Christian Faith* (Edinburgh: T & T Clark, 1928).

———. *On the Glaubenslehre: Two Letters to Dr. Lücke*. Trans. James Duke and Francis Fiorenza. Atlanta: Scholars Press, 1981.

———. *Hermeneutik*. Ed. Heinz Kimmerle. Heidelberg: Carl Winter Universitätsverlag, 1959. Trans. James Duke and Jack Forstman under the title *Hermeneutics: The Handwritten Manuscripts* (Atlanta: Scholars Press, 1977).

———. *Kurze Darstellung des theologischen Studiums*, Kritische Ausgabe. Ed. Heinrich Scholz. Leipzig: A. Deichert, 1910.

Schlichting, W. *Biblische Denkform in der Dogmatik*. Zürich: Theologischer Verlag, 1971.

Schmidt, Karl. L. "Marcion und wir. Die Gegenwartsbedeutung von Harnacks Marcion." *Kartell-Zeitung. Organ des Eisenacher Kartells akademisch-theologischer Vereine* 31 (1920/21), 83-85.

Schneider, Johannes. "Historische und pneumatische Exegese." *Neue Kirchliche Zeitschrift* 42:12 (1931), 711-733.

Schnur, Harald. *Schleiermachers Hermeneutik und ihre Vorgeschichte im 18.Jahrhundert*. Stuttgart: Verlag J. B. Metzler, 1994.

Schütz, Roland. "Kritisches zur Theologie der Krisis." *Theologische Studien und Kritiken: Beiträge zur Theologie und Religionswissenschaft* (1925), 263-288.

Seeberg, Erich. "Zum Problem der pneumatischen Exegese." In *Sellin-Festschrift*. Leipzig: Deichert 1927, 127-137.

———. "Das Problem der pneumatischen Exegese." In *Menschwerdung und Geschichte*. Stuttgart: W. Kohlhammer Verlag, 1938, 138-148.

Seeberg, Reinhold. "Zur Frage nach dem Sinn und Recht einer pneumatischen Schriftauslegung." *Zeitschrift für systematische Theologie* (1927), 3-59.

Smart, James D. *The Divided Mind of Modern Theology*. Philadelphia: Westminster, 1967.

Smend, Rudolf. "Nachkritische Schriftauslegung." In *Parrhesia: Karl Barth zum achtzigsten Geburtstag*. Zürich: Evangelischer Verlag Zürich, 1966, 215-37.

Steinmetz, Rudolf. [Review of Rom I]. *Theologisches Literaturblatt* 41 (1920), 323-325.

Stendahl, Krister. "Biblical Theology: A Program." In *Interpreter's Dictionary of the Bible*, 1. Nashville: Abingdon Press, 1962, 418-432.

Strathmann, Hermann. [Review of Rom II]. *Die Theologie der Gegenwart* 17 (1923), 261-262.

Streetman, Robert F. "Romanticism and the Sensus Numinis in Schleiermacher." In *The Interpretation of Belief. Coleridge, Schleiermacher, and Romanticism*. Ed. David Jasper. London: MacMillan, 1986, 104-125.

Stuhlmacher, Peter. "Historische Kritik und theologische Schriftauslegung." In *Schriftauslegung auf dem Wege zur biblischen Theologie*. Göttingen: Vandenhoeck & Ruprecht, 1975.

Thiel, John. "Barth's Early Interpretation of Schleiermacher." In *Barth and Schleiermacher: Beyond the Impasse?* Eds. J. Duke and R. Streetman. Philadelphia: Fortress, 1988, 11-22.

Thielicke, Helmut. *Modern Faith & Thought*. Trans. Geoffrey Bromiley. Grand Rapids: Eerdmans, 1990.

Thiselton, Anthony. "Schleiermacher's Hermeneutics of Understanding." In *New Horizons in Hermeneutics*. Grand Rapids: Zondervan, 1992, 204-236.

Thurneysen, Eduard. "Die Anfänge." In *Antwort: Karl Barth zum siebzigsten Geburtstag*. Eds. Rudolf Frey, et al. Zürich: Evangelischer Verlag, 1956, 831-864.

———. *Suchet Gott, so werdet ihr leben!* Bern: G.A. Bäschlin, 1917.
———. *Das Wort Gottes und die Theologie.* Munich: Chr. Kaiser Verlag, 1924.
Tice, Terrence. "Interviews with Karl Barth and Reflections on his Interpretation of Schleiermacher." In *Barth and Schleiermacher: Beyond the Impasse?* Eds. James Duke and Robert Streetman. Philadelphia: Fortress, 1988, 43-62.
Torm, Friedrich. *Hermeneutik des Neuen Testaments.* Göttingen: Vandenhoeck und Ruprecht, 1930.
Torrance, James B. "Interpretation and Understanding in Schleiermacher's Theology: Some Critical Questions." *Scottish Journal of Theology* 21 (1968), 268-82.
Torrance, Thomas F. "Hermeneutics According to F. D. E. Schleiermacher." *Scottish Journal of Theology* 21 (1968), 257-67.
Traub, Friedrich. "Wort Gottes und pneumatische Schriftauslegung." *Zeitschrift für Theologie und Kirche* 8 (1927), 83-111.
Troeltsch, Ernst. "Historiography." In *Encyclopaedia of Religion and Ethics.* Vol. 6. Ed. James Hastings. New York: Charles Scribner's Sons (1925), 716-723.
———. *Der Historismus und seine Probleme.* Tübingen: J. C. B. Mohr (Paul Siebeck), 1922.
———. "Über historische und dogmatishe Methode in der Theologie." In Ernst Troeltsch, *Gesammelte Schriften*, 2. Tübingen: J. C. B. Mohr (Paul Siebeck), 1913, 729-753. Trans. James Luther Adams and Walter E. Bense under the title "Historical and Dogmatic Method in Theology" in *Religion in History* (Minneapolis: Fortress Press, 1991, 11-32).
———. "Rückblick auf ein halbes Jahrhundert der theologischen Wissenschaft" (1908). In *Theologie als Wissenschaft.* Ed. Gerhard Sauter. Munich: Chr. Kaiser Verlag, 1971, 73-104. Trans. Robert Morgan amd Michael Pye under the title "Half a Century of Theology: A Review" in *Ernst Troeltsch: Writings on Theology and Religion*, eds. Robert Morgan and Michael Pye (Atlanta: John Knox Press, 1977, 53-81).
Veldhuizen, Adriaan van. [Review of Rom I]. *Nieuwe theologische studiën: praktisch maandschrift voor godgeleerdheid* 2 (1919), 109.
Wach, Joachim. *Das Verstehen: Grundzüge einer Geschichte der hermeneutischen Theorie im 19. Jahrhundert.* Tübingen: J. C. B. Mohr (Paul Siebeck), I-III, 1926-1933.
———. "The Interpretation of Sacred Books." *Journal of Biblical Literature* 55 (1936), 59-63.
Wallace, Mark I. "Karl Barth's Hermeneutic: A Way beyond the Impasse." *Journal of Religion* 68 (July 1988), 396-410.
———. *The Second Naiveté: Barth, Ricoeur, and the New Yale Theology.* Macon, GA: Mercer University Press, 1990.
Ward, Graham. *Barth, Derrida and the Language of Theology.* Cambridge: University Press, 1995.
Warnke, Georgia. *Gadamer: Hermeneutics, Tradition, and Reason.* Stanford: University Press, 1987.
Webb, Stephen H. *Re-figuring Theology: The Rhetoric of Karl Barth.* Albany, NY: State University of New York Press, 1991.
Weiß, Peter. "Die Hermeneutik Friedrich Schleiermachers und Rudolf Bultmanns im Vergleich." *Theologische Zeitschrift* 46 (1990), 124-161.
Werner, Martin. [Review of Rom I]. *Evangelisches Schulblatt: Organ des Evangelischen Schulvereins der Schweiz* 54 (1919), 400.
Wernle, Paul. *Die Anfänge unserer Religion.* Freiburg: J. C. B. Mohr (Paul Siebeck), 1901.
———. *Der Christ und die Sünde bei Paulus.* Freiburg: J. C. B. Mohr (Paul Siebeck), 1897.
———. *Einführung in das theologische Studium.* Tübingen: J. C. B. Mohr (Paul Siebeck), 1908, 1911, 1921.
———. *Paulus als Heidenmissionar.* Freiburg: J. C. B. Mohr (Paul Siebeck), 1899.

———. "Der Römberbrief in neuer Beleuchtung" [Review of Rom I]. *Kirchenblatt für die reformierte Schweiz* 34 (1919), 163-164, 167-169.

———. *Die synoptische Frage*. Freiburg: J. C. B. Mohr (Paul Siebeck), 1899.

———. *Was haben wir heute an Paulus?* Basel: Helbing & Lichtenhahn, 1904.

West, Cornel. "Schleiermacher's Hermeneutics and The Myth of The Given." *Union Seminary Quarterly Review* 34 (1979), 71-84.

Wharton, James A. "Karl Barth as Exegete and His Influence on Biblical Interpretation." *Union Seminary Quarterly Review* 28 (Fall 1972), 5-13.

Wilke, Sabine. "Authorial Intent Versus Universal Symbolic Language: Schleiermacher and Schlegel on Mythology, Interpretation, and Communal Values." *Soundings* 74 (1991), 411-425.

Windisch, Hans. [Review of Rom I]. *Theologische Literaturzeitung* 45 (1920), 200-201.

Wittig, Joseph. "Neue religiöse Bücher" [Review of Rom II]. *Hochland: Monatsschrift für alle Gebiete des Wissens, der Literatur und Kunst* 21 (1923/24), 420.

Wobbermin, Georg. *Systematische Theologie: nach religionspsychologischer Methode*, 1-3. Leipzig: J. C. Hinrich'sche, 1913-1925.

Wuhrmann, Wilhelm. [Review of Rom I]. *Schweizerische theologische Zeitschrift* 37 (1920), 59-60.

Index of Names

Achelis, Ernst Christian, 174, 176
Anzinger, Herbert, 8
Asmussen, Hans, 30
Ast, Friedrich, 47, 79, 153, 156, 255
Augustine, 55, 129, 181, 208, 212, 224
Bachmann, Philipp, 15, 16, 26
Bakker, Nicolaas, 7
Barth, Franz Albert, 69
Barth, Fritz, 69, 110, 122, 173, 292
Barth, Nelly, 14, 271-272
Baur, F. C., 149
Beck, J. T., 69, 118, 123, 135, 250, 266, 278, 288
Beintker, Michael, 8, 72, 103
Boehmer, Julius, 121
Brunner, Emil, 16, 19, 263
Buddeus, J. F., 36, 152
Bultmann, Rudolf, x, xi, 13, 16, 27, 28, 30-33, 40, 41, 43, 47, 51, 57, 60-61, 68, 77, 92-93, 97, 111, 120, 124, 194-196, 199, 202, 203, 219, 249
Buxtorf, Karl, 98
Calvin, John, 2, 7, 9, 23, 24, 26, 29, 58, 60, 69, 81, 98, 103, 118-119, 176, 179, 181, 184, 185, 196, 212, 232, 233, 238, 249, 250-253, 258, 266, 278, 288
Cassirer, Ernst, 43
Childs, Brevard, xiv, 9
Cohen, Hermann, 43
Cunningham, Mary Kathleen, 5, 6, 9
Deißner, Kurt, 121
de Wette, Wilhelm Leberecht, 142
Dilthey, Wilhelm, 32-33, 40, 43-50, 53, 59, 61, 107-109, 117, 124, 130, 132, 133, 149, 155, 156, 158-167, 169, 191, 192, 200, 203, 206, 217
Drewes, Hans-Anton, xiv
Drews, Paul, 174, 176
Ebeling, Gerhard, 32-34, 40, 48
Ebner, Ferdinand, 43
Eichendorff, Joesph, 171
Eichholz, Georg, 124, 192
Epprecht, Robert, 15-16, 18-19

Ernesti, J. A., 45, 54, 152, 159
Fascher, Erich, 27, 48, 123
Feuerbach, Ludwig, 39, 44, 219
Fichte, J. G., 107, 159, 200, 204
Frei, Hans, xii, xiv, 45-47, 71, 72, 145-149, 151, 262, 264
Freud, Sigmund, 39
Fuchs, Ernst, 32-33, 43
Fueter, Karl, 18, 19
Gadamer, Hans-Georg, xiv, 3, 4, 32, 45, 48, 91, 150, 151, 167, 192, 199-207, 274
Gerber, Ernst, 16, 18-19
Godet, F., 83, 123, 127, 266, 278, 283, 289
Goethe, J. W., 55-56, 59, 60, 64, 79, 89, 114, 129, 130, 156, 163, 175, 179, 182, 218, 237, 238
Grünewald, Matthias, 141, 193, 229
Hadorn, Friedrich, 16, 18
Harnack, Adolf von, 15, 51, 52, 105, 134, 139, 166, 170, 173, 209, 235, 260
Hegel, George Wilhelm Friedrich, 43, 158, 161, 211
Heidegger, Martin, 32-33, 40, 43-44, 47, 158, 203
Hengel, Martin, xv
Herder, Johann Gottfried von, 131, 142-151, 153, 155, 157, 159, 164, 166-169, 179, 191, 200, 211, 219, 260
Herrmann, Wilhelm, 70-73, 97, 134, 169-171, 173, 175, 235
Hirsch, Emanuel, 107
Homer, 59, 131, 238
Hunsinger, George, 6, 222
Husserl, Edmund, 43
Jameson, Frederic, 165
Jülicher, Adolf, 15-20, 27, 55-56, 58, 83, 96, 100, 108, 115, 117-121, 127, 191, 198, 231, 232, 240, 247, 248, 250, 268, 278, 283, 288, 289
Jüngel, Eberhard, 42, 54, 100, 110, 111, 116, 123

Kant, Immanuel, 2, 37, 70, 73, 129, 150, 159, 170, 177, 200, 204, 205, 218, 228, 260
Kelsey, David, xiv, 99
Kierkegaard, Soren, 212, 225
Kimmerle, Heinz, 32, 164
Klaiber, Christoph, 149
Kutter, Hermann, 134
Lao-Tzu, 55-56, 64, 79, 89, 218, 237
Lewis, C. S., xiv, 111
Lessing, G. E., 37, 45, 108, 179, 260
Lindbeck, George, xiv, 74, 225
Lindemann, Walter, 7
Lietzmann, Hans, 83, 118, 120, 127, 201, 231, 250, 278, 283, 288, 289
Lipsius, Richard A., 83, 127, 266, 278, 283, 289
Loew, Wilhelm, 15, 17-19, 108, 174
Lücke, Friedrich, 156
Lüdemann, Hermann, 169
Luther, Martin, 2, 55, 69, 77, 98, 162, 163, 179-182, 184, 195, 212, 232, 233, 235, 236, 246, 250, 252, 258
Marcion, 15, 22, 55, 118
Marti, Karl, 169
McCormack, Bruce L., xii, xiv, 1, 4, 6, 29, 43, 72, 103, 107
McGlasson, Paul, 6, 9
Melanchthon, Phillip, 179, 251
Mennicke, Carl, 16-17, 19
Natorp, Paul, 43
Niebergall, Friedrich, 243, 279, 285, 288
Nietzsche, Friedrich, 39, 44, 114-116, 161, 272, 282, 285
Novalis, Friedrich von Hardenberg, 171, 179
O'Regan, Cyril, xiv
Origen, 98
Osterwald, J. F., 36
Pestalozzi, Rudolf, 268
Pfaff, C. M., 36
Plantinga, Theodore, 166
Plato, 56, 64, 129-131
Ragaz, Leonhard, 134, 271
Ranke, Leopold, 44, 132, 150
Rieger, Carl Heinrich, 278
Ritschl, Albrecht, 70, 97, 171, 260

Robinson, James M., 27, 32, 33, 42, 246
Rosenstock-Huessy, Eugen, 43
Rosenzweig, Franz, 43
Rothe, Richard, 69
Sartorius, Karl Achilles, 69
Schelling, F. W. J., 69, 159
Schiller, Friedrich, 171, 175, 179, 182
Schlatter, Adolf, 122-123, 242, 248
Schleiermacher, F. D. E., xi, 2-4, 6-7, 11, 25, 32-33, 37-40, 43, 45, 47-54, 59, 61, 63, 68-70, 79, 91, 109, 117, 124, 129, 132, 142-144, 149-161, 163-171, 175, 176, 179, 183, 187, 188, 191-193, 197, 199, 200-207, 219, 220, 222, 223, 225, 227, 229, 239, 240, 249, 255-258, 260
Schmidt, Hermann, 8, 269
Schmidt, Karl Ludwig, 15, 137
Schneider, Johannes, 27, 48
Schweitzer, Albert, 161
Steck, Rudolf, 134, 169
Steinmetz, Rudolf, 16, 18
Stelzendorf, 107
Stendahl, Krister, 242, 261
Strathmann, Hermann, 91, 121
Strauss, David Friedrich, 98, 149, 161, 219
Thurneysen, Eduard, 7, 14, 19-26, 35, 43, 68, 76, 134-136, 186, 235, 265-275, 291
Tillich, Paul, xv, 9, 218
Troeltsch, Ernst, 70, 96-96, 105, 107, 137, 142, 144, 166-169, 177, 188, 191, 260
Turrettini, J. A., 36, 46, 150, 159
van Veldhuizen, Adriaan, 16
von Balthasar, Hans Urs, 1
von Wartenburg, Yorck, 107
Wach, Joachim, 47, 48
Warnke, Georgia, 200, 203
Weiss, Johannes, 83, 186, 266, 278, 283, 289
Werenfels, S., 36
Wernle, Paul, 16-20, 56, 82, 92, 105, 128-138, 144, 148, 166, 173, 181, 185-188, 191-193, 198, 236, 239, 240
Windisch, Hans, 15, 18
Wobbermin, Georg, 166-169
Wolf, Friedrich, 47, 79, 153, 156, 159
Wolff, C., 36
Zahn, Adolf, 83, 127, 278, 283, 289

Index of Subjects

a priori, 6, 36-38, 41-42, 59, 87, 139, 220, 242
a priori- a posteriori procedure, 36-38, 41
actualism, 5-6, 49-50, 57, 222-223
"ad hoc" hermeneutical principles, 5, 8, 50, 81-82
Alexandrian, 15, 22, 82
analogia fidei, 121, 237
Anschauung, 178-180, 182, 184, 222, 224-225
anthropology (See common humanity), 39, 40, 72, 101, 110, 164, 168, 187, 190, 206-207   211
"anti-historical," 107, 170
apostles, 55, 57, 59, 63, 77, 90-91, 95, 109, 125-126, 189-191, 197, 199, 204, 215-217, 221, 224, 229, 233-235, 257, 260, 262, 281, 284
aptitude, 63
art of understanding, 32, 47, 133, 152, 205,
attentiveness, 33-34, 64, 82-83, 87, 125, 139 141, 144, 185, 188-191, 197, 202-203, 207, 250-251, 277, 280, 286, 291
Aufhebung, 54, 140, 193
author, 8, 11, 18, 22, 45, 89, 116, 99, 122, 145-158, *passim*
— about the, 125-128, 192f., 278-279, 282-284, 289
— biblical, 67, 98, 122, 180-181, 184f., 233-234, 255, 258
— identification with, 163, 187, 189f., 258f.
— individuality of, 127, 130, 133, 152f., 163f., 171f., 187f.
— standing *with* the author, 59, 95, 97, 125-128, 142, 192f., 281, 284
— the mind of, 45, 50, 59, 145-158, 188f., 234
— "to understand an author better than he understood himself," 150-153, 165, 199f., 219f.
— "until I almost forget that I am not the author," 117-124, 192f., 257f.

biblicist, 16, 22-23, 57, 59, 82
Bible passim
— reading the Bible "like any other book," 46, 50-51, 55, 89, 131
biblical attitude, 57, 63, 89
biblical realism, 74, 262
biblical scholars, 22, 26, 46, 83-84, 86, 96-98, 100-101, 109-111, 127, 161, 166, 197, 242, 251
biblicism, 57-58, 77, 82, 179
biography, 158, 161, 189, 201, 203, 205, 220
break with liberalism, 1-7, 11, 14, 39, 65-67, 77, 134, 169, 184-186, 221f., 257
common humanity, 148-149, 153, 155, 167, 187, 211
comparative interpretation (See historical interpretation), 45, 153-158, 164, 239, 255
congeniality (*Kongenialität*), 16, 192, 258f.
contemporaneity, 82, 147f., 242f., 247f., 260-261
context, 100-111, 126-133, 146, 162, 190-191, 195-196, 205, 227, 243, 251, 264, 278, 281, 283-284, 288, 290
critical, 126, 129, 145, 153, 185, 196, 198, 230, 250, 261, 284, 288
deconstruction (deconstructionists), 245, 262
demythologization, 31, 61
Denkregel (rule of thought), 58f., 63
Deus dixit, 58, 87, 224
dialectical method, 1, 42, 50, 76, 78, 84-86, 116, 119, 161, 247, 249
direct identification, 223
doctrine, 71, 91, 159, 174-176, 179, 222, 250
dogmatism, 16, 181, 197
dogmatics, 9, 24-26, 29f., 40, 42, 54-55, 73, 87, 89, 97, 101, 139, 244,
"double-entry bookkeeping," 85f., 203, 243
eisegesis (See "reading in"), 112-114, 116, 241, 248, 250, 287

"emergency clause," 197-207, 264, 288
empathetic identification, 45, 131, 145f., 258f.
empathetic tradition of interpretation, 114, 142-207, 256f.
empathy (*Einfühlung*), 45, 76, 95, 104, 109, 125, 131, 141f., 185f., 258f., 281, 284
Enlightenment, 46, 131, 143, 179, 181, 219
enthusiasm, 16, 24, 120, 240, 242-243, 252, 259
epistemology, 33, 40, 46, 158, 161, 198
eschatology, 26, 74, 102f.
ethics, 25, 40, 29, 91, 99, 128, 170, 172, 178, 220
exegesis
— existential, 59, 111, 206
— pneumatic exegesis, 16, 26f., 40, 48, 56f., 123, 241, 252
— "presuppositionless," 50, 80, 96f., 285
— scientific, 92, 96f., 243
— theological, 4f., passim
— the priority of exegesis over hermeneutics, 5f., 13f., 49f.
expressivism, 145f., 229f.
faith, 44, 58, 62f., 68, 70f., 91, 97f., 104, 111, 115, 121, 128, 143, 178, 181f., 197, 222, 224f., 245, 249, 277
freedom, 36, 42, 49, 51f., 57, 71f., 82, 122, 235, 241, 246, 248, 251, 286
general anthropology, 164, 167-168, 187, 190, 206-207, 211, 260
genius, 9, 63, 103, 150f.
God,
— "all in all," 78f., 92, 101
— oneness, 77f.
— the being of, 35-49, 91
— the freedom of, 36, 42, 49, 72f., 238f.,
— the love of, 52, 64, 207f.
gnostic, 15, 22
grace, 90, 113, 210, 214, 221, 229
grammatical interpretation, 45, 84, 117, 145, 149-154, 200, 236, 255
hearing (See listening), 4, 42, 58, 62f., 81f., 87, 113, 119, 123, 131, 140f., 148, 157, 239, 246, 286f.
hermeneutical circle, 72
"hermeneutical manifesto," 3f., 10, 13f., 48, 91, 199, 203,

hermeneutical principles, 5f.,10, 22, 50, 63, 65, 78, 89, 95, 115, 120, 125, 194f., 262, 264
hermeneutical "problem," 31, 33, 35f., 41f., 48f., 60, 62, 150, 207, 217,
hermeneutics
— biblical, 8, 43, 47, 51-53, 130,
— general, 47f., 88f., 132, 150f., 206, 255f., 264
— special, 47f., 88f., 132, 152f., 255f., 264
— of suspicion, 197
— of trust, 184f., 264
— of understanding, 60, 152, 205f.,
— the art of, 152, 205
historians, 66, 80, 104, 106, 109, 123, 132f., 139, 166, 231f., 243, 278, 282
historical-criticism, 8, 17f., 22, 26, 53, 82f., 86, 99f., 133, 145, 149, 161, 169f., 231f., 248, 290-291
historical-psychological (approach to interpretation), 95, 109, 126, 128f., 134, 137-142, 180, 183, 190f., 201f., 216f., 231f., 257, 281, 284, 288
historical relativism, 172f., 183
historicism, 114, 49, 70f., 119, 142, 147, 167f., 251, 261
historiography, 44, 105, 158, 161, 177
History
— *Geschichte*, 103f., 262f.
—*Historie*, 103f., 183, 262f.
history of religions school, 70, 127, 129, 133, 141f., 166f., 177, 188, 278, 283
Holy Scripture, passim
Holy Spirit (See Spirit), 39, 55, 56f., 81, 88f., 115, 131, 156f., 181, 245, 255f., 264
indirect identification, 223-224
individualism, 163, 171-176, 183
individuality, 45, 77, 130, 153-159, 163-164, 185, 187, 190-191, 196, 206, 211, 255-256
inspiration, the doctrine of (See verbal inspiration), 18, 27, 81, 92, 98-100, 118, 122, 156, 181, 184-185, 196-197, 222, 224, 226, 255-256, 290-291
intuition, 45, 133, 148, 150f., 155, 178, 180, 187, 211
language, 13, 45, 144f., 152, 175f., 183, 195f., 221-228, 231, 238, 240, 246-247, 256, 262, 279, 283-284,

Index of Subjects 311

letter, the, 67, 139, 162, 181, 183, 221f., 227, 230, 249
"linguistic competence," 63, 152f.
listening (See hearing), 111, 113, 131, 144, 148, 250-251, 258
"living context," 100-111, 146, 202, 243, 281, 284, 288
love, 3, 30, 52, 83, 125f., 130f., 141, 148f., 171, 184f., 207f., 221, 277, 280, 286
Lutheran, 36, 195
memory, 86f., 279, 285
method, 2-5, 13, 15, 18, 20-22, 27-30, 34, 40-42, 49-50, 53, 55-58, 64, 65, 72, 89, 91, 95-96, 99, 112, 114, 118, 125, 129, 131, 133, 154-156, 158, 160-161, 163, 166, 168f., 172, 177, 183, 188, 194, 196, 202, 209, 231, 235, 238, 251, 255, 259, 262, 281, 284, 287-288, 290-291
miracle, 140, 177, 208-210, 209, 213, 216, 227
mistrust, 97, 99, 194, 263, 288
misunderstanding, 14, 73, 83, 100, 103, 205-206, 255, 281, 284
mitdenken (thinking with), 126f.
Miterleben, 133
Nachbildung, 44-45, 59, 162
Nachdenken, 45, 58f., 126
Nacherleben, 59, 162, 169
Nachfühlen, 44-45, 59, 162
Nachverständnis, 44-45, 59, 162
naivete, 16, 50, 74, 117, 97, 116, 161, 197, 242, 268, 289
"Neo-orthodoxy," 1, 263
Neo-Protestantism, 36, 38, 41, 58, 246
neutrality, 115-116, 105-106, 160, 222
New Hermeneutic, 32-33, 40-41, 48, 60
objectivity, 36, 44-46, 52, 84, 96, 121, 133, 160, 162, 164-165
openness, 60, 62, 75, 80-82, 100, 103-104, 109, 111, 166, 196, 219, 243-244, 246, 279, 284-286, 290,
paraphrase, 240-250
part (See whole), 78-84, 86, 90, 92, 101, 251, 279
participation, 88, 95-120, 125-126, 138, 143, 184, 192-194, 210, 230, 269-272, 280-281, 284-286, 288, 290, 292
personality, 65, 68, 118, 127, 133-142, 144, 152-153, 156-157, 162-167, 178, 182, 187-188, 190-192, 205, 232, 256, 260-261
phenomenology, 43, 141, 168, 172, 261
piety, 39, 66-68, 84, 123, 141, 174, 179-180, 183-184, 186, 189-190, 209, 221, 224-226, 229, 277
positivism, 70, 161, 165, 169, 241, 287
post-modern, 5, 50, 113, 197, 220, 245, 262
prayer, 28, 210, 258
preaching, 23, 25, 35, 40, 71-72, 139, 229, 249, 252, 265, 280, 286, 287
prejudice, 22, 57, 60, 80, 84, 95-97, 109, 115, 126, 128, 148-149, 230, 281, 284
presuppositions, 1-2, 7, 10, 23, 27, 35-38, 42, 55, 58, 80-82, 84, 86-88, 95-96, 108-115, 146-150, 154-155, 171, 187-190, 198, 200, 208, 211, 221, 226, 230, 236, 249, 260, 281, 284
privileged interpretation, 46, 50, 53-55, 115-116
prophecy, the concept of, 258f.
prophetic interpretation, 16, 153, 249, 258f., 279, 283
prophets, 16, 55, 57, 59, 63, 67, 77, 90-91, 95, 108-109, 125-126, 129-130, 181, 188-191, 197, 215-217, 233-235, 252, 259-260, 281, 284, 290-291
psychological interpretation, 27, 45, 117, 130, 138-142, 152-154, 159, 164, 168-169, 231-232, 255
psychologism, 49, 70f., 142, 167f., 261f.
psychologists, 26, 139
psychology, 27, 39, 59, 102, 121, 128, 132-133, 137, 151, 163-165, 168, 256
"reading in" (See also eisegesis), 96, 112f., 241, 248, 287
reductionism, 49, 142, 156, 191, 231-232, 262
Reformation, 29, 97-98, 122, 128, 162, 177, 203, 251, 257
Reformed, 15-16, 19, 23-25, 29, 36, 55, 69, 136, 176, 184, 195, 233-234, 236-238, 263
reformers, 2, 9, 58, 129, 179, 187, 212, 227, 256
relationship of faithfulness (*Treueverhältnis*), 192-198, 219
"relative conditions of hearing," 62f., 258

Index of Subjects

religion, 26, 38, 66f., 107, 123f., 133f., 141f., 166, 168, 170f., 179, 183, 188f., 219, 221, 241,

revelation, 1, 34-38, 42, 52, 55, 57-58, 62, 67-68, 72, 74-77, 80, 86-87, 90-91, 98-99, 101-110, 137, 143-144, 172-183, 188-190, 209, 211, 216, 218, 222-228, 233, 236-237, 251, 258, 260
Romanticism, 19, 45, 131, 137f., 142-145, 148, 150-152, 159-161, 165, 171, 173, 175-176, 179, 184, 200, 222, 247, 256
Sache, 66, 74-78, 84, 86, 90, 92, 131, 146, 200, 203
Sachlichkeit, 52, 65, 70-75, 92-93, 118, 125, 184, 189, 202-203, 219, 183, 250, 264, 288
Sachkritik, 249f.
salvation-history (*Heilsgeschichte*), 102f.
science,
— "dominant science of exegesis," 83f., 95f., 116f., 125, 127, 185-186, 190-191, 194, 201, 216-217, 239, 244, 281, 284
— exegetical (scientific exegesis), 28, 55, 92, 95f., 116, 198, 262
— human (*Geisteswissenschaft*), 44, 47f., 137, 160
— "in general," 52f., 95f.
— scientific, 16, 28, 36, 46f., 52f., 67, 70, 96f., 120f., 125, 129f., 139, 151f.,164f., 172f., 177, 194, 205, 230f., 243, 263, 277-278, 282, 287-288
school of the Holy Spirit, 56-64, 89
source, 7, 15, 23, 25, 36, 48, 55, 76-77, 85, 97, 99, 104, 126, 132, 172, 174, 182, 206, 216, 224, 233-235, 280, 286
Spirit (See Holy Spirit), 28, 66, 77, 89, 98f., 181f., 194f., 222, 224, 227, 251f., 258f., 292
sympathy (See *Kongenialität*), 16, 95, 109, 126, 134, 146, 163,167, 185, 190-193, 207, 209, 216-218, 242, 258, 261, 284, 287
theological revolution, 4-5, 13-14, 34-35, 48, 61, 91, 258
translation, 231, 246f.
trust, 125-126, 132, 172, 174, 183, 184f., 192-198, 219, 263, 278, 281-282, 284, 288
truth, 55, 85-95, 107-108, 110, 113, 131, 138, 141, 143, 146, 158, 171, 175, 179, 198, 200-205, 212, 248-252, 255, 258-259, 262, 264
understanding, 12, 23, 28, 31-34, 37, 40-41, 44-49, 59-64, 76, 79, 81, 85f., 90, 93, 95, 97, 101, 103, 108f., 112, 115, 117, 119f., 125-207, 230f., 238f., 244, 255, 257f., 278, 280-284, 286, 288-290, 292
unhistorical (*unhistorisch*), 105f., 236
"universal rule of interpretation," 79f., 85f.
verbal inspiration, the doctrine of (See inspiration), 98-100, 224, 233, 238, 250-252, 288
virtuoso, 3, 9-10, 227, 255
whole (See part), 78-84, 86, 90, 92, 101, 251, 279, 283
witness, 223f.

www.ingramcontent.com/pod-product-compliance
Lightning Source LLC
Chambersburg PA
CBHW021354290426
44108CB00010B/236